¡Acción!

LEVEL 1
Second Edition

VICKI GALLOWAY
DOROTHY JOBA
ANGELA LABARCA

GLENCOE
McGraw-Hill

New York, New York   Columbus, Ohio   Mission Hills, California   Peoria, Illinois

Glencoe/McGraw-Hill

A Division of The **McGraw·Hill** Companies

Copyright © 1998 by Glencoe/McGraw-Hill. All rights reserved. Except as permitted under the United States Copyright Act, no part of this publication may be reproduced or distributed in any form or by any means, or stored in a database or retrieval system, without prior written permission of the publisher.

Printed in the United States of America.

Send all inquiries to:
Glencoe/McGraw-Hill
15319 Chatsworth Street
P.O. Box 9609
Mission Hills, CA 91395-9609

ISBN 0-02-640034-0 (Teacher's Wraparound Edition)
ISBN 0-02-640063-4 (Teacher's Wraparound Edition, Part A)
ISBN 0-02-640067-7 (Teacher's Wraparound Edition, Part B)

1 2 3 4 5 6 7 8 9   RRW   03 02 01 00 99 98 97 96

CONTENTS

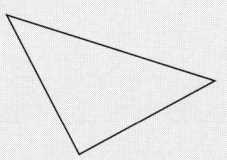

Introduction	4
Features and Benefits	5
Series Components	12
Student Edition	12
Teacher's Wraparound Edition	13
Writing Activities Workbook	16
Lesson Quizzes	16
Testing Program	16
Transparency Binder	16
Diversiones Masters	17
Estructura Masters	17
Audio Program	17
Student Tape Manual	17
Video Program	17
Computer Software	17
Level 1 in Two Volumes	17
Cooperative Learning	19
Pacing	22
Student Portfolios	24

INTRODUCTION

Welcome to the world of ¡Acción!, the junior high and high school Spanish series by Glencoe/McGraw-Hill. ¡Acción! is more than a catchy title. It is a communication-based language program that emphasizes the active involvement of the learner in all stages of instruction. As your students become active partners in gaining proficiency in all four language skills and in acquiring cultural awareness, you will find that teaching Spanish becomes more rewarding than ever before. And this Teacher's Wraparound Edition provides you with an abundance of practical suggestions and resources to make learning even more successful. ¡Acción! offers features that will encourage students to become motivated, enthusiastic learners in all phases of instruction. These features include:

- a communication-based curriculum
- contextualized learning
- learner-centered instruction
- cooperative learning
- a developmental approach to grammar
- a contextualized approach to vocabulary
- an integrated, participatory approach to culture

FEATURES AND BENEFITS

A Communication-based Curriculum

Perhaps the main challenge in the Spanish classroom today is finding ways to engage students in meaningful, communicative activities. The learner-based approach in the ¡Acción! series maximizes the amount of time students spend in developing language skills and cultural awareness in order to communicate effectively. All aspects of the instructional design—from the presentation of new material, to testing and evaluation—engage learners in the process of communicating in Spanish. Students are actively involved in comprehending and responding appropriately to oral and written messages within authentic cultural contexts.

As you use ¡Acción! Level 1 in your classroom, you will quickly see how it integrates vocabulary, grammatical structures, and culture to emphasize the main objective: to communicate meaningfully with others in Spanish. Language functions are used as the organizing principle for integrating these linguistic and cultural elements. The activities in this series have been carefully developed to motivate students to socialize, request information, perform specific tasks, and discuss issues and ideas relevant to their personal interests through appropriate listening, speaking, reading, and writing formats. And in each lesson, the wealth of authentic materials and cultural insights encourage communication within real-life contexts that reflect the diversity of the contemporary Spanish-speaking world. This Teacher's Wraparound Edition offers an easy-to-follow, step-by-step guide to using these materials most effectively in order to make your classroom one in which communication in Spanish flows as naturally and spontaneously as possible through all phases of instruction: presentation, practice, evaluation, and reentry.

Contextualized Learning

An essential characteristic of the communication-based classroom is contextualized learning. This means that everything students learn is presented within a context, or set of circumstances, that could actually take place in real life. There are no isolated lists of material, no unrelated sequences of practice items designed solely to focus on grammatical forms. Verb forms are described by the function, or purpose, they fulfill. Vocabulary is presented topically. Culture comes alive through authentic documents, photos, and activities, all of which are integrated into the lesson. All presentation of material is reinforced immediately by practice that immerses students in personalized, youth-oriented contexts. Language becomes a means to an end, rather than an end in and of itself.

This emphasis on contextualized learning engages students both intellectually and psychologically. When learners are actively engaged, they are more successful in achieving the objectives of each lesson. In contextualized learning, success for all learners is assured if they are adequately prepared to engage in the learning activity, carefully guided through it, and positively reinforced for their participation. In the ¡Acción! series, students are always given clear, concrete instructions for completing each learning activity in the Student Text. The Teacher's Wraparound Edition offers additional, easy-to-follow steps that help to prepare students for specific stages in the learning process. Both the Student Text and the Teacher's Wraparound Edition detail techniques for acknowledging and rewarding students.

Learner-centered Instruction

Today's classroom is comprised of students who not only have diverse learning styles, but who may also, in a collective sense, represent any number of cultural backgrounds. The emphasis on learner-centered instruction in the ¡Acción! series anticipates this classroom composition and offers ideas for responding positively to such diversity. Specific teaching suggestions accompany each lesson, guiding the teacher in setting up a cooperative learning environment that values diversity and encourages all students to become personally invested in their own learning. The emphasis on meeting and respecting the needs of all learners encourages students to support each other in the process of developing language proficiency and cultural awareness.

The Teacher's Wraparound Edition gives a variety of suggestions and extra activities for students who have special learning needs. Specific ideas in the section called *Reteaching* will help those students who have difficulty mastering the important lesson concepts. The topic *For the Native Speaker* offers activities specifically designed for students who have some native proficiency in Spanish. The learner-centered approach in ¡Acción! offers each student, regardless of background, learning style, or special need, resources to achieve success in developing proficiency in Spanish.

Cooperative Learning

Another key to the effective development of language skills in the communication-based classroom is cooperative learning. The basic principle of cooperative learning states that all students are active partners not only in their own learning, but in that of their classmates as well. ¡Acción! includes numerous paired and grouped activities, and, as a result, peer interaction becomes an integral part of the learner-centered classroom. Students work with each other to achieve the same objective: meaningful communication in Spanish.

The Teacher's Wraparound Edition assists you in applying cooperative learning strategies. Additional background information on the topic of cooperative learning can be found in this Teacher's Manual on page 19. In this section you will find a complete discussion of suggestions to make your classroom come alive as students actively work together to achieve proficiency.

A Developmental Approach to Grammar

As you become familiar with the instructional design of the ¡Acción! series, you will notice that it employs a developmental approach to learning grammar. In teaching certain key verbs, this approach means that students become well-acquainted with the function of each verb form, as reflected in a specific verb ending, prior to exposure to the complete verb paradigm. By function, we mean a communication act which serves a particular purpose. For example, in Level 1 **(Capítulo 2, Lección 1),** the singular forms of the verb **ser** are presented under the functional topic: How to Identify and Describe People and Things ("To identify yourself, use **soy**...; to identify someone or something, use **es**...; to question someone you speak to informally, use **eres**..."). In this example, and in many other instances, students practice each verb form in a variety of real-life contexts that makes each form meaningful to them.

Why does ¡Acción! employ a developmental approach to the teaching of grammar? Experience shows that students need time and adequate practice to develop proficiency in using grammatical forms effectively. Research also indicates that what is learned together is stored together, and consequently, retrieved together in active language usage. As an example, when the learner's mind is flooded with all forms of present tense -ar verbs in the same lesson, there are two predictable results: there is usually insufficient time to practice all forms for student mastery; and the student tends to confuse the forms on recall.

The developmental approach in the ¡Acción! series gives students sufficient time to become well-versed in using each specific grammatical form in a context that reinforces its communicative function. In Level 1, the principal structures presented in this approach include present tense and regular preterit tense verb forms, descriptive and possessive adjectives, and **gustar** + indirect object pronouns. Grammar topics are recycled at appropriate intervals. Specific references to lessons in which related forms are treated are given in the Teacher's Wraparound Edition under the topic *Structure Focus*.

A Contextualized Approach to Vocabulary

A key characteristic of the ¡Acción! series is its contextualized approach to presenting, practicing, testing, and recycling vocabulary. The initial contextualization occurs through the thematic presentation in the *Vocabulario* section of each lesson. A glance at any *Vocabulario* presentation will indicate the vocabulary theme (greetings; occupations; foods; going places; etc.). In each lesson, the presentation begins with a lead-in introductory phrase, or exchange, that establishes the context (**¿Qué quieres hacer? Quiero...**) This is followed by a series of individual vocabulary items or phrases that naturally occur within this context (**ir a casa, comprar algo, leer revistas, escuchar discos [Capítulo 1, Lección 2]**). Clear, colorful visuals help to clarify the meaning of each word or phrase, and further establish the context. This system of presenting vocabulary thematically, visually, and with contextualized labeling, helps students to organize and group new words, and relate them to vocabulary from other lessons.

In each lesson, practice activities involve students in tasks that are inherently valuable communication acts. At the same time, these and many other activities promote long-term vocabulary retention by deliberately recycling words into new and different situations and contexts. The end-of-chapter *Repaso* further recycles vocabulary by asking students to use words taught in the chapter lessons at a more integrated, recombined level. For example, in the *Repaso* for **Capítulo 2,** students are asked to "think of as many words as you can to talk about what you do on Sundays, according to the following categories." The activity is accompanied by a semantic "map" with the phrase, **los domingos** at the center, and the following categories around the perimeter: **¿por qué?, ¿cuándo?, ¿dónde?, ¿qué?** In this way, students are asked to use numerous words and phrases they have learned previously in a new, more consolidated context.

Words presented in each *Vocabulario* are integrated to the fullest extent possible into all other sections of the lesson. For example, they appear as preview in the *¡A comenzar!* section of each lesson. They are reinforced through their natural contextual link to the grammar structures presented later in the lesson. Vocabulary is reentered in the *Cultura viva* section, and further reentered in the closing *Finalmente* section where the lesson's vocabulary is summarized. The *Finalmente* speaking and writing activities *(A conversar* and *A escribir)* recombine vocabulary with the lesson's grammatical structures by asking students to communicate both conversationally and in writing on specific situational topics. In later lessons, vocabulary that was actively introduced at an earlier stage is recycled within new, appropriate contexts in order to ensure that these words are not forgotten. Deliberate and conscientious recycling of active vocabulary is perhaps the best approach to ensure that words and phrases are stored by the learner for long-term retention.

The Teacher's Wraparound Edition provides several support mechanisms to assist teachers in vocabulary presentation and practice. These include reteaching suggestions for students who may require yet another approach to mastering the vocabulary; additional (but optional) words that are related to those taught in the student text under the heading *When Students Ask;* and alternate words that are commonly used in certain areas of the Spanish-speaking world, presented here under the topic *Regionalisms*. The emphasis that ¡Acción! places on integrating vocabulary learning into all phases of developing proficiency in Spanish is among its most pedagogically-sound features.

Integrated Development of All Four Language Skills

The ¡Acción! series maximizes its communication-based curriculum by integrating into all phases of instruction the development of the four language skills: listening, speaking, reading, and writing. Students may frequently use reading and listening skills when carrying out speaking or writing activities. For example, in a paired practice format, Students A and B may be asked to fill out an order form for T-shirts. Student A reads the items on the order form to Student B and then writes down Student B's response to each item. At the same time, Student B listens to Student A read the form and then tells Student A his or her preferences. The partners are then asked to reverse roles. In this way, the activity has involved students in all four skills in order to complete the task. Regardless of which skills are being practiced, students may often need to brainstorm on the specific task as an initial, preparatory step. For example, in **Capítulo 2, Lección 3,** students are asked to "converse with a classmate about your plans for tomorrow. Use the following expressions: **Voy a..., Necesito..., Quiero..., Pienso...**" For activities such as this one, students can perform the task more readily if they are given a few minutes to think about the task and rehearse their statements mentally. You may want to encourage students to write down some key words on a sheet of paper before beginning the activity.

A closer look at how the ¡Acción! series treats the development of each language skill illustrates how they are integrated in both the Student Text and in the ancillary materials.

Listening

In the typical Spanish classroom, the teacher is the primary source for listening to a variety of spoken utterances. Sometimes what the teacher says in Spanish is specifically related to a section in the Student Text. At other times, teachers may wish to speak to students about themselves and their daily activities, as well as to talk to students about their own activities and interests. Above all, we urge you to use as much spoken Spanish in the classroom as possible in order to maximize listening, and to make the study of Spanish a real-life, dynamic experience for your students.

In addition to teacher talk in general, the ¡Acción! series provides numerous opportunities for developing the listening skill. The opening ¡A comenzar! of each lesson includes a dialogue, or some other contextualized presentation, which may either be read aloud by the teacher, or listened to using the audio cassette accompanying the lesson. Each lesson includes oral activities, many of which are designed as whole class practice. For these, the teacher may model each practice item in the activity. In the case of paired and small-group activities, the teacher may wish to do these initially as whole class activities so that students have the opportunity to hear the teacher model the practice items.

In the Student Text there is an emphasis on interaction with other classmates where listening to what a classmate says is critical to completing the activity. This is especially true in the case of paired and small-group activities. In this way, students are made responsible for what they hear. The directions to these activities include having students record the information they hear from their classmates by taking notes and reporting back to the class, or at other times, by writing a paragraph summarizing the information they heard.

The vocabulary and grammar structures highlighted in each lesson of ¡Acción! are further practiced through the Audio Program (Cassette or Compact Disc). These listening activities are accompanied by a Student Tape Manual containing tasks based on the information they heard from the recording for students to carry out. These contextualized tasks include following directions while looking at a map, writing down telephone numbers and addresses, and summarizing conversations, to name a few. For each section of the lesson, there is a corresponding recorded listening activity of this contextualized nature.

Additional practice in listening comprehension is provided through the Video Program (Videocassette or Videodisc), which includes a Video Activities Booklet. The Video Program features a variety of native speakers from various regions of the Spanish-speaking world, highlighted by those from the three main locales of the Student Text: San Antonio, Madrid, and Miami. The Video Activities Booklet offers contextualized activities that combine reading, writing, and speaking with the input students receive through listening. Students learn listening comprehension strategies as they focus on specific tasks each time they hear and see a given video segment.

The Teacher's Wraparound Edition offers many suggestions that promote listening comprehension development. Teachers have access to detailed guidelines as well as scripts of listening-based material. These scripts include presentation, review, reteaching, expansion, and additional practice.

Specifically, teachers may wish to use the *Total Physical Response* activities in the Teacher's Wraparound Edition in order to emphasize the listening skill.

Speaking

Critical to the success of this communication-based series is the emphasis on speaking. Within each lesson, from the introduction of new material to the last summary activity, students are encouraged to speak within purposeful, real-life contexts. The speaking topics are both relevant and interesting and will motivate students to want to speak. Throughout the series, students are asked to express their personal likes and dislikes, opinions, and preferences through surveys, interviews, role-playing, and other task-oriented activities. Non-threatening formats that include paired and small-group activities further encourage students to express themselves conversationally in Spanish. All speaking activities are performed within the framework of the vocabulary and grammar structures taught in a particular lesson, plus words and structures that were taught in earlier lessons. The vocabulary and structures students are expected to use in each speaking activity are modeled through one or more examples **(Por ejemplo)** so that students understand how to express themselves. In many instances, students are provided with a group of key vocabulary words from which they may choose in order to express themselves on a personal level.

In Level 1, **(Capítulo 5, Lección 2),** students learn "how to describe something they don't know the word for" (circumlocution). This valuable technique for communicating a message successfully, even when a key word is not known or remembered furthers the students' progress toward learning how to communicate in the real world. Also in Level 1, students learn how to use hesitation words, or space fillers, such as **bueno, pues,** and **a ver,** thereby learning yet another communicative technique for "buying time" while they think of how to express themselves in Spanish. Additional devices that help students to express themselves are a) learning how to summarize ideas with expressions such as **entonces** and **por eso;** and b) learning how to express ideas in sequence using **primero, después, luego,** and **entonces.** Many of the *Cultura viva* topics guide students in how they should express themselves within an authentic cultural context. These considerations include formal versus informal speech, expressions of courtesy, gestures, and use of diminutives.

Because speaking is such an integral part of the series, Speaking Tests are included as part of the Testing Program accompanying *¡Acción!* Level 1.

Reading

Each lesson in the *¡Acción!* series consistently integrates reading with listening, speaking, and writing. What is unique in this series, however, is the approach it takes in its implicit development of reading strategies that will result in students being able to read authentic Spanish materials. Students are constantly asked to read authentic texts such as telephone listings, advertisements, announcements from newspapers and magazines, invitations, tourist brochures, mail order forms, television listings, weather reports, floor plans of a house, and numerous other real-world documents for the factual information they provide. These documents frequently provide the information necessary for the completion of an activity in the Student Text. In Level 1, **(Capítulo 1, Lección 3)** for example, students are asked to read a brochure from San Antonio in order to give the correct telephone number of each place described in the brochure. Authentic texts such as this serve to reinforce, through their content, the lexical and grammatical structures presented in a particular lesson. By their attractive color and design, they not only provide a direct connection to the real world, they also make learning more interesting and enjoyable.

The widespread use of authentic texts in the Student Edition means that learners will not immediately understand everything they read in a given document, nor are they expected to. However, students are encouraged to guess at the meaning of unknown words. The Teacher's Wraparound Edition topic *Learning from Realia* provides key questions that teachers may wish to use in order to help students derive maximum benefit from these readings. Beginning with Level 1, Chapter 4, the *Cultura viva* readings are accompanied by strategies for reading Spanish texts for greater understanding.

In addition to the authentic documents previously described, there is a longer, more comprehensive *Lectura* in the final lesson of each chapter. Each of these readings has been chosen on the basis of its appealing content, its thematic link to the chapters, and for its level of reading difficulty. The activities that accompany the *Lectura* focus on pre-reading and post-reading strategies and activities that will allow students to read successfully in Spanish. Students are guided to read globally, to work with cognates and word derivation, and to interact with the content of the reading in other meaningful ways. For each *Lectura,* the Teacher's Wraparound Edition gives more suggestions to the teacher for helping students to develop sound reading strategies.

Students are asked to read on many other occasions in each lesson of the *¡Acción!* series. For example, students may begin an activity by first reading a passage, then reacting to it through a speaking or writing format. At times students may need to read a list of items accompanying an activity in order to complete a listening comprehension task in the Audio or Video Programs.

Writing

¡Acción! integrates writing with other skills by asking students to write what they have already learned to read, understand aurally, and say. One of these three language skills often becomes the stimulus for writing. For example, students may be asked to write a response to an invitation. They may be directed to complete a form with information they hear from either the Audio or the Video Program. On other occasions they may be asked to categorize vocabulary they have rehearsed orally by listing activities according to those they want to do and those they don't want to do. At other times, students may need to write down information they hear from their partner in order to report back to the entire class. In these ways, students are asked to write in contexts where writing is the most natural form of expression. At the same time, these activities allow students to express their own views, reactions, and interests within a writing framework that provides guidance in syntax and sentence structure.

The *A escribir* activity at the end of each lesson provides a more open-ended context for students to express themselves in writing. As students progress through the Level 1 textbook, the writing activities become progressively more open-ended as students acquire more control of Spanish.

Context and purpose help the student to know what to write, as well as how to express the written message. Such guidance saves students from the frustration of writing beyond their knowedge and ability levels. It also saves you, the teacher, from reading and correcting written activities in which students have exceeded their capacity to write successfully.

In addition to those activities that are specifically designed to develop the writing skill, the *¡Acción!* series offers many other opportunities. For example, as a preliminary step for a given activity, students may be asked to write down a list of words that they will want to use in carrying out the main activity. In this way, students are asked to organize their thoughts so that they are better prepared to carry out a communicative task. Many of the speaking activities are easily converted to a writing format. Suggestions for reporting and summarizing oral activities in the Teacher's Wraparound Edition are easily adaptable for writing practice. Finally, the Teacher's Wraparound Edition provides specially designed written activities for students who are native speakers of Spanish, since it is frequently the writing skill that poses the greatest challenge for these learners.

An Integrated and Participatory Approach to Culture

The *¡Acción!* series places great importance on developing student awareness of the culture in which the target language is spoken. Researchers tend to agree that competency in cultural behaviors is inextricably linked to proficiency in a second language. Rather than relegate culture to one isolated section, in the *¡Acción!* series it appears throughout the lesson, integrated into the presentation and practice of both vocabulary and structures. There is abundant use of authentic documents that reflect the cultural themes. These authentic materials are often used as a point of departure for communicative activities. Ancillary materials further integrate cultural themes with language practice—most notably in the Audio and Video components. Both of these components present Spanish-speakers in culturally authentic contexts. Moreover, they include interesting and challenging activities based on these real-life, culturally authentic models. Similarly, the lesson's grammatical structures and vocabulary are integrated into activities designed to reinforce the cultural themes of the *Cultura viva.* Students are challenged to perform personalized linguistic tasks within cultural contexts.

The basic organization of the Student Text reflects an emphasis on the integration of culture and language. Each two-chapter sequence features a specific geographic locale. A storyline involving characters who live in each locale unites the language taught in those two chapters. Exploring the lives of people who live in a specific city also brings that locale to life. This approach also minimizes students' tendency to stereotype by encouraging them to distinguish among the various cultures in which Spanish is spoken. In Level 1, San Antonio, Madrid, and Miami serve as points of departure from which students explore the entire Spanish-speaking world. This approach enables the teacher to treat both the cultural and linguistic diversity that characterizes the Hispanic world in a comprehensive, yet systematic way.

In Level 1, two cities that serve as points of departure are located in the United States. This offers several advantages.

1. Students can relate to characters who in many ways live similar lives.
2. Students find that their study of Spanish has a more immediate personal relevance as they learn to appreciate Spanish as an important language in the United States. They may even come to realize that gaining proficiency in Spanish can enhance their own future personal and career opportunities.
3. Students gain a deeper understanding of the role that Hispanics have played in the history of the United States and greater appreciation of the Hispanic influence in this country.
4. Some students may learn to recognize the wealth of Spanish language and Hispanic culture in their immediate environment. As a result, they may become interested in watching local Spanish television, listening to Spanish radio programs, reading Spanish newspapers and magazines, or going to Hispanic restaurants, movies, and museums. They may become motivated to look for everyday signs of Spanish language and culture in offices, buses, or phone books. They may begin speaking Spanish with native speakers in school, at work, or in their neighborhoods. Once students can relate what they learn in the classroom to their own lives, they tend to become avid learners.

The integrated, contextualized approach to learning culture in the *¡Acción!* series may be the key in assisting your students in developing cultural awarenesss and competency. This feature is reinforced by a section called *Critical Thinking Activity* in the Teacher's Wraparound Edition. These activities guide students in analyzing what culture is and how it affects all people. Other approaches often leave students asking themselves and you, "Why do they do (say) it that way?" Too often, teachers are at a loss for a response. The *Critical Thinking Activities* in this Teacher's Wraparound Edition anticipate that question by offering you guidelines and insights to help your students become critical thinkers. The notes encourage students to compare culturally determined behaviors and beliefs with their own. As they compare, they gain a greater understanding and acceptance of cultural differences by focusing as much on what people share as human beings, as on the cultural differences that separate them.

SERIES COMPONENTS

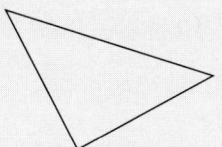
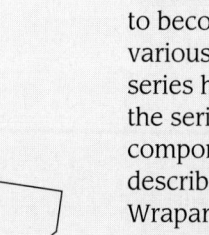

In order to adapt the learner-centered, communication-based curriculum in *¡Acción!* to your own teaching style, you may want to become more familiar with the various resources the *¡Acción!* series has to offer. Each level of the series consists of the following components, all of which are described in detail in this Teacher's Wraparound Edition.

- **Student Edition**
- **Teacher's Wraparound Edition**
- **Writing Activities Workbook, Student Edition**
- **Writing Activities Workbook, Teacher's Annotated Edition**
- **Audio Program (Cassette or Compact Disc)**
- **Student Tape Manual, to accompany the Audio Program**
- **Student Tape Manual, Teacher's Edition with Tapescript, to accompany the Audio Program**
- **Transparency Binder**
- *Estructura* **Masters**
- *Diversiones* **Masters**
- **Video Program (Videocassette or Videodisc)**
- **Video Activities Booklet, to accompany the Video Program**
- **Computer Software: Practice and Test Generator**
- **Bell Ringer Review Blackline Masters**

- **Situation Cards**
- **Lesson Quizzes with Answer Key**
- **Testing Program with Answer Key**

Level 1: Student Edition

¡Acción! Level 1 consists of six chapters, each of which is subdivided into six lessons. Geographically, Level 1 focuses on three specific locales in the Spanish-speaking world, devoting two chapters to each locale as the setting for a storyline involving specific characters who live in that area. The following specific cities are featured:

Capítulos 1–2 San Antonio
Capítulos 3–4 Madrid
Capítulos 5–6 Miami

Organization of the Student Text

The lessons in each chapter contain the following sections:

- ¡A comenzar!
- Vocabulario
- Cultura viva 1
- Estructura 1
- Cultura viva 2
- Estructura 2
- Finalmente

12 *Teacher's Manual*

¡A comenzar! This opening section introduces the lesson's objectives via a concise summary of the language functions that students are expected to perform by the end of the lesson. Examples of these language functions are found in the dialogue (letter, postcard, form, etc.) that follows. This presentation also serves to introduce the recurring characters and develop the storyline that continues over two chapters. *Actividades preliminares* are included as part of the lesson opener, offering students immediate, controlled practice in using one or more of the language functions just introduced.

Vocabulario New words are presented in thematic groups. These words are further arranged under a lead-in phrase that establishes the conversational context. The presentation includes a wide range of colorful, well-designed visuals that further aid in establishing context. The *Actividades* that follow reinforce new words and phrases by engaging students in personalized language tasks that recombine previously learned vocabulary and structures with those new to the lesson.

Cultura viva 1 This is the first of the two culture presentations in each lesson. The *Cultura viva* frequently develops a cultural theme introduced in the opening dialogue. This section includes activities which provide students with an opportunity to use the target language to express cultural insights in real-life contexts.

Estructura 1 This section presents a grammar topic in functional, how-to terms. The focus is on what linguistic structure (verb form, adjective, article) is needed in order to express a specific language function or task. Contextualized activities immediately practice the grammatical structures by relating them to tasks that students are asked to perform in a variety of formats: alone, with one classmate, in a group, with the entire class.

Cultura viva 2 This section of the lesson serves the same purpose as the first culture presentation by offering additional cultural insights into the Spanish-speaking world. Integrated activities continue to reinforce the language and cultural material presented in the lesson.

Estructura 2 This section presents an additional structure topic in functional, student-centered terms. As in the case of *Estructura 1*, contextualized practice allows students to immediately use the structure in personalized formats.

Finalmente Each lesson ends with a summary section that serves two purposes. *Situaciones* provide an opportunity for the learner to apply the lesson's vocabulary, structures and even culture points, in two guided, yet open-ended activities. The *A conversar* provides detailed guidelines for students to work in pairs to perform specific oral language tasks. *A escribir* does the same with real-life contexts that elicit a writing task.

Repaso de vocabulario This section provides students with a list of the lesson vocabulary, organized by communicative topics (**Preguntas, La familia, Lugares,** etc.). This list offers students easy access to a vocabulary study aid. It also serves as a ready reference as they perform the *Situaciones* activity on this same page of the Student Text.

End of Chapter *Repaso*

The chapter *Repaso* serves several purposes. The *¿Recuerdas?* section asks students to remember, and express in Spanish, the communicative functions that have been taught throughout the six lessons that comprise the chapter. The activities that follow reinforce these communicative functions by asking students to use them at a higher, more integrated level. These activities reinforce the concept that language learning is continuous, and that what is learned today is related to what is learned the next day.

The Teacher's Wraparound Edition

A unique component of this series is the Teacher's Wraparound Edition (TWE) which you are currently reading. It is labeled "wraparound" because its design offers the teacher consistent, specific suggestions in the left, right, and bottom margins that surround or "wrap around" each two-page spread of the Student Text. The Student Text, as it appears in the Teacher's Wraparound Edition, has been slightly reduced in size in order to provide more space for teacher notes. The TWE provides techniques for working with every aspect of the Student Text. It offers, in essence, a complete set of lesson plans, previewing and expansion techniques, and alternatives that you can adapt to your own teaching style and to the learning styles of your students. Its purpose is to save valuable teacher preparation time. A closer look at the various types of support that the notes provide may help you decide how you can most effectively use this Teacher's Wraparound Edition to its fullest advantage.

There are two basic categories of notes provided in the Teacher's Wraparound Edition:

1. primary topics which appear in the left- or right-hand margins relate most directly to the material on the corresponding pupil page,
2. secondary topics (found at the bottom margin) that complement the material on the pupil page by offering additional related strategies. These topics include *Getting Ready for the Lesson; Total Physical Response* activities; *Cooperative Learning;* and activities *For the Native Speaker.*

Description of Primary Teacher's Wraparound Topics

Lesson Objectives At the beginning of each lesson is a list of the communicative functions that students will be able to perform by the end of that lesson. These concise, clearly stated objectives tell in essence the purpose of the lesson and guide you in teaching it most effectively.

Lesson Resources The beginning of each lesson also provides references to all ancillary materials designed to supplement that lesson in the Student Text. These include the Writing Activities Workbook, Transparency Binder, Audio Program and accompanying Student Tape Manual, *Diversiones* Masters, *Estructura* Masters, Testing Program, Lesson Quizzes, Video Program with accompanying Activities Booklet, and Computer Software: Practice and Test Generator. As you come to each section within the lesson, the most appropriate of these ancillary components are listed once again for easy reference. Such access to the many resources for presenting, practicing, applying, and testing the material allows you to plan exciting, varied lessons that efficiently integrate all four language skills with cultural awareness.

Bell Ringer Reviews These activities provide reentry of earlier vocabulary and structures as independent student work at the beginning of the class, when the teacher is frequently engaged in various administrative duties, and when students may otherwise be waiting for teacher direction. They are also designed to assist students in "switching gears" from the previous class. For ease of use, the Bell Ringer Reviews appear consistently in four locations in each lesson:

1. at the beginning of the lesson;
2. with the introduction of vocabulary;
3. with the introduction to *Estructura 1;*
4. with the introduction to *Estructura 2.*

Presentation Suggestions and strategies for presenting the material featured in each lesson section (*¡A comenzar!, Vocabulario, Cultura viva 1* and *2, Estructura 1* and *2,* and *Finalmente*) are given in notes at the beginning of that section. These presentation notes include suggestions for what to do and say, as well as ways to involve students actively in the presentation process. These suggestions prepare students to be more receptive to the new material they are about to encounter. The following teacher notes merit a more detailed description.

Presentation to *Estructura 1* and *2* The notes in this section are designed to expand the ways in which the teacher can assist students in carrying out the functions in the lesson. They stress practice in all four language skills. These suggestions are also designed to facilitate the developmental approach to presenting and practicing structure.

Structure Focus These notes highlight which verb forms, or other grammatical structures, are featured in the lesson. In addition, they give the teacher an overview of how the entire grammar strand is presented in the Student Text.

Actividades All sections of each lesson include practice activities for immediate application. Many notes refer to these activities and serve to:

1. provide responses to all practice activities;
2. suggest ways of extending a given activity;
3. suggest additional related activities to supplement those in the Student Text.

When Students Ask This marginal note offers teachers immediate access to vocabulary items that are related by topic to those presented in the *Vocabulario* of each lesson. It enables the teacher to anticipate students' curiosity and be prepared to expand on each lesson's vocabulary as needed. Teachers may elect to include this optional vocabulary in practice activities, as they choose. However this vocabulary is not tested as part of the Testing Program accompanying the series.

Regionalisms The incorporation of regional variations of vocabulary items allows the teacher to maximize the realism of the

14 *Teacher's Manual*

Student Text by pointing out that there are other, equally appropriate ways of saying the same thing in different regions of the Spanish-speaking world.

Reteaching The emphasis that the ¡Acción! series places on learner-centered instruction includes options to meet all student needs. Consequently, this note offers teachers an alternate approach for students who experience difficulty in learning the lesson vocabulary or grammar. The topic Reteaching also appears at the end of the Estructura 1 and Estructura 2 sections of the lesson, providing yet another approach to presenting the grammar topics. The Reteaching suggestions may also be used for reentry and review.

Did You Know? These notes provide additional background information on various aspects of each Cultura viva topic. This information may be shared with the class, as the teacher chooses.

Critical Thinking Activities The questions in these notes are designed to encourage students to develop analytical skills. By working with culture within a critical thinking framework, students can focus on both similarities and differences when comparing diverse Hispanic cultures with each other, and with non-Hispanic cultures in the United States.

Additional Primary Teacher Wraparound Topics

Classroom Management These are alternate suggestions for grouping students for specific tasks that appear in the Student Text. These notes appear at appropriate times in the lesson and allow for flexibility in adapting the presentation and practice to diverse teaching styles. In addition, suggestions for varying the classroom grouping and seating arrangements by alternating among whole class, small group, and paired activities, offer teachers options for meeting the needs of different learning styles and interests.

Learning from Photos and Realia These notes highlight special features of the photos and authentic documents that appear on specific pages of the Student Text. They encourage teachers to explore with their students the wealth of language and cultural information that such photos and authentic texts bring to the lesson. These notes also offer specific techniques and activities for integrating these colorful, real-life additions to the text into the lesson, using them to their fullest advantage. The notes include questions, many of which are designed to assist learners in developing both reading and critical thinking skills.

Description of Secondary Teacher Wraparound Topics

Located along the bottom margin, these topics complement the material in the Student Text by offering additional related strategies that will help to meet the objectives of the lesson.

Getting Ready for the Lesson These explicit suggestions serve to preview the lesson's vocabulary, grammar, and cultural themes before students are asked to open their textbooks. These notes encourage the teacher to maximize the important preview phase of instruction. They are designed to prepare students for success in achieving the lesson objectives, and to motivate them to want to explore the lesson in depth by linking *what they already know* with the new material they are about to learn. The techniques used in this segment, including the use of visual and audio resources, provide comprehensible, contextualized input in order to stimulate students' interest and involvement in the lesson about to be presented.

Total Physical Response Activities Each *Vocabulario* section is supported by suggestions to reinforce learning of vocabulary items through in-class aural comprehension based on the Total Physical Response Method developed by James J. Asher. The principal objective of the TPR activities is to focus student attention on spoken cues as they perform physical tasks in response to teacher commands. A second objective is to assist learners in developing listening strategies in the target language in a non-threatening and supportive way.

TPR activities relieve students of the need to speak, while nevertheless allowing them to demonstrate their ability to understand spoken Spanish. An additional benefit of TPR is that it provides a change of pace, due to the physical movements required, as students respond to commands in Spanish. Moreover, these activities often apply cooperative learning principles since they tend to involve students in interactive situations as they help each other to accomplish the TPR tasks.

Pronunciation The ¡Acción! series treats Spanish pronunciation as an integral part of second language learning, offering in both the Audio and Video Programs many real-life models for students to emulate. These real-life models are presented without conscious discussion of how to pronounce individual sounds or words, thereby eliminating the need to devote long periods of valuable in-class time to such non-communicative activities.

On the other hand, the ¡Acción! series does offer teachers flexibility and options for adapting the text to their own teaching style. Consequently, teachers who wish to focus more directly on pronunciation practice will find in each lesson short verses that practice one or more of the Spanish sounds that tend to be difficult for native English speakers. Since their content reinforces the *Cultura viva* topics, the pronunciation verses are located on the corresponding page in the Teacher's Wraparound Edition. These same pronunciation verses have been recorded, and appear at the end of each lesson of the Audio Program. They are also available in overhead transparency format. The Pronunciation Transparencies are located in the **Transparency Binder** for ¡Acción! Level 1.

For the Native Speaker Each Teacher's Wraparound Edition lesson includes activities designed primarily for students who are native speakers of Spanish. These notes offer suggestions for challenging students both to explore their own cultural background and to develop greater fluency in understanding, speaking, reading, and writing Spanish. These notes offer activities that can substitute for or expand on those in the Student Text, as the teacher chooses. They also offer suggestions for integrating these activities into the total classroom management.

Cooperative Learning These suggestions provide guidelines for peer interaction in order to carry out specific activities in the Student Text. As discussed earlier, cooperative learning reflects two basic principles:

1. each learner is responsible for his or her learning, and responsible as well for maintaining a positive classroom environment that supports the learning process for all students;
2. all members of the class respect each other and the contribution that each individual makes to the learning process.

The Cooperative Learning notes that appear in the Teacher's Wraparound Edition offer detailed suggestions for maximizing peer interaction through specific grouping techniques. For a more detailed description of Cooperative Learning and suggestions for implementing it in the classroom, see page 19.

The Writing Activities Workbook

This ancillary component provides additional writing practice to reinforce all vocabulary and structures presented in the lesson. As is the case in the Student Text, writing activities are contextualized. The workbook employs a variety of stimuli to elicit written responses including art, hand-written notes, and authentic documents. The *Repaso* pages, located at the end of each workbook chapter, correspond to each *Repaso* in the Student Text and give additional practice for these cumulative activities. The Writing Activities Workbook is also available in the form of a Teacher's Annotated Edition which includes responses to each activity.

Lesson Quizzes

Individual quizzes, in a contextualized format, are provided for each *Vocabulario, Estructura 1,* and *Estructura 2* section of each lesson. They are designed to quickly tell both student and teacher how well the content of a specific section of the lesson has been mastered. An Answer Key is included at the back of the Lesson Quizzes booklet.

The Testing Program

The Testing Program accompanying this Second Edition of ¡Acción! includes one Achievement Test per lesson, as well as a more comprehensive Achievement Test for each chapter. Each test measures all five language skills (listening, speaking, reading, writing, culture). An Answer Key is provided in the Testing Program booklet immediately following the Achievement Tests. All tests are prepared on Blackline Masters. The Testing Program booklet, along with the recorded version of the listening tests, are packaged in the **Testing Program with Cassette (Compact Disc) Binder.**

The Speaking Tests have been separated from the listening, reading, writing, and culture tests to allow greater flexibility in their administration. Due to the time-consuming nature of testing the speaking skill, you may wish to test only a few students on any given day while the remainder of the class works independently. The Speaking Tests include two formats: teacher-student tests; and paired student tests, in which students are asked to converse on a specific topic. Suggestions for presenting and evaluating the Speaking Tests are given at the front of the Testing Program booklet.

The Testing Program booklet also contains Lesson and Chapter Proficiency Tests. These measure mastery of the vocabulary and structures on a more global, whole-language level. The Proficiency Tests can be used as an option to the Achievement Tests, or they may complement them.

Transparency Binder

There are four categories of transparencies comprising the Level 1 Transparency Binder:

1. *Vocabulario* **Transparencies** are reproductions of each of the *Vocabulario* presentations in the Student Textbook. All accompanying words and phrases have been deleted to allow for greater flexibility in their use.
2. **Pronunciation Transparencies** present the short verses located in the Teacher's Wraparound Edition that practice the Spanish sounds that tend to be difficult for native English speakers.
3. **Map Transparencies** are reproductions of the maps found at the beginning of the *¡Acción!* Level 1 textbook.
4. **Fine Art Transparencies** are full-color reproductions of works by well-known Spanish-speaking artists including Velázquez, Goya, Rivera, and many others. Background information about the artist and his or her work, and student activity sheets are included.

Diversiones **Masters**

These Blackline Masters offer lively, alternate activities that practice lesson vocabulary and structures. Crossword puzzles and other word games, realia-based activities, and a variety of other formats are part of the *Diversiones* Masters booklet.

Estructura **Masters**

These activities, on Blackline Masters, further reinforce each *Estructura* topic, lesson by lesson, through contextualized formats.

An Answer Key is included at the back of the *Estructura* Masters booklet.

Audio Program

The Audio Program (Cassette or Compact Disc) contains the following content designed to reinforce each lesson in the Student Text:

- the dialogue (or other presentation format) found in the opening *¡A comenzar!* of each lesson
- *Vocabulario* activity
- *Estructura 1* activity
- *Estructura 2* activity
- *Situaciones: A conversar* and *A escribir* activities
- *Pronunciación* activity
- *Repaso* activity

Student Tape Manual

The Student Tape Manual contains the follow-up activities to which students respond as they listen to the recorded material in each lesson of the Audio Program. Many of these activities include visuals as well as authentic documents to create a real-life, contextualized listening experience. With the exception of the opening dialogue (or other contextualized format), all recordings contain new material that has been developed to complement and directly reinforce each section of the Student Text.

Student Tape Manual, Teacher's Annotated Edition

The annotated edition of the Student Tape Manual includes all material found in the Student Edition. Also, the Teacher's Annotated version contains the complete tape script. Answers to each activity are also provided. For teachers who wish to include pronunciation, each lesson of the Student Tape Manual, Teacher's Annotated Edition includes one or more *Pronunciación* verses. These short rhymes are related in theme and content to the corresponding *Cultura viva* topics in the Student Text. Each verse contains one or more critical sounds for students to listen to and repeat after the model speaker.

Video Program

The hour-long Video Program (Videocassette or Videodisc) is divided into six major segments that correlate to the six chapters of the Student Text. Each chapter of the video is divided into four components:

- **Chapter Opener**
- **Lecciones**
- **Enfoque cultural**
- **Te toca a ti**

The Chapter Opener sequence captures the flavor of each of the three Spanish-speaking cities featured in Level 1: San Antonio, Madrid, and Miami. Following this introduction is a series of short segments lasting from 30 seconds to 2 minutes each. These segments feature vocabulary, structure, and culture topics from each lesson in the Student Text. The *Enfoque cultural* brings to life some of the cultural highlights presented in the chapter. *Te toca a ti* serves as a visual or audio presentation designed to elicit active oral or written production on the part of the student. All video segments were shot on location and feature real people in real life situations using authentic, unscripted language.

Video Activities Booklet

The Video Activities Booklet provides follow-up tasks that are directly related to the video segments. All activities are contextualized and offer clear student

Teacher's Manual **17**

instructions regarding what to watch and listen for. The Video Activities Booklet includes a Teacher's Manual, Culture Notes, and a complete transcript of the video soundtrack.

Computer Software: Practice and Test Generator

Available for Apple II, Macintosh and IBM-compatible computers, this software program provides materials for both students and teacher. The Practice disks provide students with new, additional practice items for the vocabulary, grammar and culture topics in each lesson of the Student Text. Immediate feedback is given, along with the percentage of answers that students answered correctly, so that with repeated practice, students can track their performance.

The Test Generator allows the teacher to print out ready-made tests, or customize a ready-made test by adding or deleting test items. The computer software comes with a Teacher's Manual as well as a printed transcript of all practice and test items.

¡Acción! Level 1 in Two Volumes

¡Acción! Part A and ¡Acción! Part B is a two-volume edition of ¡Acción! Level 1. It is designed primarily for junior high and intermediate programs where the Level 1 material is normally covered in two years. This split Level 1 edition is also appropriate for other language program configurations. The split edition is available both in Student Editions and Teacher's Wraparound Editions.

¡Acción! Part A consists of Level 1, Chapters 1–3. ¡Acción! Part B begins with a Repaso, and continues with Level 1, Chapters 4–6. The Repaso contains new, communication-based activities that recycle all material taught in Part A. The Teacher's Wraparound Edition of Part B includes page references indicating where each vocabulary and structure was initially presented in the first volume of the two-volume edition.

¡Acción! Part A and Part B include the following components: Student Text, Teacher's Wraparound Edition, and Writing Activities Workbook. The Transparency Binder, Lesson Quizzes, Audio Program, Video Program, Diversiones Masters, Estructura Masters, and Computer Software: Practice and Test Generator, are totally compatible with the split edition of Level 1.

COOPERATIVE LEARNING

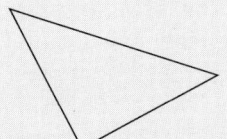
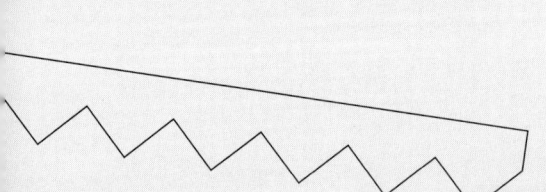

Cooperative Learning provides a structured, natural environment for student communication that is both motivating and meaningful. The affective filter that prevents many students from daring to risk a wrong answer when called upon to speak in front of a whole class can be minimized when students develop friendly relationships in their cooperative groups and when they become accustomed to multiple opportunities to hear and rehearse new communicative tasks. The goal of Cooperative Learning is to provide opportunities for learning in an environment where students contribute freely and responsibly to the success of the group. The key is to strike a balance between group goals and individual accountability. Group (team) members plan how to divide the activity among themselves, then each member of the group carries out his or her part of the assignment. Cooperative Learning provides each student with a "safe," low-risk environment rather than a whole-class atmosphere. As you implement Cooperative Learning in your classroom, we urge you to take time to explain to students what will be expected of every group member—listening, participating, and respecting other opinions.

In the Teacher's Wraparound Edition, Cooperative Learning activities have been written to accompany each lesson of the Student Textbook. These activities have been created to assist both the teacher who wants to include Cooperative Learning for the first time, and for the experienced practitioner of Cooperative Learning as well.

Classroom Management: Implementing Cooperative Learning Activities

Many of the suggested Cooperative Learning activities are based on a four-member team structure in the classroom. Teams of four are recommended because there is a wide variety of possible interactions. At the same time the group is small enough that students can take turns quickly within the group. Pairs of students as teams may be too limited in terms of possible interactions, and trios frequently work out to be a pair with the third student left out. Teams of five may be unwieldy in that students begin to feel that no one will notice if they don't really participate.

If students sit in rows on a daily basis, desks can be pushed together to form teams of four. Teams of students who work together need to be balanced according to as many variables as possible: academic achievement in the course, personality, ethnicity, gender, attitude, etc. Teams that are as heterogeneous as possible will ensure that the class progresses quickly through the curriculum.

Following are descriptions of some of the most important Cooperative Learning structures, adapted from Spencer Kagan's *Structural Approach to Cooperative Learning*, as they apply to the content of *¡Acción!* Level 1.

Roundrobin Each member of the team answers a question in turn, or shares an idea with teammates. Responses should be brief so that students do not have to wait long for their turn.

Example from *¡Acción!* Level 1, page 142, *Los días de la semana:* Teams recite the days of the week in a roundrobin fashion. Different students begin additional rounds so that everyone ends up needing to know the names of all the days. Variations include starting the list with a different day or using a race format, i.e., teams recite the list three times in a row and raise their hands when they have finished.

Roundtable Each student in turn writes his or her contribution to the group activity on a piece of paper that is passed around the team. If the individual student responses are longer than one or two words, there can be four pieces of paper with each student contributing to each paper as it is passed around the team.

A to Z Roundtable Using *¡Acción!* Level 1, page 71, *Actividad A,* students take turns adding one word at a time to a list of words associated with school in A to Z order. Students may help each other with what to write and correct spelling. Encourage creativity when it comes to the few letters of the alphabet that don't begin a specific travel word from their chapter lists. Teams can compete in several ways: first to finish all 28 letters; longest word; shortest word; most creative response.

Numbered Heads Together
Numbered Heads Together is a structure for review and practice of high consensus information. There are four steps:

Step 1: Students number off in their teams from 1 to 4.
Step 2: The teacher asks a question and gives the teams some time to make sure that everyone on the team knows the answer.
Step 3: The teacher calls a number.
Step 4: The appropriate student from each team is responsible to report the group response.

Answers can be reported simultaneously, i.e., all students with the appropriate number either stand by their seats and recite the answer together, or they go to the chalkboard and write the answer at the same time. Answers can also be reported sequentially. Call on the first student to raise his or her hand or have all the students with the appropriate number stand. Select one student to give the answer. If the other students agree, they sit down, if not they remain standing and offer a different response.

Example from *¡Acción!* Level 1, Chapter 3, page 230, Telling time:
Step 1: Using a blank clock face on an overhead transparency, or the chalkboard, the teacher adjusts the hand on the clock.
Step 2: Students put their heads together and answer the question: ¿Qué hora es?
Step 3: The teacher calls a number.
Step 4: The appropriate student from each team is responsible to report the group response.

Pantomimes Give each team one card. Have each team decide together how to pantomime for the class the action identified on the card. Each team presents the pantomime for ten seconds while the rest of the teams watch without talking. Then each of the other teams tries to guess the phrase and writes down their choice on a piece of paper. (This is a good way to accommodate kinesthetic learning styles as well as vary classroom activities.)

Example from *¡Acción!* Level 1, Chapter 1, pages 14–15 *Vocabulario:*

The teacher writes the following sentences on slips of paper and places them in an envelope.

1. *Leer revistas.*
2. *Hablar por teléfono.*
3. *Estudiar.*
4. *Escuchar discos.*
5. *Jugar tenis.*
6. *Hacer la tarea.*
7. *Comprar algo.*
8. *Bailar.*
9. *Jugar baloncesto.*
10. *Hablar con el/la maestro(a).*

Each team will draw one slip of paper from the envelope and decide together how to pantomime the action for the class. As one team pantomimes their action for 30 seconds, the other teams are silent. Then the students within

20 *Teacher's Manual*

each team discuss among themselves what sentence was acted out for them. When they have decided on the sentence, each team sends one person to write it on the chalkboard.

Inside/Outside Circle Students form two concentric circles of equal number by counting off 1-2, 1-2 in their teams. The "ones" form a circle shoulder to shoulder and facing out. The "twos" form a circle outside the "ones" to make pairs. With an odd number of students, there can be one threesome. Students take turns sharing information, quizzing each other, or taking parts of a dialogue. After students finish with their first partners, rotate the inside circle to the left so that the students repeat the process with new partners. For following rounds alternate rotating the inside and outside circles so that students get to repeat the identified tasks, but with new partners. This is an excellent way to structure 100% student participation combined with extensive practice of communication tasks.

Other suggested activities are similarly easy to follow and to implement in the classroom. Student enthusiasm for Cooperative Learning activities will reward the enterprising teacher. Teachers who are new to these concepts may want to refer to Dr. Spencer Kagan's book, *Cooperative Learning*, published by Resources for Teachers, Inc., Paseo Espada, Suite 622, San Juan Capistrano, CA 92675.

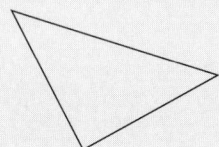

PACING

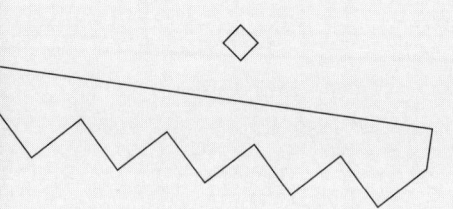

Sample Lesson Plans

¡Acción! Level 1 has been developed so that it may be completed in one school year. However, it is up to the individual teacher to decide how many lessons will be covered. Although completion of the textbook by the end of the year is recommended, it is not necessary. Many of the key structures, and much of the vocabulary taught in Level 1 are reviewed in new contexts in *¡Acción!* Level 2. The establishment of lesson plans helps the teacher visualize how a chapter can be presented. By emphasizing certain aspects of the program and de-emphasizing others, the teacher can change the focus and the approach of a lesson to meet students' needs and to suit his or her own teaching style and techniques. Sample lesson plans are provided below. They include some of the suggestions and techniques that have been described earlier in this Teacher's Manual.

STANDARD PACING 36 lessons x 6 = 216 days; 180 day school year completes 27 lessons (4.5 chapters)

	Class	Homework
Day 1	¡A comenzar! (with Audio Program)	Preview *Vocabulario*
Day 2	*Vocabulario* (with transparencies) Student textbook activities	Exercises from Writing Activities Workbook
Day 3	*Cultura viva 1* Student textbook activities *Estructura 1* Student textbook activities	 Exercises from Writing Activities Workbook Exercises from *Estructura* Masters
Day 4	*Cultura viva 2* Student textbook activities *Estructura 2* Student textbook activities	 Exercises from the Writing Activities Workbook Exercises from *Estructura* Masters
Day 5	Audio Program/Video Program	Review for test
Day 6	Test	

Note: Use activities found in the Teacher's Wraparound Edition notes, such as Cooperative Learning, TPR, or Additional Practice activities to fill in each day's teaching.

ACCELERATED PACING 36 lessons x 5 = 180 days

	Class	Homework
Day 1	¡A comenzar! (with Audio Program) Vocabulario (with transparencies) Student textbook activities	Exercises from the Writing Activities Workbook
Day 2	Audio Program: Vocabulario Cultura viva 1 Student textbook activities Estructura 1 Student textbook activities	Exercises from the Writing Activities Workbook
Day 3	Audio program: Estructura 1 Cultura viva 2 Student textbook activities Estructura 2 Student textbook activities	Exercises from the Writing Activities Workbook
Day 4	Audio Program: Estructura 2, Situaciones Video Program Cooperative Learning, TPR, etc.	Review for test Exercises from Estructura Masters
Day 5	Test A conversar/A escribir	

Note: Alternately, you may wish to do each Audio Program activity at the end of the corresponding lesson part. On day 4, start with the video and then end the class with the test. (36 lessons = 144 days)

BLOCK SCHEDULING 22 lessons = 90 days; 180 day school year completes 18 lessons (3 4/6 chapters)

	Class	Homework
Day 1	¡A comenzar! (with Audio Program) Vocabulario (with transparencies) Student textbook activities Cultura viva 1 Student textbook activities TPR, Teacher's Wraparound Edition activities	Exercises from Writing Activities Workbook
Day 2	Estructura 1 Student textbook activities Cultura viva 2 Student textbook activities Estructura 2 Student texbook activities	Exercises from Writing Activities Workbook Exercises from Writing Activities Workbook
Day 3	Audio Program/Video Program Cooperative Learning Teacher's Wraparound Edition activities	Exercises from Estructura Masters Review for test
Day 4	Test A conversar activity	A escribir activity

Note: Alternately, you may wish to do the next lesson's ¡A comenzar! and vocabulary sections after the test has been completed on Day 4. This will allow a 3 1/2 day pace.

STUDENT PORTFOLIOS

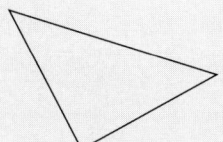
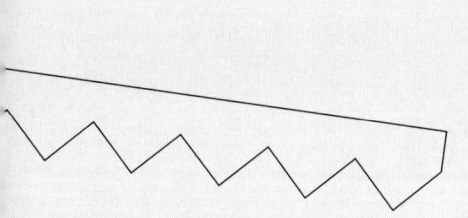

The use of student portfolios to represent long-term individual accomplishments in learning Spanish offers several benefits. With portfolios, students can keep a written record of their best work and thereby document their own progress as learners. For teachers, portfolios enable us to include students in our evaluation and measurement process. For example, the content of any student's portfolio may offer an alternative to the standardized test as a way of measuring student writing achievement. Assessing the contents of a student's portfolio can be an option to testing the writing skill via the traditional writing section on the chapter or unit test. There are as many kinds of portfolios as there are teachers working with them. Perhaps the most convenient as well as permanent portfolio consists of a three-ring binder to which each student will add during the school year, and in which the student will place his or her best written work. In the *¡Acción!* series, selections for the portfolio may come from the *A escribir* section of the student textbook as well as other activities within a given lesson. Additional portfolio sources can be found in the Writing Activities Workbook and the Video Activities Booklet. The teacher is encouraged to refer actively to students' portfolios so that they are regarded as more than just a storage device. For example, over the course of the school year, the student may be asked to go back to earlier entries in his or her portfolio in order to revise certain assignments, or to develop an assignment further by writing in a new tense, e.g., the *pretérito*. In this way the student can appreciate the amount of learning that has occurred over several months time.

Portfolios offer students a multidimensional look at themselves. A "best" paper might be the one with the least errors, or one in which the student reached and synthesized a new idea or went beyond the teacher's assignment. The Student Portfolio topic is included in each chapter of the Teacher's Wraparound Edition as a reminder that this is yet another approach the teacher may wish to use in the Spanish classroom.

Marilynn Pavlik
Lyons Twp. High School
La Grange, Illinois

Carol F. Robison
Hingham Public Schools
Hingham, Massachusetts

Bonnie S. Schuster
Fairfax County
Reston, Virginia

Judith Snyder
Fresno Unified School
  District
Fresno, California

Mary Thomas
Northside Independent
  School District
San Antonio, Texas

María J. Treviño
Northside Independent
  School District
San Antonio, Texas

María Elena Villalba
Miami Palmetto Senior High
Miami, Florida

Kathie Vogt
Florissant, Missouri

María Elena Watkins
Edgewood Independent
  School District
San Antonio, Texas

Rosanne Webster
Minerva-DeLand School
Fairport, New York

Rosemary Weddington
Franklin County High School
Frankfort, Kentucky

Janet M. Wohlers
Weston Public Schools
Weston, Massachusetts

Acknowledgments

The authors and editors would like to express their deep appreciation to the numerous Spanish teachers throughout the United States who advised us in the development of these teaching materials. Their suggestions and recommendations were invaluable. We wish to give special thanks to the educators whose names appear below.

Program Consultant

C. Ben Christensen
San Diego State University
San Diego, California

Educational Reviewers

Kristine Aarhus
Everett, Washington

Marilyn V.J. Barrueta
Yorktown High School
Arlington, Virginia

D.H. Bell
Nogales Unified
　School District #1
Nogales, Arizona

Mary M. Carr
Lawrence North
　High School
Indianapolis, Indiana

Jacky Castellow
Woodinville High School
Woodinville, Wahington

Gail B. Heffner Charles
Walnut Ridge High School
Columbus, Ohio

Desa Dawson
Del City Senior High School
Del City, Oklahoma

Irma Díaz de León
San Antonio Independent
　School District
San Antonio, Texas

Linda Erdman
Huntington Beach Union
　High School District
Huntington Beach,
　California

Janet Ghattas
Weston Public Schools
Weston, Massachusetts

Paula Hirsch
Windward School
Los Angeles, California

Margarita Esparza Hodge
Northern Virginia
　Community College
Alexandria, Virginia

Anne G. Jensen
Campbell Union HIgh
　School District
San Jose, California

Nancy Kilbourn
Simi Valley Unified
Simi Valley, California

María A. Leinenweber
Glendale Unified School
　District
Glendale, California

Cheryl Montana-Sosa
Oakdale Bohemia
　Junior High
Oakdale, New York

VeAnna Morgan
Portland Public Schools
Portland, Oregon

John Nionakis
Hingham Public Schools
Hingham, Massachusetts

Gail R. Pack
McKinney Independent
　School District
McKinney, Texas

Photography

Front Cover: Glencoe photo; inset, Curt Fischer

Bettmann Archives: 370, 479; Fischer, Curt: 255, 334, 345, 444; Franken, Owen/Stock, Boston: 363; Frerck, Robert/Odyssey Productions: 242, 255, 258 (Madrid Post Office, train station, musicians, woman serving food), 260, 261, 263, 274, 281, 282, 284, 288, 296, 298, 302, 303, 307, 308, 312, 328, 332, 343, 365, 366, 367, 368, 376, 377, 378, 388, 389, 390, 392, 393, 394, 396, 401, 413, 427, 430, 431, 438, 440, 455, 456, 457, 461, 463, 465, 476, 483; Gscheidle, Gerhard: 242, 243, 246, 254, 255, 258 (woman in phone booth), 263, 271, 284, 286, 299, 302, 342, 375, 392, 394, 410, 418, 423, 435; Halaska, Jan/The Image Works: 330; Menzel, Peter/Stock, Boston: 240–241; Nettis, Joseph/Stock, Boston: 287; Pavloff, Nick: 247, 278, 323, 327, 335, 347, 354, 359, 371, 379, 404–405, 406, 414, 415, 419, 423, 426, 430, 431, 445, 451, 459, 462, 470, 471; Putnam, Sarah/The Picture Cube: 398, 399.

Illustration

Accardo, Anthony: 248, 349, 380; Christensen, Polly (handwriting): 249, 250, 267, 274, 298, 323, 330, 356; Dyen, Don: 256, 257, 280, 324, 360, 361, 386, 387, 420, 421, 460; Fiorentino, Al: 188, 189, 432, 433; Loehle, Richard: 244, 268, 269, 292, 293, 336, 337, 372, 373, 408, 409 446, 447, 472, 473; Miyamoto, Masami: 304, 434; Schofield, Dennis: 252, 276, 339, 340, 341, 422, 424, 436, 449, 453, 478.

Realia

Courtesy of: AT&T: 487; El Diario de las Américas: 442; Diario El País: 273; Hallmark: 245, 325, 364, 466; Hernández Family: 405 (Quinceañera); Hombre de Mundo: 398; The Madrid Zoo: 266, 272; Más Magazine: 270; Ritmo Magazine: 322; Tú Magazine: 314.

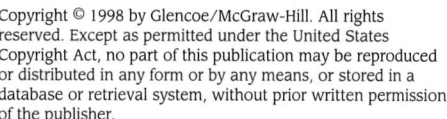

Copyright © 1998 by Glencoe/McGraw-Hill. All rights reserved. Except as permitted under the United States Copyright Act, no part of this publication may be reproduced or distributed in any form or by any means, or stored in a database or retrieval system, without prior written permission of the publisher.

Printed in the United States of America.

Send all inquiries to:
Glencoe/McGraw-Hill
15319 Chatsworth Street
P.O. Box 9609
Mission Hills, California 91346-9609

ISBN 0-02-640066-9 (Student Edition)
ISBN 0-02-640067-7 (Teacher's Wraparound Edition)

1 2 3 4 5 6 7 8 9   RRC   02 01 00 99 98 97 96

¡Acción!

LEVEL 1B

Second Edition

VICKI GALLOWAY
DOROTHY JOBA
ANGELA LABARCA

GLENCOE
McGraw-Hill

New York, New York   Columbus, Ohio   Mission Hills, California   Peoria, Illinois

---

Dr. Vicki Galloway is Associate Professor of Spanish at the Georgia Institute of Technology. She served for six years as State Consultant for Foreign Languages and International Studies in South Carolina. She was formerly Project Director at ACTFL and served as editor of *Foreign Language Annals*. She has taught at the secondary and university levels and has presented numerous teacher-development workshops at the state, regional, and national level. Her publications have appeared in the ACTFL Foreign Language Education Series, *The Modern Language Journal, The Northeast Conference Reports,* and the American Educational Research Association.

Dr. Dorothy J. Joba teaches Spanish, Latin American Studies, and history in the Glastonbury Connecticut Public Schools. She frequently speaks on topics related to those areas at local, regional and national conferences and is a reviewer for professional publications in foreign languages and the social sciences. She has lived and traveled extensively in Latin America and Spain, often directing study groups for teachers and students. Dr. Joba also teaches courses in Spanish and Latin American Studies for the University of Connecticut.

Dr. Angela Labarca is Full Professor of Spanish at the Georgia Institute of Technology. She has had extensive teaching and administrative experience both in the United States and in her native country of Chile. She has participated in the training of foreign language teachers and is a regular presenter at international and domestic conferences. Dr. Labarca has written books on second language acquisition, coauthored Spanish and ESL textbooks, and has written articles that have appeared in *Studies in Second Language Acquisition, Hispania,* and *The Modern Language Journal*.

Contenido

Repaso

1	En la escuela	**R-2**
2	Gente y cosas	**R-7**
3	Después de las clases	**R-12**
4	Lugares	**R-17**
5	Actividades	**R-22**
6	Situaciones	**R-27**
7	Nuevos amigos	**R-31**

CAPÍTULO 4

¿Cómo son los españoles?

Lección 1	**Querida señora Rivera**	242
Vocabulario	Los parientes (family relationships)	244
Cultura viva 1	Don y doña	247
Estructura 1	How to Indicate Possession and Ownership: Su/sus pp. 227 248 364	248
Cultura viva 2	Una tarjeta postal de Madrid	250
Estructura 2	How to Talk About What Others Like to Do: Le(s) + gusta pp. 39 63 251 272	251
Finalmente		253
Lección 2	**¿Cuántos años tiene José Luis?**	254
Vocabulario	Quiero ser... (occupations and professions)	256
Cultura viva 1	¿Quieres comprar algo?	260
Estructura 1	How to Say How Much or How Many: Adjectives of quantity	261
Cultura viva 2	La lotería	263
Estructura 2	How to Count from 100 to 500 pp. 24 192 264 275 352	264
Finalmente		265
Lección 3	**No comprendo a la abuela**	266
Vocabulario	Tengo... (common pets and other animals)	268
Cultura viva 1	Los abuelos	271
Estructura 1	How to Describe Other People's Likes and Dislikes: Le gusta(n)/Les gusta(n) pp. 39 63 251 272	272
Cultura viva 2	Kim escribe en su diario	274
Estructura 2	How to count from 600 to the Thousands pp. 24 192 264 275 352	275
Finalmente		277

Page references within the blue bars indicate the developmental approach to specific grammar topics.

Lección 4	**El álbum de familia**	**278**
Vocabulario	¿Cómo es? Tiene... (describing people)	280
Cultura viva 1	¡Vamos a tomar el tren!	283
Estructura 1	How to Talk About Specific People: The personal **a**	284
Cultura viva 2	Toledo, Ávila y Segovia	286
Estructura 2	How to Say What You Must Do: **Tener que** + infinitive pp. 214 217 287	287
Finalmente		289
Lección 5	**¡Qué divertido es Madrid!**	**290**
Vocabulario	En los ratos libres... (entertainment/diversions)	292
Cultura viva 1	El cine y la tele en España	295
Estructura 1	How to State Preferences: The verb **preferir**	296
Cultura viva 2	¡Me gusta esta ciudad!	298
Estructura 2	How to Talk About Another or Others: **Otro**	299
Finalmente		301
Lección 6	**Escribe la señora Rivera**	**302**
Vocabulario	¿Qué vas a hacer... ? (months and dates)	304
Cultura viva 1	Los jóvenes españoles	307
Estructura 1	How to Request Information: Summary of Question Words	308
Cultura viva 2	Los Angeles: Una ciudad bilingüe	310
Estructura 2	How to Describe What People Can and Can't Do: The verb **poder**	311
Finalmente		313
Lectura	Correo vía satélite	314
Repaso		316

Page references within the blue bars indicate the developmental approach to specific grammar topics.

CAPÍTULO 5

¡Me gusta vivir en Miami!

Lección 1	**¡Gran oferta!**	322
Vocabulario	¿Me puedes hacer un favor? (asking favors)	324
Cultura viva 1	Aquí pueden hablar español	327
Estructura 1	How to Request Favors: Object pronoun **me** pp. 328 331 343 391 412 424	328
Cultura viva 2	Una tarjeta postal a la Argentina	330
Estructura 2	How to Offer Favors: Object pronoun **te** pp. 328 331 343 391 412 424	331
Finalmente		333
Lección 2	**¿Cómo se dice "T-shirt"?**	334
Vocabulario	¿Qué es? ¿Para qué sirve? (describing things)	336
Cultura viva 1	La música latina	339
Estructura 1	How to Describe Something You Don't Know the Word For	340
Cultura viva 2	El español en el trabajo	342
Estructura 2	How to Request, Offer, and Describe Favors: **Me** and **te** with conjugated verbs pp. 328 331 343 391 412 424	343
Finalmente		345
Lección 3	**Tienes que practicar el español**	346
Vocabulario	Soy… (nationalities and languages)	348
Cultura viva 1	La televisión en español	351
Estructura 1	How to Give Dates and Count to a Million pp. 24 192 264 275 352	352
Cultura viva 2	Una carta a la Argentina	354
Estructura 2	How to Say Where People Went: The preterit of **ir**	355
Finalmente		357
Lección 4	**Nuestro idioma**	358
Vocabulario	Te invito a mi casa. (leisure activities)	360
Cultura viva 1	Cuba linda	363
Estructura 1	How to Say What People Possess: **Nuestro(s)/nuestra(s)** pp. 227 248 364	364

Page references within the blue bars indicate the developmental approach to specific grammar topics.

Cultura viva 2	La Argentina	366
Estructura 2	How to Say With Whom You Do Things: The preposition **con**	367
Finalmente		369

Lección 5 — Somos todos americanos — 370

Vocabulario	¿Cúanto tiempo hace que... ? (time expressions)	372
Cultura viva 1	Los cubanoamericanos	375
Estructura 1	How to Say What You Did, What I Did: **Yo** and **tú** forms of the preterit of **-er** and **-ir** verbs	
	pp. 376 395 415 427 440 451 480	376
Cultura viva 2	Una carta de la Argentina	379
Estructura 2	How to Report What Someone Says or Hears: The verbs **decir** and **oír**	380
	How to Request Things: The verb **pedir**	380
Finalmente		383

Lección 6 — El idioma es muy importante — 384

Vocabulario	Los quehaceres de la casa (household chores)	386
Cultura viva 1	Los diminutivos	390
Estructura 1	How to Say What You Do to or for Another Person: Indirect object pronoun **le**	
	pp. 328 331 343 391 412 424	391
Cultura viva 2	El lenguaje: algo muy frágil	394
Estructura 2	How to Say What You Did and Ask What a Friend Did: **Yo** and **tú** forms of the preterit of **-ar** verbs	
	pp. 376 395 415 427 448 451 480	395
Finalmente		397
Lectura	Los ritmos de la música afrocubana invaden la Plaza España de Madrid	398
Repaso		400

Page references within the blue bars indicate the developmental approach to specific grammar topics.

CAPÍTULO 6

De visita en Miami

Lección 1	¡Liquidación de temporada!	406
Vocabulario	Quisiera comprar... (clothing)	408
Cultura viva 1	Los anuncios	411
Estructura 1	How to Say What You Do for Others: Indirect object pronoun **les**	
	pp. 328 331 343 391 412 424	412
Cultura viva 2	¡Tío Lucas y Rafael ya están en Miami!	414
Estructura 2	How to Say What You and Others Did in the Past: Preterit **nosotros** forms	
	pp. 376 395 415 427 440 451 480	415
Finalmente		417

Lección 2	¿Vamos al centro comercial?	418
Vocabulario	¿Qué clase de ropa buscas? (clothing)	420
Cultura viva 1	La Pequeña Habana	423
Estructura 1	How to Say What People Do for You and Others: Object pronoun **nos**	
	pp. 328 331 343 391 412 424	424
Cultura viva 2	La comida cubana	426
Estructura 2	How to Write About the Past: Irregular **yo** forms of certain **-ar** verbs in the preterit	
	pp. 376 395 415 427 440 451 480	427
Finalmente		429

Lección 3	Aquí se dice "guagua"	430
Vocabulario	El parque está... (giving directions/modes of transportation)	432
Cultura viva 1	Los dialectos de un idioma	436
Estructura 1	How to Say That Someone is Coming: The verb **venir**	437
Cultura viva 2	Una carta a los abuelos	439
Estructura 2	How to Say What Someone Did in the Past: Third person singular forms of the preterit	
	pp. 376 395 415 427 440 451 480	440
Finalmente		443

Page references within the blue bars indicate the developmental approach to specific grammar topics.

Lección 4	**Un regalo especial**	**444**
Vocabulario	¿Qué tiempo hace? (weather expressions)	446
Cultura viva 1	Las estaciones del año	450
Estructura 1	How to Talk About What Others Did: Third person plural forms of the preterit	
	pp. 376 395 415 427 440 **451** 480	451
Cultura viva 2	La temperatura	453
Estructura 2	How to Refer to People and Things Already Mentioned: Direct object pronouns	454
Finalmente		457
Lección 5	**En el centro comercial**	**458**
Vocabulario	Tengo… (expressing feelings and conditions)	460
Cultura viva 1	Las tallas	462
Estructura 1	How to Make Comparisons of Numbers and Amounts: **Más/menos… que; tanto… como**	463
Cultura viva 2	La quinceañera	466
Estructura 2	How to Make Comparisons Based on Characteristics: **Tan… como; Más/Menos… que**	467
Finalmente		469
Lección 6	**¿Qué talla, por favor?**	**470**
Vocabulario	¿Cuánto(a)… ? (asking for descriptions)	472
Cultura viva 1	El sistema métrico	476
Estructura 1	How to Distinguish One Thing from Another: **Este/ese**	477
Cultura viva 2	José Martí	479
Estructura 2	How to Talk About the Past: Summary of the preterit	
	pp. 376 395 415 427 440 451 **480**	480
Finalmente		483
Lectura	Permita que el SeaEscape le lleve en un crucero por un día	484
Repaso		486

Page references within the blue bars indicate the developmental approach to specific grammar topics.

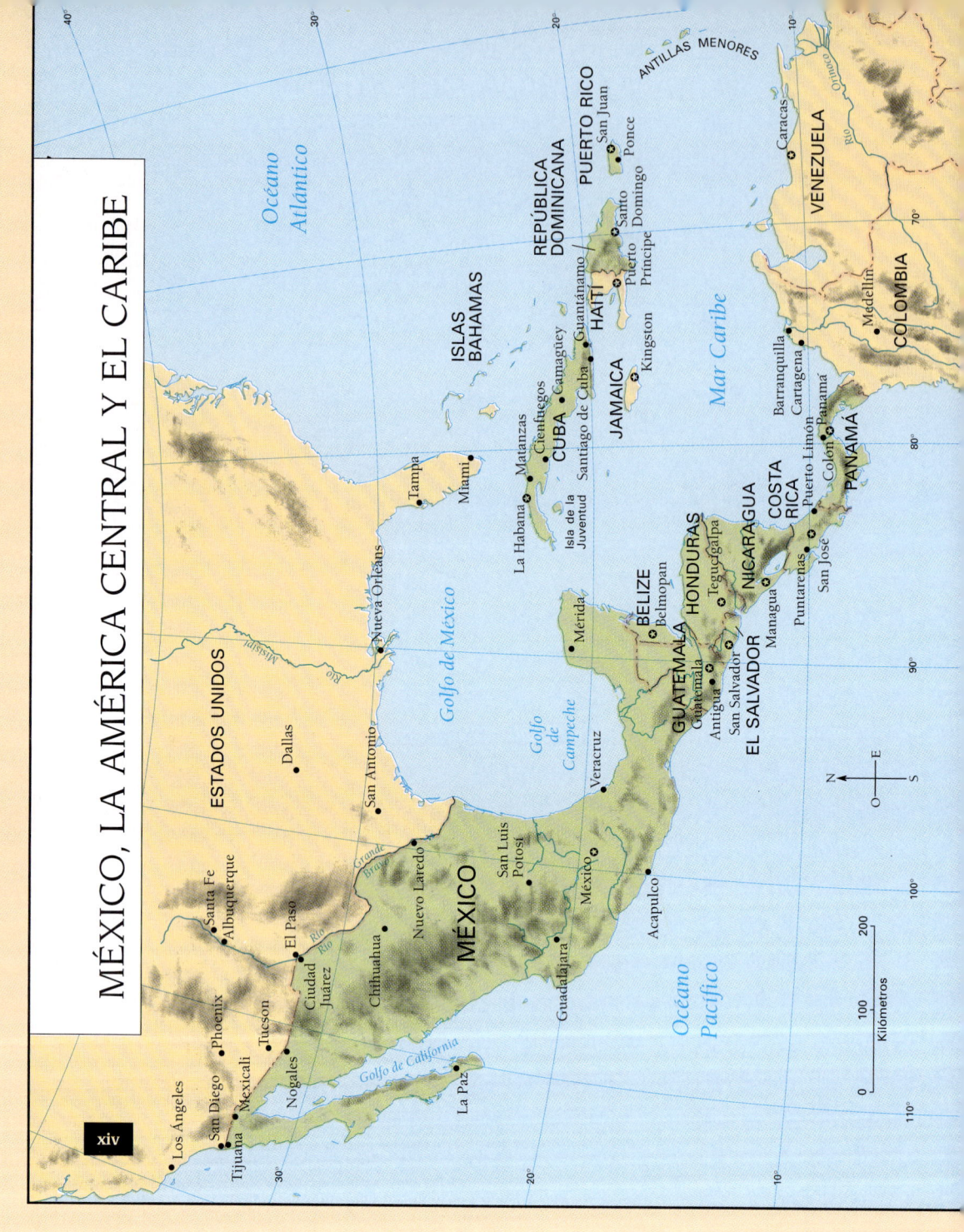

Repaso

Enlace

En la escuela

Bell Ringer Review

Directions to students: Copy the names of the following countries and write the name of the capital beside each one.
1. México
2. Argentina
3. España
4. Panamá
5. Venezuela

Actividad A
Estructura Review

Following are the Estructura topics reviewed in this activity, and the lessons where these topics were first introduced.
1. Informal greetings: Capítulo 1, Lección 1 (p. 4)
2. Formal greetings: Capítulo 1, Lección 3 (p. 27)
3. Use of **señor, señora, señorita** Capítulo 1, Lección 3 (p. 27)

Vocabulario Review

Actividad A reviews vocabulary from the following lessons:
Capítulo 1, Lección 1 (p. 6)
Capítulo 1, Lección 3 (p. 27)

Actividad A Answers
1. Buenos días, señora Garza. ¿Cómo está usted?
2. Buenas tardes, señor Hernández. ¿Cómo está usted?
3. Hola, Carlos. ¿Cómo estás?
4. Buenas tardes, señorita Guzmán. ¿Cómo está usted?
5. Hola, Paula. ¿Cómo estás?

Actividad B
Estructura Review

Following are the Estructura topics reviewed in this activity, and the lessons where these topics were first introduced.
1. Asking where someone is from: Capítulo 1, Lección 1 (p. 4)
2. Telling where one is from: Capítulo 1, Lección 1 (p. 4)

1 En la escuela

A **Buenos días.** How would you greet the following people you meet at school at the following times of day?

Por ejemplo:
Srta. Varela
Buenas noches, señorita Varela. ¿Cómo está usted?

1. Sra. Garza
2. Sr. Hernández
3. tu amigo Carlos

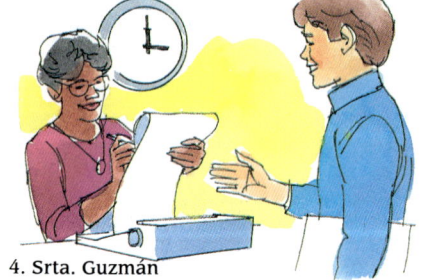

4. Srta. Guzmán

5. tu compañera de clase Paula

B **¿De dónde son?** Below are some new students in school. Tell the country and city the people below are from.

Por ejemplo:

Paco: los Estados Unidos, de Nueva York
Paco es de los Estados Unidos, de Nueva York.

1. Antonio y Luisa: los Estados Unidos, de Los Ángeles
2. Carlos y Lupe: México, de la Ciudad de México
3. Roberto: la República Dominicana, de Santo Domingo
4. Paula: Ecuador, de Quito
5. Carmen: Argentina, de Buenos Aires
6. Lucas: Venezuela, de Caracas
7. Marisol: Costa Rica, de San José
8. Juan José: Puerto Rico, de San Juan

3. Third person singular of ser: Capítulo 2, Lección 1 (p. 83)
4. Third person plural of ser: Capítulo 2, Lección 1 (p. 87)

Vocabulario Review
Actividad A reviews vocabulary from the following lesson:
Capítulo 1, Lección 1 (p. 9)

Actividad B Answers
1. Antonio y Luisa son de los Estados Unidos, de Los Ángeles.
2. ... son de México, de la Ciudad de México.
3. ... es de la República Dominicana, de Santo Domingo.
4. ... es de Ecuador, de Quito.
5. ... es de Argentina, de Buenos Aires.
6. ... es de Venezuela, de Caracas.
7. ... es de Costa Rica, de San José.
8. Juan José es de Puerto Rico, de San Juan.

Actividad C
Estructura Review
Following are the Estructura topics reviewed in this activity, and the lessons where these topics were first introduced.

1. Numbers (0–20): Capítulo 1, Lección 3 (p. 24)
2. Telling at what time something happens: Capítulo 1, Lección 3, (pp. 28–29)
3. Use of **de** for specifics: Capítulo 1, Lección 4 (p. 43)
4. Numbers (20–100): Capítulo 3, Lección 3 (p. 192)

Vocabulario Review
Actividad C reviews vocabulary from the following lessons:
Capítulo 1, Lección 3 (p. 24)
Capítulo 1, Lección 4 (pp. 34–35)

Actividad C Answers
Answers will vary but may include the following:
La clase de español es a las ocho.
La clase de matemáticas es a las...
La clase de ciencia es a las...
La clase de historia es a las...
La clase de arte es a las...
La clase de francés es a las...

Actividad D
Estructura Review
Following are the Estructura topics reviewed in this activity, and the lessons where these topics were first introduced.

1. Telling at what time something happens: Capítulo 1, Lección 3 (pp. 28–29)
2. **Me/te gusta(n)** + object(s): Capítulo 1, Lección 6 (p. 63)
3. Third person singular of **ser:** Capítulo 2, Lección 1 (p. 83)
4. **Tengo/tienes:** Capítulo 3, Lección 5 (p. 214)

C 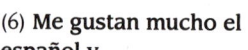 **El horario.** Write out a schedule of the courses you are taking, using the Spanish names of the courses. Tell the class your schedule. Your teacher will provide the names of courses you don't know how to say in Spanish.

Por ejemplo:
> La clase de álgebra es a la una y veinte y tres.

D **Las clases de este año.** Converse with a classmate about your impressions of school so far this year. Find out the following:
1. what classes you are taking
2. who your teachers are
3. if the classes meet in the morning or afternoon
4. which classes you like and don't like

Por ejemplo:

ESTUDIANTE A	ESTUDIANTE B
(1) ¿Qué clases tienes?	(2) **Por la mañana tengo inglés, historia, geometría y, claro, español.**
(3) ¿Quién es tu maestro de historia?	(4) **Es la señora Kent.**
(5) ¿Qué clases te gustan más?	(6) **Me gustan mucho el español y...**

E Los ideales. Use the list of qualities below to describe the following people.

1. an ideal friend
2. boyfriend or girlfriend **(novio[a])**
3. teacher

Say three things about each person. Compare your ideals with those of a classmate. Do you have anything in common?

Por ejemplo:

> El (La) amigo(a) ideal debe ser simpático(a) y divertido(a). No debe ser arrogante.

aburrido(a)
alto(a)
amable
antipático(a)
aplicado(a)
arrogante
bajo(a)
bueno(a)
delgado(a)
deprimente
diferente
difícil
divertido(a)
elegante
feo(a)
generoso(a)
gordo(a)
impaciente
inteligente
joven
malo(a)
perezoso(a)
popular
puntual
raro(a)
simpático(a)
sociable
tacaño(a)
tonto(a)

Vocabulario Review
Actividad D reviews vocabulary from the following lessons:
Capítulo 1, Lección 2 (p. 14)
Capítulo 1, Lección 3 (p. 27)
Capítulo 1, Lección 4 (p. 34)

Actividad D Answers
Answers will vary but should follow the model.

Actividad E
Estructura Review
Following are the Estructura topics reviewed in this activity, and the lessons where these topics were first introduced.

1. Nouns (gender, number): Capítulo 1, Lección 4 (p. 42)
2. Use of adjectives ending in **-o/-a**, **-e**, or a consonant: Capítulo 2, Lección 2 (p. 96)
3. **Deber** + infinitive: Capítulo 3, Lección 1 (pp. 160–162)

Vocabulario Review
Actividad E reviews vocabulary from the following lessons:
Capítulo 1, Lección 2 (pp. 14–15)
Capítulo 2, Lección 1 (pp. 78–79)
Capítulo 2, Lección 2 (pp. 92–93)
Capítulo 2, Lección 3 (pp. 104–105)

Actividad E Answers
Answers will vary but should follow the model.

Class Management
You may wish to do Actividad E as a whole class activity initially. Then you may want to have students work in small groups to write down their descriptions. Small group descriptions may be shared with the class.

Actividad F
Estructura Review
Following are the Estructura topics reviewed in this activity, and the lessons where these topics were first introduced.

1. Use of **de** for specifics: Capítulo 1, Lección 4 (p. 43)
2. Third person singular of **ser**: Capítulo 2, Lección 1 (p. 83)
3. Third person plural of **ser**: Capítulo 2, Lección 1 (p. 87)
4. Use of adjectives ending in **-o/-a, -e,** or a consonant: Capítulo 2, Lección 2 (p. 96)

Vocabulario Review
Actividad F reviews vocabulary from the following lessons:
Capítulo 1, Lección 4 (p. 34)
Capítulo 2, Lección 1 (p. 79)
Capítulo 2, Lección 2 (pp. 92–93)

Actividad F Answers
Answers will vary.

Actividad G
Estructura Review
Following are the Estructura topics reviewed in this activity, and the lessons where these topics were first introduced.

1. Informal greetings: Capítulo 1, Lección 1 (p. 4)
2. **Me/te gusta** + infinitive: Capítulo 1, Lección 4 (p. 39)
3. **Quiero/quieres ir:** Capítulo 1, Lección 5 (p. 55)
4. **Vivo en** + place: Capítulo 3, Lección 1 (p. 161)
5. Present tense of **-ir** verbs: Capítulo 3, Lección 1 (p. 167)

Vocabulario Review
Actividad G reviews vocabulary from the following lessons:
Capítulo 1, Lección 1 (p. 6)
Capítulo 1, Lección 2 (pp. 14–15)
Capítulo 1, Lección 5 (p. 49)
Capítulo 3, Lección 1 (p. 161)

Actividad G Answers
¡Hola! Me llamo...
¡Qué tal!
¿Qué te gusta hacer?
¿Quieres ir...?
¿Dónde vives?
¿Cuál es tu número de teléfono?

F **Descripciones.** A new student asks you to describe the following.

Por ejemplo:

> dos de tus clases
> *La clase de ciencias es muy interesante pero es un poco difícil. La clase de música es...*

1. dos amigos(as)
2. dos maestros
3. dos libros
4. dos equipos de tu escuela
5. dos de tus clases

G **¡Hola!** Greet and introduce yourself to a classmate. Ask how he or she is. Find out what your classmate likes to do. Invite him or her to go someplace after school. Find out your classmate's address and phone number.

2 Gente y cosas

A **¿Cuántos saben...?** On a piece of paper, write the activities below. Working in groups of five, see who can find the greatest number of people in the group who know how to do each one. Write the name of the person next to each activity. Report back to the class.

Por ejemplo:
   patinar

ESTUDIANTE A
Oye, Tina, ¿sabes patinar?

(A la clase): Tina sabe patinar.

ESTUDIANTE B
Sí, sé patinar.

1. andar en monopatín
2. esquiar
3. tocar un instrumento musical
4. jugar fútbol
5. nadar
6. patinar sobre hielo
7. cocinar
8. bailar
9. dibujar
10. sacar fotos

Gente y cosas

Bell Ringer Review
Describe two of your classmates in terms of personality and physical characteristics.
Por ejemplo: Jason es simpático, generoso y divertido. Es bastante alto.

Actividad A
Estructura Review
Following is the Estructura topic reviewed in this activity, and the lesson where it was first introduced.
Se/sabes + infinitive: Capítulo 1, Lección 5 (p. 52)

Vocabulario Review
Actividad A reviews vocabulary from the following lessons:
Capítulo 1, Lección 2 (pp. 14–15)
Capítulo 1, Lección 5 (p. 48)

Actividad A Answers
Answers will vary but should include the use of **sé** and **sabe(s)**.

Class Management
You may wish to refer to the Teacher's Manual for suggestions regarding small group work.

Actividad B
Estructura Review
Following is the Estructura topic reviewed in this activity, and the lesson where it was first introduced.
Nouns (gender, number): Capítulo 1, Lección 4 (pp. 42–43)

Vocabulario Review
Actividad B reviews vocabulary from the following lessons:
Capítulo 1, Lección 3 (p. 24)
Capítulo 1, Lección 4 (p. 34–35)
Capítulo 2, Lección 1 (p. 79)
Capítulo 2, Lección 2 (pp. 92–93)
Capítulo 2, Lección 5 (pp. 130–131)
Capítulo 2, Lección 6 (p. 142)
Capítulo 3, Lección 5 (pp. 210–211)
Capítulo 3, Lección 6 (pp. 227–228)

Actividad B Answers
1. el equipo
2. la pregunta
3. el cantante
4. el guitarrista
5. la mantequilla
6. viejo
7. adentro
8. la carne
9. el viernes
10. la moneda
11. el horno
12. enojado
13. aquí
14. el trabajo
15. entonces

B Categorías. In each group of words below, there is one word that doesn't belong. Tell what it is.

Por ejemplo:

la tienda, el restaurante, la ropa, la casa
la ropa

1. el fútbol, el equipo, el baloncesto, el béisbol
2. el cuaderno, el lápiz, el bolígrafo, la pregunta
3. el martes, el sábado, el cantante, el jueves
4. el guitarrista, el francés, la química, la historia
5. la mantequilla, el agua, el refresco, la gaseosa
6. verde, morado, viejo, azul
7. quince, treinta, adentro, sesenta
8. la camiseta, el cartel, la carne, la grabadora
9. el viernes, el televisor, el estéreo, la computadora
10. la moneda, la silla, el armario, la cama
11. el baño, el horno, la sala, la habitación
12. enojado, tercero, quinto, primero
13. esta tarde, a veces, por la noche, aquí
14. el muchacho, la compañera, el trabajo, la maestra
15. joven, guapo, entonces, divertido

CARTA
SERVICIO E I. V. A. 6% INCLUIDO
RESTAURANTE
3ª categoría

...S Y JUGOS DE FRUTA
...anja 200
.... 615
.... 1.225
.... 1.485
...go) 1.050
.... 520
.... 310
.... 615
a y tomate 285
on pollo y jamón) 1.335
.... 1.475

...DO
...UMADOS

SOPAS
e hora (de pescados y mariscos) 640
.... 370
.... 310
huevo 395

...ero

HUEVOS 700
.... 410
tos con salmón ahumado 410
tos con champiñón 700
.... 410

ASADOS Y PARRILLAS
.... 1.550
.... 1.690
COCHINILLO ASADO 515
CORDERO ASADO 620
Pollo asado 1/2 640
Pollo en cacerola 1/2 950
Pechuga «Villeroy» 745
Perdiz estofada (o escabechada) 1/2 .... 1.290
Chuletas de cerdo adobadas 1.175
Filete de ternera con patatas 1.090
Escalope de ternera con patatas 1.550
Ternera asada con guisantes 1.550
Solomillo con patatas 1.295
Solomillo con champiñón 1.180
Entrecot a la plancha, con guarnición
Ternera a la Riojana

POSTRES 260
.... 350
.... 350
.... 350
Cuajada 350

C La comida. Arrange each of the following foods below into its appropriate category.

1. **bebidas** (beverages)
2. **carnes**
3. **legumbres**
4. **almidones** (starches)
5. **productos lácteos** (milk products)
6. **postres**

D El menú. The Spanish Club is looking for suggestions for what to serve at their banquet. Working with a classmate, write a note with your suggestions for the following.

Por ejemplo:

   El primer plato debe ser...

1. el primer plato
2. el segundo plato
3. el tercer plato
4. el postre
5. las bebidas

R-9

Actividad C
Vocabulario Review
Actividad C reviews vocabulary from the following lesson:
Capítulo 2, Lección 5 (pp. 130–131)

Actividad C Answers
bebidas: jugo, leche, té
carnes: hamburguesa, jamón
legumbres: frijoles, tomates
almidones: cereal, arroz, papas
productos lácteos: leche, queso, mantequilla, helado
postres: helado, pastel, fruta

Actividad D
Estructura Review
Following are the Estructura topics reviewed in this activity, and the lessons where these topics were first introduced.

1. **Deber** + infinitive: Capítulo 3, Lección 1 (p. 160)
2. Ordinal numbers: Capítulo 3, Lección 2 (p. 179)

Vocabulario Review
Actividad D reviews vocabulary from the following lessons:
Capítulo 2, Lección 5 (pp. 130–131)
Capítulo 3, Lección 2 (p. 176)

Actividad D Answers
Answers will vary but may include the following:

1. El primer plato debe ser ensalada.
2. El segundo plato debe ser sopa de tomate.
3. El tercer plato debe ser pollo, arroz y legumbres.
4. El postre debe ser helado y pastel.
5. Las bebidas deben ser leche, jugo y refrescos.

Actividad E
Estructura Review
Following is the Estructura topic reviewed in this activity, and the lesson where it was first introduced.
Concept of the infinitive: Capítulo 2, Lección 2 (p. 99)

Vocabulario Review
Actividad E reviews vocabulary from the following lessons:
Capítulo 1, Lección 2 (pp. 14–15)
Capítulo 2, Lección 5 (pp. 130–131)
Capítulo 3, Lección 1 (pp. 162–163)
Capítulo 3, Lección 5 (pp. 210–211)
Capítulo 3, Lección 6 (pp. 222–223)

Actividad E Answers
Answers will vary but may include the following:
1. hamburguesas, huevos, jamón...
2. agua, café, gaseosa, jugo...
3. libros, revistas...
4. la tele, un partido...
5. la maleta, el pasaporte, la cámara...
6. la calculadora, el coche, el estéreo...
7. el lápiz, el bolígrafo...
8. la bicicleta, la mochila, el tomate...
9. la camiseta, el cuaderno, la lechuga...
10. el coche, la chaqueta, el cielo...
11. la leche, el pan, el papel...
12. el queso, el lápiz...

Actividad F
Estructura Review
Following is the Estructura topic reviewed in this activity, and the lesson where it was first introduced.
The verb **hay**: Capítulo 3, Lección 3 (p. 195)

Vocabulario Review
Actividad F reviews vocabulary from the following lessons:
Capítulo 1, Lección 2 (pp. 14–15)
Capítulo 1, Lección 4 (pp. 34–35)
Capítulo 1, Lección 5 (p. 49)
Capítulo 3, Lección 1 (pp. 162–163)
Capítulo 3, Lección 3 (pp. 188–189)
Capítulo 3, Lección 6 (pp. 227–228)

E Cosas, cosas y más cosas. With a classmate, list all the things that you can think of that could fit the descriptions below.

Por ejemplo:
> para jugar
> *los videojuegos, el fútbol americano, el tenis...*

1. para comer
2. para tomar
3. para leer
4. para ver
5. para viajar
6. para usar
7. para escribir
8. rojo
9. verde
10. azul
11. blanco
12. amarillo

F ¿Qué hay? Tell what there is in each of the following places.

Por ejemplo:
> en la cafetería de la escuela
> *Hay mesas, sillas, ventanas...*

1. en las clases
2. en tu habitación
3. en la cocina
4. en la sala
5. en el centro comercial
6. en la mochila
7. en la fiesta
8. en la maleta de un turista
9. en un edificio grande

G **Descripciones.** Give examples of the following people and things, according to the descriptive words.

Por ejemplo:

las ciudades de tu estado: grande / pequeño
_____ es una ciudad grande y _____ es una ciudad pequeña.

1. los videojuegos: nuevo / viejo
2. las películas: bueno / malo
3. los cantantes: guapo / feo
4. las cantantes: fenomenal / malo
5. las actrices: bueno / malo
6. las tiendas: caro / barato
7. los libros: emocionante / aburrido
8. los programas de televisión: divertido / triste
9. los equipos: formidable / malo
10. las comidas de un restaurante: bueno / malo
11. los deportistas: sensacional / regular

Actividad F Answers
Answers will vary.

Actividad G
Estructura Review
Following are the Estructura topics reviewed in this activity, and the lessons where these topics were first introduced.

1. Nouns (gender, number): Capítulo 1, Lección 4 (pp. 42–43)
2. Present tense of **ser:** Capítulo 2, Lección 1 (pp. 83 and 87)
3. Use of adjectives ending in **-o/-a, -e,** or a consonant: Capítulo 2, Lección 2 (p. 96)

Vocabulario Review
Actividad G reviews vocabulary from the following lessons:
Capítulo 1, Lección 5 (pp. 48–49)
Capítulo 2, Lección 1 (pp. 78–79)
Capítulo 2, Lección 2 (pp. 92–93)
Capítulo 2, Lección 5 (pp. 130–131)

Actividad G Answers
Answers will vary but may include the following:

1. ... es un videojuego nuevo y ... es un videojuego viejo.
2. ... es una película buena y... es una película mala.
3. ... es un cantante guapo y... es un cantante feo.
4. ... es una cantante fenomenal y... es una cantante mala.
5. ... una actriz buena y... es una actriz mala.
6. ... es una tienda cara y... es una tienda barata.
7. ... es un libro emocionante y ... es un libro aburrido.
8. ... es un programa divertido y... es un programa triste.
9. ... es un equipo formidable y ... es un equipo malo.
10. ... es una comida buena y... es una comida mala.
11. ... es un(a) deportista sensacional y... es un(a) deportista regular.

Después de las clases

Bell Ringer Review
Directions to students: Write a menu for breakfast and lunch for three consecutive days.

Actividad A
Estructura Review
Following are the Estructura topics reviewed in this activity, and the lessons where these topics were first introduced.
1. Third person singular of **-ar/-er** verbs: Capítulo 2, Lección 5 (p. 134)
2. Singular and plural usage of days of the week: Capítulo 2, Lección 6 (p. 149)
3. Present tense of **-ir** verbs: Capítulo 3, Lección 1 (p. 167)

Vocabulario Review
Actividad A reviews vocabulary from the following lessons:
Capítulo 1, Lección 2 (pp. 14–15)
Capítulo 1, Lección 4 (pp. 34–35)
Capítulo 1, Lección 5 (pp. 48–49)
Capítulo 2, Lección 3 (pp. 104–105)
Capítulo 2, Lección 6 (pp. 142–143)
Capítulo 3, Lección 1 (pp. 162–163)

Actividad A Answers
1. Los sábados lava el coche.
2. Los miércoles hace ejercicio.
3. Los jueves ve partidos.
4. Los lunes va al parque.
5. Los viernes trabaja en el centro comercial.

Extension
After doing actividad A you may wish to extend the activity by asking students to say what Raquel does each day of a given week.

3 Después de las clases

A **El calendario.** Tell what Raquel does on each of the days below, according to her calendar.

Por ejemplo:
   los martes
   Los martes juega boliche.

1. los sábados
2. los miércoles
3. los jueves
4. los lunes
5. los viernes

R-12

B **¿Qué quieres hacer?** School is dismissed early today. List eight things you want to do in your free time and put them in order of preference. Choose from the list below or think of activities of your own.

Por ejemplo:

> Primero quiero ir al cine. Después quiero...

comer
hablar con
comprar
ir a (al, a la)
escuchar
leer
ver
jugar
preparar

Actividad B
Estructura Review
Following are the Estructura topics reviewed in this activity, and the lessons where these topics were first introduced.
1. **Quiero/quieres** + activity: Capítulo 1, Lección 2 (p. 18)
2. Putting events in sequence—"now, then, afterward": Capítulo 2, Lección 3 (pp. 102–103)

Vocabulario Review
Actividad B reviews vocabulary from the following lessons:
Capítulo 1, Lección 2 (pp. 14–15)
Capítulo 1, Lección 4 (pp. 34–35)
Capítulo 1, Lección 5 (pp. 48–49)
Capítulo 2, Lección 3 (pp. 104–105)

Actividad B Answers
Answers will vary but may include the following:
Primero quiero comer. Después quiero ir al cine. Luego quiero escuchar discos. Después quiero ver la tele y jugar baloncesto. Ahora quiero preparar la tarea y leer.

Actividad C
Estructura Review
Following are the Estructura topics reviewed in this activity, and the lessons where these topics were first introduced.
1. **Me/te gusta** + infinitive: Capítulo 1, Lección 4 (p. 39)
2. **Quiero/quieres** + infinitive: Capítulo 1, Lección 2 (pp. 18–19)
3. Use of **a la/al** + place: Capítulo 1, Lección 5 (p. 55)

Vocabulario Review
Actividad C reviews vocabulary from the following lessons:
Capítulo 1, Lección 2 (pp. 14–15)
Capítulo 1, Lección 4 (pp. 34–35)
Capítulo 1, Lección 5 (pp. 48–49)
Capítulo 2, Lección 3 (pp. 104–105)
Capítulo 2, Lección 4 (p. 118)

Actividad C Answers
Answers will vary but should follow the model. You may wish to have each student prepare his or her list prior to working with a partner.

C **Gustos.** Make two lists, one of your five favorite weekend activities and another of at least three things you don't like to do.

   Me gusta...   No me gusta...

A classmate will ask you about your list and invite you to go to appropriate places. Decide what time you will go there and report your plans to the class.

Por ejemplo:

ESTUDIANTE A	ESTUDIANTE B
(1) ¿Qué te gusta hacer?	(2) **Me gusta andar en monopatín, jugar baloncesto...**
(3) ¿Quieres ir al parque esta tarde (mañana, el sábado por la mañana, etc.)?	(4) **Sí, cómo no. Gracias.**

Tossa de Mar, España.

D ¿Qué hay en la fiesta? Yolanda's family gave her a big birthday party. Working with a classmate, describe what you see and where you see each item. Make five statements.

Por ejemplo:

ESTUDIANTE A
Afuera hay una piscina.

ESTUDIANTE B
Y en la mesa hay mucha comida. Por ejemplo, hay papas fritas y hamburguesas. A la derecha hay...

Actividad D
Estructura Review
Following are the Estructura topics reviewed in this activity, and the lessons where these topics were first introduced.

1. Use of location descriptors: Capítulo 3, Lección 3 (p. 188–189)
2. The verb **hay**: Capítulo 3, Lección 3 (p. 195)

Vocabulario Review
Actividad D reviews vocabulary from the following lessons:
Capítulo 2, Lección 5 (pp. 130–131)
Capítulo 3, Lección 3 (p. 188)
Capítulo 3, Lección 6 (pp. 222–223)

Actividad D Answers
Answers will vary but may include the following:
Adentro hay un televisor. Afuera hay una piscina, unas mesas y unas sillas.

Actividad E
Estructura Review
Following are the Estructura topics reviewed in this activity, and the lessons where these topics were first introduced.

1. Third person plural of **-ar/-er** verbs: Capítulo 2, Lección 5 (p. 137)
2. Third person plural of **-ir** verbs: Capítulo 3, Lección 1 (p. 167)

Vocabulario Review
Actividad E reviews vocabulary from the following lessons:
Capítulo 1, Lección 2 (pp. 14–15)
Capítulo 1, Lección 5 (pp. 48–49)

Actividad E Answers
Answers will vary but may include the following:
Hablan con los amigos, comen hamburguesas, bailan, juegan, etc.

Actividad F
Estructura Review
Following are the Estructura topics reviewed in this activity, and the lessons where these topics were first introduced.

1. First and second person singular of **llamarse**: Chapter 1, Lesson 1 (p. 4)
2. Asking and telling where one is from Capítulo 1, Lección 1 (p. 4)
3. **Soy, eres, es**: Capítulo 2, Lección 1 (p. 83)
4. Singular and plural use of the days of the week: Capítulo 2, Lección 6 (p. 149)
5. Summary of present tense forms: Capítulo 3, Lección 1 (pp. 170–171)

Vocabulario Review
Actividad F reviews vocabulary from the following lessons:
Capítulo 1, Lección 1 (p. 4)
Capítulo 1, Lección 1 (p. 9)
Capítulo 1, Lección 5 (p. 48–49)
Capítulo 2, Lección 3 (pp. 104–105)
Capítulo 2, Lección 6 (p. 142)
Capítulo 3, Lección 1 (p. 160)
Capítulo 3, Lección 1 (p. 162–163)

Actividad F Answers
Answers will vary.

E **¿Y qué hacen?** Now tell all the activities that Yolanda and her guests are doing at the party on page E15.

Por ejemplo:
> Nadan en la piscina, comen mucho, bailan...

F **Entrevista.** Find out the following information about a classmate. Write down his or her answers. Then introduce him or her to the class.

Por ejemplo:
> ¿Cómo se llama?

ESTUDIANTE A	ESTUDIANTE B
¿Cómo te llamas?	Me llamo Tim Martínez.

(A la clase:) Se llama Tim Martínez.

1. ¿Cómo está?
2. ¿De dónde es?
3. ¿Dónde vive?
4. ¿Qué hace después de las clases? ¿los fines de semana? ¿de vacaciones?
5. ¿Cuándo sale con los amigos?

4 Lugares

A En Madrid. Tell what floor each of the following persons or things is on.

Por ejemplo:
> la oficina del Sr. Ortiz
> *Está en el primer piso.*

1. los servicios
2. la basura
3. la cafetería
4. la biblioteca
5. el vestíbulo

Lugares

Bell Ringer Review
Directions to students: Turn your paper sideways and write the days of the week in Spanish across the top. Then under each day, write two activities you do after school.

Actividad A
Estructura Review
Following are the Estructura topics reviewed in this activity, and the lessons where these topics were first introduced.

1. Ordinal numbers (to décimo): Capítulo 3. Lección 2 (p. 179)
2. Present tense of **estar** for location: Capítulo 3, Lección 2, (p. 182)

Vocabulario Review
Actividad A reviews vocabulary from the following lessons:
Capítulo 3, Lección 2 (p. 176)
Capítulo 3, Lección 3 (p. 188)

Actividad A Answers
1. Los servicios están en la planta baja.
2. La basura está en el sótano.
3. La cafetería está en el segundo piso.
4. La biblioteca está en el tercer piso.
5. El vestíbulo está en la planta baja.

Actividad B
Estructura Review
Following are the Estructura topics reviewed in this activity, and the lessons where these topics were first introduced.

1. Nouns (gender, number): Capítulo 1, Lección 4 (pp. 42–43)
2. Concept of the infinitive: Capítulo 2, Lección 2 (p. 99)

Vocabulario Review
Actividad B reviews vocabulary from the following lessons:
Capítulo 1, Lección 2 (pp. 14–15)
Capítulo 1, Lección 4 (pp. 34–35)
Capítulo 1, Lección 5 (pp. 48–49)
Capítulo 2, Lección 3 (pp. 104–105)
Capítulo 2, Lección 5 (pp. 130–131)
Capítulo 2, Lección 6 (pp. 142–143)
Capítulo 3, Lección 1 (pp. 162–163)
Capítulo 3, Lección 6 (pp. 222–223)

Actividad B Answers
Answers will vary but may include the following:

1. estudiar, leer
2. montar en bicicleta, jugar tenis
3. ir al cine, manejar un coche
4. estudiar, aprender
5. nadar, esquiar
6. descansar, dormir
7. comprar, jugar videojuegos
8. cocinar, comer
9. hablar, bailar
10. escuchar, ver
11. comprar, buscar

B Actividades. List at least two activities you associate with the following places. Use infinitives.

Por ejemplo:

    el campo
    montar a caballo, practicar deportes, dar un paseo...

1. la biblioteca
2. el parque
3. la ciudad
4. la escuela
5. la playa
6. tu habitación
7. el centro comercial
8. la cocina
9. la fiesta
10. el concierto
11. el supermercado

Músicos y bailarines en Los Ángeles, California.

C **¿Para qué van allí?** Working with a classmate, tell why you go to the places below. Which pair of students can come up with the most complete list of activities for each place?

Por ejemplo:

Vamos a casa cuando queremos (necesitamos)...

Actividad C
Estructura Review
Following are the Estructura topics reviewed in this activity, and the lessons where these topics were first introduced.

1. **Quiere/quieres** + infinitive: Capítulo 1, Lección 2 (p. 18)
2. Use of **a la/al** + place: Capítulo 1, Lección 5 (p. 55)
3. Concept of the infinitive: Capítulo 2, Lección 2 (p. 99)
4. Summary of the present tense forms: Capítulo 3, Lección 1 (pp. 170–171)

Vocabulario Review
Actividad C reviews vocabulary from the following lessons:
Capítulo 1, Lección 2 (pp. 14–15)
Capítulo 1, Lección 4 (p. 24)
Capítulo 1, Lección 5 (pp. 48–49)
Capítulo 2, Lección 3 (pp. 104–105)
Capítulo 2, Lección 5 (pp. 130–131)
Capítulo 2, Lección 6 (pp. 142–143)
Capítulo 3, Lección 1 (pp. 162–163)
Capítulo 3, Lección 6 (pp. 222–223)

Actividad C Answers
Answers will vary but may include the following:

1. Vamos a la escuela cuando queremos estudiar, aprender, hablar con los maestros.
2. Vamos al parque cuando queremos dar un paseo, correr, montar en bicicleta.
3. Vamos a la habitación cuando queremos dormir, estudiar, escuchar música.
4. Vamos a la cocina cuando necesitamos cocinar, comer algo, tomar algo.
5. Vamos a la sala cuando queremos ver la tele, leer, escuchar la radio, escuchar discos.
6. Vamos a la tienda de música cuando queremos comprar discos y casetes.
7. Vamos a la playa cuando queremos nadar.

Actividad D
Estructura Review
Following are the Estructura topics reviewed in this activity, and the lessons where these topics were first introduced.
1. Telling at what time something happens: Capítulo 1, Lección 3 (p. 28)
2. First person singular of **-ar/-er** verbs: Capítulo 2, Lección 4 (p. 122)
3. First person singular of **-ir** verbs: Capítulo 3, Lección 1 (p. 167)
4. Present tense of **estar** for location: Capítulo 3, Lección 2 (p. 182)

Vocabulario Review
Actividad D reviews vocabulary from the following lessons:
Capítulo 1, Lección 2 (pp. 14–15)
Capítulo 1, Lección 3 (p. 24)
Capítulo 1, Lección 4 (pp. 34–35)
Capítulo 1, Lección 5 (pp. 48–49)
Capítulo 2, Lección 3 (pp. 104–105)
Capítulo 2, Lección 5 (pp. 130–131)
Capítulo 2, Lección 6 (pp. 142–143)
Capítulo 3, Lección 6 (pp. 222–223)

Actividad D Answers
Student B's answers will vary, but may include the following:
1. **Estoy en la cafetería de la escuela. Tomo leche y como pan.**
2. **... en la clase de historia. Leo y contesto preguntas.**
3. **... en la clase de educación física. Practico deportes.**
4. **... en la cafetería. Como una hamburguesa, papas fritas y tomo un refresco.**
5. **... en la clase de inglés. Escribo una composición.**
6. **... en la clase de música. Canto.**
7. **... en el centro comercial. Trabajo en una tienda.**
8. **... en casa. Estudio, leo y escribo.**

D **Todo el día.** Find out where a classmate normally is at the following times of day and what he or she usually does there.

Por ejemplo:

(de la mañana)

ESTUDIANTE A	ESTUDIANTE B
(1) ¿Dónde estás a las ocho de la mañana?	(2) Estoy en la clase de español.
(3) ¿Y qué haces?	(4) **Pues, hablo con mis compañeros, escucho casetes o escribo.**

 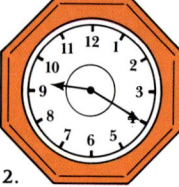 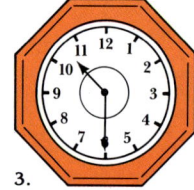 

1. (de la mañana) 2. (de la mañana) 3. (de la mañana) 4. (de la tarde)

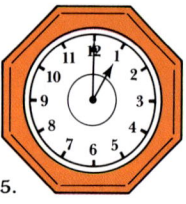 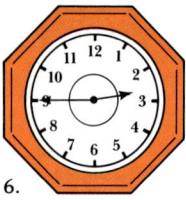 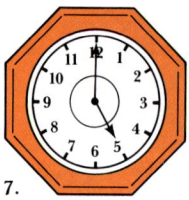 

5. (de la tarde) 6. (de la tarde) 7. (de la tarde) 8. (de la noche)

E **¿Adónde piensan ir?** Working in groups of three and using the list of places below, find out where each member of your group plans to go and what he or she wants or needs to do in each place. Appoint a spokesperson to report back to the class.

Por ejemplo:

ESTUDIANTE A
(1) ¿Adónde piensan ir esta noche?

ESTUDIANTE B
(2) Yo pienso ir al cine porque quiero ver una película.

ESTUDIANTE C
(3) Yo también. Y después pienso ir al centro porque necesito comprar un regalo.

(A la clase): Bill y Rita piensan ir al cine porque quieren ver… Y después Rita piensa ir al centro porque necesita… Bill y yo pensamos… Y luego yo pienso…

el centro comercial
el estadio
la casa de _____
el restaurante
el parque
la ciudad
el baile
la piscina
el centro
el concierto
el campo
la cafetería
la fiesta
el trabajo
el supermercado

Actividad E
Estructura Review
Following are the Estructura topics reviewed in this activity, and the lessons where these topics were first introduced.

1. Use of **a la/al** + place: Capítulo 1, Lección 5 (p. 55)
2. **Pienso/piensas ir** + infinitive: Capítulo 2, Lección 2 (p. 99)
3. Concept of stem change: Capítulo 2, Lección 4 (p. 122)
4. Summary of present tense forms: Capítulo 3, Lección 1 (pp. 170–171)

Vocabulario Review
Actividad E reviews vocabulary from the following lessons:
Capítulo 1, Lección 2 (pp. 14–15)
Capítulo 1, Lección 4 (pp. 34–35)
Capítulo 1, Lección 5 (pp. 48–49)
Capítulo 2, Lección 3 (pp. 104–105)
Capítulo 2, Lección 6 (pp. 142–143)

Actividad E Answers
Answers will vary but should include **pienso, piensa, piensan,** and **pensamos.**

Class Management
You may wish to do Actividad E as a whole class activity initially. The teacher takes the role of Student A, calling on individual students to take the roles of Students B and C. Then do Activity E once more, working in groups of three.

Actividades

Bell Ringer Review

Directions to students: Write down the following places on a sheet of paper. Draw a picture that represents each place. Then write down two activities you can do in each place.
el campo   la ciudad   el gimnasio

Actividad A
Estructura Review

Following are the Estructura topics reviewed in this activity, and the lessons where these topics were first introduced.

1. Quiero/quieres + infinitive: Capítulo 1, Lección 2 (p. 18)
2. Concept of the infinitive: Capítulo 2, Lección 2 (p. 99)
3. How to give telephone numbers: Capítulo 3, Lección 3 (p. 192)

Vocabulario Review

Actividad A reviews vocabulary from the following lessons:
Capítulo 1, Lección 2 (pp. 14–15)
Capítulo 1, Lección 3 (p. 24)
Capítulo 1, Lección 5 (pp. 48–49)
Capítulo 2, Lección 3 (pp. 104–105)

Actividad A Answers
1. 677 93 52
2. 994 20 42
3. 893 40 92 (892 44 61)
4. 834 62 89
5. 493 72 58
6. 824 57 22
7. 593 74 39

---

5 Actividades

A La guía telefónica. Tell what number you would call if you wanted to do the following in Madrid.

Banco Guipuzcoano
OFICINA PRINCIPAL: P° de la Castellana, 45
CENTRALITA PARA TODOS LOS SERVICIOS: 893 40 92   892 44 61

hotel residencia EUROPA
Plena Puerta del Sol
Habitaciones todas con baño
95228 MADRID
Carmen 8
834 62 89

AUTO - ESCUELA CENTRO AFUERA
• CLASES TEÓRICAS Y PRÁCTICAS SIN INTERRUPCIÓN DE 7 A 22 HORAS
• MEDIOS AUDIOVISUALES
Pl Santa Ana, 13   824 57 22

✷ VIPS
ABIERTO HASTA LAS 3 DE LA MADRUGADA
CAFETERÍA-RESTAURANTE
TIENDA
VÍDEO CLUB
JULIÁN ROMEA, 4   677 93 52
(Entre semana cierra a la 1)

CHUQUENA
Zapatos
Tienda: Narváez, 61 • 593 74 39

SÍ idiomas
•INGLÉS•
•FRANCÉS - ALEMÁN•
• LABORATORIO DE IDIOMAS
• ENSEÑANZA INDIVIDUAL
• CLASES DE CONVERSACIÓN Y VÍDEO
• MÉTODO PROPIO
• CURSOS INTENSIVOS DE VERANO Y SÁBADOS
Bravo Murillo, 179 - 1º
METRO ESTRECHO   493 72 58

PAPELERÍA Y LIBRERÍA MUNDIAL
Un Mundo de Papelería a su Servicio
Útiles Escolares y para Oficinas
Centro Calle 42 No. 3 - 60
Calle San Agustín
TELÉFONO: 994 20 42

1. Quieres comer algo.
2. Necesitas comprar un bolígrafo y papel.
3. Tú y tus amigos necesitan cambiar dinero.
4. Vas a Madrid pero no tienes dónde dormir.
5. Quieres aprender francés.
6. Quieres aprender a manejar un coche.
7. Quieres comprar zapatos nuevos.

B **El fin de semana.** Ask four classmates what they usually do on weekends. Then report back to the class about the similarities and differences in their activities. Choose from the list below or think of additional activities.

andar en monopatín
bailar
comprar algo
dar paseos
dormir mucho
escuchar música
ganar dinero
ir a...
hacer la tarea
jugar...
montar a caballo
montar en bicicleta
patinar (sobre hielo)
trabajar
ver partidos

Por ejemplo:

ESTUDIANTE A
¿Qué haces los fines de semana?

ESTUDIANTE B
Voy a fiestas y también duermo mucho.

(A la clase): Jan va a fiestas. Rob y Laura escuchan música. Todos dormimos mucho.

Actividad B
Estructura Review
Summary of present tense forms:
Capítulo 3, Lección 1, (pp. 170–171)

Vocabulario Review
Actividad B reviews vocabulary from the following lessons:
Capítulo 1, Lección 2 (pp. 14–15)
Capítulo 1, Lección 5 (pp. 48–49)
Capítulo 2, Lección 3 (pp. 104–105)
Capítulo 2, Lección 6 (pp. 142–143)

Actividad B Answers
Answers will vary.

Class Management
You may want to encourage students to take notes on what each person in the group says so that students can report back to the class.

Actividad C
Estructura Review

Following are the Estructura topics reviewed in this activity, and the lessons where these topics were first introduced.

1. Formation of the negative: Capítulo 1, Lección 2 (p. 18)
2. First person singular of **-ar/-er** verbs: Capítulo 2, Lección 4 (p. 122)
3. Third person singular of **-ar/-er** verbs: Capítulo 2, Lección 5 (p. 134)
4. First and third person singular of **-ir** verbs: Capítulo 3, Lección 1 (p. 167)

Vocabulario Review

Actividad C reviews vocabulary from the following lessons:
Capítulo 1, Lección 2 (pp. 14–15)
Capítulo 1, Lección 4 (pp. 34–35)
Capítulo 1, Lección 5 (pp. 48–49)
Capítulo 2, Lección 2 (pp. 92–93)
Capítulo 2, Lección 3 (pp. 104–105)
Capítulo 2, Lección 4 (p. 118)
Capítulo 2, Lección 6 (pp. 142–143)

Actividad C Answers

Answers will vary but should include the first and third person singular forms of each verb.

Actividad D
Estructura Review

Following are the Estructura topics reviewed in this activity, and the lessons where these topics were first introduced.

1. Present tense of **ir** + **a** + place/infinitive: Capítulo 2, Lección 3 (pp. 108–109)
2. First person singular of **-ar/-er** verbs: Capítulo 2, Lección 4 (p. 122)
3. Singular and plural usage of days of the week: Capítulo 2, Lección 6 (p. 149)
4. First person singular of **-ir** verbs: Capítulo 3, Lección 1 (p. 167)

C ¿**Bastante o demasiado?** For the activities below, write down which you do not do enough of and which you do too much of. Then give your list to a classmate who will report to the class.

Por ejemplo:

escuchar / hablar
No escucho bastante. A veces hablo demasiado.

(A la clase): Kate no escucha bastante y a veces habla demasiado.

1. estudiar
2. practicar
3. aprender
4. jugar
5. trabajar
6. dormir
7. comer
8. leer
9. escribir
10. visitar amigos
11. ahorrar
12. salir por la noche

D Mis actividades. List what you do at the following times.

Por ejemplo:

los viernes por la noche
A veces voy al cine con mis amigos. A veces juego videojuegos en casa.

1. después de las clases
2. los domingos
3. cuando no es posible salir por la noche
4. cuando sales por la noche con tus amigos
5. los sábados con tu familia
6. en las vacaciones
7. cuando estás aburrido(a)

E ¿Y tú? Find out if a classmate does each of the activities you listed in activity **D**. Place a check next to each of your classmate's activities. Report back to the class, comparing your and your partner's activities.

Por ejemplo:

ESTUDIANTE A	ESTUDIANTE B
Los viernes por la noche, ¿vas al cine con los amigos?	Sí. (No, veo la tele).

(A la clase): Los viernes por la noche, Didi y yo vamos al cine con los amigos. (Los viernes por la noche, a veces yo voy al cine, pero Didi ve la tele).

Vocabulario Review
Actividad D reviews vocabulary from the following lessons:
Capítulo 1, Lección 2 (pp. 14–15)
Capítulo 1, Lección 4 (pp. 34–35)
Capítulo 1, Lección 5 (pp. 48–49)
Capítulo 2, Lección 2 (pp. 92–93)
Capítulo 2, Lección 3 (pp. 104–105)
Capítulo 2, Lección 4 (p. 118)
Capítulo 2, Lección 6 (pp. 142–143)

Actividad D Answers
Answers may vary but may include the following:

1. A veces voy a la biblioteca. A veces estudio.
2. Voy a la iglesia. A veces voy al parque.
3. A veces estudio. A veces veo la tele.
4. ... vamos al cine. ... vamos a fiestas.
5. ... vamos a la playa. ... vamos a las tiendas.
6. ... voy a la playa. ... trabajo.
7. ... veo la tele. ... leo un libro.

Actividad E
Estructura Review
Following are the Estructura topics reviewed in this activity, and the lessons where these topics were first introduced.

1. Present tense of **ir** + **a** place/infinitive: Capítulo 2, Lección 3 (pp. 108–109)
2. Singular and plural usage of days of the week: Capítulo 2, Lección 6 (p. 149)
3. Summary of present tense forms: Capítulo 3, Lección 1 (pp. 170–171)

Vocabulario Review
Actividad E reviews vocabulary from the following lessons:
Capítulo 1, Lección 2 (pp. 14–15)
Capítulo 1, Lección 4 (pp. 34–35)
Capítulo 1, Lección 5 (pp. 48–49)
Capítulo 2, Lección 2 (pp. 92–93)
Capítulo 2, Lección 3 (pp. 104–105)
Capítulo 2, Lección 4 (p. 118)
Capítulo 2, Lección 6 (pp. 142–143)

Actividad E Answers
Answers will vary.

Actividad F
Estructura Review
Following are the Estructura topics reviewed in this activity, and the lessons where these topics were first introduced.

1. **Soy, eres, es:** Capítulo 2, Lección 1 (p. 83)
2. **Somos, son:** Capítulo 2, Lección 1 (p. 87)
3. Use of adjectives ending in -**o**/-**a**, -**e**, or a consonant: Capítulo 2, Lección 2 (p. 96)
4. Present tense of **ir** + **a** + place/infinitive: Capítulo 2, Lección 3 (pp. 108–109)
5. Singular and plural usage of days of the week: Capítulo 2, Lección 5 (p. 149)
6. Summary of present tense forms: Capítulo 3, Lección 1 (pp. 170–171)
7. Present tense of **tener:** Capítulo 3, Lección 5 (p. 217)
8. **Mi(s), tu(s):** Capítulo 3, Lección 6 (p. 227)

Vocabulario Review
Actividad F reviews vocabulary from the following lessons:
Capítulo 1, Lección 2 (pp. 14–15)
Capítulo 1, Lección 4 (pp. 34–35)
Capítulo 1, Lección 5 (pp. 48–49)
Capítulo 2, Lección 3 (pp. 104–105)
Capítulo 2, Lección 5 (pp. 130–131)
Capítulo 2, Lección 6 (pp. 142–143)
Capítulo 3, Lección 1 (pp. 162–163)
Capítulo 3, Lección 6 (pp. 222–223)

Actividad F Answers
Answers will vary.

F **Mi compañero y yo.** Compare yourself to a classmate, answering the questions below.

Por ejemplo:

¿Qué deportes practican?
Ali juega baloncesto, pero yo juego béisbol. (Ali y yo jugamos tenis todos los fines de semana, etc.).

1. ¿Qué saben hacer?
2. ¿Qué leen?
3. ¿Qué programas ven?
4. ¿Adónde van los fines de semana?
5. ¿Qué hacen después de las clases?
6. ¿Cómo son?
7. ¿Qué comen por la mañana? ¿por la tarde?
8. ¿Qué tienen en casa?

Escenas de Puerto Rico.

6 Situaciones

A Reacciones. How would you react to the following statements? Choose from the list below.

Por ejemplo:

> No me gusta el helado.
> *¡No me digas! (¡Qué raro!)*

¡Qué aburrido!	¡Qué tonto!
¡Qué va!	¡Qué pena!
¡No me digas!	¡Qué horror!
¡Qué raro!	¡Qué feo!
¡Qué difícil!	¡Qué antipático!
¡Qué suerte!	¡Qué perezoso!
¡Qué listo!	

1. Voy a correr en un maratón.
2. Quiero estudiar latín.
3. Siempre saco una A en todos los exámenes.
4. Me gusta comer papas fritas con mermelada.
5. Durante las vacaciones Oscar estudia en la biblioteca todos los días.
6. No recuerdo mi número de teléfono.
7. Inés tiene un coche nuevo.
8. En la casa de la familia Yáñez todos los cuartos son anaranjados.
9. El maestro de ciencias prepara un examen para el primer día de clases.
10. La familia Blanco no va de vacaciones porque el señor Blanco está muy enfermo.
11. No me gusta estudiar ni trabajar, pero me gusta dormir, comer y descansar.

B ¿Y tú? Now make three statements about yourself. Tell them to a classmate who will react using the expressions from the list in activity **A**. Reverse roles.

Situaciones

Bell Ringer Review
Directions to students: Draw three circles on your paper. Write one of the following words in each circle: **película fiesta vacaciones** Around each circle write all the words or expressions you can think of that are related to the principal word. Connect each word to the circle with a straight line.

Actividad A
Estructura Review

1. **Quiero/quieres** + infinitive: Capítulo 1, Lección 2 (p. 18)
2. **Me/te gusta** + infinitive: Capítulo 1, Lección 4 (p. 39)
3. Use of adjectives ending in **-o/-a, -e**, or a consonant: Capítulo 2, Lección 2 (p. 96)
4. Summary of present tense forms: Capítulo 3, Lección 1 (pp. 170–171)
5. Present tense of **tener**: Capítulo 3, Lección 5 (p. 217)

Vocabulario Review
Capítulo 1, Lección 2 (pp. 14–15)
Capítulo 1, Lección 4 (pp. 34–35)
Capítulo 1, Lección 5 (pp. 48–49)
Capítulo 1, Lección 6 (p. 60)
Capítulo 2, Lección 1 (pp. 78–79)
Capítulo 2, Lección 2 (pp. 92–93)
Capítulo 2, Lección 3 (pp. 104–105)
Capítulo 2, Lección 6 (pp. 142–143)
Capítulo 3, Lección 1 (pp. 162–163)

Actividad A Answers
Answers may vary but may include the following:

1. ¡Que horror!
2. ¡Qué aburrido!
3. ¡Qué listo(a)!
4. ¡No me digas!
5. ¡Qué raro!
6. ¡Qué tonto(a)!
7. ¡Qué suerte!
8. ¡Qué feo!
9. ¡Qué antipático!
10. ¡Qué pena!
11. ¡Qué va!

Actividad B Answers
Answers will vary.

Actividad C
Estructura Review
Following are the Estructura topics reviewed in this activity, and the lessons where these topics were first introduced.

1. Present tense of **ir** + **a** + place/infinitive: Capítulo 2, Lección 3 (pp. 108–109)
2. **Deber** + infinitive: Capítulo 3, Lección 1 (pp. 160–162)
3. Summary of present tense forms: Capítulo 3, Lección 1 (pp. 170–171)

Vocabulario Review
Actividad C reviews vocabulary from the following lessons:
Capítulo 1, Lección 4 (p. 35)
Capítulo 2, Lección 5 (pp. 130–131)
Capítulo 3, Lección 5 (pp. 210–211)

Actividad C Answers
Answers will vary but the list might include the following items:
recibir el pasaporte
recordar los cheques de viajero
hacer la maleta
estudiar el mapa
recordar los números de teléfono

Actividad D
Estructura Review
Following are the Estructura topics reviewed in this activity, and the lessons where these topics were first introduced.

1. Numbers (0–20): Capítulo 1, Lección 3 (p. 24)
2. Concept of the infinitive: Capítulo 2, Lección 2 (p. 99)
3. **Deber** + infinitive: Capítulo 3, Lección 1 (pp. 160–162)
4. Numbers (20–100): Capítulo 3, Lección 3 (p. 192)
5. Use of the indefinite article: Capítulo 3, Lección 5 (p. 214)

Vocabulario Review
Actividad D reviews vocabulary from the following lessons:
Capítulo 1, Lección 4 (p. 35)
Capítulo 2, Lección 5 (pp. 130–131)
Capítulo 3, Lección 5 (pp. 210–211)

Actividad D Answers
Answers will vary according to local prices.

C **¡Buen viaje!** You're going to Spain for a week. Work with a classmate to compose a list of all the things you need to do first. Which group can come up with the most comprehensive list?

Por ejemplo:

ESTUDIANTE A
Si vamos a España, debemos llevar los pasaportes.

ESTUDIANTE B
Y no debemos olvidar los cheques de viajero.

D **¿Cuánto debe pagar?** Tell a foreign visitor how much he or she should pay in dollars for the following.

Por ejemplo:
   un casete
   Usted debe pagar ocho dólares.

1. una revista
2. unos zapatos
3. una hamburguesa
4. una comida en un restaurante bueno
5. un sandwich
6. un videojuego
7. una calculadora pequeña
8. una mochila
9. una camiseta

E **¿Cuánto dinero?** Now tell the visitor how much he or she should pay to do the following.

Por ejemplo:
>ir al cine
>*Para ir al cine usted debe pagar cinco dólares.*

1. jugar boliche
2. esquiar
3. comer en la cafetería de la escuela
4. ver un partido en el estadio
5. ir a un concierto
6. alquilar (rent) un vídeo

F **¿Cómo están?** Tell how you and the people below feel when in the following situations.

Por ejemplo:
>Haces muchos ejercicios.
>*Estoy cansado(a).*
>La maestra tiene un coche nuevo.
>*Está muy contenta.*

1. Necesitas preparar la cena.
2. Sacas buenas notas en las clases.
3. Tu amigo saca malas notas.
4. Tu amiga va a ver a tu conjunto favorito.
5. Quieres salir con tus amigos pero necesitas limpiar tu habitación.
6. José necesita estudiar todo el fin de semana.
7. Marta no tiene dinero.
8. Tu fiesta es un desastre porque los chicos no quieren bailar.
9. El examen de historia es demasiado difícil.
10. Estás en la cama porque tienes mononucleosis.
11. En el examen de geografía dos estudiantes escriben que Barcelona es la capital de España.
12. Tú y tus compañeros no tienen clases mañana.

Actividad E
Estructura Review
1. Numbers (0–20): Capítulo 1, Lección 3 (p. 24)
2. Concept of the infinitive: Capítulo 2, Lección 2 (p. 99)
3. **Ir** + **a** + a place: Capítulo 2, Lección 3 (pp. 108–109)
4. **Deber** + infinitive: Capítulo 3, Lección 1 (pp. 160–162)
5. Numbers (20–100): Capítulo 3, Lección 3 (p. 192)

Vocabulario Review
Actividad E reviews vocabulary from the following lessons:
Capítulo 1, Lección 2 (pp. 14–15)
Capítulo 1, Lección 4 (p. 35)
Capítulo 1, Lección 5 (pp. 48–49)
Capítulo 2, Lección 3 (pp. 104–105)
Capítulo 2, Lección 6 (p. 143)

Actividad E Answers
Answers will vary according to local prices.

Actividad F
Estructura Review
1. Use of adjectives ending in **-o/-a, -e,** or a consonant: Capítulo 2, Lección 2 (p. 96).
2. Present tense of **estar**: Capítulo 3, Lección 2 (p. 182)
3. **Estar** + adjectives: Capítulo 3, Lección 4 (p. 203)

Vocabulario Review
Actividad F reviews vocabulary from the following lessons:
Capítulo 2, Lección 1 (p. 79)
Capítulo 3, Lección 4 (p. 200)

Actividad F Answers
Answers will vary but may include the following:
1. Estoy ocupado(a).
2. Estoy emocionado(a).
3. Está deprimido.
4. Está contenta.
5. Estoy triste.
6. Está triste.
7. Está deprimida.
8. Estoy enojado(a).
9. Estoy nervioso(a).
10. Estoy enfermo(a).
11. Están equivocados(as).
12. Estamos contentos(as).

Actividad G
Estructura Review

1. Use of adjectives ending in **-o/-a**, **-e** or a consonant: Capítulo 2, Lección 2 (p. 96)
2. Summary of present tense forms: Capítulo 3, Lección 1 (pp. 170–171)
3. Present tense of **estar**: Capítulo 3, Lección 2 (p. 182)
4. **Estar** + adjectives: Capítulo 3, Lección 4 (p. 203)

Vocabulario Review

Capítulo 1, Lección 2 (pp. 14–15)
Capítulo 1, Lección 4 (pp. 34–35)
Capítulo 1, Lección 5 (pp. 48–49)
Capítulo 2, Lección 3 (pp. 104–105)
Capítulo 2, Lección 6 (pp. 142–143)
Capítulo 3, Lección 1 (pp. 162–163)
Capítulo 3, Lección 4 (p. 200)

Actividad G Answers
Answers will vary.

Actividad H
Estructura Review

1. **Me/te gusta** + infinitive: Capítulo 1, Lección 4 (p. 39)
2. First person singular of **-ar/-er** verbs: Capítulo 2, Lección 4 (p. 122)
3. First person singular of **-ir** verbs: Capítulo 3, Lección 1 (p. 167)
4. Present tense of **estar** for location: Capítulo 3, Lección 2 (p. 182)
5. **Estar** + adjectives: Capítulo 3, Lección 4 (p. 203)

Vocabulario Review

Capítulo 1, Lección 2 (pp. 14–15)
Capítulo 1, Lección 4 (pp. 34–35)
Capítulo 1, Lección 5 (pp. 48–49)
Capítulo 2, Lección 3 (pp. 104–105)
Capítulo 2, Lección 6 (pp. 142–143)
Capítulo 3, Lección 1 (pp. 162–163)
Capítulo 3, Lección 4 (p. 200)

Actividad H Answers
Answers will vary but should include the following words and phrases:

1. Estoy en...
2. Veo...
3. Answers will vary.
4. Estoy con...
5. Me gusta... No me gusta...
6. Estoy... porque...

G **Situaciones.** Tell situations when you and others have any of the following feelings.

Por ejemplo:
> Estoy aburrido(a) cuando...
> *Estoy aburrido cuando juego boliche.*

1. Estoy contento(a) cuando...
2. Mis maestros están enojados cuando...
3. Mis amigos(as) están nerviosos(as) cuando...
4. Estoy deprimido(a) cuando...
5. Mis amigos(as) y yo estamos enojados(as) cuando...
6. Mi maestro está contento cuando...

H **De vacaciones.** Think back to a special day last summer. Imagine that you're reliving that day and write a short letter to a friend to describe it. Use the following questions as a guide. Start your letter with **Querido(a)** _____ and end with **Tu amigo(a),** _____.

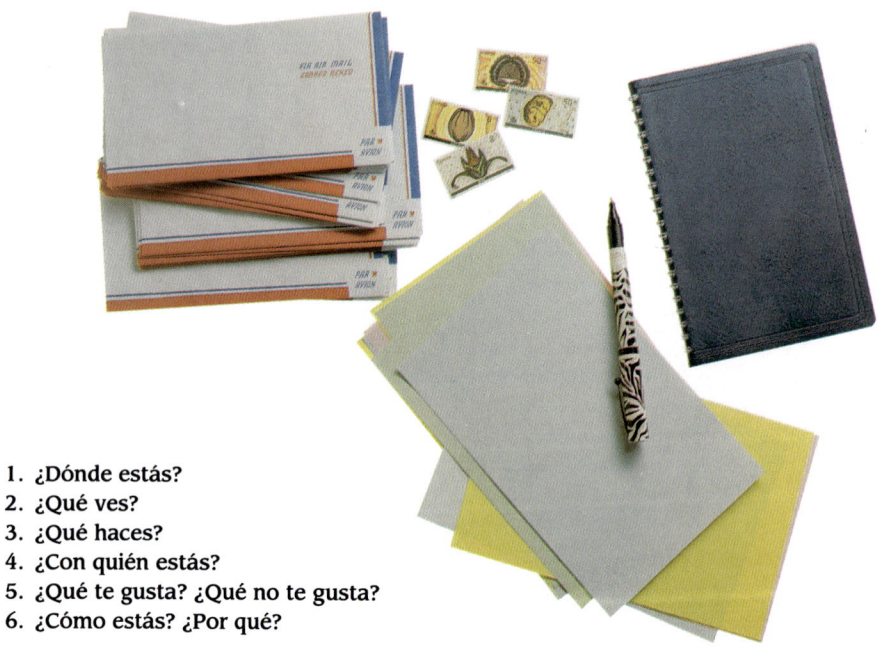

1. ¿Dónde estás?
2. ¿Qué ves?
3. ¿Qué haces?
4. ¿Con quién estás?
5. ¿Qué te gusta? ¿Qué no te gusta?
6. ¿Cómo estás? ¿Por qué?

7 Nuevos amigos

A **El día típico.** A new student asks you and your classmates what a typical school day is like. Answer her questions.

Por ejemplo:

¿A qué hora salen ustedes de casa?
Salimos a las siete o a las siete y media.

1. ¿A qué hora llegan a la escuela?
2. ¿Cuántas clases tienen?
3. ¿Qué estudian?
4. ¿Dónde toman el almuerzo?
5. ¿Qué comen?
6. ¿Qué hacen después de las clases?
7. ¿A qué hora salen de la escuela?
8. ¿A qué hora toman la cena?
9. ¿Dónde hacen la tarea?
10. Cuando salen por la noche, ¿adónde van?

B **Las visitas.** Some exchange students from Spain will be spending Saturday and Sunday in your area. Plan three different events for each day, one in the morning, one in the afternoon and one in the evening.

Por ejemplo:

El sábado por la mañana vamos a nadar en la piscina. Por la tarde…

Nuevos amigos

Bell Ringer Review
Directions to students: How are the following people feeling? Write complete sentences using the following names and adjectives. **Por ejemplo:** Lourdes/enojado
Lourdes está enojada.
1. Antonio y Josefa/enamorado
2. Paco/emocionado
3. Tina y Susan/contento
4. Marta/tranquilo

Actividad A
Estructura Review
Following are the Estructura topics reviewed in this activity, and the lessons where these topics were first introduced.

1. Telling at what time something happens: Capítulo 1, Lección 3 (p. 28)
2. Third person plural of **-ar/-er** verbs: Capítulo 2, Lección 5 (p. 137)
3. First person plural of **-ar/-er** verbs: Capítulo 2, Lección 6 (p. 146)
4. First and third person plural of **-ir** verbs: Capítulo 3, Lección 1 (p. 167)
5. Use of **cuántos(as):** Capítulo 3, Lección 3 (p. 195)
6. Present tense of **tener:** Capítulo 3, Lección 5 (p. 217)
7. Telling time: Capítulo 3, Lección 6 (p. 230)

Vocabulario Review
Capítulo 1, Lección 2 (pp. 14–15)
Capítulo 1, Lección 3 (p. 24)
Capítulo 1, Lección 5 (pp. 48–49)
Capítulo 2, Lección 3 (pp. 104–105)
Capítulo 2, Lección 5 (pp. 130–131)
Capítulo 2, Lección 6 (pp. 142–143)
Capítulo 3, Lección 1 (pp. 162–163)
Capítulo 3, Lección 6 (p. 227)

Actividad A Answers
Answers will vary, however students should use the **nosotros** form of the verb in each response.

Actividad B
Estructura Review
Following are the Estructura topics reviewed in this activity, and the lessons where these topics were first introduced.

1. Present tense of **ir** + **a** + place/infinitive: Capítulo 2, Lección 3 (pp. 108–109)
2. Singular and plural usage of days of the week: Capítulo 2, Lección 6 (p. 149)

Vocabulario Review
Capítulo 1, Lección 2 (pp. 14–15)
Capítulo 1, Lección 4 (pp. 34–35)
Capítulo 1, Lección 5 (pp. 48–49)
Capítulo 2, Lección 3 (pp. 104–105)
Capítulo 2, Lección 4 (p. 118)
Capítulo 2, Lección 6 (pp. 142–143)
Capítulo 3, Lección 1 (pp. 162–163)

Actividad B Answers
Answers will vary.

Actividad C
Estructura Review
1. Telling at what time something happens: Capítulo 1, Lección 3 (p. 28)
2. Present tense of **ir** + **a** + place/infinitive: Capítulo 2, Lección 3 (pp. 108–109)
3. Third person plural of **-ar/-er** verbs: Capítulo 2, Lección 5 (p. 137)
4. First person plural of **-ar/-er** verbs: Capítulo 2, Lección 6 (p. 146)
5. Singular and plural usage of days of the week: Capítulo 2, Lección 6 (p. 149)
6. First and third person plural of **-ir** verbs: Capítulo 3, Lección 1 (p. 167)
7. The verb **hay**: Capítulo 3, Lección 3 (p. 195)

Vocabulario Review
Capítulo 1, Lección 2 (pp. 14–15)
Capítulo 1, Lección 4 (pp. 34–35)
Capítulo 1, Lección 5 (pp. 48–49)
Capítulo 2, Lección 3 (pp. 104–105)
Capítulo 2, Lección 4 (p. 118)
Capítulo 2, Lección 5 (pp. 130–131)
Capítulo 2, Lección 6 (pp. 142–143)
Capítulo 3, Lección1 (pp. 162–163)

C **Quieren saber.** Answer the Spanish students' questions about life in your area.

1. ¿A qué hora llegan ustedes a la escuela?
2. ¿A qué hora comen ustedes aquí? ¿Qué comen en la cafetería?
3. ¿Qué equipos hay en la escuela?
4. ¿Qué clases necesitan tomar?
5. ¿Qué hacen después de las clases?
6. ¿Adónde van los fines de semana?
7. ¿Qué idiomas entienden?
8. ¿Qué música escuchan?
9. ¿Salen mucho por la noche? ¿Adónde van?
10. ¿Trabajan mucho? ¿Y duermen mucho? ¿Duermen en clase?

D **En mi pueblo.** Advise visitors to your area what they should do and see using the verbs below. Give good reasons.

Por ejemplo:
> visitar
> *Si visitan mi pueblo (ciudad), deben visitar el estadio. Es nuevo y grande, y los fines de semana hay partidos buenos.*

1. ver
2. ir a
3. sacar fotos de
4. comprar
5. hablar con
6. llevar
7. visitar

La misión de San Juan Capistrano, California.

Actividad C Answers
Answers will vary.

Actividad D
Estructura Review
1. Third person singular of **ser**: Capítulo 2, Lección 1 (p. 83)
2. Third person plural of **ser**: Capítulo 2, Lección 1 (p. 87)
3. Use of adjectives ending in **-o/-a**, **-e** or a consonant: Capítulo 2, Lección 2 (p. 96)
4. Concept of the infinitive: Capítulo 2, Lección 2 (p. 99)
5. **Deber** + infinitive: Capítulo 3, Lección1 (pp. 160–162)
6. Present tense of **estar** for location: Capítulo 3, Lección 2 (p. 182)
7. The verb **hay** Capítulo 3, Lección 3 (p. 195)

E Gustos. You've just met a classmate and want to find out more about him or her. Ask the following information.

Por ejemplo:

actor favorito / ¿quién?

ESTUDIANTE A	ESTUDIANTE B
¿Quién es tu actor favorito?	Mi actor favorito es _____.

1. dirección / ¿cuál?
2. clase favorita / ¿cuándo?
3. amigos / ¿quiénes?
4. habitación / ¿cómo?
5. cantante favorito / ¿quién?
6. actriz favorita / ¿quién?
7. número de teléfono / ¿cuál?

F Preguntas fáciles. Make a list of questions to ask a classmate about himself or herself using the following question words.

Por ejemplo:

¿adónde?
¿Adónde vas los sábados? (¿Adónde piensas ir de vacaciones?, etc.)

1. ¿cuándo?
2. ¿a qué hora?
3. ¿dónde?
4. ¿cómo?
5. ¿por qué?
6. ¿qué?

G Quiero saber. Make a list of ten questions you would ask a classmate to get to know him or her better. Then get together in groups of three. Combine your questions to come up with fifteen final questions.

Por ejemplo:

¿Te gusta correr? ¿Qué te gusta hacer los sábados por la tarde?

Vocabulario Review
Capítulo 1, Lección 5 (pp. 48–49)
Capítulo 2, Lección 1 (pp. 78–79)
Capítulo 2, Lección 2 (pp. 92–93)
Capítulo 2, Lección 3 (pp. 104–105)
Capítulo 2, Lección 6 (pp. 142–143)
Capítulo 3, Lección 1 (p. 176)
Capítulo 3, Lección 5 (pp. 210–211)
Capítulo 3, Lección 6 (pp. 222–223)

Actividad D Answers
Answers will vary.

Actividad E
Estructura Review
1. Telling at what time something happens: Capítulo 1, Lección 3 (p. 28)
2. Third person singular of **ser**: Capítulo 2, Lección 1 (p. 83)
3. Third person plural of **ser**: Capítulo 2, Lección 1 (p. 87)
4. Giving phone numbers: Capítulo 3, Lección 3 (p. 192)

Vocabulario Review
Capítulo 2, Lección 1 (pp. 78–79)
Capítulo 2, Lección 4 (p. 118)
Capítulo 3, Lección 4 (p. 176)
Capítulo 3, Lección 3 (p. 192)
Capítulo 3, Lección 6 (pp. 227–228)

Actividad E Answers
Answers will vary.

Actividad F
Vocabulario Review
The vocabulary used in this activity will vary according to each student's response. The chapter, lesson and page number of **Acción, Level 1, Part A** in which the interrogative words are first introduced are listed below.
¿Qué? Capítulo 1, Lección 2 (p. 14)
¿A qué hora? Capítulo 1, Lección 3 (p. 28)
¿Cómo? Capítulo 2, Lección 1 (pp. 78–79)
¿Cuándo? Capítulo 2, Lección 4 (p. 118)
¿Por qué? Capítulo 2, Lección 5 (p. 128)
¿Dónde? Capítulo 3, Lección 2 (p. 176)

Actividad F Answers
Answers will vary.

Actividad G
Estructura and Vocabulario Review
The structure and vocabulary used in this activity will vary with each student's response.

Actividad G Answers
Answers will vary.

Chapter Overview

Cultural setting

Chapter 4 continues with the characters Kim and Pilar in Madrid. The main cultural issues are: the role of the grandmother in the Spanish family; and the conflict between tradition and rapid, revolutionary change in lifestyles. This latter concept is crucial to an understanding of today's Spain.

Rationale

A This chapter serves to consolidate, recombine, and transfer various structural elements previously learned and to expand their concepts into the learning of new yet similar structures. For example:
- the function of expressing likes and dislikes using **gustar**, familiar in terms of concept, and practiced in terms of first and second persons, is now expanded to third person
- the function of third person reporting is elaborated by summative, concluding, and paraphrasing devices (**Parece que...** , **Dice que...** ,**Creo que...**)

B The concept of past time is developed (specifically, the preterit of the verb **ir**) in a nondisruptive fashion, as an undercurrent, via the **Cultura viva 2** in odd-numbered lessons. The preterit will be formally and systematically introduced in Chapters 5 and 6.

CAPÍTULO 4

Estructura

This chapter focuses on the following structure topics:
- the possessive adjectives **su** and **sus** to talk about what belongs to others;
- the **gustar** construction with **le** and **les** to talk about likes and dislikes of others;
- the verb **tener** for age and personal physical description;
- the adjectives of quantity **todo(s),** **mucho(s),** and **poco(s);**
- counting from 100 to the thousands;
- the use of the personal **a;**
- the use of **tener que** + infinitive to talk about obligation;
- the verb **preferir** for stating and asking preferences and the use of **otro;**
- a summary of interrogative words; and
- the use of **poder** + infinitive to talk about people's abilities.

¿Cómo son los españoles?

C A summary of question words is presented to consolidate students' ability to request information.

We hope you enjoy the remainder of your stay in Spain!

Video

The video is an optional component, intended to reinforce the vocabulary, structures, and cultural content in each lesson. Please refer to the Video Activities Booklet for suggestions on how to use this resource.

Lección 1 (0)

Lección 2 (219)

Lección 3 (353)

Lección 4 (606)

Lección 5 (657)

Lección 6 (744)

Enfoque cultural (844)

¡Te toca a ti! (955)

Pacing

The six lessons comprising Chapter 4 will each require approximately 5–6 days. However, pacing will vary according to the length of the class, the age of the students, student aptitude and the number of ancillary materials employed.

Student Portfolio

Writing assignments include the following:

Lesson 1: p. 253, A escribir; Workbook, p. 109
Lesson 2: p. 265, A escribir; Workbook, p. 117
Lesson 3: p. 277, A escribir
Lesson 4: p. 282, Act. C
Lesson 5: p. 301, A escribir; Workbook, p. 133, Act. B
Lesson 6: p. 309, Act. A;

CAPÍTULO 4

Lección 1

Objectives

By the end of this lesson, students will be able to:

1. talk about what others like to do
2. talk about what belongs to others
3. identify family members
4. describe what someone or something seems to be like

Lesson 1 Resources

1. Workbook, pp. 108–113
2. Vocabulario Transparency
3. Pronunciation Transparency P-4.1.1
4. Audio Cassette 4.1 Compact Disc 5
5. Student Tape Manual, pp. 87–90
6. Bell Ringer Review Blackline Masters, p. 22
7. Computer Software: Practice & Test Generator
8. Video (cassette or disc)
9. Video Activities Booklet, pp. A49–A50
10. Estructura Masters, pp. 43–44
11. Diversiones Masters, pp. 43–44
12. Situation Cards
13. Lesson Quizzes, pp. 73–75
14. Testing Program

Bell Ringer Review

Directions to students: Draw a clock that represents each of these times.

1. Son las diez menos diez y seis.
2. Son las doce y cinco.
3. Es la una y veinte y cinco.
4. Son las cuatro y cuarto.
5. Son las siete menos quince.

¡A comenzar!

Presentation

A. Lead students through each of the four functions given on page 242, progressing from the English

---

CAPÍTULO 4

Lección 1

Querida señora Rivera

¡A comenzar!

The following are some of the things you will be learning to do in this lesson.

When you want to...	You use...
1. tell someone you speak to formally what he or she likes to do	**A usted le gusta** + activity.
2. describe what something or someone seems to be like	**Parece...**
3. talk about what belongs to others 　　one thing 　　more than one	 **su** **sus**
4. identify family members	**los hermanos, la mamá, el papá, la abuela,** etc.

Now find examples of the above words and phrases in the following letter.

Getting Ready for Lesson 1

You may wish to use one or more of the following suggestions to prepare students for the lesson:

1. Talk to students about your family. Bring in photos if you have them. As you name each family member, tell what each likes to do, what his or her interests are, where each lives, and what each does. For example:

Aquí tengo una foto de mi hermana. Se llama Rachel. Le gusta nadar, jugar tenis y esquiar. También le gusta leer novelas policiales de viajar. Rachel es de aquí pero ahora vive en Houston. Es agente de viajes. Trabaja en una agencia muy grande.

2. Describe what students in your class like to do, giving some statements that are not correct. For example:

Kim le escribe una carta a su maestra de español que vive en Los Ángeles.

Madrid
10 de julio

Querida señora Rivera:

Sé que a usted le gusta recibir cartas de sus estudiantes. Pues, aquí estoy en Madrid con Pilar. No tengo tiempo para contar toda mi confusión con la planta baja y el primer piso. ¡Qué lío! Pero por fin estoy aquí en casa de los Mestre. ¡Qué simpáticos son! Pilar manda abrazos para todos.

El apartamento parece bastante pequeño para toda la gente que vive aquí. Son Pilar y sus tres hermanos, su mamá y su papá, y la abuela doña Beatriz. La abuela es del campo, pero no sé cuándo regresa a su pueblo.

Saludos afectuosos de
Kim

Actividades preliminares

A Ask your teacher three questions about what he or she likes to do.

Por ejemplo:
¿A usted le gusta jugar tenis?

B Your family has agreed to host Javier, a foreign exchange student from Argentina. On a separate sheet of paper, complete the following letter to Javier. Use Kim's letter to Sra. Rivera as a guide.

_____ Javier:

¡Hola! Me llamo _____. Vivo en _____. Mi casa (apartamento) es bastante _____ y (no) me gusta porque _____.

En mi familia somos _____, _____ y yo. A mi familia le gusta _____ pero no le gusta _____. ¿Qué te gusta hacer a ti? Todos esperamos tu visita.

Tu amigo(a) _____

243

Vocabulario

Vocabulary Teaching Resources
1. Vocabulario Transparency 4.1
2. Workbook, pp. 108–109
3. Cassette 4.1
4. Student Tape Manual, p. 88
5. Lesson Quizzes, p. 73

Bell Ringer Review
Directions to students: Unscramble the following sentences:
1. maleta aquí mi está
2. en escritorio tu habitación tu está
3. mis mochila están en libros la
4. nuevos son bolígrafos tus

Presentation
Have students open their books to the Vocabulario on page 244. Begin introducing the new vocabulary on this page by modeling the phrase, **Los parientes son . . .** Then model each member of the family. For example: **la tía, el tío, los tíos; la prima, el primo, los primos;** etc. Have students repeat after you in unison. For each person in the Vocabulario, you may want to ask students, **¿Cómo es?** Have students describe their brothers and sisters by asking **¿Cómo es tu hermano(a)? ¿Tienes un/a hermano(a) mayor? ¿menor?** Ask individual students if he or she is an only child (**hijo[a] único[a]**).

Vocabulario

Los parientes

los tíos — la tía, el tío
los primos — la prima, el primo
los padres — la madre (la mamá), el padre (el papá)
los hijos — la hija, el hijo
el hermano mayor, la hermana menor — los hermanos
el abuelo, la abuela — los abuelos

244 CAPÍTULO 4

Total Physical Response

Getting Ready
Make twelve individual poster strips and label as follows: **Sr. Gómez, Sra. Gómez, Jorge-17 años, Estela-11 años, el abuelo, la abuela, el tío, la tía, la prima, el primo, la hija, el hijo.** Hand out one poster strip each to twelve different students, all of whom will stand up in front of the class.

New Words
señala   señalen
saluda   saluden
dile

Pre-Activity
Make up a short story using the names of the students on the strips and tell how they are related to each other.

A **¿Dónde viven tus parientes?** Make a list of six of your relatives and tell where each one lives.

B **La familia de mi compañero(a) de clase.** Ask a classmate the following questions and take notes. The class will then exchange notes and read the descriptions. See if you can guess who is being described.

1. ¿Dónde está tu casa? ¿Cómo es?
2. ¿Cuántas personas son en tu familia?
3. ¿Cuántos hermanos tienes?
4. ¿Quién es el/la mayor de la familia?
5. ¿Quién es el/la menor de la familia?
6. ¿Tienes muchos primos? ¿Quién es tu primo(a) favorito(a)? ¿Cómo es?

Lección 1 245

When Students Ask

You may want to give students the following additional vocabulary to allow them to talk about their families.

la madrastra
el padrastro
el/la hijastro(a)
el/la hermanastro(a)
el/la hijo(a) único(a)
Es soltero(a).
Está casado(a).
Está muerto(a).
Está(n) separado(s).
Está(n) divorciado(s).

Actividades

Actividades A and B Answers
Answers will vary.

Additional Practice
After doing Actividad B, you may wish to reinforce the learning with the following:
As a written assignment, have students describe the things each person in their family does. For example: **Mi mamá trabaja todo el día. Luego regresa a casa y prepara la comida y limpia la casa. Mi hermano menor va a la escuela y después juega con sus amigos o ve la tele.**

Learning From Realia

You may want to have students look at the greeting cards on page 245 and have them guess what occasion the cards celebrate. You may also want to have them guess what the word "**querida**" means.

TPR 1

Señalen al padre.
Señalen a la abuela.
Saluden al abuelo.
Señalen a los hijos.
Escriban el nombre del hijo del Sr. Gómez.
Saluden al tío.
Escriban el nombre de la prima de Jorge.
Saluden a los padres.

TPR 2

(Distribute the poster strips to a new group of students.)

Señala al primo de Estela.
Indica a la abuela de los hijos.
Camina hacia el tío.
Saluda a la abuela de _____.
Habla con la madre de Estela.
Mira a los tíos de _____.
Ve al abuelo y dile "Buenos días".

Actividad C Answers
Answers will vary.

Class Management
You may want to have students work in pairs when doing Actividad C. Partners can take turns asking each question and writing down their partner's response.

Actividad D Answers
Answers will vary.

Additional Practice
After doing Actividades A, B, C, and D, you may wish to reinforce the learning with the following activities:

1. Your assignment for Spanish class is to write a brief composition about a favorite relative. Use the questions below as a guide.
   a. ¿Quién es tu pariente favorito?
   b. ¿Dónde vive?
   c. ¿Cómo son ustedes similares?
   d. ¿Cómo son diferentes?
   e. ¿Qué hacen ustedes?
2. Have students think of a person (either famous or local) whose family would be familiar to classmates. Have them identify this person only in terms of a relative. Classmates will guess who the person is. For example:
   Su hermana mayor está en el equipo de baloncesto de la escuela. Or: **Su abuelo es el señor X.**

Reteaching
Have students tell one piece of advice they would give to each member of their family. For example: **A mi mamá: Debes descansar más.**

C **Tengo mucha familia.** Talk about three of your favorite relatives, using the questions below as a guide.

1. ¿Cómo son?
2. ¿Dónde viven?
3. ¿Qué hacen durante las vacaciones?
4. ¿Vas a su casa a veces?
   ¿Cuándo? ¿Qué hacen ustedes?

D **La familia de Pilar.** Describe what each member of Pilar's family seems like to you, based on their appearance in the photo below.

1. La madre de Pilar parece _____.
2. El padre de Pilar parece _____.
3. El hermano mayor parece _____.
4. Los hermanos menores parecen _____.
5. La abuela parece _____.

246 CAPÍTULO 4

For the Native Speaker
Write a character sketch (50–75 words) of one of your relatives. You may want to talk about where your relative lives, his or her immediate family, where they live, occupation, interests, etc. Include information on that person's good and bad qualities.

Cooperative Learning
Have students bring photos of their favorite relative to class. In pairs, have them share information about their relative. As a whole class activity, have each student tell what he or she found out about their partner's relative. Students should also describe the relative to the class, and show the photo, in order for the class to verify that the description is correct.

CULTURA VIVA 1

Don y doña

Cuando Kim habla con la abuela de Pilar, dice "doña Beatriz". Los títulos "don" y "doña" se usan cuando "señor" y "señora" parecen demasiado formales. También hay otra diferencia: "don" y "doña" se usan con el nombre de la persona y no con el apellido.

Por ejemplo:

señor Jorge García   don Jorge
señora Ana Vilas   doña Ana

Actividad

Which title would you use to refer to the following people?

1. your teachers
2. your principal
3. an old friend of the family
4. an athletic coach

Cultura viva 1

Reading Strategies
1. Have students identify the cognates in this reading. Write them on the chalkboard.
2. Read the **Cultura viva** on this page, then do the **Actividad**.

Did You Know?
Don and **doña** were originally titles of nobility. Now they are used to show respect to someone of higher social position or to an older person. The titles are capitalized only at the beginning of a sentence.

They are also used with the first and last name together (**don Mario Escobar, doña Tomasa Rivera**). The abbreviations for **don** and **doña** are **D.** and **Da.**

Critical Thinking Activity
What are some titles of respect in English? When do you use these titles and to whom might you say them?

Actividad

Actividad Answers
1. Señor/señora/señorita.
2. Señor/señora/señorita.
3. Don/doña.
4. title choice would depend on the coach/athlete relationship.

Pronunciation

1. Use Pronunciation Transparency P-4.1.1, or write the pronunciation activity on the chalkboard. Have students copy it into their notebooks.
   **Don Zacarías Tudela
   viene del pueblo Morela.
   Es buen zapatero
   calzado de cuero.
   Su mujer doña Nora
   es de Zamora
   y goza de la zarzuela.**
2. You may wish to play the recorded version of this activity, located at the end of Cassette 4.1.
3. Have students repeat words and phrases individually and in unison. You may wish to focus on the /z/ sound as in *Zacarías; zapatero; calzado; Zamora; goza; zarzuela*

Estructura 1

Structure Teaching Resources
1. Workbook, pp. 110–111
2. Cassette 4.1
3. Student Tape Manual, p. 88
4. Estructura Masters 4.1
5. Lesson Quizzes, p. 74

Bell Ringer Review
Directions to students: Draw a tree on your paper with several branches. Each branch represents a part of your family. Draw leaves on the branches and write one person's name on each leaf and what relation that person is to you. Write these words in Spanish.

Structure Focus
In this lesson, the presentation of possessive adjectives is limited to **su** and **sus**. The possessive adjectives **mi(s)** and **tu(s)** were taught in Chapter 3, Lesson 6. The possessive adjective **nuestro** will be presented in Chapter 5, Lesson 4.

Presentation
Lead students through steps 1–2 on page 248. For additional examples, you may want to use the photo of the Mestre family on page 246. Point to each individual and tell how he or she is related to someone else. For example, **Doña Beatriz es la abuela de Pilar. Es su abuela.**

Estructura 1

How to Indicate Possession and Ownership **Su / sus**

You have already learned to say the following things about what people have.

- To talk about what you own, using **mi** and **mis**.

  Tengo mi libro y mis lápices.

- To talk to a friend about what he or she has, using **tu** and **tus**.

  Maricarmen, ¿tienes tu libro y tus lápices?

- To talk about what someone else has, using **de**.

  Es el libro de Jaime. Son los libros del maestro.

1. To talk about what someone else owns or what other people own, you will use **su** or **sus**. **Su** or **sus** can mean "his," "her," or "their." Use **su** with one thing owned and **sus** with more than one.

   Pilar y su familia viven en un apartamento. Su apartamento es bonito y cómodo.

   José Luis tiene una colección de trofeos. Sus trofeos son muy grandes.

2. You also use **su** or **sus** to mean "your" when talking to one person formally or to more than one person both formally and informally (**usted** or **ustedes**).

   Señor Mestre, su casa está en la calle Goya, ¿verdad?

   Señora Mestre, sus abuelos son del campo, ¿no?

   José Luis y Pilar, ¿tienen su tarea para la clase de inglés?

"*¿Son sus maletas, señora?*"

248 CAPÍTULO 4

A **¡Qué mala memoria!** Bruno is so forgetful in the morning that his sister must make sure he has everything. What are the things she checks?

Por ejemplo:
> lápices
> *Quiere saber si tiene sus lápices.*

1. libros
2. bolígrafos
3. dinero
4. papel
5. cuaderno
6. tareas
7. mochila

B **¿Quién está preparado?** Check to see what a classmate has brought—or not brought—to class today. Make a list of five items to ask about. Reverse roles. Then report back to the class.

Por ejemplo:

el libro | sí | no
* | ✓ |*

ESTUDIANTE A
John, ¿tienes tu libro?
(A la clase:) John tiene su libro.

ESTUDIANTE B
Sí.

C **¿Y usted, maestro?** Ask your teacher about the following. Use the suggestions below or think of some of your own. Your teacher will then ask you about the same things.

Por ejemplo:
> coche
> *¿Cómo es su coche? (Su coche es nuevo, ¿verdad?, Su coche es grande, ¿no?)*

1. casa o apartamento
2. ciudad
3. calle
4. familia
5. amigos

Lección 1 **249**

Actividades

Actividad A Answers
1. Quiere saber si tiene sus libros.
2. ... sus bolígrafos.
3. ... su dinero.
4. ... su papel.
5. ... su cuaderno.
6. ... sus tareas.
7. ... su mochila.

Actividad B Answers
Answers will vary, however Student A should use the possessive adjectives **tu** and **su** in his or her responses.

Actividad C Answers
Answers will vary, however if students use the suggestions given, they will say, ¿Como es su casa (apartamento)? ¿Cómo es su ciudad? ¿Cómo es su calle? ¿Cómo es su familia? ¿Cómo son sus amigos?

Extension
After doing Actividad C, you may wish to extend it in the following way. Have students think of additional questions they could ask for each of these topics. You may wish to divide students into groups of three to four and assign each group one of the topics. Provide five minutes for groups to think of as many questions as they can on their topic. As you respond to the questions, have students take notes. For homework, have students prepare a description of "**Mi maestro(a).**"

Reteaching
Hold some of your personal items up for the class to see (pen, paper, pencils, books, etc.) Have individual students identify each object using **Es su...** or **Son sus...**

Cultura viva 2

Reading Strategies

1. Read the letter aloud to the class. You may wish to have each student read one line from the letter.
2. Lead students through the **Actividad** on this page. The concept of past time is introduced passively in this **Cultura viva,** specifically through the preterit of the verb **ir**. The preterit is formally and systematically presented in Chapters 5 and 6 of *¡Acción! 1*.
3. You may wish to refer to the *¡Acción! 1* Fine Art Transparencies.

Did You Know?

The Museo del Prado in Madrid contains one of the finest art collections in the world. It was founded by the royal Spanish family over two centuries ago.

El Escorial is a combination church, monastery, palace, and burial place. It is located about 30 miles northwest of Madrid. It was built by King Felipe II between 1563 and 1584 and contains 300 rooms, 88 fountains, and 86 staircases. King Felipe dedicated El Escorial to Saint Lawrence because Felipe's soldiers defeated the French on Saint Lawrence's Day. Many Spanish Monarchs are buried in El Escorial.

Critical Thinking Activity

The Museo del Prado in Madrid contains one of the finest art collections in the world. Do you know of any similar museum in the U.S. or in another country? Why do you think Spaniards are proud of the Museo del Prado? Give some reasons.

Actividad

Actividad Answers
1. **Fui.**
2. **Vi.**
3. Answers will vary but should use **fui** and **vi.**

CULTURA VIVA 2

Una tarjeta postal de Madrid

> Madrid
> 23 de julio
>
> Querida señora Rivera:
> ¡Hola! ¿Cómo está usted? ¡Madrid es estupendo! El jueves pasado fui con Pilar al Museo del Prado donde vi las pinturas que estudiamos en clase. Anoche fui al cine donde vi una película en español. Para mí todavía es un poco difícil entender las películas en español, pero practico el idioma todos los días y ahora creo que hablo bastante bien. Mañana pensamos visitar El Escorial. Adiós y hasta luego.
>
> Saludos de
> Kim

Las Meninas de Velázquez.

Actividad

Answer the following questions about what happened in the past.

1. What word does Kim use to say she went somewhere?
2. What word does she use to say that she saw something?
3. Use these two words to tell a place you went last week **(la semana pasada)** and something you saw there.

Por ejemplo:

La semana pasada _____ a (a la, al) _____ y vi _____.

CAPÍTULO 4

Estructura 2

How to Talk about What Others Like to Do   **Le(s) + gusta**

You have already learned to say what you like to do and to ask a friend or family member if he or she likes to do something.

Me gusta ir a España. ¿Te gusta viajar?

1. To say what someone else likes to do, use **le gusta** + activity.

    A Jorge le gusta ahorrar dinero.

2. To say what someone to whom you speak formally likes to do, you also use **le gusta** + activity.

    A usted le gusta jugar tenis, ¿verdad?

3. To say what more than one person likes to do, use **les gusta** + activity.

    A los estudiantes les gusta hablar español.

4. When speaking to more than one person about what they like to do, also use **les gusta** + activity.

    ¿A ustedes les gusta escuchar discos?

    Notice that in each case, when you are talking about what people like to do, the word **gusta** does not change.

5. In the above examples, the words **a Jorge, a usted, a los estudiantes,** and **a ustedes** clarify who the **le** or **les** is in each case. These words are not necessary if the meaning of **le** or **les** is already clear.

    Mi hermano favorito es José Luis. Le gusta bailar.

6. When you want to emphasize what you like to do or contrast it with what a friend likes to do, use **a mí** and **a ti**.

    Tú y yo somos diferentes. A mí me gusta ir a la playa y a ti te gusta dar paseos por el campo.

    You may also use the phrases **a mí** and **a ti** by themselves.

    A Pilar le gusta jugar tenis. A mí no. ¿Y a ti?

Lección 1

Actividades

Actividad A Answers
A Kim le gusta leer, sacar fotos, tocar la guitarra, nadar, dibujar, escuchar música, correr y jugar tenis.

Actividad B Answers
Answers will vary.

Actividad C Answers
Answers will vary, however Student A should remember to use the familiar **te gusta** form in asking the questions.

Additional Practice
After doing Actividades A, B, and C, you may wish to reinforce the lesson by doing the following activities:

1. Choose a member of your family and say what he or she likes or doesn't like to do. **Por ejemplo: A mi hermano Todd le gusta jugar tenis pero no le gusta estudiar.**
2. Write what you think three of your teachers like to do in their free time. **Por ejemplo: Al señor Nolan le gusta esquiar.**
3. On a slip of paper write down four things you like and don't like to do. Also describe some of your favorite possessions. Divide into small groups and appoint a spokesperson. The spokesperson for each group will then read to the class what each student has written. Can the class guess who wrote each slip of paper? **Por ejemplo: Le gusta comer helado. También le gusta jugar baloncesto y nadar. No le gusta estudiar. Su disco favorito es . . .**

Reteaching

Have students write down five activities their friends like to do.

A **La maleta.** Judging from the contents of Kim's suitcase, what do you think she likes to do? Say six things.

Por ejemplo:
   A Kim le gusta escuchar música.

B **¿Qué les gusta?** What do the following people like to do?

Por ejemplo:
   tus compañeros de clase
   A mis compañeros de clase les gusta hablar español.

1. tus amigos
2. tus padres
3. los deportistas
4. tus hermanos
5. los actores
6. los maestros

Now compare what you like to do with each of the above groups.

Por ejemplo:
   A mis amigos les gusta correr pero a mí no.
   (A mis amigos les gusta correr y a mí también).

C **Mis compañeros y yo.** Interview a classmate to find out if he or she likes to do the following. Reverse roles. A third classmate (**Estudiante C**) takes notes and reports back to the class about your similarities and differences.

Por ejemplo:
   ¿Le gusta escribir? ¿Qué escribe?

ESTUDIANTE A
(1) ¿Te gusta escribir?
(3) ¿Qué escribes?

ESTUDIANTE B
(2) **Sí, me gusta.**
(4) **Escribo cartas.**

ESTUDIANTE C
A Bill le gusta escribir. Escribe cartas.

1. ¿Le gusta leer? ¿Qué lee?
2. ¿Le gusta ver películas? ¿Qué películas ve?
3. ¿Le gusta ver la tele? ¿Qué programas ve?
4. ¿Le gusta practicar deportes? ¿Qué deportes practica?
5. ¿Le gusta salir por la noche? ¿Adónde va?

Cooperative Learning

Each team selects someone from the team to write about. Like investigative reporters, they divide up the research topics: classes, family, after-school activities, address, etc. Students compile their notes and write one composition. Each team member is responsible for writing what he or she discovered. The final copies are posted on the bulletin board.

Finalmente

Situaciones

A conversar
1. Choose a musician, musical group, actor, actress, or athlete whom you admire. Describe him or her to a classmate. Reverse roles.
2. What else do you know about the celebrity? Describe his or her likes and dislikes. Describe his or her family.

A escribir You have been asked to write an article for the Spanish Club newspaper about a member of your Spanish class. Choose someone you know well.
1. Include the person's name (**Se llama...**) and address.
2. Tell what grade (**el...grado**) the person is in.
3. Describe the person by telling what he or she likes and doesn't like to do.
4. Also describe his or her family.

Repaso de vocabulario

PREGUNTAS
¿Le gusta?
¿Les gusta?

POSESIÓN
su
sus

OTRAS PALABRAS Y EXPRESIONES
a mí
a ti
parece

LA FAMILIA
los abuelos
   la abuela
   el abuelo
los hermanos (mayores / menores)
   la hermana (mayor / menor)
   el hermano (mayor / menor)
los hijos
   la hija
   el hijo

los padres (los papás)
   la madre (la mamá)
   el padre (el papá)
el/la pariente
los primos
   la prima
   el primo
los tíos
   la tía
   el tío

Lección 1

Finalmente

Situaciones

Lesson 1 Evaluation
The A conversar and A escribir situations on this page are designed to give students the opportunity to use as many language functions and as much vocabulary from this lesson as possible. The A conversar and A escribir are also intended to show how well students are able to meet the lesson objectives.

Presentation

Prior to doing the A conversar and A escribir on this page, you may wish to play the Situaciones listening activities on Cassette 4.1 as a means of helping students organize the material.

For the Native Speaker

Pretend you're a reporter for the school newspaper assigned to write an article about a new student in your school. Ask him or her questions such as the following and write the article:
What are your favorite colors? What are your favorite foods? What do you do every day? Which are your favorite classes? What did you do last weekend? What music do you like? What do you like to do in your free time? How many people are there in your family?

CAPÍTULO 4

Lección 2

Objectives

By the end of this lesson, students will be able to:

1. tell how much something costs
2. tell how old someone is
3. identify people's professions
4. use numbers from 100 to 500
5. express an opinion

Lesson 2 Resources
1. Workbook, pp. 114–119
2. Vocabulario Transparencies
3. Pronunciation Transparency P-4.2.1
4. Audio Cassette 4.2 Compact Disc 5
5. Student Tape Manual, pp. 91–95
6. Bell Ringer Review Blackline Masters, p. 23
7. Computer Software: Practice & Test Generator
8. Video (cassette or disc)
9. Video Activities Booklet, pp. A51–A52
10. Estructura Masters, pp. 45–47
11. Diversiones Masters, pp. 45–46
12. Situation Cards
13. Lesson Quizzes, pp. 76–79
14. Testing Program

Bell Ringer Review

Directions to students: Fill in each category below with the names of your own relatives.

hermanos: padres:
primos: tíos:
abuelos:

¡A comenzar!

Presentation

A. Lead students through each of *(continued)*

254

CAPÍTULO 4

Lección 2

¿Cuántos años tiene José Luis?

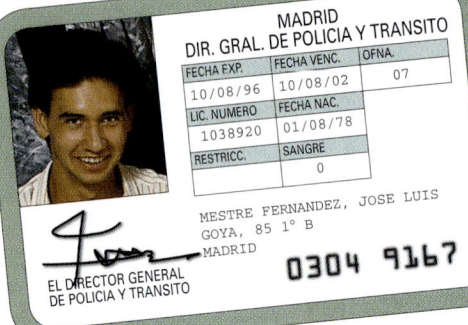

¡A comenzar!

The following are some of the things you will be learning to do in this lesson.

When you want to...	You use...
1. ask how much something costs	¿Cuánto vale?
2. ask about someone's age	¿Cuántos años tiene?
3. say what someone is studying to be	Estudia para + profession.
4. express an opinion	Creo que...
5. give someone's profession	Es ingeniero(a) / empleado(a) de banco, etc.

Now find examples of the above words and phrases in the following conversation.

254

Getting Ready for Lesson 2

You may wish to use one or more of the following suggestions to prepare students for the lesson:

1. Tell students that you need to buy a gift for a friend or relative's birthday. Tell something the person likes to do. Mention an appropriate gift, and ask how much it costs. For example: **Necesito comprar un regalo para mi hermana. El lunes es su cumpleaños. Sé que le gusta escuchar música. ¿Debo comprar unos casetes? ¿Cuánto vale un casete?** Write some possible prices on the board, including some that are outrageously high or low. Ask students to choose an appropriate price.
2. Show illustrations of items students might wish to buy. Ask individual students **¿Cuánto vale?** Allow students to

Pilar y Kim están en un almacén en el centro de Madrid.

PILAR: Necesito comprar un regalo para mi hermano mayor. El jueves es su cumpleaños. Sé que le gusta jugar tenis. ¿Te gusta esta raqueta de tenis?
KIM: Sí, mucho. ¿Cuánto vale?
PILAR: No sé. Creo que no es muy cara.
KIM: ¿Cuántos años tiene José Luis?
PILAR: El jueves cumple diez y nueve años.
KIM: ¿Y qué estudia en la universidad?
PILAR: Estudia para ingeniero.
KIM: Tu papá es ingeniero también, ¿no?
PILAR: Sí, trabaja para la RENFE.
KIM: ¿Y tu mamá?
PILAR: Mi madre es empleada de banco.

Actividad preliminar

Give the age of each of the following people. Then tell if each is younger or older than you.

Por ejemplo:
>tu hermano
>*Mi hermano tiene once años. Es menor que yo.*

1. tu amigo(a) favorito(a)
2. tu hermano(a)
3. un(a) vecino(a) (neighbor)
4. un(a) compañero(a) de clase

255

Vocabulario

Vocabulary Teaching Resources
1. Vocabulario Transparencies 4.2
2. Workbook, pp. 114–115
3. Cassette 4.2
4. Student Tape Manual, p. 92
5. Lesson Quizzes, p. 76

Bell Ringer Review

Directions to students: Copy the following relatives on your paper. Beside each person write three words that best describe that person. Then write down that person's favorite activity. If the person listed below is not in your family, choose someone else to describe. Follow the model.

Mamá: simpática, amable, bonita. Le gusta esquiar.
1. tu tío favorito
2. tu papá
3. tu hermano(a)
4. tu primo(a)

Presentation

A. Have students open their books to the Vocabulario on pages 256 and 257. Model each new word, beginning each time with the phrase **Quiero estudiar para...** Have students repeat each phrase in unison. Ask individual students whether or not they want to be one of the professionals listed in the Vocabulario. For example, **Tom, ¿quieres ser periodista?** Encourage students to give a complete response. For example, **Sí, quiero ser periodista.**

B. Ask individual students, **¿Para qué quieres estudiar?** Encourage them to give a complete response. For example, **¿Quiero estudiar para dentista.**

Vocabulario

Quiero ser...
Quiero estudiar para...

- dentista
- periodista
- electricista
- enfermero(a)
- policía   mujer policía
- arquitecto(a)
- carpintero(a)
- bombero(a)
- mecánico(a)
- abogado(a)

256 CAPÍTULO 4

Total Physical Response

Getting Ready
Use Vocabulario Transparencies 4.2 and color transparency pens.

New Words
rectángulo   cuadro
triángulo   círculo

TPR

(Pairs of students.)

Toquen al mecánico.
Escriban el número 20 sobre el supervisor.
Hagan dos círculos azules en el bombero.
Indiquen al dentista con un círculo negro.
Cubran al agricultor.

Lección 2 **257**

C. Point to the art in the Vocabulario and ask individual students, **¿Es doctor o doctora?**, etc.
D. Have students identify the professions of some currently well-known people. You may also wish to provide names of local people or TV characters.
E. Have students rank five professions that interest them: **Primero... Segundo... Tercero... Etc.**

When Students Ask

You may wish to give students the following additional vocabulary to allow them to talk about professions:
el/la camarero(a)
el/la agente de viajes
el/la vendedor/a
el/la plomero(a)
el/la cocinero(a)
el/la secretario(a)
el/la programador/a
el/la cartero(a)
el/la fotógrafo(a)
el/la banquero(a)
el/la agente de bienes raíces
el/la peluquero(a)

Regionalisms

You may wish to tell students that in some parts of the Spanish-speaking world the following word is an alternative to the one presented in the Vocabulario.
la fábrica (la factoría) (Puerto Rico)

Pongan dos triángulos verdes en el doctor.
Muéstrenme el veterinario.
Hagan dos cuadros negros en el electricista.
Pongan dos rectángulos anaranjados en el policía.
Escriban el número 16 sobre el ingeniero.
(Repeat with **tú**.)

Actividades

Actividad A Answers
Answers will vary.

Actividad B Answers
1. A Enrique le gusta dibujar casas y edificios y estudiar matemáticas. / Creo que estudia para arquitecto.
2. ... maestra (ama de casa) (profesora).
3. ... ingeniera.
4. ... estudian para mecánicos.
5. ... estudia para periodista.
6. ... mujer de negocios (dueña de una compañía, supervisora).

Additional Practice
After doing Actividades A and B, you may wish to reinforce the learning with the following: Have students name the occupations they associate with the following objects, places, or activities.
1. dibujar, casas, edificios, apartamentos (arquitecto[a])
2. animales (veterinario[a])
3. hospitales, personas enfermas, inyecciones (doctor/a)
4. periódicos, computadoras, lápiz, bolígrafo, cuaderno, grabadora (periodista)
5. escuela, estudiantes, libros, enseñar, exámenes, tareas (maestro[a], profesor/a)
6. construir, sillas, mesas, muebles, casas, camas, escritorios (carpintero[a])
7. lámparas, refrigerador, horno, estéreo (electricista)
8. coches, motos, autobuses, motores (mecánico[a])
9. limpiar, comprar comida y ropa, cocinar, ayudar (ama de casa)

Learning From Realia
You may want to have students look at the ads from the Madrid yellow pages on page 258. Have students imagine that they're in Madrid and have the following problems. What number should they call?
1. Tienes un problema legal.
2. Necesitas ir al dentista.
3. La lámpara de tu habitación no funciona.

Actividades

A Ocupaciones. Using the **Vocabulario** on pages 256 and 257, make a list of the occupations that appeal to you and another list of those that don't. Use the following headings.

| Las ocupaciones que me gustan | Las ocupaciones que no me gustan |

B ¿Qué le gusta hacer? A classmate describes what various people like to do. Decide what profession each is preparing for, based on these descriptions.

Por ejemplo:

    Marta / estudiar biología y zoología, jugar con animales

ESTUDIANTE A	ESTUDIANTE B
A Marta le gusta estudiar biología y zoología y jugar con animales.	Creo que estudia para veterinaria.

1. Enrique / dibujar casas y edificios, estudiar matemáticas
2. Inés / cuidar (care for) niños, leer libros y aprender cosas nuevas
3. Dolores / estudiar matemáticas y trabajar con computadoras
4. Luis y Raúl / estudiar mecánica, trabajar con coches y motores
5. Mauricio / escribir, sacar fotos, saber qué pasa
6. Anita / ganar dinero, ahorrar dinero, tomar decisiones, trabajar en una oficina

For the Native Speaker
Write a letter to several professionals such as a firefighter, a dentist, a lawyer, a doctor, etc., asking general biographical information about their profession. Some of the questions you could ask are: What preparation is required? Likes, dislikes regarding their job? Salary ranges? Years of study required? Have native speakers share their letters with the class.

C Cien por ciento. The people below are describing what percentage of their time they spend doing different activities related to their jobs. For each, tell what you think his or her profession is.

Por ejemplo:

> Juan: Trabajo cincuenta por ciento del tiempo con una computadora. El treinta por ciento del tiempo contesto el teléfono.
> *Creo que es empleado de oficina (de banco, etc.).*

1. Víctor: Paso sesenta por ciento del día en el hospital y veinte por ciento en la oficina donde veo a mis pacientes. Por la noche descanso y leo libros de medicina.
2. Roberto: Paso setenta por ciento de mi tiempo afuera. Saco fotos en la calle y escribo artículos para el periódico.
3. Gloria: Paso noventa por ciento del día en casa. Es un trabajo muy difícil y no gano dinero. Limpio, cocino, voy de compras y trabajo todo el día.
4. Alicia: Paso todo el día afuera en el campo donde manejo un tractor.
5. Yolanda: Paso ochenta por ciento de mi tiempo en mi oficina y veinte por ciento afuera donde visito a los animales.

D ¿Por qué? Choosing from the list of professions in the **Vocabulario**, tell two things you would like to be and two you would not like to be. Tell why, using reasons such as those below.

trabajar afuera	hacer trabajos manuales
trabajar adentro	trabajar con animales
trabajar con la gente (people)	ganar mucho dinero
trabajar con los números	reparar cosas

Por ejemplo:

> bombero
> *Quiero ser bombero porque me gusta trabajar afuera, hacer trabajos manuales y trabajar con la gente.*

Lección 2   259

Actividad C Answers
1. Creo que es doctor.
2. ... periodista.
3. ... ama de casa.
4. ... agricultora.
5. ... veterinaria.

Actividad D Answers
Answers will vary.

Additional Practice
After doing Actividades A, B, C, and D, you may wish to reinforce the learning with the following activity: Have students select occupations from the Vocabulario list that they would not want to have, and tell why. For example: **No quiero ser doctor/a porque no me gusta estudiar ciencias. No quiero ser ama de casa porque no me gusta limpiar la casa.**

Have students identify professions, based on the following questions:
1. ¿A quién visitas si te duelen las muelas? (Point to your jaw.)
2. ¿A quién visitas si estás enfermo?
3. ¿Quién escribe artículos para el periódico?
4. ¿Quién enseña a los estudiantes?
5. ¿Quién construye casas y edificios?
6. ¿Quién trabaja afuera en el campo?
7. ¿A quién llamas si las lámparas no funcionan?
8. ¿A quién llamas si hay emergencias?
9. ¿A quién visitas si tienes problemas con el coche?
10. ¿A quién visitas si tu gato o tu perro está enfermo?

Reteaching
Ask students to open their books to the Vocabulario on pages 256 and 257 and tell which of the following two categories each occupation falls under: **los que trabajan adentro; los que trabajan afuera.** You may want to write these categories on the chalkboard.

Cultura viva 1

Reading Strategies

1. Read the **Cultura viva** on this page. Ask students to guess at the meaning of any new words they find in the reading.
2. On the chalkboard, make a list of items and services that are available in an **almacén**.

Did You Know?

The majority of stores in large cities in Spain close during lunch time and reopen in the afternoon at around five o'clock. However, that custom is changing. Major department stores, such as **El Corte Inglés** and **Galerías Preciados**, remain open during lunch time.

Critical Thinking Activity

Compare what is sold in **El Corte Inglés** and in **Galerías Preciados** with what is sold in department stores in your city.

Actividad

Actividad Answers
1. ... discos./Están abajo en el sótano.
2. ... revistas./ ... el sótano.
3. ... una cámara./(Las cámaras) están... el sótano.
4. ... una maleta./(Las maletas) ... arriba en la segunda planta.
5. ... un sandwich y un refresco./ ... la sexta planta.
6. ... perfume./(Los perfumes)... abajo en la planta baja.

Additional Practice

You may wish to reinforce the lesson with the following: Match the Spanish and English words related to shopping. Write down the clues that helped you decide.

1. tienda   a. department store
2. almacén   b. specialty store
3. sucursal   c. branch of a department store

CULTURA VIVA 1

¿Quieres comprar algo?

En Madrid y en otras ciudades españolas hay muchas tiendas pequeñas, pero mucha gente prefiere comprar en los grandes almacenes. Hay dos almacenes principales en Madrid con sucursales en otras ciudades grandes. Son El Corte Inglés y Galerías Preciados. Venden una gran variedad de productos y también ofrecen muchos servicios para sus clientes. Por ejemplo, allí puedes comprar muebles, alimentos y ropa, y también puedes cambiar dinero y hacer reservaciones para viajes.

EDIFICIO MODA

1° SÓTANO Imagen y Sonido. Discos. Microinformática. Fotografía. Fumador. Papelería. Librería. Tienda de la Naturaleza. Turismo.

B PLANTA BAJA Complementos de Moda. Perfumería y Cosmética. Joyería. Bisutería. Bolsos. Relojería. Marroquinería. Stand Dunhill. Cartier. Bombonería Godiva.

1ª PLANTA Señoras. Confección. Punto. Peletería. Boutiques Internacionales. Lencería y Corsetería. Futura Mamá. Tallas Especiales. Complementos de Moda.

2ª PLANTA Caballeros. Confección. Ante y Piel. Boutiques. Ropa Interior. Sastrería a Medida. C. Gourmet. Artículos de Viajes. Complementos de Moda.

3ª PLANTA Infantil: Niños/as (4 a 10 años). Confección. Boutique. Complementos Bebés. Carrocería. Canastillas. Confección Bebé. Zapatería Bebé. **Chicos/as (11 a 14 años).** Confección Boutique Agua Viva. Complementos. Juguetería.

4ª PLANTA Zapatería. Señoras, Caballeros y Niños. Deportes. Confección. Deportiva. Zapatería Deportiva Armería. Marcas Internacionales. Complementos.

5ª PLANTA Juventud. Confección. Tienda Vaquera. Lencería y Corsetería.

6ª PLANTA Promociones y Ferias. Cosas (regalos juventud). **Servicios:** Cafetería. Restaurante. Pizzería. Bufé.

Actividad

You are at the information desk on the **planta baja** of **El Corte Inglés.** Your friend asks where the following items can be purchased. Use the directory to tell which floor each item is on and whether it is up or down.

Por ejemplo:
    zapatos

ESTUDIANTE A
Perdón, señorita (señor), quisiera comprar zapatos.

ESTUDIANTE B
Están arriba en la cuarta planta.

1. discos
2. libros y revistas
3. una cámara
4. una maleta
5. un sandwich y un refresco
6. perfume

Pronunciation

1. Use Pronunciation Transparency P-4.2.1, or write the pronunciation activity on the chalkboard. Have students copy it into their notebooks.

   Hay dos empleados
   detrás del mostrador.
   Vienen diez clientes,
   cada uno comprador.
   El primero paga quince
   porque es un gran señor.
   Y cinco pagan cinco y
   dos pagan tres
   y uno paga dos
   y otro paga seis.
   ¿Cuánto pagan los diez?

2. You may wish to play the recorded version of this activity, located at the end of Cassette 4.2.

Estructura 1

How to Say How Much or How Many *Adjectives of quantity*

To ask how much or how many, you have used **¿cuántos?** or **¿cuántas?**

¿Cuántos discos quieres comprar?
¿Cuántas muchachas hay en tu clase?

1. You can also use the singular form of these words.

   ¿Cuánto dinero necesitas?
   ¿Cuánta leche debo comprar?

2. When you want to ask how much one thing costs, you say **¿Cuánto vale?** for one thing and **¿Cuánto valen?** for more than one.

   ¿Cuánto vale el disco?
   ¿Cuánto valen las camisetas?

3. When you want to ask someone's age, you say **¿cuántos años?** and the appropriate form of **tener**.

   ¿Cuántos años tienes?
   ¿Cuántos años tienen tus hermanos?

¿Cuántos casetes tienes?

4. To tell how much or how many, you can use a specific number or the following words. Note that these words can be used to describe one thing or more than one.

poco / poca / pocos / pocas	a little, few
mucho / mucha / muchos / muchas	a lot, many
todo / toda / todos / todas	every, all

   ¿Tienes muchas camisetas? No, tengo pocas.

   Luis está enfermo. Debe pasar toda la semana en casa.

   En mi escuela, muchos estudiantes estudian español. Pocos estudian latín.

   Mañana Ana va a estudiar todo el día. Todas sus clases son difíciles.

Lección 2   **261**

Actividades

Actividad A Answers
Answers will vary.

Extension
After doing Actividad A, you may wish to extend the learning by having students ask each other how old the following are. For example: **tu casa**

ESTUDIANTE A	ESTUDIANTE B
¿Cuántos años tiene tu casa?	Tiene diez años.

1. la escuela
2. los Estados Unidos
3. el coche de tus padres
4. un libro viejo en la biblioteca

Actividad B Answers
Answers will vary but must include the **yo** form of the verb.

Actividad C Answers
Answers will vary, however students should use **poco, mucho,** and **todo** when they report to the class.

Additional Practice
After doing Actividades A, B, and C, you may wish to reinforce the lesson by doing the following:
A new exchange student asks you questions about your school and city. Play the roles with a classmate. **Por ejemplo: cines en la ciudad**

ESTUDIANTE A	ESTUDIANTE B
¿Hay muchos cines en la ciudad?	Hay pocos. (Hay muchos, No hay muchos).

1. piscinas en la ciudad
2. restaurantes buenos
3. exámenes en la clase de inglés
4. fiestas en la clase de español
5. bailes en la escuela
6. partidos de baloncesto
7. estudiantes aplicados
8. deportistas buenos
9. tarea en las clases

Reteaching

Ask students questions about what there is in the classroom using **poco, mucho, todo**.

Actividades

A **Mis hermanos.** Ask if your classmate has brothers or sisters. Also find out how old they are. Report back to the class about who's older and younger in your classmate's family.

Por ejemplo:

ESTUDIANTE A	ESTUDIANTE B
(1) ¿Tienes hermanos?	(2) Sí, tengo una hermana.
(3) ¿Y cuántos años tiene?	(4) Bueno, mi hermana tiene diez y nueve años.

(A la clase:) Sara tiene una hermana mayor.

B **¿Todos los días?** Describe your routine by completing the following sentences.

1. Todos los sábados...
2. Todos los domingos...
3. En muchas clases...
4. Muchas veces...
5. Pocas veces...
6. Todas las noches...

C **Mis compañeros.** Working in groups of three or four, poll your classmates using the following questions. Report back to the class.

Por ejemplo:
¿Cuántos piensan comer en la cafetería hoy?

(A la clase:) Todos pensamos comer en la cafetería hoy. (Muchos estudiantes piensan comer afuera. Pocos piensan comer en la cafetería. Nadie (nobody) piensa comer en la cafetería hoy, etc.).

¿Cuántos...
1. ... quieren ser doctores? ¿abogados? ¿ingenieros?
2. ... tienen una familia grande?
3. ... tienen abuelos en casa?
4. ... viven en un apartamento? ¿en una casa?
5. ... tienen una colección en casa?
6. ... practican deportes?

CULTURA VIVA 2

La lotería

¿Qué es una lotería? Pues, compras un billete que lleva un número. Si seleccionan tu número, ganas mucho dinero. En España hay muchas loterías. En una lotería, el ganador recibe cincuenta por ciento del dinero y el otro cincuenta por ciento es para el estado, o el gobierno. Las ganancias del estado pagan muchos servicios. Por ejemplo, se usan para los niños que no tienen padres y para las viudas (señoras que ya no tienen esposos). Una de las loterías más grandes es la de la ONCE (Organización Nacional de Ciegos). Con las ganancias de esta lotería se pagan los salarios de los vendedores de billetes y también se mantienen escuelas para los ciegos (personas que no pueden ver).

Actividades

A The above tells about the Spanish lottery. What do you know about how a lottery works? In the paragraph above, find five people or groups of people who benefit from the lottery system. Which one receives the most money?

B Complete the following sentence:
Si gano la lotería, pienso comprar _____, _____ y _____.

Cultura viva 2

Reading Strategies
1. On the chalkboard, write several key words that are used in this reading: **billete; ganar; ganador; ganancias.** You may want to give students the meaning of these words.
2. Now do the **Actividades** on this page.

Did You Know?
Spain is not the only Spanish-speaking country that has a lottery. Many other countries have some type of lottery system, including Mexico and Colombia.

Critical Thinking Activity
Is there a lottery in your state? What are some advantages and disadvantages of a lottery?

Actividades

Actividad A Answers
1. el estado o el gobierno
2. los niños que no tienen padres
3. las señoras que ya no tienen esposos (viudas).
4. los vendedores de billetes
5. los ciegos

Los ciegos ganan más dinero.

Actividad B Answers
Answers will vary.

Estructura 2

Structure Teaching Resources
1. Workbook, p. 119
2. Cassette 4.2
3. Student Tape Manual, p. 93
4. Estructura Masters 4.2
5. Lesson Quizzes, pp. 78–79

Bell Ringer Review

Directions to students: On your paper, draw a picture that represents the following professions:

1. bombero
2. ama de casa
3. agricultor
4. periodista
5. carpintero
6. abogada

Structure Focus

The numbers from 100 to 500 are presented in this lesson. Numbers 600 and on will be taught in Chapter 4, Lesson 3.

Presentation

Lead students through steps 1–3 on page 264. You may first want to review numbers by tens. For step 2, you may wish to model the numbers from 200 to 500, having students repeat each number in unison.

Actividad

Actividad Answers
Las tarjetas postales valen trescientas sesenta y cinco pesetas.
El bolígrafo vale ciento ochenta pesetas.
El cartel vale cuatrocientas pesetas.
La camiseta vale quinientas cincuenta pesetas.
El refresco vale sesenta y cinco pesetas, y el pastel vale ciento sesenta pesetas. El total es doscientas veinte y cinco pesetas.

Estructura 2

How to Count from 100 to 500

You have learned that the word **cien** is used for 100.

Necesito cien pesetas, por favor.

1. For numbers between 101 and 199, use **ciento**.

    El televisor vale ciento cincuenta dólares.

2. Below are the words for 200, 300, 400, and 500.

    doscientos(as) **cuatrocientos(as)**
    trescientos(as) **quinientos(as)**

    Notice that the ending you use for 200 to 500 (**-os** or **-as**) depends on whether you are describing masculine or feminine words.

    ¿Cuántos discos tiene José? ¡Tiene doscientos!
    ¿Cuántas páginas tiene el libro? Tiene trescientas páginas.

3. Follow the hundreds with single- and double-digit numbers.

    105 ciento cinco
    240 doscientos cuarenta
    590 quinientos noventa

Actividad

¿Cuánto vale? Pilar has just purchased the items below. Tell how much each one costs.

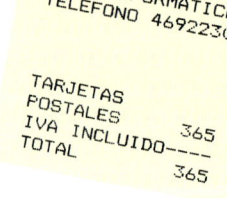

Cooperative Learning

Have students bring or draw pictures of what they want to purchase. They should write the price of the item on the back. In teams, they will take turns showing their picture and asking teammates for the price. The one who is closest to the correct price gets to hold the picture. At the end, the member with the most pictures wins a prize.

Finalmente

Situaciones

A conversar It's the year after your graduation and you happen to see a former classmate. Greet each other and converse about the following.

1. where each of you lives and what your home is like
2. your possessions
3. your daily activities

A escribir You are preparing to interview a local Hispanic professional. Write down questions you will ask this person to obtain the following information.

1. name and profession
2. name and address of his or her company
3. what he or she likes and dislikes about the job
4. what a student must do to prepare for this kind of work

Repaso de vocabulario

PREGUNTAS
¿Cuánto vale?
¿Cuántos años tiene(s)?

OCUPACIONES
el/la abogado(a)
el/la agricultor/a
el ama de casa (f.)
el/la arquitecto(a)
el/la bombero(a)
el/la carpintero(a)
el/la dentista
el/la doctor/a
el/la dueño(a)
el/la electricista
el/la empleado(a)
el/la enfermero(a)
el hombre de negocios
el/la ingeniero(a)
el/la mecánico(a)
la mujer de negocios
la mujer policía
el/la periodista
el policía
el/la profesor/a
el/la supervisor/a
el/la veterinario(a)

NÚMEROS
ciento
doscientos(as)
trescientos(as)
cuatrocientos(as)
quinientos(as)

CANTIDADES
mucho(a)
poco(a)
todo(a)

LUGARES
la compañía
la fábrica

EXPRESIONES
Creo que...
estudiar para

Lección 2   265

For the Native Speaker

Native speakers will write 2–3 sentences describing a profession without naming it. For example: **Mi trabajo a veces es peligroso pero al mismo tiempo me da mucha satisfacción. Pongo mi vida siempre en peligro para que el público común tenga tranquilidad.** The class guesses the profession **(policía)**.

CAPÍTULO 4

Lección 3

Objectives

By the end of this lesson, students will be able to:

1. talk about what others like and dislike
2. tell how something or someone appears to be
3. identify household pets and common zoo animals
4. use numbers from 600 to the thousands

Lesson 3 Resources
1. Workbook, pp. 120–125
2. Vocabulario Transparencies
3. Pronunciation Transparency P-4.3.1
4. Audio Cassette 4.3 Compact Disc 6
5. Student Tape Manual, pp. 96–100
6. Bell Ringer Review Blackline Masters, p. 24
7. Computer Software: Practice & Test Generator
8. Video (cassette or disc)
9. Video Activities Booklet, pp. A53–A54
10. Estructura Masters, pp. 48–49
11. Diversiones Masters, pp. 47–48
12. Situation Cards
13. Lesson Quizzes, pp. 80–84
14. Testing Program

Bell Ringer Review

Directions to students: List the people in your immediate family according to their ages.
Por ejemplo: Mi mamá tiene treinta y cinco años. Mi hermano mayor tiene diez y nueve años.

CAPÍTULO 4

Lección 3

No comprendo a la abuela

¡A comenzar!

The following are some of the things you will be learning to do in this lesson.

When you want to...	You use...
1. talk about one thing that someone likes	A + person + **le gusta** + thing.
2. talk about several things that someone likes	A + person + **le gustan** + things.
3. say how something or someone appears to be	Parece que...

Now find examples of the above words and phrases in the following postcard.

Getting Ready for Lesson 3

You may wish to use one or more of the following suggestions to prepare students for the lesson:

1. Tell students that you are trying to decide on a pet to buy and are having difficulty making a decision. Use the first Vocabulario Transparency 4.3 or some other source to talk about various types of pets. Weigh the pros and cons of each. For example:
Quisiera tener un animal en casa pero no sé qué animal comprar. Quizás un perro (show picture). **Dicen que los perros son muy buenos, pero si tengo un perro, no puedo viajar. Quizás un gato** (show picture). **Dicen que los gatos son muy independientes y que no les gustan las personas.**

Kim le escribe una tarjeta postal a la señora Rivera.

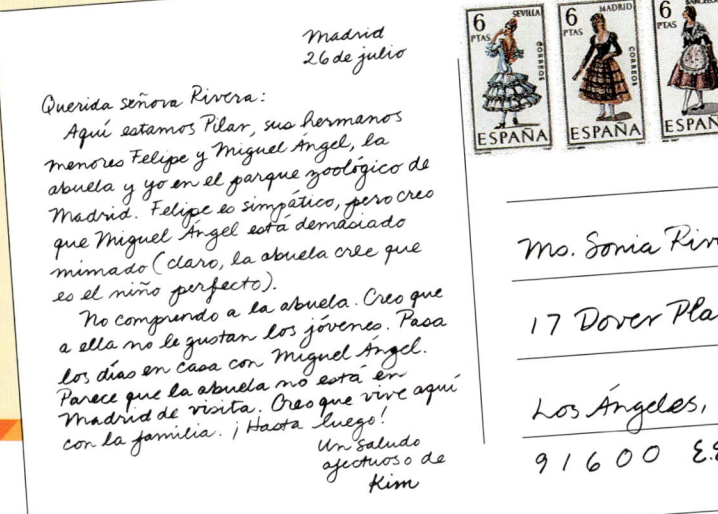

Madrid
26 de julio

Querida señora Rivera:
 Aquí estamos Pilar, sus hermanos menores Felipe y Miguel Ángel, la abuela y yo en el parque zoológico de Madrid. Felipe es simpático, pero creo que Miguel Ángel está demasiado mimado (claro, la abuela cree que es el niño perfecto).
 No comprendo a la abuela. Creo que a ella no le gustan los jóvenes. Pasa los días en casa con Miguel Ángel. Parece que la abuela no está en Madrid de visita. Creo que vive aquí con la familia. ¡Hasta luego!
   Un saludo
   afectuoso de
     Kim

Ms. Sonia Rivera
17 Dover Place
Los Ángeles, CA
91600 E.E.U.U.

Actividades preliminares

Say whether you know that the following statements are true or whether you're not entirely sure. Begin each statement with **Sé que...** or **Parece que...**

Por ejemplo:
  Madrid es una ciudad divertida.
  Parece que Madrid es una ciudad divertida.

1. José Luis es hermano de Pilar.
2. Madrid es la capital de España.
3. Pilar vive en Madrid.
4. José Luis saca buenas notas en la universidad.
5. Kim y Pilar son buenas amigas.

267

Vocabulario

Vocabulary Teaching Resources
1. Vocabulario Transparencies 4.3
2. Workbook, pp. 120–121
3. Cassette 4.3
4. Student Tape Manual, p. 97
5. Lesson Quizzes, p. 80

Bell Ringer Review
Directions to students: Write down three occupations you would like to have and three you would not like to have. Give reasons for your choices.

Presentation
A. Have students open their books to the Vocabulario on pages 268 and 269. Model each new word on these pages. Begin each phrase on page 268 with **Tengo...** Have students repeat each phrase in unison. Then model each new word on page 269, beginning with the phrase, **En el parque zoológico cuidan...**

B. You may wish to survey the class to find out the most popular pets in the Vocabulario. Rank them using **primero, segundo, tercero, etc.** Do the same for the zoo animals.

C. You may wish to call attention to where descriptive words are placed. For example, **gato negro y blanco, peces dorados, perro pequeño.** Have students add their own descriptions to these animals. For example, **un gato independiente, peces dorados aburridos, un caballo perezoso, un perro gordo, una serpiente verde, un conejo blanco, etc.**

Vocabulario

Tengo...
- una tortuga
- un caballo viejo
- un canario amarillo
- un ratoncito blanco
- unos peces dorados
- un periquito azul
- un gato negro
- un conejo blanco
- un perro pequeño

268 CAPÍTULO 4

Total Physical Response

Getting Ready
For **TPR 1**, make three to five copies of the Vocabulario Transparencies. Cut out the animals and distribute one to each student. There should be enough illustrations so that every student has one or two. For **TPR 2**, have one set of illustrations on the front table.

New Words
lleven   dame   denme

TPR 1
(After each command, say **Muéstrenmelos(las)** in order to check for accuracy.)
Pongan los conejos blancos en el piso.
Denme los monos.
Levanten las manos si tienen un ratoncito blanco.

En el parque zoológico cuidan...

- los pingüinos
- los leones
- los monos
- los tigres
- los elefantes
- los osos
- los gorilas
- los camellos
- las llamas
- las serpientes

Lección 3 **269**

D. You may want to have students describe the zoo animals on page 269. For example: **Los pingüinos son blancos y negros. Son muy divertidos.**

When Students Ask

You may wish to give students the following additional vocabulary to allow them to talk about other animals:

la vaca	el burro
la pantera	el cerdo
el toro	la oveja
el rinoceronte	el chivo
el gallo	el cocodrilo
el hipopótamo	la vicuña
la gallina	la cebra
el caimán	el ciervo
el pato	la jirafa
la mariposa	el lobo
la rana	el zorro

Regionalisms

You may wish to tell students that in some parts of the Spanish-speaking world the following words or phrases are alternatives to those presented in the Vocabulario.
el mono (el chango) (Mex. and Central Am.) **(el mico)**;
la serpiente (la culebra)

Lleven los elefantes a mi escritorio.
Levanten los pies si tienen un perro.
Denme los caballos viejos.
Lleven los pingüinos a la ventana.
Pongan los camellos debajo de la mesa.
Lleven los peces dorados a la pared.
Denme los osos.
Lleven los gatos negros a la puerta.
(Repeat with different animals.)

TPR 2

Dale el oso a ____.
Dame el periquito azul.
Lleva las llamas a la pared.
Escribe "leones" en la pizarra.
Esconde los gorilas en tu libro.
Pon el conejillo de indias en tu mesa.
Entrega los tigres a ____.
Toca las serpientes y camina a la puerta.
(Repeat commands with other animals.)

Actividades

Actividades

A **Preferencias.** Ask a classmate which animals presented in the **Vocabulario** he or she likes. Then report to the class.

Por ejemplo:

ESTUDIANTE A	ESTUDIANTE B
¿Te gustan los gatos?	Sí, (No, no) me gustan.

(A la clase:) A Mary (no) le gustan los gatos.

B **¿Cómo son los animales?** Use the following traits to describe the animals listed below.

bonito	misterioso
divertido	paciente
feo	peligroso (dangerous)
grande	pequeño
independiente	perezoso
inteligente	simpático
listo	tímido

Por ejemplo:

   los gatos
   Los gatos son (parecen) independientes y misteriosos.

1. los perros
2. las serpientes
3. los caballos
4. los conejos
5. los leones
6. los osos
7. los pingüinos
8. los monos
9. los gorilas
10. los canarios
11. las tortugas
12. los ratoncitos
13. los camellos
14. las llamas

C **De vacaciones.** Write a note to your neighbor thanking him or her for agreeing to take care of your pet while you're on vacation. Answer the following questions to provide information about your pet. If you don't have a pet, think of a friend's or relative's pet.

1. ¿Cómo es?
2. ¿Cuándo come?
3. ¿Qué le gusta hacer?
4. ¿Qué no le gusta hacer?
5. ¿Dónde duerme?
6. ¿Qué más necesita?

Here is the first line of your letter.

Querido(a) _____:

Gracias por cuidar a *(nombre del animal)*...

Actividades

Actividades A Answers
Answers will vary.

Classroom Management
You may wish to have pairs of students interview each other on all items in the Vocabulario. Each partner will take notes on the other's responses. Then each partner will report back to the class.

Actividades B and C Answers
Answers will vary.

Reteaching

Using the Vocabulario on pages 268 and 269, ask students to make a list of animals for each of the following categories:
1. animals they have
2. animals they want to have
3. animals they don't like

For the Native Speaker
Write a letter of application for a job in an animal hospital. Give complete autobiographical data, explain why you want the job, your qualifications, your available work hours, etc.

Cooperative Learning
Teams will brainstorm and make a complete list of animals and their traits. They will then place a star next to the animal they like the most and write a sentence stating why. Compile the lists from each team to see how many of the same animals were chosen in the class.

CULTURA VIVA 1

Los abuelos

En las culturas hispanas, los abuelos son muy importantes en la familia. Cuidan y supervisan a los niños (sus nietos) y controlan muchas de las actividades de la casa. Algunos viven en sus propias casas, pero la mayoría vive con un hijo o una hija. Allí, hacen el trabajo de la casa, preparan la comida o hacen las compras. Todos respetan las opiniones y recomendaciones de los abuelos.

Actividades

A According to the above reading, which of the following activities do many Hispanic grandparents do?

Por ejemplo:

limpiar la casa
Sí, limpian la casa.

1. cocinar
2. cuidar a los niños
3. ir de compras
4. descansar todo el día
5. expresar sus opiniones
6. ver la tele todo el día
7. jugar con los niños
8. ir a discotecas
9. ganar dinero
10. vivir con sus hijos
11. dar recomendaciones

B Answer the following questions about your grandparent(s).

1. ¿Dónde viven tus abuelos?
2. ¿Hablas por teléfono con ellos?
3. ¿A tus abuelos les gustan los jóvenes? ¿Les gustan tus amigos?
4. ¿Les gusta tu música? ¿Les gusta tu ropa?

Lección 3

Cultura viva 1

Reading Strategies
1. Have students identify and describe the people in the top photo on page 271.
2. Read the **Cultura viva** aloud to the class, or have students read silently to themselves.

Did You Know?
From an early age, children in Hispanic cultures are taught to respect and help the elderly.

Critical Thinking Activity
Imagine that your grandparents were living with you. How would your life change? Is it a good idea for grandparents to live with their children and grandchildren?

Actividades

Actividad A Answers
1. Sí, cocinan.
2. Sí, cuidan a los niños.
3. Sí, van de compras.
4. No, no descansan todo el día.
5. Sí, expresan sus opiniones.
6. No, no ven la tele todo el día.
7. Sí, juegan con los niños.
8. No, no van a discotecas.
9. No, no ganan dinero.
10. Sí, viven con sus hijos.
11. Sí, dan recomendaciones.

Actividad B Answers
Answers will vary.

Additional Practice
Ask students what advice Pilar's grandmother would give to the following members of her family.
Por ejemplo:
Pilar va a las discotecas todos los fines de semana.
No debes ir a las discotecas todos los fines de semana.

1. Los hermanos menores no sacan buenas notas.
2. José Luis sale todas las noches con una chica diferente.
3. Pilar nunca ahorra dinero.

Pronunciation
1. Use Pronunciation Transparency P-4.3.1, or write the pronunciation activity on the chalkboard. Have students copy it into their notebooks.

   Basta de jugar,
   basta de correr.
   Cierra ya tus ojos,
   sol de mi querer.

   Arrorró, mi niño,
   arrorró, mi sol,
   arrorró, pedazo
   de mi corazón.

2. You may wish to play the recorded version of this activity, located at the end of Cassette 4.3.
3. These are two traditional lullabyes grandmothers sing to children. Take them slowly. If students cannot produce the **rr**, focus on the other elements of pronunciation here.

Estructura 1

Structure Teaching Resources
1. Workbook, pp. 122–123
2. Cassette 4.3
3. Student Tape Manual, p. 98
4. Estructura Masters 4.3
5. Lesson Quizzes, pp. 81–82

Bell Ringer Review
Directions to students: What do animals eat? Make two headings on your paper: **carnivores** and **herbivores.** Then look at the animals shown on pages 268 and 269 in your text. List the meat eaters and the plant eaters in the appropriate columns on your paper.

Structure Focus
In this lesson, the presentation of **gustar** is limited to **Le gusta(n)** and **Les gusta(n)**. **Le(s) gusta** + infinitive was taught in Chapter 4, Lesson 1. Students learned to use **me gusta** and **te gusta** in Chapter 1, Lesson 4; and **me gustan** and **te gustan** in Chapter 1, Lesson 6.

Presentation
Lead students through steps 1–3 on page 272. For additional examples you may want to make statements about students in the class. For example, **A José le gusta estudiar. A Luisa le gusta nadar. A Janey y a Paula les gustan los deportes. A Julio no le gustan las tareas.** Etc. Have students react to the above statements.

Estructura 1

How to Describe Other People's Likes and Dislikes   **Le gusta(n) / Les gusta(n)**

You have already learned to say what another person likes and doesn't like to do.

> **A Kim le gusta viajar. También le gusta sacar fotos.**

You have also learned to say what two or more people like and don't like to do.

> **A mis compañeros les gusta bailar. No les gusta cantar.**

1. To say that someone likes one thing, use **le gusta** + object.
   > **A Pilar le gusta el parque zoológico.**
   > **A Kim le gusta Madrid.**

2. To say that someone likes more than one thing, use **le gustan** + objects.
   > **A José Luis le gustan sus clases.**
   > **A Miguel Ángel le gustan las serpientes.**

3. To say what more than one person likes or does not like, use **les gusta** or **les gustan**.
   > **A los estudiantes les gusta la señora Rivera.**
   > **A los hermanos de Pilar les gustan las vacaciones.**
   > **¿A ustedes les gustan los bailes de la escuela?**
   > **A mis padres no les gusta la tele.**

272 CAPÍTULO 4

Actividades

A **¿Qué le gusta?** List at least two likes and dislikes for the following people.

Por ejemplo:
> un amigo
> *A mi amigo Tom le gustan los videojuegos.*
> *No le gustan los exámenes de historia.*

1. tu amigo(a)
2. tu mamá o tu papá
3. tu primo(a)
4. tu maestro(a) de español
5. tu hermano(a)
6. un/a compañero(a) de clase

B **¿Qué les gusta?** Complete the sentences below to describe differences in the interests of the following groups of people.

1. A los niños les gusta(n)...
2. A los jóvenes les gusta(n)...
3. A los padres les gusta(n)...
4. A los abuelos les gusta(n)...
5. A los maestros les gusta(n)...

C **Animales.** List two animals you like and two you don't like.

Por ejemplo:
> Me gustan los perros pero no me gustan los gatos.

Then compare the results in a small group, announcing the similarities and differences to the class.

Por ejemplo:
> A Mark y a Chris les gustan los osos pero no les gustan los elefantes.

Lección 3   **273**

Cultura viva 2

Reading Strategies

1. Read the **Cultura viva** on this page. Have students guess what **diario** means, given the context.
2. Lead students through the **Actividades**. The concept of past time is introduced passively here. The preterit is formally and systematically presented in Chapters 5 and 6 of ¡Acción! 1.

Did You Know?

La calle Serrano is probably the most expensive shopping area of Madrid. One can find many fashionable stores there. The Plaza Mayor is in the heart of old Madrid. It is surrounded by 136 houses built in the 17th century. Most of the houses have remained in the same family, generation after generation. **Paella** is a Valencian rice dish with a variety of seafood.

Critical Thinking Activity

What regional dishes do you associate with various parts of the United States?

Actividades

Actividad A Answers
Sola: ir a un concierto en la Plaza Mayor.
Acompañada: ir a la casa de Maura, ir de compras en la calle Serrano, a comer paella. Fui. Fuimos.

Actividad B Answers
La semana pasada, luego, ayer, después del concierto.
All refer to times in the past.

Actividad C Answers
En la calle Serrano: vi gente elegante y cosas demasiado caras en las tiendas.
En la Plaza Mayor: vi un concierto y un grupo de estudiantes norteamericanos.

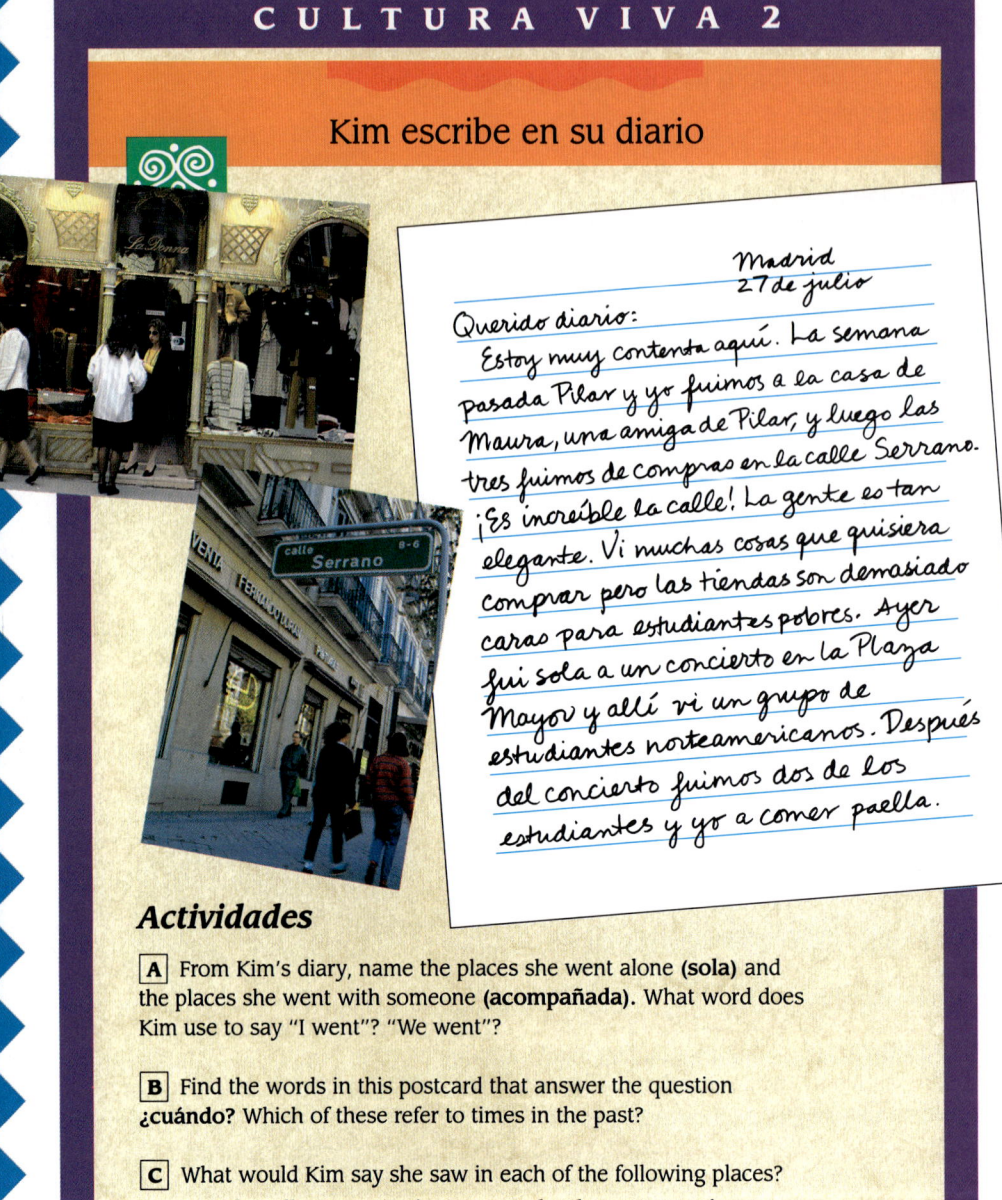

CULTURA VIVA 2

Kim escribe en su diario

> Madrid
> 27 de julio
>
> Querido diario:
> Estoy muy contenta aquí. La semana pasada Pilar y yo fuimos a la casa de Maura, una amiga de Pilar, y luego las tres fuimos de compras en la calle Serrano. ¡Es increíble la calle! La gente es tan elegante. Vi muchas cosas que quisiera comprar pero las tiendas son demasiado caras para estudiantes pobres. Ayer fui sola a un concierto en la Plaza Mayor y allí vi un grupo de estudiantes norteamericanos. Después del concierto fuimos dos de los estudiantes y yo a comer paella.

Actividades

A From Kim's diary, name the places she went alone (**sola**) and the places she went with someone (**acompañada**). What word does Kim use to say "I went"? "We went"?

B Find the words in this postcard that answer the question **¿cuándo?** Which of these refer to times in the past?

C What would Kim say she saw in each of the following places?
En la calle Serrano vi _____. En la Plaza Mayor vi _____.

Estructura 2

How to Count from 600 to the Thousands

You have learned that the numbers for 200, 300, 400, and 500 end either in **-os** or **-as**, depending on what you are describing.

> **El televisor vale trescientos dólares.**
> **Hay doscientas personas en el estadio.**

1. The numbers from 600 to 900 work the same way. They are:

600	seiscientos(as)
700	setecientos(as)
800	ochocientos(as)
900	novecientos(as)

2. The word for 1,000 is **mil**. To say 2,000, 3,000, 4,000, and so on, you say:

    dos mil, tres mil, cuatro mil, etc.

3. Notice how numbers are combined. To give numbers in the thousands in Spanish, use a period instead of a comma, as in the last three examples.

115	ciento quince
231	doscientos treinta y uno
355	trescientos cincuenta y cinco
1.400	mil cuatrocientos
2.800	dos mil ochocientos
3.335	tres mil trescientos treinta y cinco

4. When you combine numbers, as in the examples above, only the numbers that indicate "hundreds" (200, 300, 400, etc.) change endings, depending on whether you are describing masculine or feminine nouns.

    > **Hay doscientas quince muchachas en la escuela.**
    > **Y hay doscientos veinte y dos muchachos.**
    >
    > **El coche vale nueve mil quinientos dólares.**
    > **El trofeo vale tres mil cuatrocientas pesetas.**

Lección 3   **275**

Actividad

Actividad Answers

Answers will vary but should include the following:
El teléfono portátil vale setecientos cincuenta dólares.
El estéreo vale seiscientos noventa y cinco...
La videocasetera vale seiscientos veinte...
El viaje a Miami vale mil cuatrocientos...
La moto vale mil cien...
El viaje a España vale tres mil doscientos veinte y cinco...

Reteaching

Bring in store ads from local newspapers that show prices. As you read the prices, have students tell you or point to the item you are referring to.

Learning from Realia

You may want to have students look at the clothing store ad on page 276 and tell the cost of the most expensive and least expensive items in the ad.

Actividad

¡Qué suerte! On a TV game show, you have won $6,500 and now you must decide how to spend the money. Choose from the selection of prizes below.

Por ejemplo:

Quiero la bicicleta. Vale quinientos treinta y cinco dólares. También quiero _____. Vale _____.

el teléfono portátil $750

el estéreo $695

el viaje a Miami $1400

la videocasetera $620

la bicicleta $535

la moto $1100

el viaje a España $3225

276 CAPÍTULO 4

Finalmente

Situaciones

A conversar You want to buy a pet at the mall. A classmate will play the role of the salesclerk.

1. Ask the salesclerk what pets the store has.
2. Ask about the age, colors, and other characteristics of three pets the salesclerk has mentioned.
3. Ask about the cost of each one.
4. Make a selection.

A escribir On a separate sheet of paper, complete the application for part-time work at the local veterinary clinic.

¿Cómo se llama? _____
¿Cuál es su dirección? _____
¿Cuál es su número de teléfono? _____
¿Cuántos años tiene? _____
¿Por qué quiere trabajar en la clínica? _____
¿Qué animales le gustan más? _____
¿Hay animales que no le gustan? _____
¿Cuántas horas quiere trabajar? _____ ¿Qué días? _____
¿Tiene experiencia? _____ ¿Dónde? _____

Repaso de vocabulario

ANIMALES
el caballo
el camello
el canario
el conejo
el elefante
el gato
el gorila
el león
la llama
el mono
el oso
el periquito
el perro
el pez dorado
   (pl. los peces dorados)
el pingüino
el ratoncito
la serpiente
el tigre
la tortuga

NÚMEROS
seiscientos(as)
setecientos(as)
ochocientos(as)
novecientos(as)
mil

PERSONAS
los/las jóvenes
el/la niño(a)

OTRAS PALABRAS Y EXPRESIONES
cuidar
Parece que...
el parque zoológico

Lección 3 **277**

Finalmente

Situaciones

Lesson 3 Evaluation
The A conversar and A escribir situations on this page are designed to give students the opportunity to use as many language functions and as much vocabulary from this lesson as possible. The A conversar and A escribir are also intended to show how well students are able to meet the lesson objectives.

Presentation
Prior to doing the A conversar and A escribir on this page, you may wish to play the Situaciones listening activities on Cassette 4.3 as a means of helping students organize the material.

Note. Before administering Capitulo 4, Lecciones 1–3 Test, refer students to ¿Recuerdas? Lecciones 1–3, on page 316.

For the Native Speaker
Directions to students: Set up an imaginary zoo using either stuffed animals or pictures from magazines. Choose several animals and give descriptions of each, pretending you are a guide taking tourists through the zoo. The descriptions can be done in writing and orally.

CAPÍTULO 4

Lección 4

Objectives

By the end of this lesson, students will be able to:

1. describe someone's physical characteristics
2. say what they and others have to or must do
3. talk about specific people using the personal **a**

Lesson 4 Resources
1. Workbook, pp. 126–129
2. Vocabulario Transparency
3. Pronunciation Transparency P-4.4.1
4. Audio Cassette 4.4 Compact Disc 6
5. Student Tape Manual, pp. 101–104
6. Bell Ringer Review Blackline Masters, p. 25
7. Computer Software: Practice & Test Generator
8. Video (cassette or disc)
9. Video Activities Booklet, pp. A55–A56
10. Estructura Masters, pp. 50–52
11. Diversiones Masters, pp. 49–50
12. Situation Cards
13. Lesson Quizzes, pp. 85–87
14. Testing Program

Bell Ringer Review

Directions to students: Practice the following numbers in Spanish. Write them out in words on your paper and pronounce them out loud.
600, 700, 800, 900, 1.000

¡A comenzar!

Presentation

A. Lead students through each of the four functions given on page 278, progressing from the English *(continued)*

CAPÍTULO 4

Lección 4

El álbum de familia

¡A comenzar!

The following are some of the things you will be learning to do in this lesson.

When you want to...	You use...
1. describe someone's characteristics	**pelirrojo(a), rubio(a),** etc.
2. talk about someone's features	**ojos azules, pelo negro, frenos en los dientes, bigote,** etc.
3. say what someone must do	**Tiene que** + activity.
4. talk about specific people	... **a** + person

Now find examples of the above words and phrases in the following conversation.

Getting Ready for Lesson 4

You may wish to use the following suggestion to prepare students for the lesson: Bring to class photos of your family that you may have used in Lesson 1 of this chapter (or use the Vocabulario Transparency). Show the photos (or transparency) as you describe what the people look like. As you describe hair color, eye color, etc., you may wish to have students raise their hands if these descriptions also apply to them.

Kim y Pilar miran fotos de la familia de Pilar.

PILAR: Mira, Kim, aquí hay una foto de mis tíos. A la derecha está mi tía Elena. Es periodista. Es muy divertida. Ya ves que es muy guapa. Tiene pelo negro y ojos azules.
KIM: ¿Y quién es el niño con frenos en los dientes?
PILAR: Es José Antonio, el hijo de tía Elena. A ver... ¿ves a la pelirroja con anteojos? Es mi otra tía, Lidia, que trabaja en la RENFE. Siempre está muy ocupada. Tiene que trabajar mucho, incluso los fines de semana. Ahora, ¿ves al hombre con bigote?
KIM: ¿El señor alto que está a la izquierda?
PILAR: Sí. Es Juan Ignacio, el esposo de mi tía Lidia. Enseña historia en la universidad y escribe novelas policiales.
KIM: ¿Y quién es la niña rubia?
PILAR: Es Paloma, la hija de Lidia y Juan Ignacio.

Actividades preliminares

A The following relatives appear in the photo Pilar shows Kim.

Elena   José Antonio   Lidia   Paloma   Juan Ignacio

Based on Pilar's explanation, tell who is being described.

1. Es el esposo de Lidia.
2. Es periodista.
3. Son los primos de Pilar.
4. Es la hija de Lidia.
5. Es el hijo de Elena.
6. Es profesor y escritor.
7. Es pelirroja y tiene anteojos.
8. Tiene pelo negro y ojos azules.
9. Tiene frenos en los dientes.

B Think of four people you enjoy seeing. Tell when or where you usually see them.

Por ejemplo:

Veo a mi prima Inés los fines de semana.

279

Vocabulario

Vocabulary Teaching Resources
1. Vocabulario Transparency 4.4
2. Workbook, pp. 126–127
3. Cassette 4.4
4. Student Tape Manual, p. 102
5. Lesson Quizzes, p. 85

Bell Ringer Review
Directions to students: Write a note to a friend telling him or her what kind of new pet you want and some qualities it should have.

Presentation
Have students open their books to the Vocabulario on page 280. Model each new word beginning each phrase with **Tiene...** Have students repeat each phrase in unison. Ask students to name someone in the class who has one of the physical characteristics in the Vocabulario. For example, ¿Quién tiene pelo lacio? ¿Quién tiene pelo corto? Etc.

When Students Ask
The following additional vocabulary may be provided to allow students to describe people's hair or skin color:
moreno(a)
trigueño(a)
castaño(a)

Vocabulario

¿Cómo es? Tiene...
- pelo lacio
- pelo negro
- pelo rizado
- ojos azules
- Usa anteojos.
- barba
- ojos verdes
- pelo largo
- pelo corto
- ojos negros
- frenos en los dientes
- Es pelirroja.
- Usa lentes de contacto.
- Es rubio.
- bigote
- ojos de color café

280 CAPÍTULO 4

Total Physical Response

Getting Ready
For **TPR 1**, give students construction paper to cut out a blue circle, a green rectangle, a black square, and a brown triangle.

New Word
la figura

TPR 1
Si tienen ojos azules, levanten el círculo azul.
Si tienen ojos negros, muéstrenme el cuadro negro.
Si tienen ojos verdes, muéstrenme el rectángulo verde.
Miren a la persona a su derecha o izquierda.
Levanten la figura del color de sus ojos.

Actividades

A Mis compañeros de clase. Give the name of at least one classmate who has the following characteristics.

Por ejemplo:

    ojos negros
    Carlos tiene ojos negros.

1. ojos azules
2. pelo corto
3. ojos de color café
4. anteojos
5. pelo rubio
6. frenos en los dientes
7. pelo negro
8. lentes de contacto
9. pelo rizado

¿Cómo es él? ¿Y ella?

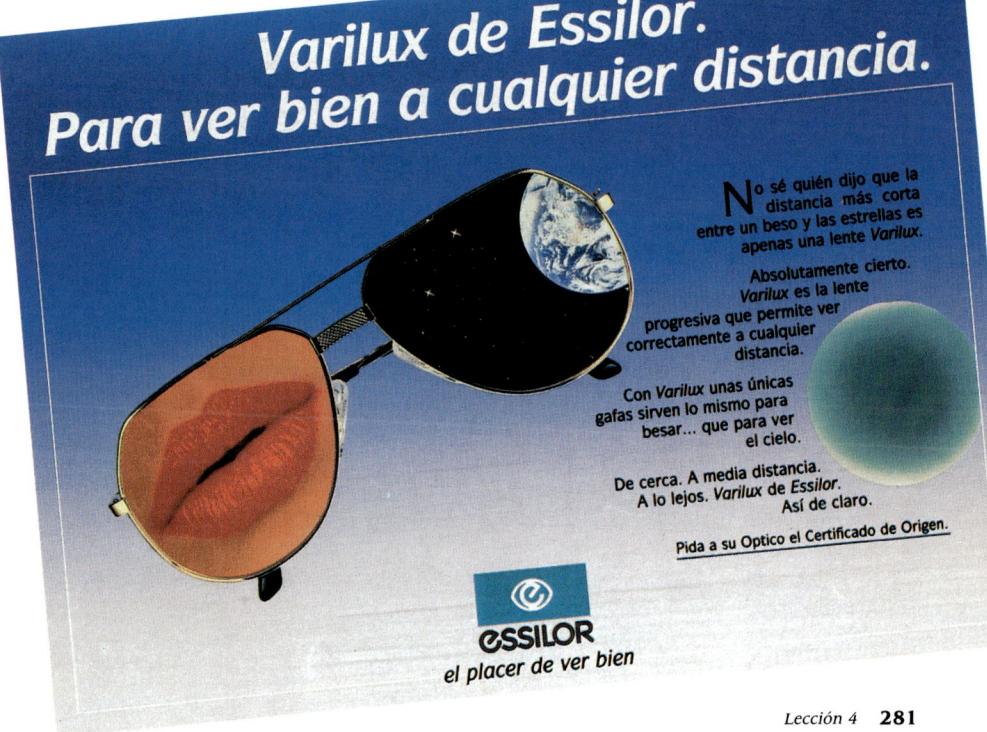

Varilux de Essilor.
Para ver bien a cualquier distancia.

No sé quién dijo que la distancia más corta entre un beso y las estrellas es apenas una lente *Varilux*.

Absolutamente cierto. *Varilux* es la lente progresiva que permite ver correctamente a cualquier distancia.

Con *Varilux* unas únicas gafas sirven lo mismo para besar... que para ver el cielo.

De cerca. A media distancia. A lo lejos. *Varilux de Essilor.* Así de claro.

Pida a su Optico el Certificado de Origen.

essilor
el placer de ver bien

Regionalisms

In some parts of the Spanish-speaking world the following words or phrases are are alternatives to those presented in the Vocabulario.
los frenos (el aparato, los frenillos);
los anteojos (las gafas) los lentes (los espejuelos) (Caribbean);
pelirrojo(a) (colorín[ina]) (Chile)

Actividades

Actividades A, B, and C Answers
Answers will vary.

Reteaching

Using the vocabulary items on page 280, describe an imaginary person to the class. Have each student draw the person you are describing on a piece of paper. Then have each student share his or her drawing with the class.

Muéstrenme la figura del color de los ojos de su madre.
(Repeat with other family members.)

TPR 2

Levanten las manos si tienen pelo rubio.
Toquen los pies si tienen pelo corto.
Pongan la cabeza en su escritorio si tienen pelo rizado.
Quítense los anteojos.

Cierren los ojos si tienen lentes de contacto.

TPR 3

Habla con una chica con pelo corto.
Saluda a un chico con barba o bigote.
Sonríe a una chica con pelo rubio.
Dale tu número de teléfono a un(a) chico(a) con ojos azules.
(Interchange commands and words.)

Learning From Photos

You may want to have students look at the photo on page 282 and have them describe hairstyles for Spanish male and female teens, based on what they see in the photo.

Unos viajeros jóvenes en la Estación de Atocha.

B **No somos gemelos.** Think of a friend and compare what the two of you look like, what characteristics you have in common, and what you like to do. Complete the following statements.

1. Mi amigo(a) se llama _____.
2. Los (Las) dos somos (tenemos) _____.
3. A _____ le gusta _____, y a mí también (pero a mí _____).

C **Mis parientes.** Choose two of your favorite relatives and describe each one as completely as you can, answering the following questions.

Por ejemplo:

¿Usan anteojos?
Mi prima Kay usa anteojos pero mi tío Luke usa lentes de contacto.

1. ¿De qué color tienen los ojos y el pelo?
2. ¿Cuántos años tienen?
3. ¿Qué les gusta? ¿Qué no les gusta?
4. ¿Dónde viven?
5. ¿Cómo son?

282 CAPÍTULO 4

For the Native Speaker

You may wish to give descriptions of celebrities who will be recogized by native speakers. For example, Menudo, Gloria Estefan, Emilio Estévez, Paul Rodríguez. Don't reveal the name of the celebrity. Students will guess who the celebrities are. See who can identify the greatest number of celebrities after listening to the description. As an option, you may wish to have native speakers describe these celebrities to others.

Cooperative Learning

Have students bring in photos of their relatives. In teams they will take turns describing the photos and share the information with the class.

CULTURA VIVA 1

¡Vamos a tomar el tren!

La RENFE (Red Nacional de los Ferrocarriles Españoles) es el sistema nacional de trenes. Viajar en tren es muy popular y muy rápido en España. Hay varias clases de trenes: el tranvía es el más lento porque tiene muchas paradas en todos los pueblos pequeños. El rápido y el expreso son, claro, más rápidos. Pero el más rápido y el más cómodo de todos es el famoso Talgo. Durante los 260 "días azules", es posible comprar billetes más baratos y ahorrar dinero.

Actividades

A When are train tickets cheaper?

B Scan the following ad for information on a special student card (**la tarjeta joven**) for the railway system. Find out the following.

1. ¿Cuántos años debes tener para usar la tarjeta?
2. ¿Cuánto vale la tarjeta?
3. ¿Cuándo es posible viajar?
4. ¿Cuántos kilómetros necesitas viajar?
5. ¿Dónde compras la tarjeta?

¡¡Ésta es tu marcha!!
Tarjeta Joven de la Renfe.

Ésta es la marcha del tren. La Marcha de la Tarjeta Joven de la RENFE. Con ella, si tienes de 12 a 26 años, puedes viajar en tren a mitad de precio de la Tarifa General. Al precio que tú puedes.

Con la Tarjeta Joven no tienes excusas, cuesta sólo 2.500 ptas. y puedes recorrerte España de punta a punta siempre que salgas en días azules y a más de 100 Kms. de donde estés.

Además, por sacarte la Tarjeta, tienes un recorrido en litera gratis.

Y por si fuera poco, RENFE te dedica un super programa musical: todos los sábados, de 13.00 a 14.00 h., Emilio Aragón en directo en "Entretenidísimo." (Cadena Ser O. M. y F. M.)

Cómprala ya.
Puedes hacerlo en Estaciones, Oficinas de Viaje RENFE y Agencias de Viaje autorizadas.

RENFE
MEJORA TU TREN DE VIDA

Pronunciation

1. Use Pronunciation Transparency P-4.4.1, or write the pronunciation activity on the chalkboard. Have students copy it into their notebooks.
   Arrastrando los vagones
   sobre el riel de acero gris
   en todas las direcciones
   cruzan trenes el país.

2. You may wish to play the recorded version of this activity, located at the end of Cassette 4.4.

3. Have students repeat words and phrases individually and in unison. You may wish to focus on the following sounds:
   /rr/ arrastando; riel;
   /r/ sobre; acero; gris; direcciones; cruzan trenes

Cultura viva 1

Reading Strategies
1. Read the **Cultura viva** on this page. Have students guess the meaning of **Red Nacional de los Ferrocarriles Españoles**.
2. List on the chalkboard the four types of trains in Spain. You may wish to mention the new high speed AVE *(Alta Velocidad Española)* train that runs between Madrid and Seville.

Did You Know?
Although Spain has a good network of paved highways, and most people own a car, train travel is very common. It is efficient, fast, and inexpensive. Railways connect most major cities. Train travel is the most common form of travel throughout Europe.

Critical Thinking Activity
Based on the reading, compare Spain's train system to Amtrak. Does Amtrak go everywhere in the U.S.? Why isn't train travel as popular in the U.S. as it is in Spain? What are some advantages of train travel? Can you think of any disadvantages?

Actividades

Actividad A Answers
Durante los días azules.

Actividad B Answers
1. Debes tener de 12 a 26 años.
2. La tarjeta vale 2.500 pesetas.
3. Es posible viajar durante los días azules.
4. Necesitas viajar más de 100 Kms.
5. Compras las tarjetas en Estaciones, Oficinas de Viaje RENFE y Agencias de Viaje autorizadas.

Estructura 1

Structure Teaching Resources
1. Workbook, p. 128
2. Cassette 4.4
3. Student Tape Manual, p. 103
4. Estructura Masters 4.4
5. Lesson Quizzes, p. 86

Bell Ringer Review

Directions to students: Write the name of a classmate who has each of the following characteristics:

1. Tiene ojos azules y pelo rubio.
2. Tiene pelo negro y frenos en los dientes.
3. Tiene pelo negro y usa anteojos.
4. Tiene pelo corto, rizado y rubio.

Presentation

Lead students through steps 1–4 on page 284. For step 1, you may wish to give additional examples of the personal **a**, such as: **Veo a Carmen. También veo su libro. Escucho discos. Escucho a Sofía.** For step 2, you may wish to add examples of **a + el = al**. For example, **Veo al maestro. Busco al amigo de Karen.**

Estructura 1

How to Talk about Specific People — **The personal a**

In the following pairs of sentences, in one sentence in each pair the direct object refers to a person; in the other, the direct object refers to a thing.

> **Veo a Julia en la clase de arte. En la clase vemos muchas fotos.**
>
> **No comprendo a la maestra de geometría. No comprendo el libro tampoco.**
>
> **En julio pensamos visitar Nueva York. Allí pensamos visitar a mis abuelos.**

1. Did you notice that if a word referring to a specific person or persons follows the verb, you use **a** before that word?

   > **Los domingos visito *a* mi amiga Inés. Inés y yo vamos al parque donde siempre vemos *a* mis compañeros. También vemos *al* hermano de Inés, que juega baloncesto con sus amigos. Generalmente invito *a* Inés a tomar algo después en una cafetería.**

En el comedor del apartamento de la familia Mestre. ¿A quiénes ves?

2. Did you notice in the above paragraph that if the **a** comes before **el**, the two words combine to form **al**?

   > **Inés piensa invitar al primo de Susan a la fiesta. También va a llamar al hermano de Eva.**

3. The personal **a** also appears in questions about specific people.

   > **¿A quién llamas?**   **Llamo a Pilar.**
   > **¿A quién invitas al baile?**   **Invito a José Luis.**

4. You do not use **a** before specific people after the verb **tener**.

   > **Tengo dos hermanos.**

284 CAPÍTULO 4

Actividades

A Mi mundo. Think of three people you visit frequently. Tell when you usually visit each of them.

Por ejemplo:
> mi amigo Sam
> *Visito a mi amigo Sam los sábados por la tarde.*

B Mis amigos. Tell about the people who are important to you by answering the following questions.

Por ejemplo:
> ¿A quién llamas cuando no entiendes la tarea?
> *Llamo al hermano de Pat.*

1. ¿A quién invitas al cine?
2. ¿A quién ves cuando vas a las fiestas?
3. ¿A quién ayudas (help) con la tarea?
4. ¿A quién visitas los fines de semana?
5. ¿A quién llamas cuando tienes un problema?

C Un mensaje. When Pilar and Kim return home one day, they find a phone message Pilar's mother left. Complete it by inserting a personal **a** in the blanks where necessary.

> Pilar:
> Debes llamar ___ Maura. Parece que ___ todos van a ver ___ José Antonio porque sale para Segovia el sábado. Maura quiere saber si debe invitar ___ Felipe y ___ su novia. Sabes ___ el número de teléfono de Maura, ¿no?

Actividades

Actividad A Answers
Answers will vary, however students should use the personal **a** in each response.

Actividad B Answers
Answers will vary but should include the following:
1. Invito a ...
2. Veo a ...
3. Ayudo a ...
4. Visito a ...
5. Llamo a ...

Actividad C Answers
The personal **a** should appear before the words **Maura, José Antonio, Felipe, su novia.**

Additional Practice
After completing Actividades A, B, and C, you may wish to reinforce the lesson by having Student A ask Student B the pair of questions in No. 1 below. Student B will respond. Then Student B will ask Student C the same question. Continue until all students in the class have had a chance to both ask and answer each pair of questions. Then repeat with question No. 2, etc.

1. ¿A quién buscas?
   Busco a ____.
   ¿Qué buscas?
   Busco ____.
2. ¿A quién ves en la cafetería?
   Veo a ____.
   ¿Qué ves?
   Veo ____.
3. ¿A quién escribes?
   Escribo a ____.
   ¿Qué escribes?
   Escribo ____.
4. ¿A quién escuchas?
   Escucho a ____.
   ¿Qué escuchas?
   Escucho ____.

Cultura viva 2

Reading Strategies

1. Use the map of Spain on page 1 to show the location of each city described in the reading.
2. You may want to refer to the ¡Acción! 1 Fine Art Transparencies by El Greco at this time.

Did You Know?

Toledo is located 41 miles southwest of Madrid. Because of its many historic structures, the Spanish government has declared the entire city a national monument. The architecture of Toledo shows a strong Moorish influence. The Moors captured Toledo in 712 A.D. and made the city its headquarters for that part of Spain.

Avila is located northwest of Madrid. The walls that surround Avila are the oldest and best preserved in Spain.

Segovia is also located northwest of Madrid. Its aqueduct is still in use. Segovia's second landmark is the **Alcázar** (castle).

Critical Thinking Activity

What does the reading tell you about Spain's history? In general, how would you compare Spain's history to U.S. history?

Actividad

Actividad Answers
Answers will vary but may include the following:

1. Si estamos en Toledo debemos visitar la Catedral y la Iglesia de Santo Tomás.
2. Si estamos en Ávila debemos ver la Catedral y la Iglesia de Santa Teresa.
3. Si estamos en Segovia debemos ver el Acueducto Romano y el Alcázar.

CULTURA VIVA 2

Toledo, Ávila y Segovia

Muchos turistas que visitan Madrid hacen excursiones a tres ciudades pequeñas que están a poca distancia de la capital: Toledo, Ávila y Segovia.

Toledo es una ciudad histórica. Como tiene influencia árabe, hebrea y católica, los turistas se maravillan ante la sinagoga, la catedral, las iglesias, los monasterios y calles y edificios medievales. También visitan la casa de El Greco, uno de los pintores más famosos de España.

Ávila es una ciudad medieval, completamente rodeada por una muralla construida como protección contra los moros. En Segovia, vemos el acueducto romano que pasa por el centro de la ciudad.

EXCURSIONES Y VISITAS
VIAJES ORBE, S.A.

MEDIO DÍA EN TOLEDO

En Toledo, ciudad-museo de gran belleza artística, visitamos la Catedral y su riquísimo Tesoro, y la Iglesia de Santo Tomás, donde está la obra más importante de El Greco: "El Entierro del Conde de Orgaz." Visitamos también la Sinagoga de Santa María la Blanca y el Monasterio de San Juan de los Reyes.

Salidas julio: 9, 10, 12, 13, 14, 21, 22, y 24.

Precio por persona: 2.200 ptas.

ÁVILA-SEGOVIA

En Ávila, visitamos la Catedral y la Iglesia de Santa Teresa. Más tarde salimos para Segovia, donde comemos cochinillo asado en un restaurante típico. En esta ciudad podemos contemplar el Acueducto Romano, de unos 2.000 años de antigüedad, y visitar el Alcázar.

Salidas julio: 11, 16, 19, 20 y 21.

Precio por persona: 4.700 ptas.

Actividad

Help Kim give advice on what to see in the following cities.

1. Si estamos en Toledo, ¿qué debemos hacer?
2. ¿Y si estamos en Ávila?
3. ¿Y si estamos en Segovia?

Estructura 2

How to Say What You Must Do   **Tener que** + *infinitive*

To say what you or others must do or have to do, use a form of the verb **tener,** followed by **que** and the activity.

**Tengo que hacer la tarea.
¿Tienes que llamar a tu hermano?
José no tiene que trabajar hoy.
Todos tenemos que ganar dinero.
Raquel y su prima tienen que visitar a sus abuelos.**

Actividades

A ¡Vamos a España! A group of students is going to Spain for a week. You are in charge of giving them final instructions. Which of the following must they do? Which do they not need to do?

Por ejemplo:

> recibir el pasaporte
> *Tienen que recibir el pasaporte.*
> llevar el libro de inglés
> *No tienen que llevar el libro de inglés.*

1. saber la dirección del hotel
2. llevar cheques de viajero
3. estudiar el mapa
4. llegar temprano al aeropuerto
5. comprar regalos para la maestra
6. hablar español
7. ser muy amables
8. ahorrar cinco mil dólares

Una vista de Toledo.

B En tu casa. List five things that your parents would say you have to do at home. Use **primero, luego, después, entonces.**

Por ejemplo:

> *Primero tienes que limpiar tu habitación.*

Lección 4   287

Actividad C Answers
Answers will vary.

Classroom Management
You may wish to do Actividad D as a whole class activity initially. Take the role of Student A, calling on individual students to answer for Student B. You may want to do this as a paired activity the second time.

Actividades D and E Answers
Answers will vary.

Additional Practice
After doing Actividades A, B, C, D, and E, you may wish to reinforce the lesson by doing the following: In pairs have students invite each other to do certain things. The partner will refuse and say that he or she has to do something instead. For example:

ESTUDIANTE A	ESTUDIANTE B
¿Quieres ir al cine?	No, gracias, tengo que estudiar.

Reteaching

Have students list five things they have to do after school.

C Estoy muy ocupado. Bruno asks you to do the following things, but you think he's boring. Tell him that you have to do something else.

Por ejemplo:

¿Quieres tomar algo en la cafetería?
¡Qué pena! Tengo que ver al maestro de inglés.

1. ¿Quieres ir al centro comercial?
2. ¿Por qué no jugamos tenis?
3. ¿Quieres ir al cine el sábado?
4. ¿Por qué no vamos al partido esta noche?
5. Te gusta el fútbol, ¿verdad? ¿Quieres jugar?

D Imposible. Suggest to a classmate that the two of you do the following things. Your classmate will reject your suggestions and say something else you both have to do instead.

Por ejemplo:
ir al cine

ESTUDIANTE A	ESTUDIANTE B
¿Por qué no vamos al cine?	No. Tenemos que ir al centro.

1. ir al partido
2. tomar algo
3. bailar
4. hablar inglés
5. descansar
6. salir esta noche
7. limpiar tu habitación

¿Qué tienen que hacer los muchachos?

E Resoluciones. Think of three things that you don't do enough of Share these with a classmate. Then tell what you have to do to improve. Report back to the class.

Por ejemplo:

ESTUDIANTE A	ESTUDIANTE B
No trabajo bastante en mis clases. Tengo que trabajar más.	Nunca llevo a mi hermano menor al cine. Tengo que llevar a mi hermano al cine más.

(A la clase:) Jill dice que tiene que trabajar más. Yo también.

Finalmente

Situaciones

A conversar A classmate has witnessed a robbery. You will play the role of a police officer who asks about what the suspect looks like.

1. Find out if the person is a man or a woman.
2. Find out the person's approximate (**más o menos**) age.
3. Ask if the person is tall or short, thin or heavy.
4. Ask about the color, length, and type of hair. If it is a man, ask about facial hair and its color and length.
5. Find out if the person wears glasses.

A escribir Write a note to a classmate describing a well-known personality, such as an athlete, politican, musician, actor, or actress. Don't give the person's name; your classmate will guess whom you are describing.

1. Give the person's profession.
2. Describe what the person looks like.
3. Give one or two other details, such as the person's recent achievements or favorite activities.

Repaso de vocabulario

DESCRIPCIÓN PERSONAL	DESCRIPCIÓN DE PELO	EXPRESIÓN
los anteojos	corto	tener que
la barba	lacio	
el bigote	largo	
los dientes	pelirrojo(a)	
los frenos	rizado	
los lentes de contacto	rubio(a)	
los ojos		
el pelo		

Lección 4 289

Finalmente

Situaciones

Lesson 4 Evaluation
The A conversar and A escribir situations on this page are designed to give students the opportunity to use as many language functions and as much vocabulary from this lesson as possible. The A conversar and A escribir are also intended to show how well students are able to meet the lesson objectives.

Presentation
Prior to doing the A conversar and A escribir, you may wish to play the Situaciones listening activities on Cassette 4.4 as a means of helping students organize the material.

For the Native Speaker
Native speakers will talk about places in their countries they like and tell why. They should make a list for their classmates.

CAPÍTULO 4

Lección 5

Objectives

By the end of this lesson, students will be able to:
1. say what they and others prefer to do
2. identify television programs and pastimes
3. talk about another or others
4. report on what someone says

Lesson 5 Resources
1. Workbook, pp. 130–135
2. Vocabulario Transparencies
3. Pronunciation Transparency P-4.5.1
4. Audio Cassette 4.5 Compact Disc 6
5. Student Tape Manual, pp. 105–108
6. Bell Ringer Review Blackline Masters, p. 26
7. Computer Software: Practice & Test Generator
8. Video (cassette or disc)
9. Video Activities Booklet, pp. A57–A58
10. Estructura Masters, pp. 53–54
11. Diversiones Masters, pp. 51–52
12. Situation Cards
13. Lesson Quizzes, pp. 88–91
14. Testing Program

Bell Ringer Review

Directions to students: Draw a picture of this Halloween monster. Follow the description given of its physical characteristics. The rest is up to you and your imagination! **El monstruo es muy alto y flaco. Tiene el pelo muy rizado y verde. Tiene frenos enormes en sus dientes. También usa anteojos negros porque tiene problemas con los ojos. ¡Es muy feo!**

CAPÍTULO 4

Lección 5

¡Qué divertido es Madrid!

¡A comenzar!

The following are some of the things you will be learning to do in this lesson.

When you want to...	You use...
1. say what someone prefers to do	**Prefiere** + activity.
2. report what someone says	**Dice que...**
3. talk about other things	**otros(as)...**

Now find examples of the above words and phrases in the following letter.

Getting Ready for Lesson 5

You may wish to use one or more of the following suggestions to prepare students for the lesson:
1. Bring a TV schedule to class and describe the types of programs that are on television today and tonight. Have students respond according to their likes and dislikes. Also have them agree or disagree with your opinion of various programs. For example: **Por la mañana hay muchos concursos. Por ejemplo, a las diez hay _____. (No) Me gustan los concursos porque _____. Prefiero _____. A las seis de la tarde siempre veo las noticias, etc.**
2. Tell students some common complaints about television viewing. Have them respond in agreement (**De acuerdo**)

Kim le escribe una carta a Josh, un compañero de clase en Los Ángeles.

Querido Josh:

Aquí estoy en Madrid con Pilar. Madrid es fantástico y Pilar es sensacional, tan guapa y simpática como siempre. Por la tarde, Pilar y yo salimos con su hermano mayor, José Luis, y sus amigos. Vamos al cine y comemos tapas, o vamos a las discotecas y después tomamos un café en una de las plazas. Hay muchas discotecas — son fantásticas y tienen toda la música de los Estados Unidos, Inglaterra, Alemania y, claro, de España también. Si no salimos, a veces veo telenovelas y otros programas interesantes. Pero a Pilar no le gustan las telenovelas. Prefiere hacer otras cosas. Por ejemplo, le encanta leer.

También vive con la familia la abuela de Pilar. A la abuela no le gustan las discotecas — dice que son malas para las jóvenes. (Me gusta mucho la familia de Pilar, pero no comprendo a la abuela). Bueno, termino la carta ahora. Esta tarde empiezo un curso de arte en el Museo del Prado.

¡Hasta pronto!

Tu amiga,
Kim

Actividades preliminares

A Based on Kim's letter, tell whether the following statements are true **(Es verdad)** or false **(No es verdad)**.

1. Kim cree que Pilar es amable.
2. Kim y Pilar nunca salen por la tarde.
3. Parece que a Kim le gusta Madrid.
4. Pilar ve la tele muy poco.
5. A las chicas les gusta bailar.
6. A Kim no le gusta escribir a su maestra de español.

B Tell at what time each of the following begins and ends.

Por ejemplo:

tu primera clase
Empieza a las ocho y cuarto y termina a las nueve.

1. tu clase de español
2. tu programa favorito
3. el programa favorito de tu hermano (mamá, papá, etc.)

or disagreement **(No es verdad)**. For example:

a. Dicen que hay demasiada violencia en los programas.
b. Dicen que la violencia en la televisión causa crímenes.
c. Dicen que los jóvenes ven la tele 25 horas a la semana.
d. Dicen que la televisión es mala para los niños.
e. Dicen que los jóvenes no leen bastante porque ven demasiado la tele.
f. Dicen que los niños creen todo lo que ven en la televisión.

¡A comenzar!

Presentation

A. Lead students through each of the three functions given on page 290, progressing from the English to the Spanish for each function. Then have students find these words and phrases in the letter on page 291.

B. Introduce the Lesson 5 letter by reading it aloud or by playing the recorded version. Tell students they are going to hear Kim read a letter she wrote to a friend in Los Angeles. Have students listen to the tape to find out the following information:
  1. dos cosas que a Kim y Pilar les gusta hacer
  2. una cosa que a la abuela de Pilar no le gusta

C. Now ask students to open their books and look at the letter on page 291. Ask students to list the following:
  1. las cosas que a Kim le gusta hacer
  2. las cosas que a Pilar le gusta hacer

D. Have each student compare his or her preferences to those of Kim and Pilar. For example:
A Kim le gusta _____ pero a mí, no. Prefiero _____.
A Pilar le gusta _____ y a mí también.

E. Help students summarize what Kim says in her letter using the expression **dice que**. For example:
Kim dice que salen con José Luis y que comen...

Actividades preliminares

Actividad A Answers
1. Es verdad.
2. No es verdad.
3. Es verdad.
4. Es verdad.
5. Es verdad.
6. No es verdad.

Actividad B Answers
Answers will vary.

Vocabulario

Vocabulary Teaching Resources
1. Vocabulario Transparencies 4.5
2. Workbook, pp. 130–131
3. Cassette 4.5
4. Student Tape Manual, p. 105
5. Lesson Quizzes, p. 88

Bell Ringer Review

Directions to students: List one important thing that each member of your family has to do very soon. Follow this model: **Mi hermana Susan tiene que practicar el piano para el concierto.**

Presentation

A. Have students open their books to the Vocabulario on pages 292 and 293. Model each new word or phrase, beginning with **En los ratos libres quiero aprender a...** Have students repeat after you in unison.

B. Find out what students like to do in their spare time. For example, **¿Cuántos saben jugar cartas? ¿ajedrez? ¿Cuántos quieren aprender?** Have students respond with their preferences. For example, **¿Prefieres leer or jugar cartas? ¿Con quién juegas cartas? ¿Quién gana? ¿Qué lees? ¿Prefieres jugar ajedrez o leer libros de ciencia ficción? ¿Con quién juegas ajedrez? ¿Quién gana? ¿Cómo se llama tu libro de ciencia ficción favorito?**

C. Have students tell what things they are learning to do now in school. For example, **Aprendo a hablar español.**

D. After modeling the words and phrases on page 293, ask students to list their two favorite TV

Vocabulario

En los ratos libres quiero aprender a...

jugar cartas jugar ajedrez

A veces prefiero leer novelas...

románticas policiales de ciencia ficción

También me gusta leer revistas de...

historietas moda deportes

Y me gusta jugar juegos de mesa. **Me gusta ganar pero a veces pierdo.***

*perder (ie)

292 CAPÍTULO 4

Total Physical Response

Getting Ready
Bring to class magazine covers, novels, and TV listings of programs students will recognize. Each student should have at least one of the above.

New Words
coloquen
título

TPR 1

Pongan los programas deportivos en la pizarra.
Pongan las revistas de moda en la pared.
Coloquen las telenovelas en la pared a mi derecha.
Coloquen las novelas de ciencia ficción en la pared a mi izquierda.
Denme los programas educativos.
Denle a ____ los programas cómicos.

¿Qué clase de programa prefieres?
Prefiero ver...

 las telenovelas

 las noticias

 los concursos

 los programas deportivos

 los programas educativos   los programas cómicos

 las películas extranjeras

 las películas de terror

 las películas de aventuras

Actividades

A Las películas. List a recent movie for each of the following categories.

1. películas cómicas
2. películas de aventuras
3. películas románticas
4. películas de ciencia ficción
5. películas de terror
6. películas policiales

Lección 5 **293**

Lleven las historietas a mi escritorio.
Lleven los programas de concursos a la pared detrás del cuarto.
Levántense si prefieren las películas de aventuras.
Párense en la puerta si les gustan las revistas deportivas.
Vayan a la pizarra si prefieren las novelas de ciencia ficción.
(Interchange commands and titles.)

TPR 2
Dale tu programa de noticias a _____.
Busca un título de novela romántica y ponlo en mi escritorio.
Busca una historieta y dásela a _____.
Toma un título de la persona a tu derecha y dime cómo se llama.
Busca un programa policial y dáselo a un muchacho alto.

---

programs and tell what kind of program each is. For example:
Mis programas favoritos son ___ y ___.

When Students Ask
The following additional vocabulary may be provided to allow students to talk about their preferences.
**jugar damas
jugar damas chinas
hacer rompecabezas
jugar dominó
tejer
ver los dibujos animados**

Regionalisms
You may wish to tell students that in some parts of the Spanish-speaking world the following words or phrases are alternatives to those presented in the Vocabulario.
**las cartas (los naipes);
el juego de mesa (el juego de salón);
policial (policíaco[a])**

Actividades

Actividad A Answers
Answers will vary.

Actividades B and C Answers
Answers will vary.

Extension
After doing Actividad B, you may wish to extend it in the following ways:

1. If students disagree with the statement, have them say what should be done instead. For example:
   1. No estoy de acuerdo. Deben incluir más programas deportivos.
2. Tally on the chalkboard how many students agree and disagree with each statement. Then summarize the results. For example, Parece que (no) deben incluir más programas cómicos. Etc.

Actividad D Answers
1. Practico deportes (Juego cartas).
2. Juego cartas (ajedrez).
3. Veo programas deportivos (telenovelas).
4. Leo libros románticos (libros de terror).
5. Veo programas cómicos (programas policiales).
6. Leo novelas (biografías).
7. Me gusta leer...
8. Prefiero las películas de...
9. Cuando juego juegos de mesa...

Extension
When doing Actividad D, you may wish to extend it by keeping a tally on the chalkboard of students' preferences. Then have students summarize the results.

Reteaching

Ask individual students the following questions: ¿Qué te gusta hacer en los ratos libres? or ¿Qué prefieres hacer en tus ratos libres? or ¿Qué clase de programas prefieres? Ask other students to summarize. For example: A Raúl le gusta jugar ajedrez pero a veces prefiere leer revistas de deportes. Prefiere los programas deportivos.

B **Opinión pública.** The following are the opinions some people have expressed about U.S. television programming. For the statements you agree with, say or write **De acuerdo.** If you disagree, say or write **No estoy de acuerdo.**

1. Deben incluir más programas cómicos.
2. Existe un exceso de telenovelas.
3. Deben incluir más programas educativos.
4. Deben prohibir las películas de terror.
5. Un programa de noticias a las 7:00 de la mañana y otro a las 6:00 de la tarde es suficiente.
6. Deben incluir más programas deportivos, por ejemplo de fútbol y de otros deportes también.
7. Deben presentar más programas extranjeros.
8. Hay demasiados concursos.

C **Quiero aprender.** List five things that you would like to learn how to do some day.

Por ejemplo:
> Quiero aprender a esquiar.

D **¿Cuál prefieres?** Interview a classmate using the following questions. Then report back to the class about his or her preferences.

Por ejemplo:

ESTUDIANTE A	ESTUDIANTE B
¿Lees libros o ves la tele?	Leo libros.

(A la clase:) Bob dice que prefiere leer libros.

1. ¿Practicas deportes o juegas cartas?
2. ¿Juegas cartas o juegas ajedrez?
3. ¿Ves programas deportivos o telenovelas?
4. ¿Lees libros románticos o libros de terror?
5. ¿Ves programas cómicos o programas policiales?
6. ¿Lees novelas o biografías?
7. ¿Qué clase de revistas te gusta leer?
8. Cuando vas al cine, ¿qué clase de película prefieres?
9. Cuando juegas juegos de mesa, ¿a veces pierdes o siempre ganas? ¿y cuando practicas deportes?

For the Native Speaker

A. Have native speakers make a list of five television programs shown in their country. They should then explain what each program is about.

B. Ask native speakers to describe five different television programs shown in the U.S.

Cooperative Learning

Ask reporters from each team to exchange places with reporters from other teams in the class. After asking questions 1–9 in Actividad D, each reporter will return to his or her own team and share his or her findings from the other team.

CULTURA VIVA 1

El cine y la tele en España

A los españoles (como a los norteamericanos) les gusta mucho ir al cine. Pero en España no es raro ir a ver una película después de cenar, como a las once de la noche.

En España la televisión es muy popular también. Muchos de los canales son controlados por el gobierno. Por eso, ves menos anuncios comerciales, y los programas no siempre empiezan y terminan a la hora o a la media hora como en los Estados Unidos.

Actividad

Find at least one program in the Madrid listing below that fits each of the following categories.

1. programas extranjeros
2. de niños
3. concursos
4. cómicos
5. de noticias
6. deportivos
7. de música
8. de aventuras

DOMINGO

09.15 TVE-1 CONCIERTO

12.00 TVE-2 DOMINGO DEPORTE
Espacio deportivo que presenta MARÍA ESCARIO, y que ofrece las siguientes transmisiones:
12.15: BALONCESTO. En directo, desde el Pabellón de Villalba, se ofrece la transmisión del encuentro correspondiente a la Liga ACB, que enfrenta a los equipos del ATLÉTICO DE MADRID VILLALBA y al JOVENTUT DE BADALONA. **15.00: GOLF.** En directo, desde el campo de Valderrama se ofrece la transmisión de la última jornada del TROFEO VOLVO MASTERS. **CICLISMO:** Resumen de la Escalada al Montjuich. **GIMNASIA.** En directo, desde el Pabellón de Bruselas, transmisión de la final de la Copa del Mundo de este deporte.

13.00 CANAL+ EL GRAN MUSICAL

14.30 ANTENA-3 NOTICIAS

16.30 CANAL+ PREVIO LIGA DE FÚTBOL

17.20 TELE-5 LASSIE

17.45 TVE-1 JUEGO DE NIÑOS
XAVIER SARDÁ presenta este concurso en el que los participantes deben adivinar

19.00 TVE-2 PLAYA DE CHINA:
"EL MUNDO" (II)
Capítulo 21 de esta serie estadounidense que consta de 22 episodios. Colleen, tras el entierro de su padre, está muy confundida y se plantea el permanecer en Estados Unidos en lugar de regresar a Vietnam.

19.35 TVE-5 MISIÓN IMPOSIBLE:
"LA PRUEBA" (Capítulo 16)

19.45 TVE-2 NOTICIAS

20.00 TVE-5 EL NUEVO BENNY HILL

20.05 ANTENA-3 LA RULETA DE LA FORTUNA
Concurso presentado por IRMA SORIANO.

20.30 ANTENA-3 DIBUJOS ANIMADOS:
"EL CAMPEÓN"

21.30 TVE-2 CHEERS:
"LOS CHICOS DEL BAR"
Un antiguo compañero de equipo de Sam decide organizar en Cheers una rueda de prensa. En el transcurso de la misma va a presentar un libro autobiográfico en el que relata las juergas que él y Sam disfrutaron en su juventud

Pronunciation

Cuando vemos películas de amor no siempre creemos al actor.
Y cuando leemos libros de amor no siempre creemos al escritor.

Cultura viva 1

Reading Strategies
1. Read the Cultura viva on this page. Have students guess the meaning of canal(es) and gobierno.
2. Now do the Actividad on this page.

Did You Know?
TV is not as popular in Spain and other countries as it is in the U.S. In fact, many programs shown in Spain are imported from the U.S. American movies are popular in Spain and in many other countries.

Critical Thinking Activity
Based on the reading selection, make some comparisons between Spanish television and U.S. television.

Actividad

Actividad Answers
1. Playa de China, La ruleta de la fortuna, Cheers, El nuevo Benny Hill, Lassie, Misión imposible.
2. Juego de niños, Dibujos animados.
3. La ruleta de la fortuna.
4. El nuevo Benny Hill, Dibujos animados, Cheers.
5. Noticias.
6. Domingo deporte, Previo liga de fútbol.
7. Concierto, El gran musical.
8. Misión imposible.

Additional Practice
After completing the Actividad on page 295, you may wish to reinforce the lesson with the following: Compare the times people go to the movies in Spain with the times they go where you live. **Por ejemplo: En España van al cine ____. Donde yo vivo, van al cine ____.**

Pronunciation Notes
1. Use Pronunciation Transparency P-4.5.1, or write the pronunciation activity on the chalkboard. Have students copy it into their notebooks.
2. You may wish to play the recorded version of this activity, located at the end of Cassette 4.5.
3. Have students repeat words and phrases individually and in unison. You may wish to focus on the /r/ sound as in amor; actor; escritor.

Estructura 1

Structure Teaching Resources
1. Workbook, pp. 132–133.
2. Cassette 4.5
3. Student Tape Manual, p. 106
4. Estructura Masters 4.5
5. Lesson Quizzes, p. 89

Bell Ringer Review

Directions to students: Write these three categories across the top of your paper. Then list your preferred programs and movies in the appropriate column. Add other categories if you wish.

programas cómicos
telenovelas
películas de terror
películas policiales
películas de aventuras

Presentation

Lead students through steps 1–3 on page 296. To establish familiarity, you may wish to model each form of the verb **preferir,** having students repeat in unison. You may also wish to remind students that they have already learned the verbs **pensar** and **querer** and that these have the same stem changes as **preferir.**

Learning From Photos

You may want to have students look at the photos on page 296 and have them identify the various kinds of magazines they see.

Estructura 1

How to State Preferences   **The verb preferir**

1. When you want to state your preferences or those of others, use the appropriate form of the verb **preferir (ie),** followed by the activity you prefer to do.

SINGULAR	PLURAL
prefiero	preferimos
prefieres	preferís*
prefiere	prefieren

*This form is rarely used in the Spanish-speaking world, except for Spain.

2. When you want to ask which one someone prefers, use **¿cuál?**
   ¿Cuál película prefieres ver?
   Prefiero ver la película romántica.

3. When you want to offer someone choices, use the word **o.**
   ¿Prefieres nadar o descansar?

En un quiosco de Madrid.

Actividades

A **En los ratos libres.** Choosing from the following list, decide which types of magazines you, your family, and your friends prefer.

revistas de casa y cocina
revistas de coches
revistas de deportes
revistas policiales
revistas de historietas
revistas cómicas
revistas de moda
revistas de noticias
revistas de política
revistas financieras

1. tú
2. tu hermano(a)
3. tu mamá o tu papá
4. tú y tus amigos
5. tus abuelos

B **¿Cuál prefieres?** Interview a classmate to find out which activity from the list below he or she prefers to do. Report back to the class.

Por ejemplo:

ir al cine o jugar videojuegos

ESTUDIANTE A	ESTUDIANTE B
¿Prefieres ir al cine o jugar videojuegos?	Prefiero ir al cine (jugar videojuegos).

(A la clase:) Jill dice que prefiere...

1. salir con los amigos o descansar en casa
2. ver telenovelas o escuchar música
3. leer en la biblioteca o estudiar en casa
4. tomar un café o un refresco
5. comer tapas o papas fritas
6. practicar deportes o correr
7. comer en la cafetería de la escuela o comer afuera
8. limpiar tu habitación o estudiar
9. jugar cartas o escuchar música
10. jugar juegos de mesa o ajedrez
11. ver películas extranjeras o películas de ciencia ficción

Lección 5 **297**

Actividades

Actividad A Answers
1. Prefiero...
2. ... prefiere...
3. ... prefiere...
4. ... preferimos...
5. ... prefieren...

Actividad B Answers
Answers will vary.

Additional Practice
After completing Actividades A and B, you may wish to reinforce the lesson by doing the following activity: Name two things that you and your best friend might choose to do in the situations below.
Por ejemplo: cuando están en casa
Cuando estamos en casa, preferimos jugar juegos de mesa o escuchar música.

1. cuando salen por la noche
2. cuando están en la clase de español
3. cuando van al cine
4. cuando van a la cafetería
5. cuando van al centro comercial
6. cuando visitan a un amigo

Reteaching
Write down one thing the following members of your family prefer to do.
1. tú
2. tu hermano(a)
3. tus padres
4. tú y tus hermanos

Cultura viva 2

Reading Strategies

1. Read Kim's diary entry to the class aloud, or ask students to take turns reading one sentence each. Remind students that José Luis is Pilar's older brother.
2. Lead students through the **Actividades.** The concept of past time is introduced passively here. The preterit is formally and systematically presented in Chapters 5 and 6 of ¡Acción! 1, and reviewed in ¡Acción! 2.

Did You Know?

Spaniards tend to stay up later and go out late at night more than Americans. Spanish teenagers don't have to obey a curfew. That's why Kim and José Luis are in a café at 2 o'clock in the morning.

Critical Thinking Activity

What do you think American TV programs and movies shown in Spain tell Spaniards about life in the U.S.? Do they give a true picture of life in the U.S.?

Actividades

Actividad A Answers
Kim fue a una tienda, a la discoteca y a un café con José Luis. Kim piensa ir al Parque del Retiro y a una fiesta en casa de un amigo de Pilar.

Actividad B Answers
Kim went: **fui.**
Kim and José Luis went: **fuimos.**
Pilar went: **fue.**

Actividad C Answers
A Kim le gusta Madrid, le gusta bailar y le gustan Pilar y José Luis.

Actividad D Answers
Answers will vary.

CULTURA VIVA 2

¡Me gusta esta ciudad!

6 de agosto

Querido diario:
Ayer por la tarde fui a una tienda a comprar un regalo para la señora Rivera. Anoche fuimos a la discoteca a bailar Pilar, José Luis y yo. ¡Qué bien baila ese chico! Después, Pilar fue a casa y José Luis y yo fuimos a tomar algo en el café ¡a las dos de la noche! Mañana él y yo vamos a hacer un picnic y pasar el día en el Parque del Retiro. Dice que es muy divertido pasear en bote en el lago. Luego, por la noche, vamos a ir a una fiesta en casa de un amigo de Pilar y José Luis. ¡Me gusta esta ciudad! (También me gusta José Luis).

Actividades

A Name the places Kim went in Madrid. Name the places she is going to go.

B What word does Kim use to say she went somewhere? To say that she and José Luis went somewhere? To say Pilar went somewhere?

C What can you tell about what Kim likes?

D Compare where you went yesterday (**ayer**) to where you're going to go tomorrow. Complete the following sentences.

   Ayer fui a _____. Mañana voy a _____.

298 CAPÍTULO 4

For the Native Speaker

Have native speakers write a 2–3 minute TV commercial and present it to the class. Students can use props or illustrations in presenting their commercial. You may wish to read over the script before asking the native speakers to present it to the class.

Estructura 2

How to Talk about Another or Others — **Otro**

1. If you want to express the idea of "another" or "others," use the word **otro**. This word will come before the person(s) or thing(s) you are referring to and end in **-o, -os, -a,** or **-as**.

    ¿Quieres otra cosa? Sí, necesito otro bolígrafo.
    Muchos estudiantes son aplicados, otros son perezosos.

2. If you want to express the idea of "the other one" or "the other ones," use the word **el, la, los,** or **las** before the appropriate form of **otro**.

    ¿Te gustan los anteojos negros? No, prefiero los otros.
    ¿Hablas del chico rubio? No, hablo del otro, del pelirrojo.

Actividades

A **¿Quieres otro?** Tell whether you are satisfied with the following things or whether you want others. Explain why.

Por ejemplo:

tu cama
No me gusta mi cama. Es vieja y no es muy cómoda. Quiero otra. (Me gusta mi cama. Es nueva y grande. No necesito otra).

1. tus discos
2. tu mochila
3. tu estéreo
4. tu habitación
5. tu gaveta
6. tu libro de matemáticas
7. tu perro o tu gato

El Escorial, al norte de Madrid.

Actividad B Answers
Answers will vary.

Actividad C Answers
1. Una de las revistas es de moda, las otras son de coches.
2. Uno de los muchachos juega un videojuego, los otros juegan cartas.
3. Uno de los gatos es negro, los otros son blancos.

B ¿De acuerdo o no? Write down your preferences for each of the following topics. Then, with a partner, find out how many topics the two of you agree on. Report back to the class.

Por ejemplo:

>leer (una revista)

ESTUDIANTE A	ESTUDIANTE B
(1) ¿Quieres leer la revista *People*?	(2) Sí, me gusta. (No, prefiero leer otra).
(3) ¿Cuál prefieres?	(4) Prefiero *Sports Illustrated*.

(A la clase:) Yo prefiero la revista *People* pero Jaime dice que prefiere *Sports Illustrated*.

1. ver (una película)
2. ver (un programa de televisión)
3. practicar (un deporte)
4. ir a (un partido)
5. ser (una ocupación)
6. tener (un animal)
7. comer (una comida)
8. tomar (un refresco)

C ¿Cómo es diferente? Describe the people and things below by telling how one of each group is different from the others.

Por ejemplo:

>Uno de los muchachos no tiene anteojos, los otros tienen anteojos.

1. 2. 3.

300 CAPÍTULO 4

Finalmente

Situaciones

A conversar Converse with a classmate about leisure activities.

1. Ask what kinds of leisure activities your partner likes to do.
2. Find one activity that you both have in common and invite your classmate to do something related to that activity.
3. Agree on a day, time, and place.

A escribir Your school has decided to begin a Spanish-language collection for the library. Complete the following note to your librarian, telling all the types of books, magazines, and videos that would appeal to a wide variety of students in your school.

Estimado(a) ____:

A muchos estudiantes les gusta(n) ____, ____ y ____. Entonces, usted debe comprar ____, ____ y ____.

Repaso de vocabulario

PREGUNTAS
¿Cuál prefiere(s)?
¿Qué clase de...?

DIVERSIONES
el ajedrez
las cartas (cards)
el concurso
la historieta
el juego de mesa
la novela
el programa
la telenovela

ACTIVIDADES
aprender a
empezar (ie)
ganar (to win)
perder (ie)
terminar

DESCRIPCIONES
cómico(a)
de aventuras
de ciencia ficción
de moda
de terror
deportivo(a)
educativo(a)
extranjero(a)
policial
romántico(a)

OTRAS PALABRAS Y EXPRESIONES
Dice que
otro(a)
preferir (ie)
las noticias
los ratos libres

Finalmente

Situaciones

Lesson 5 Evaluation
The A conversar and A escribir situations on this page are designed to give students the opportunity to use as many language functions and as much vocabulary from the lesson as possible. The A conversar and A escribir are also intended to show how well students are able to meet the lesson objectives.

Presentation

Prior to doing the A conversar and A escribir on this page, you may wish to play the **Situaciones** listening activities on Cassette 4.5 as a means of helping students organize the material.

CAPÍTULO 4

Lección 6

Objectives

By the end of this lesson, students will be able to:
1. talk about what they and others can or can't do
2. tell the day and month something occurs
3. request information
4. talk about an event to take place in the future

Lesson 6 Resources
1. Workbook, pp. 136–143
2. Vocabulario Transparency
3. Pronunciation Transparency P-4.6.1
4. Audio Cassette 4.6 Compact Disc 7
5. Student Tape Manual, pp. 109–116
6. Bell Ringer Review Blackline Masters, pp. 27–28
7. Computer Software: Practice & Test Generator
8. Video (cassette or disc)
9. Video Activities Booklet, pp. A59–A63
10. Estructura Masters, pp. 55–56
11. Diversiones Masters, pp. 53–54
12. Situation Cards
13. Lesson Quizzes, pp. 92–95
14. Testing Program

¡A comenzar!

Presentation

A. Lead students through each of the four functions on page 302, progressing from the English to the Spanish for each function. Then have students find these words and phrases in the letter on page 303.

CAPÍTULO 4

Lección 6

Escribe la señora Rivera

¡A comenzar!

The following are some of the things you will be learning to do in this lesson.

When you want to...	You use...
1. tell a friend what he or she can do	**Puedes** + activity.
2. say what someone else can or can't do	**(No) Puede** + activity.
3. refer to an event to take place one day next week	**el lunes (martes, etc.) que viene**
4. to say the day and the month something occurs	**el** + date + **de** + month

Now find examples of the above words and phrases in the following letter.

302

Getting Ready for Lesson 6

You may wish to use one or more of the following suggestions to prepare students for the lesson:

1. Talk about your plans for next summer or next year. For example: **El verano que viene (el año que viene) voy a viajar a _____ (voy a trabajar en _____, voy a aprender a _____, voy a leer _____, etc.).**

2. Have students raise their hands in response to your questions about plans for next summer or next year. For example:
   a. ¿Cuántos van a trabajar?
   b. ¿Cuántos van a hacer un viaje con los padres? Etc.

Kim recibe una carta de la señora Rivera.

15 de agosto
Los Ángeles

Querida Kim:

¡Gracias por todas tus cartas y tarjetas postales! Y ¡qué bien escribes en español! Parece que te gustan mucho José Luis y su grupo y veo que puedes salir con ellos por la noche. ¡Qué experiencia para ti!

Creo que con el tiempo vas a comprender a la abuela. Es de otra generación y no puede comprender bien los intereses de los jóvenes como Pilar y tú, José Luis y los otros. Debes comprender también que, para los hispanos, la abuela es una parte muy importante de la familia. Por eso, creo que ella no va a regresar a su pueblo.

Bueno, tu mamá dice que vas a regresar a Los Ángeles el lunes que viene. ¡Quiero saber todas las noticias de tu viaje a Madrid!

Saludos afectuosos de
Sonia Rivera

P.D. Otra cosa: Si tienes tiempo antes de regresar, ¿me puedes comprar unas revistas y periódicos españoles?

Actividades preliminares

A Tell two things you plan to do on the following days next week.

Por ejemplo:
> el viernes que viene
> *El viernes que viene pienso ir al cine.*

1. el sábado que viene
2. el domingo que viene
3. el martes que viene

B Tell what time you return home in the following situations.

Por ejemplo:
> después de las clases
> *Regreso a las tres y media.*

1. después de un partido
2. después de una fiesta
3. después del cine

Vocabulario

Vocabulary Teaching Resources
1. Vocabulario Transparencies 4.6
2. Workbook, pp. 136–137
3. Cassette 4.6
4. Student Tape Manual, p. 110
5. Lesson Quizzes, p. 92–93

Bell Ringer Review

Directions to students: Write a description of one of your favorite singers, actors, or actresses. Identify his or her profession and give a description in terms of physical appearance. Then see whether the class can guess whom you have described.

Presentation

A. Have students open their books to the Vocabulario on pages 304 and 305.
Model each month of the year, beginning with **enero.** Have students repeat each month in unison.

B. Ask individual students what they like to do during different months of the year. For example, **Karen, ¿qué te gusta hacer en julio?** Encourage students to give a complete response. For example, **Me gusta nadar, montar a caballo, etc.**

C. Now have students look at the vocabulary presentation on page 305. Model the question **¿Qué vas a hacer...** Then model each new word or phrase.

D. You may wish to use Vocabulario Transparencies 4.6 when making the following statements, or you may choose to write the following on the chalkboard:

Vocabulario

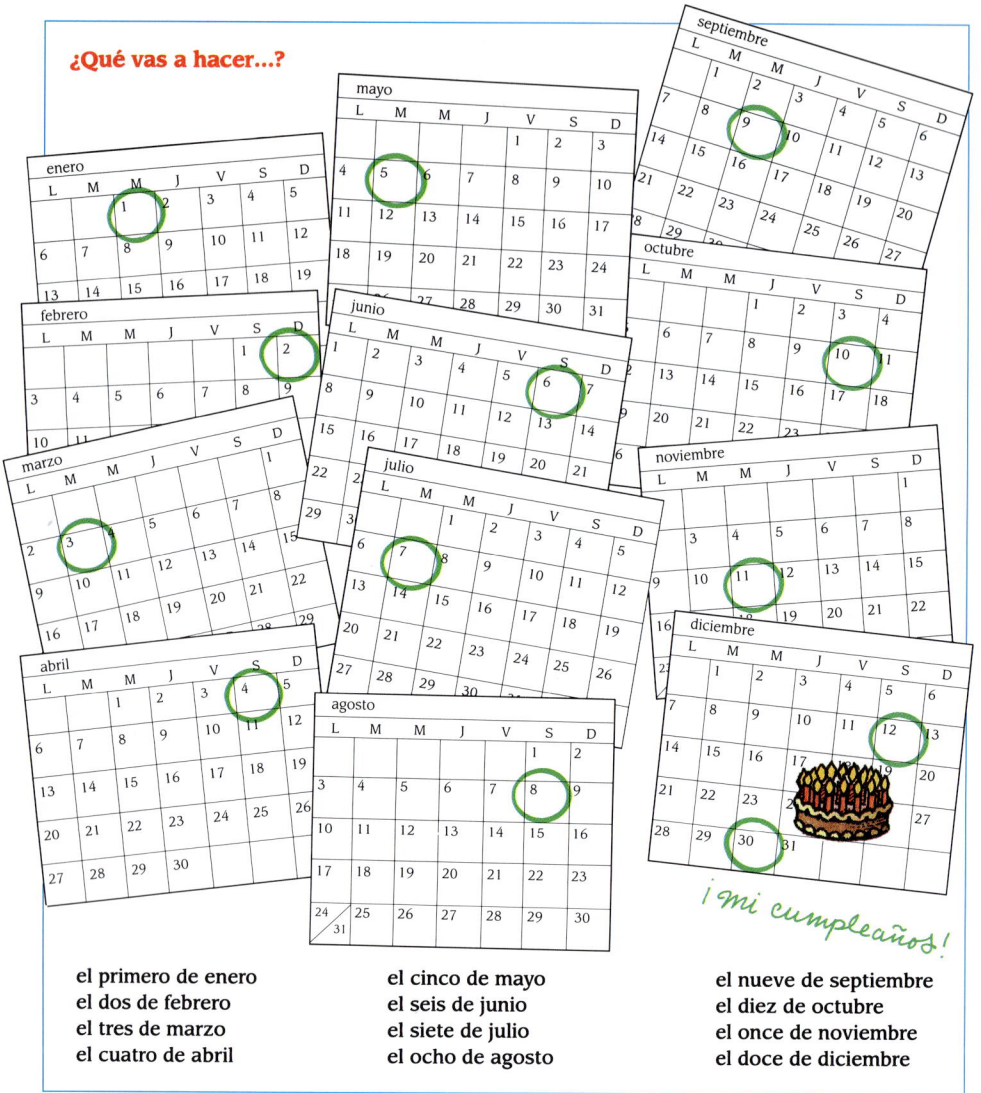

¿Qué vas a hacer...?

el primero de enero
el dos de febrero
el tres de marzo
el cuatro de abril

el cinco de mayo
el seis de junio
el siete de julio
el ocho de agosto

el nueve de septiembre
el diez de octubre
el once de noviembre
el doce de diciembre

304   CAPÍTULO 4

Total Physical Response

Getting Ready
Draw a calendar for the month of February and make one copy for each student. Write in **miércoles, viernes,** and **domingo** only. Leave blocks open for students to write in numbers. At the end of each **TPR** activity, show students a transparency of your calendar so they can match it with their own.

New Words
dibujen   corazón
cuadro   círculo
rectángulo

TPR 1

Escriban lunes en el primer cuadro.
Marquen sábado en el sexto cuadro.
Indiquen martes en el segundo cuadro.
Escriban jueves en el cuarto cuadro.

Actividades

A El año que viene. Imagine that New Year's Day is coming up. List five of your resolutions.

Por ejemplo:

El año que viene voy a hacer la tarea todos los días.

B Mis planes. Interview a classmate about his or her plans for the following times.

Por ejemplo:

esta tarde

ESTUDIANTE A
¿Qué vas a hacer esta tarde?

ESTUDIANTE B
Voy a trabajar.

1. pasado mañana
2. esta noche
3. la semana que viene
4. el miércoles que viene
5. el mes que viene
6. el año que viene

---

1. Pasado mañana hay una fiesta en la clase.
2. El año que viene no voy a dar más exámenes en la clase de español.
3. El mes que viene no hay clases.
4. La semana que viene tus padres van a vender su coche y no van a comprar otro.

Ask students to make their own statements using these time referents.

Note: In some parts of the Spanish-speaking world the *p* is dropped from **septiembre**.

When Students Ask

The following additional vocabulary may be provided to allow students to talk about expressions of time.
ahora mismo
en dos semanas, tres semanas, etc.
en tres días, cuatro días, etc.

Actividades

Actividades A and B Answers
Answers will vary.

Extension
You may wish to extend Actividad B by having each partner take notes on what the other student said. Then have each partner report back to the class.

Escriban los números en la primera semana.
Marquen los números en la segunda semana.
Indiquen los números en la tercera semana.
Escriban los números en la cuarta semana.

TPR 2

Busquen el día _____ y escriban "partido de fútbol".
Encuentren el día _____ y marquen "examen de español".
Dibujen un corazón el día 14.
Marquen el día _____ con "vacaciones".
Dibujen un círculo el lunes, día _____.
Hagan un rectángulo el jueves _____.

Actividad C Answers
Answers will vary but should include each month of the year.

Actividad D Answers
1. el 1 de enero
2. el 11 de noviembre
3. el 4 de julio
4. el 25 de diciembre
5. el 12 de octubre
6. Answers will vary.

Actividades E and F Answers
Answers will vary.

Additional Practice
After completing Actividades A, B, C, D, E, and F on pages 305 and 306, you may wish to reinforce the learning with the following activity: Write a letter to the school board protesting the change of your vacation time from summer to November, December, and January. Tell why you and your classmates want the vacation time returned to the usual months.
Por ejemplo:
Estimados señores:
Quisiéramos tener las vacaciones los meses de _____ porque _____. No queremos tener las vacaciones en _____ porque _____.

Reteaching
Using the Vocabulario on pages 304 and 305, have volunteers think of a particular month. Then they will ask the class, ¿Qué mes es? They may also want to give a clue, for example, **Es un mes cuando vemos los partidos de fútbol. Etc.** Other students will guess the month. The student who guesses correctly starts the game once again.

C Cada mes del año. Tell what you do each month of the year.

Por ejemplo:

> enero
> *En enero juego baloncesto y esquío.*

D Fechas importantes. Give the dates of the following celebrations.

Por ejemplo:

> el día de San Valentín
> *el 14 de febrero*

1. el Año Nuevo
2. el Día de los Veteranos
3. el Día de la Independencia
4. la Navidad (Christmas)
5. el Día de la Raza
6. tu cumpleaños

E ¿Vacaciones de invierno? Your school board plans to change your vacation time from summer to November, December, and January. Compare the winter vacation plan to your summer vacation plan in terms of your usual activities.

Por ejemplo:

> En junio voy a la playa, pero en noviembre no quiero (no es posible, no me gusta, etc.) ir a la playa.

F El sábado que viene. Ask two or three classmates what their plans are for the weekend. Then report back to the class, comparing your plans with those of your classmates.

Por ejemplo:

ESTUDIANTE A
¿Qué vas a hacer el sábado (domingo) que viene?

ESTUDIANTE B
Voy a ir a la biblioteca por la tarde.

(A la clase:) Yo voy a correr, pero Sue va a ir a la biblioteca y Tom va a ir al partido de baloncesto. Gina y Eva van a trabajar.

Cooperative Learning
After listing five resolutions in Actividad A, page 305, have each team choose the most interesting ones. The team recorder will list these on the board. While this is being done, others on the team can have a three-way interview of Actividad B. They should alternate asking and answering questions. Once all team reporters have written their list on the chalkboard, Actividad A's results can be discussed as a whole class activity in order to find similarities and differences among class members.

CULTURA VIVA 1

Los jóvenes españoles

A los jóvenes españoles les gusta tomar clases particulares (lecciones privadas) para aprender, por ejemplo, a tocar un instrumento, a bailar, a practicar ciertos deportes o artes marciales o aprender idiomas, especialmente inglés.

Pero los jóvenes no pasan todo el tiempo en clases. Por la noche, desde las once hasta la una o las dos de la mañana, muchos bailan, comen y conversan en las discotecas.

Actividad

Spanish teenagers like to spend free time taking lessons on things of interest to them. List the classes below that (a) you would like to take, (b) you are already taking, and (c) you already know how to do.

Por ejemplo:

Quisiera estudiar (Ya estudio, Ya sé)...

IDIOMAS	INSTRUMENTOS	DEPORTES	OTRAS CLASES
francés	guitarra	tenis	artes marciales
español	piano	vóleibol	baile moderno
chino	batería (drums)	fútbol	ajedrez
japonés	saxofón	natación	
italiano	violín	esquí	
		gimnasia	

Lección 6

Cultura viva 1

Reading Strategies

1. Read the **Cultura viva** on this page. As a class, list on the chalkboard the various activities Spanish teenagers do, according to the reading.
2. Now do the **Actividad** on this page.

Did You Know?

High school students are allowed to go to **discotecas** in Spain, even though alcoholic beverages are served.

Wine is a normal part of meals in Spain.

Since most people in Spain live in cities rather than suburban or rural areas, people have access to an extensive public transportation system. It is therefore easier for young people to go out since they don't have to rely on adults to take them to their destination.

Critical Thinking Activity

What are some similarities and differences in leisure activities of teenagers in the U.S. and in Spain? Imagine you are a Spanish teenager. What might your day be like?

Actividad

Actividad Answers
Answers will vary.

Learning from Photos

You may want to have students look at the photos on page 307. Have them choose one of the photos and imagine what plans the Spanish teenagers are making for later in the day.

Pronunciation

1. Use Pronunciation Transparency P-4.6.1, or write the pronunciation activity on the chalkboard. Have students copy it into their notebooks.
**En los ratos libres
muchos estudian inglés;
algunos escriben a amigos
en francés
y otros aprenden a jugar
ajedrez.**
2. You may wish to play the recorded version of this activity, located at the end of Cassette 4.6.
3. Have students repeat words and phrases individually and in unison. You may wish to focus on the stressed final syllable in words such as **inglés, francés,** and **ajedrez**.

Estructura 1

Structure Teaching Resources
1. Workbook, p. 138
2. Cassette 4.6
3. Student Tape Manual, p. 111
4. Estructura Masters 4.6
5. Lesson Quizzes, p. 94

Bell Ringer Review
Directions to students: On your paper list all the things you have to do at home and at school to avoid getting into trouble with your parents and your teachers.

Presentation
Lead students through steps 1–11 on pages 308 and 309. Remind students that they have learned all of these question words in previous lessons and that this is a review. You may wish to encourage students to refer to this page from now on when they need help with asking questions in Spanish.

Estructura 1

How to Request Information   *Summary of Question Words*

You have learned to request information using question words.

1. You have learned to ask where people and things are located, using **dónde**.
   ¿**Dónde** está la calle Serrano? Está a la derecha.

2. You have asked where people go, using **adónde**.
   ¿**Adónde** vas mañana? No voy a ningún lugar.

3. You have asked where people are from, using **de dónde**.
   ¿**De dónde** son ustedes? Somos de Puerto Rico.

4. You have used **cómo** with forms of the verb **ser** to ask what someone or something is like.
   ¿**Cómo** es la muchacha de Colombia? Es muy lista.

5. You have used **cómo** with **estar** to ask how people feel.
   ¿**Cómo** está, señora Dávila? Estoy bien, gracias.

6. To ask when someone does something or when something takes place, you have used **cuándo** and **a qué hora**.
   ¿**A qué hora** es el baile? Es a las ocho.
   ¿**Cuándo** sales para España? El viernes a la una y media.

7. To ask for a reason, you have used **por qué**.
   ¿**Por qué** necesitas estudiar esta noche?
   Porque tengo dos exámenes mañana.

8. You have asked "what," using **qué**.
   Oye, ¿**qué** quieres hacer esta noche? Bueno, no sé.

9. You have used a form of **cuánto** to ask how much or how many.
   ¿**Cuánto** dinero necesitas? Necesito dos dólares.
   ¿**Cuántas** chicas juegan tenis en tu escuela? Veinte y dos.

En una escuela de Madrid.

Cooperative Learning
Have students ask each other questions using each one of the question words. Students should write down the answers to the questions. Allow 5–10 minutes for practice. Then call on students to volunteer their results.

10. You have used **quién** to ask who does something and **de quién** to ask to whom something belongs.

> ¿Quién sabe hacer la tarea de español?   Marta González.
> ¿De quién es el libro?   Es de Jaime Suñer.

11. To ask someone to choose between two things, you have used **cuál**.

> ¿Cuál prefieres ver, el programa deportivo o la telenovela?
> Me gusta más el programa deportivo.

Actividades

A **La carta de presentación.** Your class has decided to exchange letters with students studying English in Spain. Write a letter introducing yourself, answering the following questions.

1. ¿Cómo te llamas?
2. ¿De dónde eres? ¿Dónde vives?
3. ¿Cuántos hermanos tienes? ¿Cuántos años tienen? ¿Cómo son?
4. ¿Cómo eres?
5. ¿Qué te gusta hacer en los ratos libres?
6. ¿Te gusta practicar deportes? ¿Cuál prefieres?
7. ¿Sales mucho con los amigos? ¿Cuándo? ¿Adónde van?
8. ¿Quién es tu músico favorito?

B **La invitación.** A classmate invites you to go someplace with a friend of his or hers this weekend. Since you don't know your classmate's friend, find out the following information.

Por ejemplo:

> ¿Quién es el/la amigo(a)?

ESTUDIANTE A	ESTUDIANTE B
¿Quién es tu amigo(a)?	Es Dana.

1. ¿Cómo es?
2. ¿De dónde es?
3. ¿Cuánto dinero van a necesitar?
4. ¿Adónde van a ir?
5. ¿Dónde van a comer?
6. ¿A qué hora van a regresar a casa?

Lección 6   **309**

Cultura viva 2

Reading Strategies
1. Read the **Cultura viva** on this page. Have students look at the photos and identify what they see that represents Hispanic culture.
2. Now do the **Actividad** on this page.

Did You Know?
Los Angeles has the largest Mexican population outside of Mexico City. It was founded by a group of Mexican settlers in 1781. Today, Hispanics account for approximately twenty-eight percent of Los Angeles' total population. Although people of Mexican ancestry make up the largest Hispanic group, many other nationalities are also represented.

Critical Thinking Activity
Do you think the percentage of Hispanics living in major U.S. cities will increase or decrease in the next five years? Give some reasons for your answer.

Actividad

Actividad Answers
1. Son de Guatemala.
2. ... Honduras.
3. ... Nicaragua.
4. ... El Salvador.
5. ... México.

Learning from Realia
You may want to have students look at the realia pieces on page 310. Have students tell what day and at what time they could watch **Desde Hollywood**. Ask students what kind of program it is. Using the restaurant ads from the yellow pages, have students tell you what number(s) they would call to make reservations at various restaurants.

CULTURA VIVA 2

Los Ángeles: una ciudad bilingüe

Kim y la señora Rivera son de Los Ángeles, California. Los Ángeles es una gran ciudad con mucha gente hispana de origen mexicano, centroamericano y sudamericano. Si visitas Los Ángeles, vas a ver que el español está por todas partes. Puedes hablar español en las calles, los restaurantes y las tiendas. Puedes leer revistas y periódicos en español. Y puedes oír español en la radio y la televisión.

Actividad

Name the countries from which the following groups of residents in Los Angeles come.

Por ejemplo:
    los costarricenses
    Son de Costa Rica.

1. los guatemaltecos
2. los hondureños
3. los nicaragüenses
4. los salvadoreños
5. los mexicanos

Guía de Restaurantes
Una guía práctica de restaurantes, según clase de comida

Colombianos
LOS ARRIEROS RESTAURANT
2619 W Sunset Bl LA 583 0074

Cubanos
EL CHORI RESTAURANT
5147 E Gage Av Bell 873 3011

Guatemaltecos
EL NAYARIT RESTAURANT
18822 W Sunset Bl LA 584 0766
GUATELINDA RESTAURANT
2220 W 7th LA........................... 485 7420
MI GUATEMALA RESTAURANT
Especialidad En Comida
Guatemalteca
695 S Hoover LA 487 4296

Español
MADRID RESTA
Comida De
Especialida
Y Tapas Típ
Diario 11-10
Especiales
Salón de Ba
1712 W Su

Filipino
Amihan Grill & T
3253 Beve
EVA'S LECHÓN
Especialis
Lechones
Diferentes
4252 W 3

310 CAPÍTULO 4

For the Native Speaker
Have native speakers make a collage of a city of the future. They should also write a description of this future city. In their writing they should include future occupations, leisure time activities, what schools will be like, etc. Have them read their description to the class.

Estructura 2

How to Describe What People Can and Can't Do *The verb* **poder**

To say what you or others can and can't do, use a form of the verb **poder (ue)**.

SINGULAR	PLURAL
puedo	podemos
puedes	podéis*
puede	pueden

*This form is rarely used in the Spanish-speaking world, except for Spain.

No puedo salir esta noche. ¿Puedes ir al cine mañana?
Pilar no puede ir con nosotros al campo.
Podemos invitar a quince personas a la fiesta.
¿Pueden ustedes traer discos a la fiesta?

Actividades

A Soy increíble. Write down four things that you can do very well.

Por ejemplo:

Puedo nadar muy bien.

B Mi compañero y yo. Now ask a classmate if he or she can do each of the things on your list from activity **A**. Take notes and report back to the class, comparing what you and your partner can do.

Por ejemplo:

ESTUDIANTE A   ESTUDIANTE B
¿Puedes nadar muy bien?   Sí, puedo. (No, no puedo).

(A la clase:) Puedo esquiar muy bien, pero Ana no puede. Ella puede montar a caballo, pero yo no puedo. Los (Las) dos podemos nadar muy bien.

Lección 6   311

Actividad C Answers
1. En mi casa, (no) puedo salir muy tarde por la noche.
2. ... (no) puedo ver la tele...
3. ... (no) puedo escuchar el estéreo...
4. ... (no) puedo tener...
5. ... (no) puedo decir...

Actividad D Answers
Answers will vary.

Actividad E Answers
Answers will vary but may include the following:
Cuando ustedes están aburridos, pueden hablar por teléfono con amigos.

Actividad F Answers
Answers will vary but may include the following:
¿Podemos comer en la clase? ¿Podemos leer el periódico de la escuela durante la clase? ¿Podemos jugar juegos de mesa? ¿cartas?

Additional Practice
After completing Actividades A, B, C, D, E, and F, you may wish to reinforce the lesson by doing the following activity: Have students make a list of their two most frequent requests of their parents. Then have them tell what their parents usually say in response to each request. **Por ejemplo:** Yo pregunto: "Mamá, ¿puedo ver la tele esta noche?" Y mi mamá dice: "No. Tienes que estudiar."

Reteaching
Write down one thing the following members of your family are able to do well.
1. tú
2. tu hermano(a)
3. tus padres
4. tu y tus padres

C Prohibido. Tell whether or not you are allowed to do the following things at home.

Por ejemplo:
> comer en la cama
> *En mi casa no puedo comer en la cama.*

1. salir muy tarde por la noche
2. ver la tele después de las diez de la noche
3. escuchar el estéreo durante la cena
4. tener un perro
5. decir (to say) **malas palabras**

D ¿Quién puede? Working in groups of three, find out whether your classmates are allowed to do the things listed in activity **C**. Take notes and report back to the class.

Por ejemplo:
> ¿Quién puede comer en la cama?
>
> (A la clase:) Ana y Curt pueden comer en la cama, pero yo no puedo.

E Cuando están aburridos. List five suggestions about what your classmates can do when they are bored.

Por ejemplo:
> Cuando ustedes están aburridos, pueden jugar con el perro.

F El último día de clases. Ask your teacher to change five class or school rules for the last day of school. How many of your requests will your teacher grant?

Por ejemplo:
> ¿Podemos tener clase afuera?

¿Quién puede contestar la pregunta?

Finalmente

Situaciones

A conversar Converse with a classmate about the next school vacation.

1. Ask your partner where he or she plans to go. Give your reaction.
2. Find out what your partner will do there.
3. Ask if your partner will go with family or friends.
4. Find out when your partner will return.
5. Reverse roles.

A escribir
1. Write a note to several friends telling them about a party at a classmate's home.
2. Give a specific date and time when the party will be.
3. Tell the various activities that all of you can do at the party.
4. Ask who can contribute **(llevar)** various items (cassettes, food, etc.).
5. Say that you need to know if they can go to the party by next Monday.

Repaso de vocabulario

EXPRESIONES DE TIEMPO
el año (que viene)
el mes (que viene)
pasado mañana
la semana (que viene)

LOS MESES
enero
febrero
marzo
abril
mayo
junio
julio
agosto
septiembre
octubre
noviembre
diciembre

ACTIVIDAD
regresar

OTRAS PALABRAS
el cumpleaños
poder (ue)

Finalmente

Situaciones

Lesson 6 Evaluation
The A conversar and A escribir situations on this page are designed to give students the opportunity to use as many language functions and as much vocabulary from this lesson as possible. The A conversar and A escribir are also intended to show how well students are able to meet the lesson objectives.

Presentation
Prior to doing the A conversar and A escribir on this page, you may wish to play the Situaciones listening activities on Cassette 4.6 as a means of helping students organize the material.

Lectura

Presentation

A. Before reading the Lectura, you may wish to have students work in groups to discuss the following questions. These questions are intended to help students think about the theme of the reading.

1. What are some advantages and disavantages of having a pen pal?
2. If you could have a pen pal from any country in the world, what country would you choose and why?
3. What qualities would you look for in a pen pal?

B. Have one student from each group report back to the class.

C. Now have students read the Lectura silently to themselves, or work with a partner. Have them answer the Actividades questions on page 315.

Lectura

You'll be able to figure out many of the words from the context in which they appear or because they look like English words that have similar meanings. First, look over the reading below. Then complete the activities, which follow.

Correo VÍA SATÉLITE

¿Quieres ponerte en contacto con amigos de todas partes? Envíanos tus datos utilizando este cupón.

Nombre: _____
Dirección: _____
Edad: _____
Pasatiempos: _____

El cupón dirígelo a:
Correo vía Satélite

Nombre: Silvia Ortiz
Dirección: Heredia, Urb. La Esperanza 15, COSTA RICA
Edad: 15 años
Pasatiempos: Coleccionar todo lo referente al joven cantante Chayanne, tomar fotografías, estudiar, ver televisión y tener amigos de diferentes nacionalidades.

Nombre: Alfonso Marín
Dirección: Calle 19 #4-56, Apto. 1117, Edificio Sabana, Bogotá, COLOMBIA
Edad: 16 años
Pasatiempos: Leer, practicar deportes, escuchar música variada, escribir poemas, salir con mis amigas y coleccionar monedas de diferentes países.

Nombre: María del Carmen Sánchez
Dirección: Rdo. Rosendo Llanes, Danlí, El Paraíso, HONDURAS
Edad: 18 años
Pasatiempos: Intercambiar correspondencia, estampillas, carteles, escuchar música romántica, leer artículos sobre la cultura de diferentes países y escribir versos.

Nombre: Eugenia Vila Ávila
Dirección: Libertad 1261, Huancayo, PERÚ
Edad: 16 años
Pasatiempos: Practicar deportes, bailar, ver los vídeos musicales de mis artistas favoritos, salir con mis amigos y mantener correspondencia con jóvenes de todo el mundo.

Nombre: Juan José Pereira
Dirección: 15668 San Miguel de Sarandón, Santiago de Compostela, La Coruña, ESPAÑA
Edad: 15 años
Pasatiempos: Escribir, practicar deportes, ir al cine y a la playa, escuchar música variada, leer artículos sobre mis artistas favoritos y viajar.

Nombre: Lilia Calas
Dirección: Calle 8° de Los Jardines #4, H. Caborca, Sonora, MÉXICO.
Edad: 14 años.
Pasatiempos: Intercambiar correspondencia con otros jóvenes, cantar, bailar, tocar piano y coleccionar todo lo referente al grupo musical Flans.

Nombre: Angélica Trujillo
Dirección: 2351 Penn Rd., El Monte, California, 91765, ESTADOS UNIDOS
Edad: 16 años
Pasatiempos: Bailar, ver televisión, leer revistas, escuchar música variada, estudiar con mis amigas, coleccionar versos, practicar deportes e ir a la playa.

Nombre: Gromyko Watts
Dirección: Santa Rosa, Weg 173, Curaçao, ANTILLAS HOLANDESAS
Edad: 17 años
Pasatiempos: Mantener correspondencia con chicos y chicas de todo el mundo, practicar deportes, ver televisión, coleccionar carteles de mis artistas favoritos.

Nombre: Griselda M. Álvarez
Dirección: Col. Serramonte 3, Senda 3, Casa # 51, EL SALVADOR
Edad: 19 años
Pasatiempos: Coleccionar calcomanías y posters, escuchar música e intercambiar correspondencia con chicos y chicas de diferentes países.

Nombre: Cinthya Miralda
Dirección: Boul. de las Rosas, 256, Loacalco, Estado de México C.P. 55700, MÉXICO.
Edad: 17 años
Pasatiempos: Dibujar, leer, escuchar música variada, planear actividades con mis amistades, practicar deportes e intercambiar correspondencia con chicas y chicos de diferentes países.

Getting Ready for Reading

You may want to discuss the following keys to successful reading with your students before having them read the Lectura on page 314:

1. Skim the following magazine columns. That is, read over the selection quickly to get the main idea.
2. Don't stop to figure out the meaning of unknown words.
3. Look for cognates. For example, **contacto, variada, planear, nacionalidades.**
4. Try to read in groups of words, instead of word-for-word.

Actividades

A The magazine column on page 314 publishes requests from young people looking for pen pals. Look at the coupon in the upper left corner. Which of the following questions do you need to answer when writing to this column?

1. ¿Cómo te llamas?
2. ¿Cuántos hermanos tienes?
3. ¿Dónde vives?
4. ¿Cuál es tu apellido?
5. ¿Adónde vas?
6. ¿Cuál es tu número de teléfono?
7. ¿Cómo eres?
8. ¿Cuántos años tienes?
9. ¿De dónde eres?
10. ¿Qué te gusta hacer?

B Determine which pastimes are the most popular for these young people by listing the activities mentioned and tallying the number of times each activity is mentioned.

Por ejemplo:

Escribir cartas: 2

Determine the five most popular activities and tell whether you like to do each of them.

C Choose one of the people who interests you the most and write a letter to him or her by responding to the questions below. Use the following format for your letter.

1. ¿Cuántos años tienes?
2. ¿En qué grado estás?
3. ¿Cómo es tu familia?
4. ¿Cómo es tu ciudad?
5. ¿Qué te gusta hacer?
6. ¿Qué haces todos los días?
7. ¿Qué estudias?
8. ¿Qué haces los fines de semana?
9. ¿Cuál es tu pasatiempo favorito? ¿Por qué?
10. ¿Cómo eres?

Estimada Raquel:
¿Cómo estás? Me llamo Julia. Tengo diez y seis años. Estoy en el décimo grado. Mi familia .....

Saludos de
Julia Allen

Actividades

Actividad A Answers
1. Sí.
2. No.
3. Sí.
4. Sí.
5. No.
6. No.
7. No.
8. Sí.
9. No.
10. Sí.

Actividades B and C Answers
Answers will vary.

Capítulo de Repaso

Repaso Resources
1. Workbook, pp. 141–143
2. Cassette 4.6
3. Student Tape Manual, pp. 115–116
4. Cumulative Test for Chapters 3 and 4, pp. 71–80

Bell Ringer Review

Directions to students: Tell how old your best friend is and describe him or her in five sentences.

¿Recuerdas?

Presentation

To review Chapter 4, call on individual students to give an example for each communicative function listed for Lecciones 1–3 and Lecciones 4–6, page 316. The numbers in parentheses on page 316 refer to the actual page(s) in Chapter 4 where each function was presented and practiced. You may wish to have your students go back to these pages for additional review and practice before continuing on to the Actividades, pages 317–319.

Lecciones 1–3 Answers

The following words and phrases are examples for each of the 14 functions listed under Lecciones 1–3. These words and phrases should be included in the students' response to each function listed below.

1. Parece...
2. Los hermanos, la mamá, el papá, etc.
3. Su... , sus...
4. Le(s) gusta...
5. ¿Cuánto vale?
6. ¿Cuántos años tiene?
7. Creo que...
8. Estudia para...
9. Es ingeniero, empleado(a) de banco, etc.
10. ¿Cuánto(s)...? ¿Cuánta(s)...?
11. Cien, doscientos, trescientos, etc.

Capítulo 4   Repaso

¿Recuerdas?

Do you remember how to do the following things, which you learned in **Capítulo 4**?

LECCIONES 1–3
1. describe what someone or something seems to be like (p. 242)
2. identify family members (p. 244)
3. describe possession or ownership (p. 248)
4. talk about what others like to do (p. 251)
5. ask how much something costs (p. 254, 261)
6. ask about someone's age (p. 254)
7. express an opinion (p. 254)
8. tell what someone is studying to be (p. 254)
9. name common occupations (pp. 256–257)
10. ask how much or how many there is of something (p. 261)
11. use numbers from 100 to 500 (p. 264)
12. identify common pets and zoo animals (pp. 268–269)
13. talk about things that others like (p. 272)
14. use numbers from 600 to the thousands (p. 275)

LECCIONES 4–6
1. describe someone's physical characteristics (p. 280)
2. talk about specific people (p. 284)
3. tell what you and others must do (p. 287)
4. report what someone says (p. 290)
5. identify pastimes (pp. 292–293)
6. tell and ask about preferences (p. 296)
7. talk about another or others (p. 299)
8. tell what will take place at a given time in the future (pp. 304–305)
9. give dates (pp. 304–305)
10. request information (pp. 308–309)
11. say what people can and can't do (p. 311)

Actividades

A Sueños. Compare your home with one you want to have. Use two paragraphs, starting one with **En mi casa...** and the other with **Pero en la casa que quiero...**

B Mi gente preferida. Find out from a classmate the following: (a) who his or her two favorite people are, (b) what they do, (c) what relationship they have to him or her, (d) what they like and dislike the most, and (e) why your classmate likes them. Then report back to the class.

C Mi horario. Tell the class about your schedule. Include the following.

1. cinco cosas que haces todos los días
2. un lugar adonde fuiste (you went) la semana pasada (Fui a...)
3. dos cosas que vas a hacer la semana que viene

D ¿Cuál es mi trabajo? Work in pairs or small groups and think of a profession. The other pairs or groups in the class will then ask yes/no questions to try to guess what the profession is.

Por ejemplo:
　　bombero
　　¿Trabaja usted en casa?
　　¿Tiene que trabajar por la noche?
　　¿Trabaja con niños?
　　¿Gana mucho dinero?

E ¿Dónde está el señor X? Draw the face of a fictitious person. On a separate sheet, describe the person, giving a name, occupation, and personality. Your teacher will distribute the drawings around the class. Read your description as a "missing person report." Which of your classmates has your "person"?

---

12. Le gusta(n)/Les gusta(n)...
13. Los elefantes, los monos, etc.
14. seiscientos(as), setecientos(as), etc.

Lecciones 4–6, Answers

The following words and phrases are examples for each of the 11 functions listed under Lecciones 4–6. These words and phrases should be included in the students' response to each function listed below.

1. Tiene barba, bigote, pelo rubio, etc.
2. Llamo a...
3. Tengo (Tienes, tiene, etc.) que...
4. Dice que...
5. Jugar cartas, jugar ajedrez, etc.
6. Preferir
7. Otro, otros, etc.
8. La semana que viene; el año que viene, etc.
9. El... de marzo de 199____
10. ¿Dónde?, ¿adónde?, ¿de dónde?, ¿cómo?, ¿a qué?, ¿cuándo?, ¿por qué?, ¿cuánto?, ¿quién?, ¿cuál?
11. Poder (ue)

Actividades

Presentation

Each practice activity in this Chapter 4 review combines several of the language functions listed on page 316. Students are asked to use the language they have learned at a higher, more integrated level, compared to the individual practice activities in Lessons 1–6 of Chapter 4.

Actividad A Answers
Answers will vary.

Actividad B Answers
Answers will vary, however the questions asked will approximate the following:
a. ¿Quiénes son las dos personas que te gustan más?
b. ¿Qué hacen estas personas?
c. ¿Son tus parientes?
d. ¿Qué les gusta(n) ¿Qué no les gusta(n)
e. ¿Por qué te gustan... ?

Actividades C, D, and E Answers
Answers will vary.

Actividad F Answers
1. ¿Por qué no vemos Club Disney?
2. ... Jazz entre amigos?
3. ... Rockopop?
4. ... Buenos días, buenos clips?
5. ... De película?
6. ... Queenie?

Actividad G Answers
Answers will vary.

Actividad H Answers
1. Don Gilberto
2. Tomás
3. Úrsula
4. Ildefonso
5. Érica
6. Roberto
7. Raquel
8. Esteban
9. Zacarías

Actividades I and J Answers
Answers will vary.

F En la tele. Using the Madrid TV listing at right, what would you suggest to a friend that the two of you watch at the following times of day?

Por ejemplo:
>a las ocho de la noche
>¿Por qué no vemos _____?

1. a las seis y media de la tarde
2. a la una de la mañana
3. a las tres de la tarde
4. a las siete y media de la mañana
5. a las siete de la tarde
6. a las diez y media de la noche

G Recomendaciones. Choose one of the programs listed in activity **F** for a member of your family and one of your friends. Tell what time it is on and why that person should watch it.

Por ejemplo:
>Mi papá debe ver... porque...

H La familia de Ildefonso. Pilar describes a family she knows in Los Angeles. Fill in the name of each family member to show their relationship. In the chart below, + means they are married; / means children.

Mi hermano dice que el año que viene, va a los Estados Unidos. Tiene un amigo, Ildefonso, que vive en Los Ángeles. Creo que la casa está en las afueras de la ciudad, en un barrio donde hay mucha gente de habla española.

Los padres de Ildefonso son españoles y amigos de mis padres. Bueno, el papá, Tomás, es español. Creo que la mamá, Úrsula, es argentina. Ildefonso es muy amable y tiene un hermano

PARA VER

Buenos días, buenos clips
7:30 / Canal +
Vídeos musicales de todo tipo y condición para comenzar el día con buen pie.

Jazz entre amigos
1:00 / TVE-1
Celebración del sexto aniversario del programa con la actuación del quinteto de Tom Harrell y la entrega de los premios de *Jazz entre amigos*.

Rockopop
15:00 / TVE-1
Programa musical con entrevistas y actuaciones, presentado por Beatriz Pécker.

Club Disney
18:30 / TVE-1
Programa infantil nuevo en emisión que incluye dibujos animados, telefilmes, juegos y concursos.

De película
19:00 / TVE-2
Espacio cinematográfico con entrevistas y reportajes sobre el Festival Internacional de Cine de San Sebastián.

Queenie
22:30 / TVE-2
Serie que trata de la historia de una niña mestiza, de padre ingles y madre india, en la Calcuta de 1931. La mezcla de su origen le complicará tremendamente la vida.

mayor, Roberto. ¡Fíjate qué guapo! Tengo una foto aquí en el escritorio. ¿Ves?

Aquí está la familia entera: la esposa de Ildefonso, Érica y el hijo, Esteban. ¿Precioso, no? Erica es norteamericana pero habla español. Y el pequeñito es el primo de Esteban, Zacarías. Es una familia de varones. La mamá de Zacarías es Raquel. Sí, Roberto está casado. Qué pena, ¿no? Pues, mira la casa. ¡Qué elegante! Y debe ser muy grande, porque todos viven allí, también el abuelo, don Gilberto. Es un señor muy divertido. Juega con los nietos todo el día.

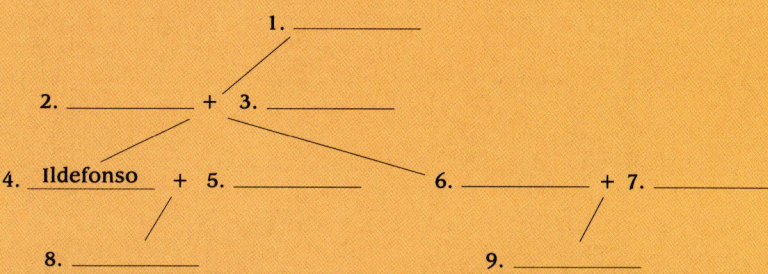

I **Ya sé muchas palabras.** List as many words as you can think of to identify and describe people in terms of the following categories.

1. los parientes
2. las ocupaciones
3. la apariencia
4. la personalidad

J **Sabelotodo.** In groups of three or four, play the Spanish version of Trivial Pursuit (**Sabelotodo**). Think of three or four questions dealing with information or vocabulary that you have studied so far in Spanish class. Use the following categories of questions:

(C) Cultura (L) Lengua (G) Geografía (CSD) ¿Cómo se dice?

Have your teacher look over your questions and then see who can stump the rest of the class.

Chapter Overview

Cultural setting

The remaining two chapters in Level 1 take place in Miami and focus on the Cuban-American population. In Chapter 5, you will meet Carmen Marín and her parents who are originally from Cuba. The Marín family now lives in the Miami area, where Carmen was born. Carmen is bilingual and Spanish is the language of her household. However Carmen's constant mixing of Spanish and English is a source of aggravation to her father, who fears that the language of his family will ultimately be lost.

Rationale

A The use of circumlocution, that is, describing things you don't know the word for, as an oral communication strategy has tremendous utility when one's communicative motives outstrip linguistic capabilities. The activities presented are designed to help students decrease "exact word" dependence and to develop greater flexibility in speech by "talking around" the unknown vocabulary. Chapter 5 also presents techniques for self-correction **(digo,...)**, stalling, and paraphrasing.

B Indirect object pronouns **(me, te, le)** are introduced through the function of asking and granting favors, first with **¿me** + conjugated form of **poder?** and later with conjugated forms of verbs such as **prestar, traer, ayudar, dar.** It is our experience that such a real life "hook" allows students to grasp more rapidly the concept of and need for indirect object pronouns in both oral and written communication.

CAPÍTULO 5

Estructura

This chapter focuses on the following structure topics:
- asking and describing favors with the indirect pronouns **me, te,** and **le;**
- requesting and giving descriptions of objects in terms of composition, appearance, and purpose;
- giving nationalities;
- giving dates and describing time periods, using **desde** and **hace...que;**
- telling where people went, using **ir** in the preterit;
- describing what belongs to you and others (our);
- telling with whom we do things, using **con;**
- identifying what people say, hear and request or order, using present tense forms of the verbs **decir, oír** and **pedir.**

¡Me gusta vivir en Miami!

The presentation of the indirect object pronouns **les** and **nos** is delayed until Chapter 6 in order to allow students digestion and familiarity time and the opportunity to both grasp the concept and begin to develop some automaticity in limited aspects of its application.

C Chapter 5 begins the development of one function of the preterit, namely serialized reporting of past events, using the high frequency verbs **ir** and **ver**.

Video

The video is an optional component, intended to reinforce the vocabulary, structures, and cultural content in each lesson. Please refer to the Video Activities Booklet for suggestions on how to use this resource.

Lección 1 (1218)

Lección 2 (1253)

Lección 3 (1452)

Lección 4 (1608)

Lección 5 (1739)

Lección 6 (1840)

Enfoque cultural (1952)

¡Te toca a ti! (2043)

Pacing

The six lessons comprising Chapter 5 will each require approximately 5–6 days. However pacing will vary according to the length of the class, the age of the students, student aptitude and the number of ancillary materials employed.

Student Portfolio

Writing assignments include the following:

Lesson 1: p. 333, A escribir
Lesson 2: p. 345, A escribir; Workbook, p. 152, Act. B
Lesson 3: p. 357, A escribir; Workbook, p. 157, Act. B
Lesson 4: p. 369, A escribir
Lesson 5: p. 383, A escribir; Workbook, p. 165, Act. B
Lesson 6: p. 397, A escribir

Lesson 1 Resources
1. Workbook, pp. 144–149
2. Vocabulario Transparency
3. Pronunciation Transparency P-5.1.1
4. Audio Cassette 5.1 Compact Disc 7
5. Student Tape Manual, pp. 117–120
6. Bell Ringer Review Blackline Masters, p. 29
7. Computer Software: Practice & Test Generator
8. Video (cassette or disc)
9. Video Activities Booklet, pp. A65–A66
10. Estructura Masters, pp. 57–58
11. Diversiones Masters, pp. 55–56
12. Situation Cards
13. Lesson Quizzes, pp. 96–98
14. Testing Program

Bell Ringer Review

Display a picture of a celebrity familiar to students, a rock star, for example. Directions to students: Study the picture on the board carefully. Then write at least five questions about this person. Use the interrogative words we have studied to form your questions.

¡A comenzar!

Presentation

A. Lead students through each of the three functions given on page *(continued)*

CAPÍTULO 5

Lección 1

¡Gran oferta!

¡A comenzar!

The following are some of the things you will be learning to do in this lesson.

When you want to...	You use...
1. ask a favor of a friend	¿**Me puedes** + activity?
2. ask a favor of several people	¿**Me pueden** + activity?
3. offer to do something for a friend	**Te puedo** + activity.

Now find examples of the above words and phrases in the following conversation and advertisement.

Carmen Marín vive en Miami. Habla por teléfono con su amiga Elena.

CARMEN: ¿Recibes la revista *Ritmo*, ¿verdad?
ELENA: Sí, ¿por qué?
CARMEN: ¿Me puedes prestar el nuevo número? Tiene un anuncio muy interesante.
ELENA: Bueno, te puedo llevar la revista esta noche después de comer. Paso por tu casa a las siete.
CARMEN: Perfecto. Muchas gracias, ¿eh? Hasta luego.

¡GRAN OFERTA! Camiseta de Gloria Estefan

Todas las tallas: pequeña, mediana, grande, extra grande
Cinco colores: blanco, azul celeste, amarillo, verde claro, rojo
De algodón Perma-Prest
$14.50 cada una, o dos por el super precio de $24.95

¡Sí, quiero aprovechar esta gran oferta!

Me pueden mandar, por favor:

Cantidad	Color	Talla	Precio	Total
2	blanco rojo	P M G XG (M)	$14.50 2=$24.95	24.95

NOMBRE: Carmen Marín
TELÉFONO: (305) 555-9783
CALLE: 2193 30 St. NW
CIUDAD: Miami ESTADO: FL ZIP CODE: 33165

Incluyo mi ☒ cheque ☐ giro postal a nombre de COLECCIÓN JUVENTUD, S. A.
Favor de cobrar a mi ☐ Visa No. ☐ Mastercard No.
Fecha de vencimiento _____ mes año   firma autorizada _____
☒ Me pueden mandar un catálogo también?

Actividad preliminar

Ask a classmate for the following favors.

Por ejemplo:

prestar cinco dólares

ESTUDIANTE A	ESTUDIANTE B
¿Me puedes prestar cinco dólares?	Sí, cómo no. (No, no puedo).

1. llamar esta noche
2. comprar un refresco
3. limpiar la habitación esta tarde
4. visitar el sábado

Vocabulario

Vocabulary Teaching Resources
1. Vocabulario Transparency 5.1
2. Workbook, pp. 144–145
3. Cassette 5.1
4. Student Tape Manual, p. 118
5. Lesson Quizzes, p. 96

Bell Ringer Review

Directions to students: Pretend you live in Argentina, where the seasons are the opposite of ours. Copy the following activities and write beside each one the names of the months in which you would most likely do each one.

1. ir a la playa
2. esquiar
3. andar en monopatín
4. tener vacaciones
5. ir a la escuela

Presentation

Have students open their books to the Vocabulario on page 324.

1. Model the question **¿Me puedes hacer un favor?** Then model each phrase, beginning each one with **Me puedes...** Have students repeat each phrase in unison.
2. Ask for volunteers to do favors for you. For example:
   Maestro(a): ¿Quién me puede prestar un lápiz?
   Estudiante: Yo (puedo)
   Maestro(a): Gracias, muy amable.
   a. dar un sello
   b. prestar un sobre
   c. llevar la carta al correo
   d. enseñar a escribir mi nombre
   e. traer la tarjeta de crédito
   f. ayudar a preparar las tareas

324

Vocabulario

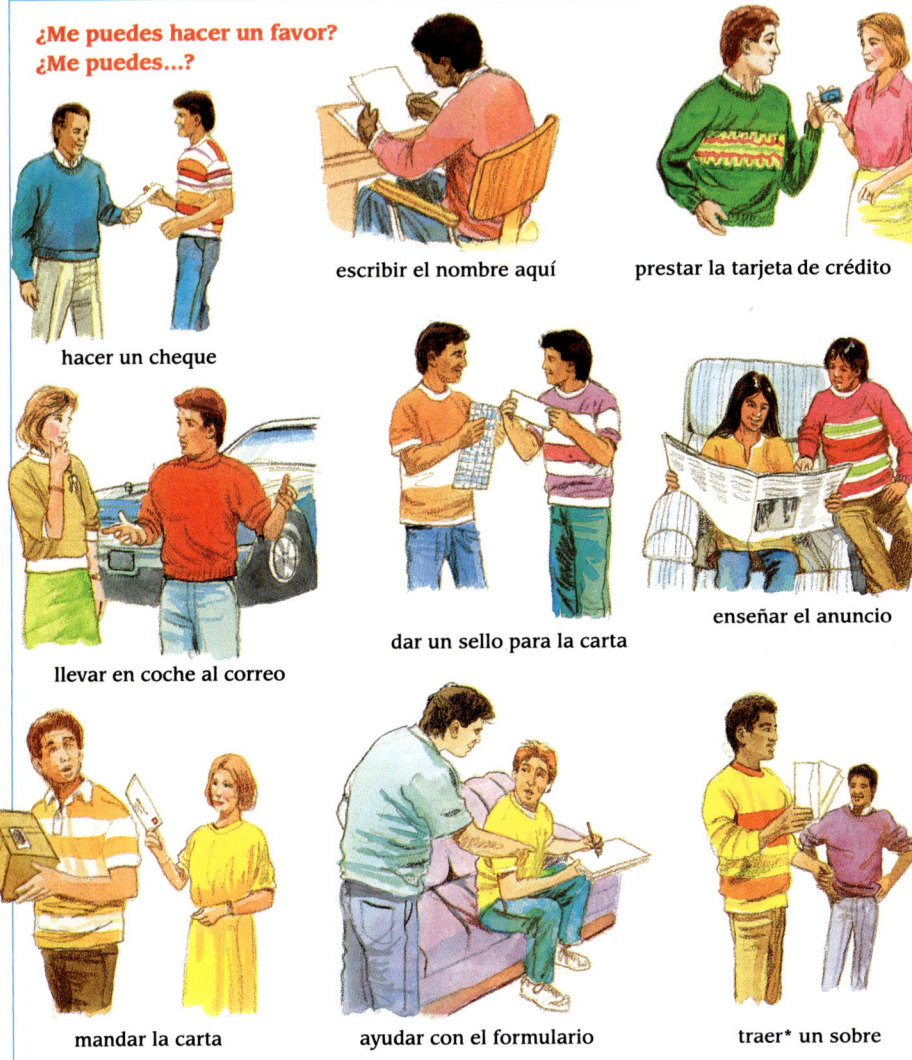

¿Me puedes hacer un favor?
¿Me puedes...?

- hacer un cheque
- escribir el nombre aquí
- prestar la tarjeta de crédito
- llevar en coche al correo
- dar un sello para la carta
- enseñar el anuncio
- mandar la carta
- ayudar con el formulario
- traer* un sobre

*The **yo** form of **traer** is **traigo**.

324 CAPÍTULO 5

Total Physical Response

Getting Ready
1. Make pictures of a check, credit card, and stamp on a sheet of paper.
2. Cut out an ad for cassettes and one for records from a magazine, and make copies of each. Draw five lines under each ad for students to fill out their order forms.
3. Number each of the above items 1 through 5.
4. Have students bring an envelope from home.

New words
llenen   firmen
miren   el costo

Muéstrenme con los dedos el número del formulario.

Actividades

A **¿Te gusta escribir cartas?** Complete the following sentences about writing and sending letters.

1. Me gusta escribir a _____.
2. Para escribir la carta, necesito _____.
3. En la dirección, escribo _____.
4. En la carta a un amigo, pregunto _____.
5. Para mandar la carta, necesito _____.
6. En el correo puedo comprar _____.

B **Por favor.** Ask a classmate if he or she can lend you the following things.

Por ejemplo:

    un bolígrafo

ESTUDIANTE A

Por favor, ¿me puedes prestar un bolígrafo?

ESTUDIANTE B

Sí, cómo no. (No, no puedo).

1. diez dólares
2. unos lápices
3. un sobre
4. tu calculadora
5. tu estéreo
6. la tarea
7. el libro de español
8. unos discos
9. dinero para comprar algo en la cafetería

Lección 1   325

Learning from Realia
You may want to have students look at the realia on page 325. Have students describe the relationship between the people shown. Have them describe what the people look like. Have students guess what the occasion is.

When Students Ask
You may wish to give students the following additional vocabulary to allow them to talk about sending and receiving mail.
por correo aéreo   el buzón
el/la cartero   el paquete
el remite

Regionalisms
You may wish to tell students that in certain parts of the Spanish-speaking world, the following words or phrases are alternatives to those presented in the Vocabulario.
el formulario (la planilla)
el sello (la estampilla, el timbre)

Actividades

Actividad A Answers
Answers will vary but may include the following.

1. ... mi abuela.
2. ... un bolígrafo (papel).
3. ... la calle, la ciudad, el estado.
4. ... si le gusta su escuela.
5. ... un sobre (un sello).
6. ... sellos.

Actividad B Answers
Estudiante A's questions should include: **Por favor, ¿me puedes prestar... ?**
Estudiante B's responses will vary, according to the model.

Indiquen con los dedos el número del cheque.
Muéstrenle el anuncio a un/a amigo(a). (Interchange commands and items.)
Miren el formulario de los discos.
Escriban su nombre en la primera línea.
Escriban dos títulos de discos en la segunda línea.
Indiquen el costo de cada disco en la tercera línea.
Marquen el total en la cuarta línea.
Escriban la fecha. Llenen el cheque con el total del primer disco. Firmen el cheque.
Marquen el número de la tarjeta en el formulario en la quinta línea.
Escriban su nombre y dirección en el sobre.
Dibujen un sello en el lugar apropiado.

Actividad C Answers
Answers will vary.

Actividad D Answers
Answers will vary but may include the following.
1. Mamá, ¿me puedes comprar una camiseta? Quiero ir a la playa y todas mis camisetas son viejas.
2. ¿Me puedes prestar unos sellos? Tengo que mandar unas cartas.
3. Mamá, ¿me puedes llevar en coche a la escuela? Necesito un libro.
4. Mamá, ¿me puedes dar diez dólares? Necesito comprar un disco.
5. ¿Me puedes prestar dinero? Tengo que llamar a mi casa.
6. ¿Me puedes traer el periódico con el anuncio? Quiero saber más del concierto.
7. ¿Me puedes enseñar la foto de tu amiga guapa? Quiero ver a la muchacha.

Reteaching
Using Vocabulary Transparency 5.1, use an transparency marker to number each of the scenes. Have students give the number of the scene you describe.
1. Quiero mandar esta carta pero no tengo sobre.
2. ¿Me puedes prestar la tarjeta de crédito?
3. ¿Cuánto vale un sello para mandar una carta a España?
4. No tengo bicicleta. ¿Me puedes llevar en coche al correo?
5. Necesito veinte dólares. ¿Me puedes hacer un cheque?
6. No entiendo qué debo escribir aquí. ¿Me puedes ayudar?

Learning from Realia
You may want to have students look at the realia on page 326. Have students guess at the meaning of "al día siguiente" and "sólo." Ask students why they think the U.S. Postal System advertises its services in Spanish.

C Regalos y préstamos. Tell five things you are willing to lend, and five things you are willing to give.

Por ejemplo:
> prestar / dar
> *Puedo prestar cinco dólares. Puedo dar mis discos viejos.*

D ¿Me puedes hacer un favor? For each problem below, request some help and give a reason.

Por ejemplo:
> No tienes coche y quieres ir al baile.
> *Papá, ¿me puedes prestar el coche? Quiero ir al baile.*
> *(Tía, quiero ir al baile. ¿Me puedes llevar?)*

1. No tienes una camiseta buena para ir a la playa.
2. Necesitas mandar unas cartas y no tienes sellos.
3. Necesitas hacer la tarea pero no tienes el libro en casa.
4. Quieres comprar el nuevo disco de tu cantante favorito pero no tienes el dinero.
5. Estás en el centro comercial y necesitas llamar a tu casa pero no tienes dinero.
6. Tu amiga dice que hay un anuncio para un concierto de tu cantante favorito pero no sabes dónde está el periódico.
7. Tu amigo dice que tiene una amiga muy guapa. Quieres ver una foto.

For the Native Speaker
You may wish to have students write a letter requesting tickets to a concert by a popular singer. They should include in the letter the price of the tickets, the date of the concert, and how many tickets they want. They should also include payment, name, address, and telephone number in the letter.

Cooperative Learning
Students work in pairs. One will describe a T-shirt to his or her partner. The partner will draw it.

CULTURA VIVA 1

Aquí pueden hablar español

Hoy día hay más o menos setecientos cincuenta mil (750.000) cubanoamericanos en la ciudad de Miami. Este número representa casi el cincuenta por ciento de la población total de la ciudad. Muchos de ellos son doctores, abogados, profesores, directores de compañías y otros profesionales. Las contribuciones de todos los cubanos al comercio y a la economía de la ciudad son muy grandes.

El éxito de los cubanos y su decisión de mantener su idioma y cultura maternos son evidentes en la gran cantidad de periódicos, revistas, programas de radio y televisión en español.

Actividad

In the above reading, see if you can determine the following.

1. what percentage of Miami's current population is Cuban
2. what professions many Cubans practice
3. how Cubans have contributed to Miami's success as a city
4. how you could use your Spanish in Miami

Pronunciation

1. Use Pronunciation Transparency P-5.1.1, or write the pronunciation activity on the chalkboard. Have students copy it into their notebooks.
   Hace mucho tiempo que vivimos en la Florida, pero nunca olvidamos nuestra isla querida.
2. You may wish to play the recorded version of this activity, located at the end of Cassette 5.1.
3. Focus on the following sound: /v/ **vivimos; olvidamos**

For the Native Speaker

Write a 150–200 word composition about a trip they once took to a neighboring city, amusement park, or other place of interest.

Cultura viva 1

Reading Strategies

1. Read the **Cultura viva** on this page. You may wish to discuss with the class some of the many ethnic groups that live in the U.S.
2. Now do the **Actividad** on this page.

Did You Know?

After Fidel Castro became dictator of Cuba in 1959, thousands of Cubans left the country. They went to the United States, Mexico, and Spain. Half a million Cubans came to the United States. The majority of those who came settled in Miami because of that city's proximity to Cuba and its similar climate.

Cubans have given Miami a strong Latin flavor. They have attracted many banks and companies that handle Latin-American trade. Cuban Americans hold many local and state political offices.

Critical Thinking Activities

1. Do a research paper on the Cuban Revolution.
2. If you had to leave the United States and live in another country where you didn't speak the language, know the customs or the culture, how do you think you would adjust to your new life?
3. Think of reasons why people leave their country for another.

Actividad

Actividad Answers

1. Almost fifty percent.
2. Professions such as medicine, law, and business.
3. Cubans have contributed to the commercial and economic life of the city.
4. By reading newspapers and magazines, by listening to the radio, and by watching TV.

Estructura 1

Structure Teaching Resources
1. Workbook, pp. 146–147
2. Cassette 5.1
3. Student Tape Manual, p. 118
4. Estructura Masters 5.1
5. Lesson Quizzes, p. 97

Bell Ringer Review
Directions to students: Copy the following words and phrases on your paper. Then draw a picture representing each one.
1. un sello
2. una tarjeta de crédito
3. una carta con un sobre
4. un cheque
5. un formulario

Structure Focus
The object pronoun **me** is presented in this lesson. Students will learn how to request favors. Students have been using **me + gusta(n)** since Chapter 1.

Presentation
1. Lead students through steps 1–3 on page 328.
2. You may want to introduce **me puedes(n)** asking students for favors. For example:
   ¿Me puedes prestar... ?
   ¿Me pueden ayudar con... ?

Actividades

Actividad A Answers
1. No, señor(a, -ita), ya escribimos bastante.
2. ... hablamos...
3. ... escuchamos...
4. ... leemos...
5. ... ayudamos...

Estructura 1

How to Request Favors   *Object pronoun* **me**

1. When you want to request help or a favor from a friend, use **¿Me puedes** + activity?

   ¿Me puedes prestar tu coche?

2. When you want to request help from someone you address formally, use **¿Me puede** + activity?

   Señorita, ¿me puede ayudar con la tarea?

3. When you want to request help from more than one person, use **¿Me pueden** + activity?

   Tíos, ¿me pueden llevar al cine?

Actividades

A **¡Qué exigente!** Your teacher makes some extra requests of the class. Tell your teacher that you and your classmates can't do what he or she asks because you already do each activity enough.

Por ejemplo:
   ¿Me pueden limpiar la clase?
   No, señor(a, -ita), ya limpiamos bastante.

1. ¿Me pueden escribir diez palabras más?
2. ¿Me pueden hablar más de la cultura hispana?
3. ¿Me pueden escuchar dos minutos más?
4. ¿Me pueden leer dos páginas más?
5. ¿Me pueden ayudar después de la clase?

Una clase de inglés en Buenos Aires, Argentina.

328   CAPÍTULO 5

B **¿Qué puedes decir?** What do you say in the following situations to get what you want? Choose either the formal or friendly form of address, depending on the person to whom you are speaking.

Por ejemplo:

Quieres ir al cine con Marta y no tienes dinero.
Marta,...
Marta, ¿me puedes prestar diez dólares? (¿Me puedes hacer un favor?)

1. Estás en el gimnasio y necesitas tu mochila que está en tu gaveta. Pablo,...
2. Estás en la oficina de la escuela y necesitas ayuda. Señorita,...
3. Estás en el correo y quieres mandar una carta. Señor,...
4. Estás en la clase de español y necesitas ayuda con la tarea. Susan,...
5. Tu cumpleaños es el sábado y quieres una grabadora nueva. Tía,...
6. El club de español va a hacer un viaje y necesitas un cheque. Mamá,...

C **Favores.** Write down the name of the person you would ask for each of the favors listed below. Then, ask the favor of each person you listed.

Por ejemplo:

hablar en inglés
Señor(a, -ita), por favor, ¿me puede hablar en inglés?

1. prestar cinco dólares
2. ayudar con la tarea
3. dar buenas notas
4. prestar el cuaderno
5. llevar en coche al centro comercial
6. comprar un regalo
7. hablar más despacio (slowly)
8. limpiar la habitación
9. prestar tus discos
10. escuchar
11. llamar esta noche
12. enseñar las fotos de tu fiesta

Lección 1 **329**

Learning from Photos

You may want to have students look at the photo on page 328. Have them formulate five questions they would like to ask the Argentine student about his English studies. Have them guess what five questions he would like to ask them about their study of Spanish.

Actividad B Answers
Answers will vary but may include the following.

1. Pablo, ¿me puedes traer mi mochila?
2. Señorita, ¿me puede ayudar?
3. Señor, ¿me puede dar un sello?
4. Susan, ¿me puedes ayudar con la tarea?
5. Tía, ¿me puedes comprar una grabadora nueva?
6. Mamá, ¿me puedes hacer un cheque?

Actividad C Answers
Answers will vary, but students must decide whether to use **puedes** or **puede,** according to whom they are addressing.

Reteaching

Directions to students: Your friend wants you to do some favors for him or her. What favors does he or she ask you? Write down four.

Cultura viva 2

Reading Strategies

1. Have students locate Argentina on the map on page xvi. Point out Mar del Plata on the map.
2. Now read the **Cultura viva** on this page.
3. Lead students through the **Actividades**. The preterit is used receptively in this **Cultura viva**. It is presented formally in Chapter 5, Lesson 3.

Did You Know?
Mar del Plata, located about 400 kilometers south of Buenos Aires, is Argentina's largest summer resort.

Critical Thinking Activity
Have teams research Argentina. Divide the class into four large groups made up of all the 1's, 2's, 3's, and 4's from each group. Each group looks up something different. For example, mountain ranges; cities; industry; immigrants; economy; government; etc. They come back and compile information. Then they return to their regular teams and share their findings. Have each team share information it has gathered with the class.

Actividades

Actividad A Answers
Disneyworld, Epcot Center.

Actividad B Answers
Sola: Epcot Center.
Acompañada: Disneyworld.

Actividad C Answers
El fin de semana pasado, la semana pasada./Both refer to the past.

Actividad D Answers
Answers will vary.

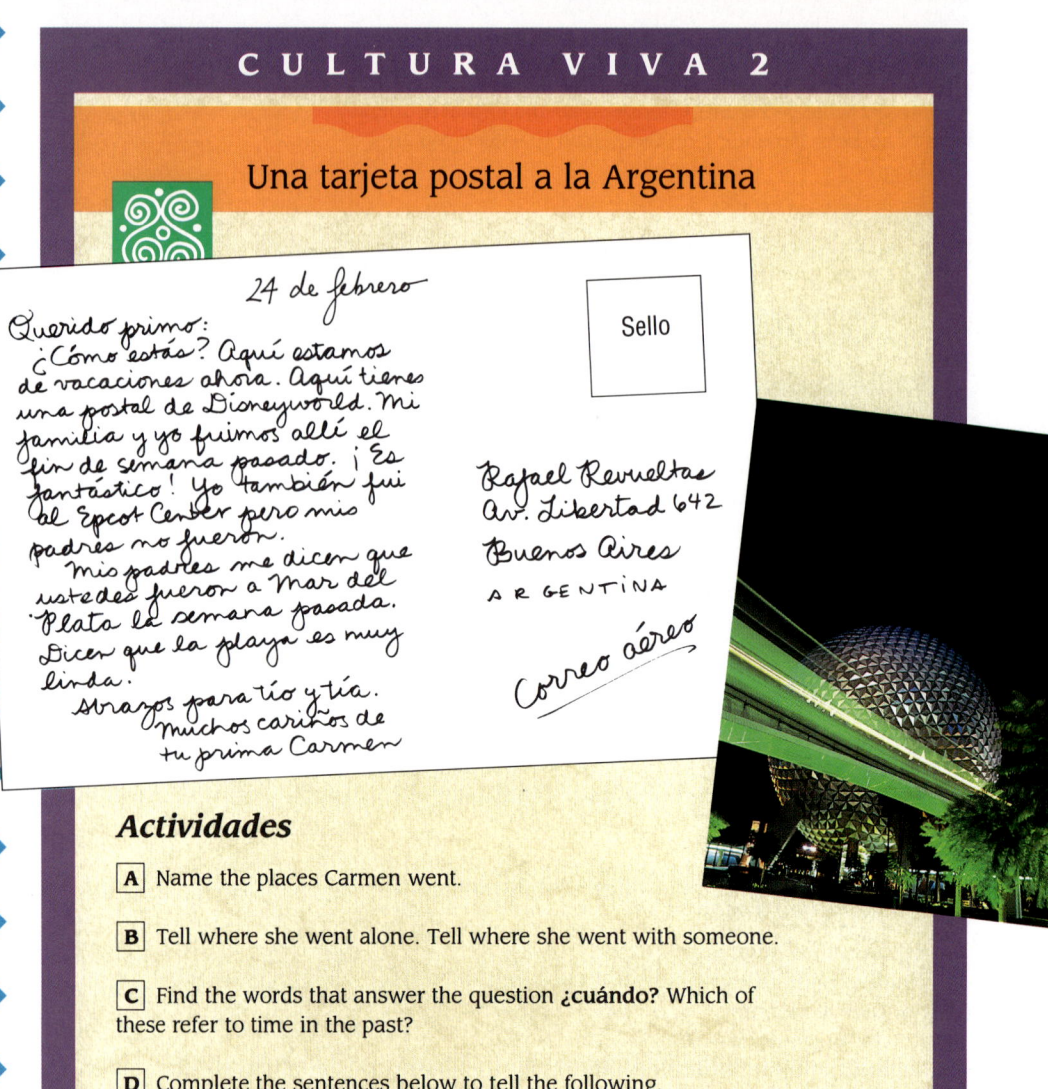

CULTURA VIVA 2

Una tarjeta postal a la Argentina

24 de febrero

Querido primo:
¿Cómo estás? Aquí estamos de vacaciones ahora. Aquí tienes una postal de Disneyworld. Mi familia y yo fuimos allí el fin de semana pasado. ¡Es fantástico! Yo también fui al Epcot Center pero mis padres no fueron.
Mis padres me dicen que ustedes fueron a Mar del Plata la semana pasada. Dicen que la playa es muy linda.
Abrazos para tío y tía.
Muchos cariños de tu prima Carmen

Rafael Revueltas
Av. Libertad 642
Buenos Aires
ARGENTINA

Correo aéreo

Actividades

A Name the places Carmen went.

B Tell where she went alone. Tell where she went with someone.

C Find the words that answer the question ¿cuándo? Which of these refer to time in the past?

D Complete the sentences below to tell the following.
1. where you went last week: **Fui a** _____.
2. where you and family members or friends went: _____ **y yo fuimos a** _____.
3. where friends or family members went without you: _____ **fueron a** _____. **Yo no fui.**

330 CAPÍTULO 5

Estructura 2

How to Offer Favors   **Object pronoun te**

You have used the word **me,** which means "to me" or "for me," when you want to request favors for yourself.

> ¿Me puedes ayudar con la tarea?

When you want to offer a favor to a friend or family member or describe what you can do for him or her, use **te,** which means "to you" or "for you."

> **Te puedo prestar mi libro.**
> **No te puedo prestar mis discos.**
> **Miguel te puede ayudar con la tarea.**
> **Mis padres te pueden llevar al centro comercial.**
> **David y yo te podemos dar cinco dólares, si quieres.**

Actividades

A Buenos amigos. Tell a classmate three things that you can do for him or her. Then say three things you cannot do.

Por ejemplo:

> **Te puedo visitar si estás enfermo(a).**
> **No te puedo ayudar con la tarea de historia.**

B El estudiante nuevo. Tell five places in your area that you and your friends can show a new student. Say something interesting about each place. Use the suggestions below or think of your own.

Por ejemplo:

> **Te podemos enseñar el zoológico. Es muy grande y divertido. Tiene muchos animales.**

el centro	una tienda	un parque
un centro comercial	un lugar secreto	una playa
un estadio	una calle	un restaurante

Lección 1 331

Actividades

Actividades Answers
Actividades A, B, and C, pp. 331–332
Answers will vary but should follow the models.

Reteaching
Ask a classmate for three favors.

Learning from Photos
You may want to have students look at the photos in the realia piece on page 332. Have them imagine that they're going on the student trip to Mexico. Based on the photos, what are some of the things that they will be able to do and see while there?

C **Donaciones.** The Spanish Club is having a sale of used items to raise money for a trip to Mexico. You have been asked to collect items. Your partner will tell you five things he or she can give you. Write down your partner's responses and report back to the class.

Por ejemplo:

ESTUDIANTE A
¿Qué me puedes dar?

ESTUDIANTE B
Te puedo dar mis tarjetas de béisbol.

Finalmente

Situaciones

A conversar You need to borrow some money from a classmate to buy a birthday gift for a friend.

1. Ask if your partner can lend you some money.
2. Your partner asks you why you need the money.
3. Tell what you plan to buy and for **(para)** whom. Then tell how much it costs.
4. Your partner hesitates about lending the money.
5. Tell what favor you can do for your partner if he or she lends you the money.
6. Your partner agrees to give you the money but asks you for a favor in return.

A escribir You have seen an advertisement for some of your favorite audio cassettes for only four dollars each. Order several cassettes. Begin your letter with **"Estimados señores"** and include the following information.

1. Give the titles of the cassettes you want to buy.
2. Give the price of each title and the total amount of your purchase **(El precio total es...)**.
3. Ask if you can pay by credit card or check.
4. Give your name, address, and telephone number.

Repaso de vocabulario

COSAS			LUGAR
el anuncio	el sobre	hacer un favor	el correo
el cheque	la tarjeta de crédito	llevar	
el favor		mandar	EXPRESIONES
el formulario	ACTIVIDADES	prestar	hacer un cheque
el nombre	ayudar	traer	por favor
	dar		
	enseñar		

Lección 1   **333**

For the Native Speaker
In pairs have students pick out sale ads from a newspaper or a magazine. Have them order merchandise from the ads. They should write to those stores with the full address on the letter and envelope.

Finalmente

Situaciones

Lesson 1 Evaluation
The **A conversar** and **A escribir** situations on this page are designed to give students the opportunity to use as many language functions and as much vocabulary from this lesson as possible. The **A conversar** and **A escribir** are also intended to show how well students are able to meet the lesson objectives.

Presentation
Prior to doing the **A conversar** and **A escribir** on this page, you may wish to play the **Situaciones** listening activities on Cassette 5.1 as a means of helping students organize the material.

Repaso de vocabulario

The words and phrases in the Repaso de vocabulario have been taught for productive use in this lesson. They are summarized here as a resource for both students and teacher. The Repaso de vocabulario also serves as a convenient resource for the A conversar and A escribir activities on this page. It also gives the teacher a source for writing either additional practice or evaluation activities such as quizzes and tests in addition to those provided by the publisher.

Lesson 2 Resources
1. Workbook, pp. 150–154
2. Vocabulario Transparencies
3. Pronunciation Transparency P-5.2.1
4. Audio Cassette 5.2 Compact Disc 7
5. Student Tape Manual, pp. 121–125
6. Bell Ringer Review Blackline Masters, p. 30
7. Computer Software: Practice & Test Generator
8. Video (cassette or disc)
9. Video Activities Booklet, pp. A67–A68
10. Estructura Masters, pp. 59–60
11. Diversiones Masters, pp. 57–58
12. Situation Cards
13. Lesson Quizzes, pp. 99–101
14. Testing Program

Bell Ringer Review

Directions to students: Several friends ask you favors this week. How do you respond? List of the following favors in the appropriate columns: **Te puedo ayudar a...** and **No te puedo ayudar a...** Remember to add **"Lo siento"** if you can't help.

lavar el coche, limpiar la casa, comprar un regalo, llevar al centro comercial, ayudar con la tarea de historia

CAPÍTULO 5

Lección 2

¿Cómo se dice "T-shirt"?

¡A comenzar!

The following are some of the things you will be learning to do in this lesson.

When you want to...	You use...
1. ask a favor of someone	¿Me + activity?
2. give the meaning of a word in Spanish	Se dice...
3. tell what things are made of	Son de + material.

Now find examples of the above words and phrases in the following conversation.

Carmen habla con su papá.

CARMEN: Oye, papá, ¿me das un cheque, por favor?
PAPÁ: ¿Para qué? A ver.
CARMEN: Mira, quiero comprar dos "T-shirts".
PAPÁ: *Camisetas*, Carmen. Y no comprendo por qué necesitas dos. Son muy caras.
CARMEN: Pero, papá, son del último "tour". Y además, son de puro "cotton".
PAPÁ: *Algodón*, Carmen. ¡Por Dios! Se dice "algodón".

Actividades preliminares

A Think of the most difficult words you know in Spanish. Write them down in English. Quiz a classmate.

Por ejemplo:

ESTUDIANTE A
¿Cómo se dice "chemistry" en español?

ESTUDIANTE B
Se dice "química". (No sé cómo se dice).

B Ask a classmate for the following items.

Por ejemplo:
    un dólar

ESTUDIANTE A
¿Me prestas un dólar, por favor?

ESTUDIANTE B
Sí, cómo no. (No tengo, No puedo, etc.).

1. papel   2. un bolígrafo   3. la calculadora   4. la tarea

¡A comenzar!

Presentation

A. Lead students through each of the three functions given on page 334, progressing from the English to the Spanish. Then have students find these words and phrases in the dialogue on page 335.

B. Introduce the Lesson 2 dialogue by reading it aloud or by playing the recorded version.

C. Now ask students to open their books and look at the dialogue as you lead them through what is said. For example:
1. ¿Qué dice Carmen para pedir el cheque?
2. Cuando Carmen pide el cheque, ¿qué dice su papá?
3. ¿Por qué quiere el cheque Carmen?
4. Cuando Carmen dice "T-shirts", ¿qué dice su papá?
5. ¿Por qué no quiere comprar las camisetas el papá?
6. Según Carmen, ¿por qué son caras?
7. Cuando Carmen dice que son de puro "cotton", ¿qué dice su papá?

D. Have students look at the dialogue and determine why Carmen's father is upset. ¿Por qué está enojado el papá de Carmen?
1. ¿porque a él no le gustan los conjuntos de rock?
2. ¿porque no le gustan las camisetas?
3. ¿porque las camisetas son muy caras?
4. ¿porque Carmen dice palabras en inglés cuando habla español?

Actividades preliminares

Actividad A and B Answers
Answers will vary.

Vocabulario

Vocabulary Teaching Resources
1. Vocabulario Transparencies 5.2
2. Workbook, p. 150
3. Cassette 5.2
4. Student Tape Manual, p. 122
5. Lesson Quizzes, p. 99

Bell Ringer Review
Directions to students: Your best friend is in the hospital and is bored. What could you buy or lend him or her to make the time pass more quickly? Make two lists under the headings **Te puedo prestar...** and **Te puedo comprar...**

Presentation
A. Have students open their books to page 336.
   1. Model each of the four words at the top of page 336. Begin each phrase with **Es...** Have students repeat each phrase in unison.
   2. Using vocabulary transparencies, point to the word and ask individual students ¿**Es una llave?** Encourage students to give a complete answer. For example: **Sí, es una llave.**
B. Have students look at the following groupings of vocabulary on pages 336–337.
   1. Model the questions ¿**Qué es?** ¿**Para qué sirve?** ¿**De qué es?** ¿**Cómo es?**
   2. Pointing to objects in the classroom, ask students the questions presented in the vocabulary. For example: **Maestro(a):** (pointing to a pencil) ¿**Qué es?** **Estudiante: Es un lápiz**

Vocabulario

¿Qué es? Es...

una llave
un bolsillo
una billetera
un reloj

¿Para qué sirve? Sirve para...

abrir la puerta
llevar cosas
saber la hora
guardar libros y otras cosas

336 CAPÍTULO 5

Total Physical Response

Getting Ready
For **TPR 1**, use transparencies and color transparency pens. For **TPR 2**, obtain real items or pictures of items to be used in the activity. Bring multiples of the same item in various materials and display them in front of the room.

New Words
echa   devuelve   ponte

TPR 1
(Whole class or pairs)
Toquen la mochila.
Apunten al armario.
Indiquen la llave.
Hagan un círculo negro en el bolsillo.
Dibujen un cuadro azul en la billetera.

¿De qué es?
Es un aparato de...
plástico
metal

Es una cosa de...
papel
goma
algodón
cuero
madera
plata
oro
vidrio

¿Cómo es? Es...
redondo(a)
cuadrado(a)
rectangular

Maestro(a): ¿Para qué sirve?
Estudiante: Sirve para escribir.
Maestro(a): ¿De qué es?
Estudiante: Es de madera.
Continue with different objects.

3. You may wish to follow up with having students find the following things in the classroom.
   a. cosas redondas
   b. cosas cuadradas
   c. cosas rectangulares

When Students Ask

You may wish to give students the following additional vocabulary to allow them to describe objects.

triangular   ovalado(a)
la tela   la seda
la lana   el poliéster

Regionalisms

You may wish to tell students that in some parts of the Spanish-speaking world the following word are alternatives to those presented in the Vocabulario.
la billetera (la cartera)
el bolsillo (la bolsa) (Perú)

Lección 2   337

Toquen el objeto de plata.
Indiquen el objeto de oro.
Apunten al objeto de papel.
Hagan dos rectángulos verdes en el objeto de madera.
(Interchange commands and items.)

TPR 2
(Individual students)
Toca el reloj de oro.

Toma agua del vaso de plástico.
Ponte la camiseta de algodón.
Echa jugo en la jarra de vidrio.
Lleva el lápiz de madera a _____.
Lleva el lápiz de metal a _____.
Guarda los zapatos de cuero en mi escritorio.
Guarda el reloj de plata en el bolsillo.
Llévale la billetera a _____.
(Interchange commands and items.)

Actividades

Actividad A and B Answers
Answers will vary.

Actividad C Answers
Answers will vary but should approximate the following.

1. Una llave es de metal. Es pequeña y delgada. Sirve para abrir la puerta.
2. Una tarjeta de crédito es de plástico. Es rectangular y delgada. Sirve para comprar cosas.
3. Un calendario es de papel. Es rectangular y tiene números y los nombres de los meses y de los días de la semana. Sirve para enseñar los días.

Actividad D Answers
Answers will vary.

Reteaching

Ask students to bring or show you objects in the classroom without mentioning the name of the object. For example:
Linda, ¿me traes (enseñas) el aparato para escuchar casetes?

1. la cosa para escribir en la pizarra
2. la cosa para limpiar la pizarra
3. la cosa para escribir en el papel
4. la cosa que abrimos cuando queremos aire fresco
5. la cosa que usas para llevar tus libros

Actividades

A ¿De qué es? Tell what five things in your classroom are made of.

Por ejemplo:
> la silla
> *La silla es de metal (madera).*

B Para mí es de oro. Name five of your most prized possessions and tell what they are made of.

Por ejemplo:
> tu radio
> *Mi radio es de plástico. (Tengo un radio de plástico).*

C Descripción. Tell what the following items are made of, what they look like, and what they are for.

Por ejemplo:
> un lápiz
> *Un lápiz es de madera y de goma. Es delgado y largo. Sirve para escribir.*

1. una llave
2. una tarjeta de crédito
3. un calendario
4. un reloj
5. una billetera
6. una mochila
7. unas monedas
8. un bolsillo
9. un televisor
10. un teléfono
11. una cámara
12. una maleta

D Adivina, buen adivinador. Prepare descriptions of three objects and see if a classmate can guess what you are talking about. In your description, answer the following questions.

¿Para qué sirve?   ¿De qué es?   ¿Cómo es?

Por ejemplo:

ESTUDIANTE A
Es un aparato para trabajar con números. Es de plástico. Es rectangular.

ESTUDIANTE B
Es una calculadora, ¿verdad?

For the Native Speaker

Directions to students: Write a newspaper ad for two objects you wish to sell. Describe the objects by giving color, size, use, appearance, and condition. Include your address or telephone number. Read the ad to the class without mentioning the name of the objects. The class guesses what objects you are selling.

CULTURA VIVA 1

La música latina

El ritmo latino, que es la base de la "salsa" y la música "disco" en los Estados Unidos, tiene su origen en Cuba y el Caribe. La música del Caribe es una combinación de ritmos africanos e hispanos. Muchos bailes como la rumba, la conga y el chachachá tienen su origen en el Caribe.

Los instrumentos de percusión son muy importantes para estos ritmos. Aquí hay algunos de los instrumentos usados en Cuba y el Caribe.

Pégate... Suave 12-60 AM
Tenemos lo que te gusta.

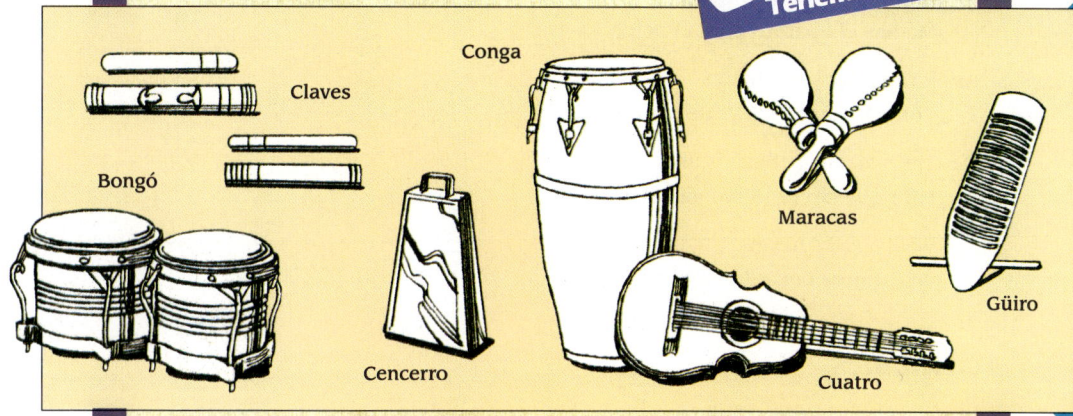

Bongó, Claves, Conga, Cencerro, Maracas, Cuatro, Güiro

Actividad

Éstas son las diez canciones más populares durante una semana en Miami.

1. ¿Qué estación de radio debes escuchar si te gustan estas canciones?
2. ¿Qué canción es la más popular?
3. ¿Qué canciones son menos (less) populares?
4. ¿Quiénes son los cantantes más populares?

SUPER Q 108 SUPER HITS

SUPER HIT	ARTISTA(S)
1. UN BUEN PERDEDOR	Franco de Vita
2. DÉJALO QUE REGRESE	Hansel y Raúl
3. TÚ Y YO	Julio Iglesias
4. ME VAS A ECHAR DE MENOS	José José
5. CREO EN EL AMOR	José Luis Rodríguez
6. EN CARNE VIVA	Charanga '76
7. SERÉ	Salsa Latina
8. AMAR A MUERTE	Luis Ángel
9. POR SI ACASO	Braulio
10. TE QUIERO TE QUIERO	Orq. Éxito

Cultura viva 1

Reading Strategies

1. Read the **Cultura viva** on this page.
2. Bring cassettes or compact discs of Latin music to play for the class. Point out the instruments mentioned in the reading so students can appreciate the strong percussion base of this music.
3. If you have a way of obtaining some of the instruments, bring them to class so that students can handle them and try to play them.

Did You Know?

Cuban composers have combined African and European musical traditions to create the Cuban sound. The combination of the guitar and the African drum gives Cuban music its characteristic beat.

Critical Thinking Activity
Working in groups, find out more information about dances such as **la rumba, la conga,** and **el chachachá.** Learn the basic steps and present them to the class.

Actividad

Actividad Answers
1. Super Q (108).
2. "Un buen perdedor".
3. "Por si acaso"; "Te quiero, te quiero".
4. Franco de Vita; Hansel y Raúl.

Pronunciation

1. Use Pronunciation Transparency P-5.2.1, or write the pronunciation activity on the chalkboard. Have students copy it into their notebooks.
   Sóngoro cosongo,
   songo be;
   Sóngoro cosongo,
   de mamey;
   Sóngoro, la negra
   baila bien;
   sóngoro de una,
   sóngoro de tré.
   (Nicolás Guillén, poeta cubano, 1902–1989)
2. You may wish to play the recorded version of this activity, located at the end of Cassette 5.2.
3. Ask students to focus on the rhythm.

Estructura 1

Structure Teaching Resources
1. Workbook, pp. 151–152
2. Cassette 5.2
3. Student Tape Manual, p. 122
4. Estructura Masters 5.2
5. Lesson Quizzes, p. 100

Bell Ringer Review
Bring a recording of "salsa" music to class. Directions to students: Turn to page 339. Listen to the music carefully and write on your paper any of the instruments shown on this page that you hear.

Structure Focus
In this lesson students will learn to circumlocute.

Presentation
Lead students through steps 1–5 on page 340.
Show the class pictures of objects they know. Ask questions. **A ver... ¿cómo se dice _____? ¿Para que sirve?**

Actividades

Actividad A Answers
1. c
2. a
3. e
4. f
5. b
6. d

Estructura 1

How to Describe Something You Don't Know the Word For

If you forget a word or don't know the word for something, you can still communicate by using the following strategies.

1. Use stalling devices to gain time to think.
   A ver... Bueno... Pues...

2. Use general terms when you can't remember a word. For example, **la cosa** (thing) or **el aparato** (mechanical thing).
   ¿Dónde está la cosa redonda?
   ¿Me das el aparato para el pelo?

3. Ask how to say something.
   ¿Cómo se dice "key"? **Se dice "llave".**

4. Describe what something is used for.
   ¿Para qué sirve? Sirve para escribir.

5. Ask what a word means.
   ¿Qué quiere decir "mochila"?

Actividades

A Descripciones. Match the following objects with their descriptions on page 341.

A.
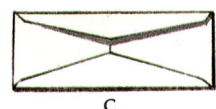
C.
B.

D.

E.
F.

340 CAPÍTULO 5

1. Es la cosa en que mandas una carta. Aquí escribes el nombre y la dirección. Tiene un sello.
2. Es el aparato de plástico con los números de cero a nueve. Ayuda mucho en las clases de matemáticas y ciencias.
3. Es el aparato que sirve para escribir algo oficial o formal. Las secretarias usan este aparato.
4. Es la cosa para llevar dinero, las tarjetas de crédito y otras tarjetas importantes.
5. Es la cosa que sirve para abrir puertas, maletas y otras cosas.
6. Es el aparato que sirve para saber qué hora es. Puede ser grande o pequeño.

B Así se dice. Describe each of the objects below to a classmate. Your classmate will tell you what you've described. Provide the following types of information:

color   size   shape   use   material   appearance   condition

Por ejemplo:

ESTUDIANTE A
Es una cosa rectangular para llevar libros. Es azul y bastante vieja.

ESTUDIANTE B
Es la mochila.

1.

3.

2.

4.

5.

Lección 2   341

Cooperative Learning

Have students think of difficult words they know in Spanish and have them write the meanings in English. In teams students will quiz each other, asking "¿Cómo se dice _____?" Teams may wish to offer clues such as "La palabra empieza con la letra *d*. Es una palabra corta, etc. At the end, each team will announce those words that were not known by the other team, which will use the dictionary to determine the meaning of each word.

Actividad B Answers
Answers will vary but may include the following.

1. Es una cosa rectangular y amarilla. Es de papel. Tiene fotos interesantes./Es una revista.
2. Es una cosa rodonda que comemos. Adentro hay carne y lechuga./Es una hamburguesa.
3. Es una cosa cuadrada y gris. Sirve para llevar ropa cuando viajamos./Es una maleta.
4. Es una cosa redonda y negra. Es de plástico. Sirve para escuchar música./Es un disco.
5. Es una cosa rectangular de madera. Sirve para guardar ropa en la habitación./Es un armario.

Additional Practice
After doing Actividades A and B, you may wish to reinforce the learning with the following. Directions to students: Ask a classmate to lend you three of the objects below. Describe the object but do not name it. Your classmate will guess what you are describing. **Por ejemplo:**

Estudiante A: ¿Me puedes prestar la cosa para escribir?
Estudiante B: ¡Ah!, quieres el bolígrafo.

la calculadora	la guitarra
el cuaderno	el estéreo
el sello	el sobre
la mochila	la billetera

Reteaching
Display an assortment of items in front of the class. For example, calculator, pen, wallet, purse, key, envelope, cassette, or backpack. Describe each item in terms of appearance, use, size, shape, and condition. Have individual students identify the item described and bring it to you.

Cultura viva 2

Reading Strategies
1. Read the **Cultura viva** on this page.
2. Using the vocabulary in the reading, discuss with students the advantages of being bilingual.

Did You Know?
Because there are many Hispanic communities in the United States, the opportunity to use Spanish in the workplace is increasing. For example, bilingual teachers are in great demand in states that have large Spanish-speaking populations. In some districts, bilingual teachers can command a higher salary than their monolingual counterparts.

Critical Thinking Activities
1. Invite a member of your community who uses Spanish in his or her work to speak to the class. Have students prepare questions to ask the visitor.
2. In groups, have students think of as many reasons as possible why Spanish would be useful in the following occupations: real estate agent, hotel manager, secretary, social worker, and doctor.

Actividad

Actividad Answers
Answers will vary.

Learning from Realia
You may want to have students look at the realia on page 342. Ask students what number the following people would call to learn more about one of the positions offered.
1. un/a doctor/a
2. una persona que quiere trabajar con abogados
3. una persona que sabe reparar coches
4. un/a secretario(a) o recepcionista

CULTURA VIVA 2

El español en el trabajo

 El papá de Carmen es abogado y trabaja en una compañía internacional en Miami. Todos los días habla inglés y español con sus clientes.

Si sabes más de un idioma, hay muchos trabajos que puedes hacer. Hay muchas instituciones y compañías en los Estados Unidos que necesitan empleados que hablen inglés y español. Por ejemplo, los bancos, hospitales y clínicas; las agencias de servicios sociales y las escuelas; toda clase de compañías internacionales; los canales de televisión, los periódicos, las estaciones de radio, compañías de aviación y muchísimas otras. Si sabes dos idiomas, no sólo tienes más oportunidades de trabajo, sino que tu trabajo puede ser más interesante.

Actividad

Based on the above reading, list five occupations in which you think you could use Spanish.

Por ejemplo:
> Empleados de bancos, compañías como...

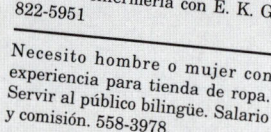

EMPLEOS

Solicito médico bilingüe para curso de enfermería con E. K. G. 822-5951

Necesito hombre o mujer con experiencia para tienda de ropa. Servir al público bilingüe. Salario y comisión. 558-3978.

Se solicita ayudante legal, preferible hablar inglés. Llamar lunes a viernes de 10 a 6 pm. 823-9831

Mecánico para trabajar en gasolinera. Debe ser bilingüe. Inf. 853-9800.

¿Necesita trabajo? Llame Avance Personal para empleos de oficina. Poco inglés necesario. Llamar 245-8761.

Estructura 2

How to Request, Offer, and Describe Favors

Me and te with conjugated verbs

You have learned to request favors and tell favors you do for others, using **me** or **te** and a form of the verb **poder**.

¿Me puedes traer mi camiseta verde?
Te puedo dar mi bolígrafo, si quieres.

1. You can use **me** and a form of other verbs to request a favor.

   ¿Me traes mi camiseta verde?
   ¿Me das el bolígrafo?
   Señorita, ¿me hace un favor?

2. You also use **me** to describe what people do or don't do for you or to you.

   Mi maestra me da buenas notas.
   Mi hermana siempre me ayuda con la tarea.
   Mis amigos no me prestan dinero.

3. To offer a favor to a friend or family member, or to describe what you do for that person, use **te**.

   Te invito a mi fiesta.
   Te voy a comprar unos discos para tu cumpleaños.

4. The following are some things friends or family might offer to do for each other.

-ar verbs		**-er** and **-ir** verbs
mandar	hablar	hacer
escuchar	llamar	leer
enseñar	dar	escribir
ayudar		abrir
prestar		traer
llevar		
guardar		
comprar		

Una familia cubanoamericana en Miami.

Estructura 2

Structure Teaching Resources

1. Workbook, pp. 153–154
2. Cassette 5.2
3. Student Tape Manual, p. 123
4. Estructura Masters 5.2
5. Lesson Quizzes, p. 101

Bell Ringer Review

Directions to students: Look around the classroom and write down the names in Spanish of as many objects as you can. Then write what each item is made of.

Structure Focus

Me and **te** with conjugated verbs are presented in this lesson. Students will learn how to request, offer, and describe favors. The object pronouns **le, les,** and **nos** will be presented in Lesson 6 of this chapter; Chapter 6, Lesson 1; and Chapter 6, Lesson 2, respectively.

Presentation

1. Lead students through steps 1–4 on page 343.
2. Ask students to lend you three different things. Tell them why you need them. For example: ¿Me das un lápiz? Tengo que escribir algo. ¿Me prestas papel? Tengo que preparar un examen. ¿Me traes el libro? Tengo que enseñar la lección.

Actividades

Actividad A Answers
Answers will vary but should include the following.

1. ... me hace favores.
2. ... me ayudan.
3. ... me llaman.
4. ... me escuchan.
5. ... me escriben.
6. ... me dan regalos.

Actividad B Answers
Answers will vary.

Actividad C Answers
1. ¿Por qué no me traes regalos de tus viajes?
2. ¿... no me das dinero cuando lavo el coche?
3. ¿... no me hablan cuando me ven?
4. ¿... no me da buenas notas cuando trabajo mucho?
5. ¿... no me das regalos para mi cumpleaños?

Additional Practice
After completing Actividades A, B, and C, you may wish to reinforce the lesson by doing the following activity. Directions to students: Write down three things you have that you are willing to exchange with a classmate. In another column, write down three things you want from a classmate.
Por ejemplo:
Tengo....
una colección de revistas de tenis
un bolígrafo negro
una raqueta de tenis
Quiero...
tu colección de discos de los Rolling Stones
tu camiseta verde
tu calculadora

Now offer your classmate a trade.

Reteaching
Have students tell you one thing their friends do for them and one their friends don't do for them. **Por ejemplo:**
Mis amigos me llevan a fiestas pero no me ayudan con mi tarea.

Actividades

A **¿Quién te hace favores?** Tell who does things for you by responding to the following questions.

Por ejemplo:

> ¿Quién te da dinero en tu familia?
> *Mi mamá me da dinero.*

1. ¿Quién te hace favores?
2. ¿Quién te ayuda cuando no entiendes algo?
3. ¿Quiénes te llaman por teléfono?
4. ¿Quiénes te escuchan cuando tienes problemas?
5. ¿Quiénes te escriben cartas o tarjetas postales?
6. ¿Quiénes te dan regalos?

B **Consecuencias.** Tell what will happen if the following favors are not granted.

Por ejemplo:

> Si no me prestas tus discos...
> *Si no me prestas tus discos, mi fiesta va a ser un poco aburrida.*

1. Si no me ayudas con la tarea...
2. Si no me traes tus discos nuevos...
3. Si mis padres no me permiten salir esta noche...
4. Si mi maestro no me da exámenes fáciles...
5. Si mis compañeros no me prestan sus vídeos nuevos...
6. Si no me guardas una silla en la cafetería...

C **¿Qué pasa?** Ask the following people why they don't do what you expect them to.

Por ejemplo:

> Tu amiga nunca te manda cartas cuando viaja.
> *¿Por qué no me mandas cartas cuando viajas?*

1. Tu amigo nunca te trae regalos de sus viajes.
2. Tu papá nunca te da dinero cuando lavas el coche.
3. Tus amigos nunca te hablan cuando te ven.
4. Tu maestra nunca te da buenas notas cuando trabajas mucho.
5. Tu primo nunca te da regalos para tu cumpleaños.

Finalmente

Situaciones

A conversar You have lost your backpack at school. Your partner is working in the office where the lost-and-found box is.

1. Greet your partner.
2. Tell your partner you don't know where your book bag is and ask for help.
3. Your partner asks what the bag is like. Describe it, telling the color, size, shape, and material.
4. Your partner asks what's in the bag. Describe the contents.
5. Your partner asks if you can come back in 15 minutes. Tell your partner why you need the book bag now.

A escribir A close friend suddenly decides you're not a good friend. Write your friend a note, listing all the favors you do for him or her. Then invite him or her to do something with you this weekend.

Repaso de vocabulario

PREGUNTAS
¿Cómo se dice?
¿De qué es?
¿Para qué sirve?

COSAS
el aparato
la billetera
el bolsillo
la cosa
la llave
el reloj

ACTIVIDADES
abrir
guardar
llevar (to carry)

MATERIALES
el algodón
el cuero
la goma
la madera
el metal
el oro
el papel

el plástico
la plata
el vidrio

FORMAS
cuadrado(a)
rectangular
redondo(a)

EXPRESIONES
se dice
sirve para

CAPÍTULO 5

Lección 3

Objectives

By the end of this lesson, students will be able to:

1. say what nationality they and others are
2. say that something has been going on since a certain date
3. tell the year in which an event occurred
4. give the year they were born
5. tell where they went at one point in the past and ask where others went

---

Lesson 3 Resources

1. Workbook, pp. 155–159
2. Vocabulario Transparencies
3. Pronunciation Transparency P-5.3.1
4. Audio Cassette 5.3 Compact Disc 7
5. Student Tape Manual, pp. 126–130
6. Bell Ringer Review Blackline Masters, p. 31
7. Computer Software: Practice & Test Generator
8. Video (cassette or disc)
9. Video Activities Booklet, pp. A69–A70
10. Estructura Masters, pp. 61–63
11. Diversiones Masters, pp. 59–60
12. Situation Cards
13. Lesson Quizzes, pp. 102–105
14. Testing Program

CAPÍTULO 5

Lección 3

Tienes que practicar el español

¡A comenzar!

The following are some of the things you will be learning to do in this lesson.

When you want to...	You use...
1. say what nationality you and others are	**Somos** + nationality.
2. say that something has been going on since a certain date	Activity + **desde** + date.
3. give a year in the twentieth century	**Mil novecientos...**
4. ask a friend or relative if he or she went somewhere	**¿Fuiste a** + place?
5. say that you went someplace yesterday	**Fui ayer.**

Now find examples of the above words and phrases in the following conversation.

346

Getting Ready for Lesson 3

You may wish to use the following suggestions to prepare students for the lesson.

1. Give students a list of events in your life, using as many cognates and familiar words as possible. Do not list events in chronological order. For example:

   a. viaje a Puerto Rico
   b. graduación de la universidad
   c. viaje a México
   d. nacimiento de mi hijo(a) _____
   e. matrimonio con _____

   Give an account of these events arranged by topics rather than chronologically. Give years in terms of the decade (for example, **en el año ochenta y cinco**). As you speak, have students record the year

Carmen habla con su padre.

PAPÁ: ¿Ya fuiste al correo a mandar el cheque?
CARMEN: Sí, papá. Fui ayer. Gracias por el cheque. Te van a gustar las "T-shirts".
PAPÁ: Carmen, tienes que practicar el español.
CARMEN: Pero, papá, estamos aquí en Miami desde mil novecientos sesenta y tres. ¿Por qué no puedo hablar inglés en casa?
PAPÁ: Bueno, porque somos cubanos y tienes que hablar bien el español.

Actividad preliminar

Ask a classmate if he or she went to the following places yesterday.

Por ejemplo:
　　al cine

ESTUDIANTE A
¿Fuiste al cine?

ESTUDIANTE B
Sí, fui con Miriam. (No, no fui).

1. al partido de _____
2. a la cafetería
3. al centro comercial
4. al trabajo
5. a la casa de _____

---

of each event. Then allow one minute for them to work with partners to put the events in chronological order, using time sequencing (**primero, luego, después**) or ordinal numbers (**primero, segundo, tercero**).

2. Use the preterit in your narrative so that students begin hearing the sounds of that tense. As long as you provide adequate contextual support and "stall time" between dates, students will have access to what you are saying. For example:
(Topic:) **Estoy casado(a) y tengo tres hijos. Mi esposo(a) se llama _____.**
(Info:) **Me casé con _____ en el año _____ en la ciudad de _____.**
(Stall time:) **¡Qué matrimonio más lindo!**

Bell Ringer Review

Directions to students: Make two columns on your paper labeled **bolsillo** and **billetera**. Then write each of the following items in the appropriate column.

1. monedas
2. llaves
3. tarjetas de crédito
4. cheques
5. fotos
6. bolígrafos
7. calculadoras
8. documentos importantes

¡A comenzar!

Presentation

A. Lead students through each of the five functions given on page 346, progressing from the English to the Spanish. Then have the students find these words and phrases in the dialogue on page 347.

B. Introduce the Lesson 3 dialogue by reading it aloud or by playing the recorded version. Have students raise their hands when they hear Carmen's father insist on something.
　El papá de Carmen insiste en algo. Según el papá, ¿qué tiene que hacer Carmen? ¿Por qué?

C. Now ask students to open their books and look at the dialogue as you lead them through what is said. For example:
　1. ¿Qué pregunta el papá de Carmen?
　2. ¿Qué palabra en español no puede recordar Carmen?
　3. Entonces, ¿qué dice su papá?
　4. ¿Está de acuerdo Carmen?
　5. ¿Desde cuándo está en los Estados Unidos la familia Marín?
　6. Carmen quiere saber por qué no puede hablar inglés en casa. ¿Qué dice su papá? Es decir, ¿la familia Marín es de qué país?

Actividad preliminar

Actividad Answers
Answers will vary.

Vocabulario

Vocabulary Teaching Resources
1. Vocabulario Transparencies 5.3
2. Workbook, pp. 155–156
3. Cassette 5.3
4. Student Tape Manual, p. 127
5. Lesson Quizzes, p. 102

Bell Ringer Review

Directions to students: Draw ten circles on a sheet of paper. In the center of each one write one of the following materials: **vidrio, oro, plata, madera, cuero, algodón, goma, papel, plástico, metal**. Draw lines out from each circle and write as many things as you can think of that are made of that material.

Presentation

A. Have students open their books to page 348. Model each new word on page 348. Begin each phrase with **Soy...** Have students repeat each phrase in unison.

B. Now have students look at the vocabulary presentation on page 349.
  1. Model the phrases **¿Qué idioma estudias? Estudio...** Have students repeat each phrase in unison.
  2. Ask which language is spoken by each of the nationalities. For example: **Los cubanos hablan español.**
  3. Using the names of well-known people from foreign countries, ask individual students questions. For example: **¿Qué es Julio Iglesias?** Encourage students to give complete responses. For example: **Es español.**

Vocabulario

348 CAPÍTULO 5

Total Physical Response

Getting Ready
Make up poster strips with the names of each nationality presented in feminine and masculine form. Distribute two per student, having students use only one strip at a time. Show Vocabulary Transparency 5.3 during the activity for reference.

New Words
pasen   al fondo de

Pre-activity
Review the world map pointing out the locations of the different countries, nationalities, and the names of the continents.

¿Qué idioma estudias?
Estudio...

español inglés francés alemán
japonés italiano chino ruso

Actividades

A **¿De dónde son?** What countries are the following people from?

Por ejemplo:
> los cubanos
> *Los cubanos son de Cuba.*

1. los hondureños
2. los colombianos
3. los guatemaltecos
4. los venezolanos
5. los ecuatorianos
6. los bolivianos
7. los dominicanos
8. los peruanos
9. los norteamericanos
10. los uruguayos
11. los costarricenses

Lección 3 349

Note: Remind students about adjective agreement and show them how to add **-es** for nationalities such as **francés**. Also point out that nationalitites and languages are not capitalized.

When Students Ask

You may wish to give students the following additional vocabulary to allow them to talk about nationalities.
vietnamita
coreano(a)
indio(a)
filipino(a)
camboyano(a)
tailandés(esa)
polaco(a)
portugués(esa)
griego(a)
yugoslavo(a)
irlandés(esa)
noruego(a)
suizo(a)
sueco(a)
jamaicano(a)
haitiano(a)

Actividades

Actividad A Answers

1. Los hondureños son de Honduras.
2. Los colombianos... Colombia.
3. Los guatemaltecos... Guatemala.
4. Los venezolanos... Venezuela.
5. Los ecuatorianos... Ecuador.
6. Los bolivianos... Bolivia.
7. Los dominicanos... la República Dominicana.
8. Los peruanos... Perú.
9. Los norteamericanos... los Estados Unidos.
10. Los uruguayos... Uruguay.
11. Los costarricenses... Costa Rica.

TPR
(After each command say **Muéstrenme su nacionalidad.**)
Levántense si son de Norteamérica.
Levanten la mano si son de Europa.
Pasen a mi derecha si son de Centroamérica.
Pasen a mi izquierda si son de la América del Sur.
Vayan al frente de la clase si son de Asia.
Vayan al fondo de la clase si son del Caribe.
Pasen a mi derecha si son de un país muy grande.
(Repeat having students use their second strip.)

Actividad B Answers

En Miami hay restaurantes argentinos, españoles, colombianos, peruanos, chinos, cubanos y japoneses. Answers will vary.

Actividad C Answers

1. Una chilena habla español.
2. Una japonesa... japonés.
3. Un italiano... italiano.
4. Un canadiense... inglés o francés.
5. Una puertorriqueña... español e inglés.
6. Un francés... francés.
7. Un norteamericano... inglés.
8. Un guatemalteco... español.
9. Una alemana... alemán.
10. Una española... español.

Reteaching

Provide a classroom map or have students use maps in their text. Directions to students: Study Central America, South America, and the Caribbean carefully. Then make an outline map of the area on your paper. Label each country and its capital. Draw a line out from each country and write the name in Spanish of the people who live there.

Learning from Realia

You may want to have students look at the realia on page 350. Have students imagine that they're in Miami and are going out to eat. Have them tell which restaurants they prefer and which they don't like. Ask them what numbers they would call to make reservations for restaurants they like.

B **Una ciudad internacional.** Tell what kinds of food you can eat in Miami based on the following restaurant ads. Then tell what kinds of restaurants there are in your area.

Por ejemplo:

En Miami hay restaurantes _____.
En mi ciudad hay restaurantes _____.

C **¿Qué idioma habla?** Tell the language that each of the following people speaks.

Por ejemplo:

una mexicana
Una mexicana habla español.

1. una chilena
2. una japonesa
3. un italiano
4. un canadiense
5. una puertorriqueña
6. un francés
7. un norteamericano
8. un guatemalteco
9. una alemana
10. una española

350 CAPÍTULO 5

For the Native Speaker

Have students write a composition about what country they would visit if they could. They should tell why they'd like to visit the country, when they would go, what they would pack, how they would get there, and what they would do there.

Cooperative Learning

Each group will create an imaginary ID of a Hispanic teenager. Each team will first choose a country of origin. The group will then locate on a map the name of a city from that country. They should include the following information to complete the ID: **apellido, nombre, dirección, nacionalidad, ocupación, edad** (age). Have the groups attach a photo to the ID.

CULTURA VIVA 1

La televisión en español

En Miami así como en Nueva York, Los Ángeles, Chicago y en casi todas las otras grandes ciudades de los Estados Unidos, puedes ver televisión en español. Hay casi 500 canales que transmiten programas en español en nuestro país.

Actividad

Using the advertisements below, tell each of the following persons the name and time of a show he or she should watch.

Por ejemplo:

Gabriela: Me gustan los concursos.
Debes ver "Super Sábados" a las cuatro de la tarde.

1. Sarita: Me gustan los programas de mujeres.
2. Paco: Yo prefiero ver programas cómicos.

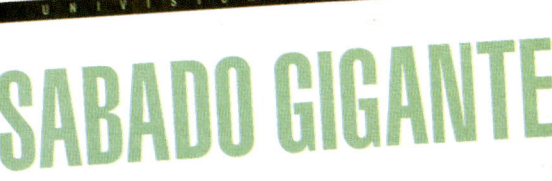

Cultura viva 1

Reading Strategies
1. Read the **Cultura viva** on this page.
2. You may wish to use the reading to discuss television programs with your students.

Did You Know?
A. **Univisión, Telemundo,** and **Galavisión** are the most important Spanish-language networks. Popular programs include sports and variety programs, movies, talk shows, sitcoms, news, and **telenovelas**.
B. Many of the programs in the U.S. are produced in a variety of Spanish-speaking countries. It is not unusual to watch a **telenovela** from Venezuela and a variety program from Puerto Rico in the same night.

Critical Thinking Activities
1. What are the advantages of being able to watch television in a foreign language?
2. Is there a Spanish-language station in your area? What channel is it? Check your local listings, and write down five programs you could watch in Spanish.

Actividad

Actividad Answers
1. Debes ver "Revista Femenina" de lunes a viernes a las tres de la tarde.
2. ... "Sábado Gigante" a las siete de la noche.

Learning from Realia
You may want to have students look at the realia on page 351. Ask students to give opinions of each of the programs (Eve, ¿qué te parece "TV mujer"?). Have them rank the programs from one to three, from most to least interesting.

Pronunciation

1. Use Pronunciation Transparency P-5.3.1, or write the pronunciation activity on the chalkboard. Have students copy it into their notebooks.
   En la tele hay muchos programas que quiero ver:
   "MTV internacional" y "TV mujer",
   "Lucha libre" y "El Show de cada día",
   "Hablemos del cine" y "La mujer policía".
2. You may wish to play the recorded version of this activity, located at the end of Cassette 5.3.
3. Have students repeat words and phrases individually and in unison. You may wish to focus on the following sound.
   /p/ programas; policía

Estructura 1

Structure Teaching Resources
1. Workbook, p. 157
2. Cassette 5.3
3. Student Tape Manual, p. 128
4. Estructura Masters 5.3
5. Lesson Quizzes, p. 103

Bell Ringer Review
Directions to students: Draw an outline map of the South American continent. Label the countries and their capitals. Write the nationality of the people who live in each country on the map.

Structure Focus
In this lesson students will learn how to give dates in terms of years, tell when they were born, say how long they have been doing certain activities, and use numbers to the millions.

Presentation
1. Lead students through steps 1–4 on page 352.
2. Ask students what year they were born. Write a few of the years on the board. Then ask students to read the years in Spanish.

Actividades

Actividad A Answers

1. g 3. c 5. f 7. a
2. e 4. b 6. d

Actividades B and C Answers
Answers will vary.

Additional Practice
After completing Actividades A, B, and C, you may wish to reinforce

---

Estructura 1

How to Give Dates and Count to a Million

You have learned to use numbers in the thousands.

> La computadora vale mil trescientos quince dólares.
> El coche vale diez mil dólares.

1. To tell the year of an event, use the numbers you have already learned. For example, the year 1997 would be the same as the number 1,997: **Mil novecientos noventa y siete.**

   Notice how to give various years in the twentieth century.

1963	mil novecientos sesenta y tres
1975	mil novecientos setenta y cinco
1980	mil novecientos ochenta

2. To give the year you were born, use **Nací en...**

   > Nací en 1978.
   > Nací en 1981.

3. To give the date on which you first started doing something, you use *activity* + **desde** + *date*.

   > Vivo en Orlando desde 1990.
   > Estudio español desde 1996.

4. A million is **un millón**. To state that there are a million of something, say **Hay un millón de...** To form the plural, add **-es** to **millón** and drop the accent mark.

   > Hay un millón de dólares en el banco.
   > Cuatro millones de personas viven en Madrid.

352 CAPÍTULO 5

LATINOS EN HOLLYWOOD
AHORA Y ANTES

Antonio Banderas
Mambo Kings, Philadelphia, Miami Rhapsody, Desperado, Assassins, Don't Talk to Strangers

Emilio Estevez
The Outsiders, The Breakfast Club, Stake Out, Stake Out II

Cameron Díaz
The Mask, Feeling Minnesota

Andy García
The Untouchables, Black Rain, Internal Affairs, When A Man Loves A Woman

Salma Hayek
Desperado, From Dusk Til Dawn

Raúl Julia
Kiss of the Spider Woman, Addams Family, Addams Family Values

Esai Morales
Bad Boys, La Bamba

Edward James Olmos
Stand and Deliver

Elizabeth Peña
Down and Out in Beverly Hills, La Bamba

Paul Rodríguez
DC Cab, Born in East LA

Charlie Sheen
Red Dawn, Platoon, Wall Street

Jimmy Smits
The Believers, Old Gringo, Mi Familia; Romero

Actividades

A Estudiante de historia. Tell the year in which each of the following events took place, choosing from the list on the right.

Por ejemplo:

independencia de los Estados Unidos
1776 (mil setecientos setenta y seis)

1. Los primeros hombres llegan a la luna (moon). a. 1492
2. asesinato del presidente Kennedy b. 1787
3. asesinato del presidente Lincoln c. 1865
4. Constitución de los Estados Unidos d. 1876
5. asesinato de Martin Luther King, Jr. e. 1963
6. Alexander Graham Bell inventa el teléfono. f. 1968
7. Cristóbal Colón llega a América. g. 1969

B ¿Desde cuándo? Tell how long you have been doing the following things.

Por ejemplo:

¿Desde cuándo vives aquí?
Vivo aquí desde 1988.

1. ¿Desde cuándo practicas tu deporte favorito?
2. ¿Desde cuándo estudias español?
3. ¿Desde cuándo sabes leer?
4. ¿Desde cuándo eres miembro de un club?
5. ¿Desde cuándo eres amigo(a) de *(nombre de la persona)*?

C Autos usados. A favorite relative is thinking of buying you a used car. Look at the ads to the right. Decide on a model you like, tell how much it costs, then tell the telephone number your relative needs to call for further information.

Por ejemplo:

Me gusta el Mazda. Vale ocho mil cincuenta dólares. Debes llamar al ocho, cincuenta y ocho, sesenta y ocho, treinta.

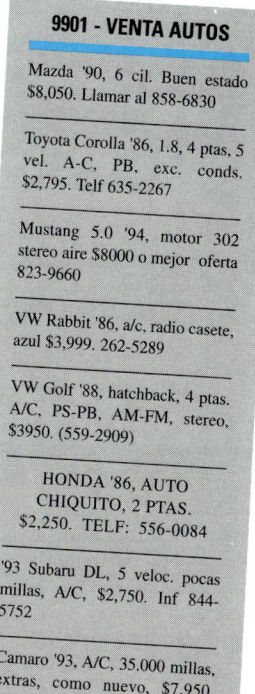

9901 - VENTA AUTOS

Mazda '90, 6 cil. Buen estado $8,050. Llamar al 858-6830

Toyota Corolla '86, 1.8, 4 ptas. 5 vel. A-C, PB, exc. conds. $2,795. Telf 635-2267

Mustang 5.0 '94, motor 302 stereo aire $8000 o mejor oferta 823-9660

VW Rabbit '86, a/c, radio casete, azul $3,999. 262-5289

VW Golf '88, hatchback, 4 ptas. A/C, PS-PB, AM-FM, stereo, $3950. (559-2909)

HONDA '86, AUTO CHIQUITO, 2 PTAS. $2,250. TELF: 556-0084

'93 Subaru DL, 5 veloc. pocas millas, A/C, $2,750. Inf 844-5752

Camaro '93, A/C, 35.000 millas, extras, como nuevo, $7,950. Telf. 860-1721

Cultura viva 2

Reading Strategies
1. Read the **Cultura viva** on this page. Have a different student read each sentence in Alicia's letter.
2. Have students identify and describe the people in the photos on page 354.
3. Have students take the role of Alicia's brother and write a response to the letter. Then have them compare their letter to the one on page 379.

Did You Know?
In writing letters, Hispanics tend to be more effusive and cordial than Americans are. When writing to friends and relatives, it is common to open with **Querido(a)...** or **Queridísmo(a)...** and to close with a phrase such as **Un fuerte abrazo de tu hijo (prima, tío, hermana que te quiere mucho...)**.

Critical Thinking Activity
Write a letter inviting someone you like very much to spend two weeks with you and your family. Use the letter in **Cultura viva 2** as a model.

Actividades

Actividad A Answers
1. hermanos
2. Cuba; Miami
3. está demasiado ocupado; descansar

Actividad B Answers
¿No fuiste al doctor? ¿Fuiste a...?

Learning from Photos
You may want to have students look at the photos on page 354. Have them describe each person physically. Then have them describe what the person appears to be like **(El tío Lucas parece...)**.

354

CULTURA VIVA 2

Una carta a la Argentina

La mamá de Carmen le escribe a su hermano Lucas, el papá de Rafael.

> Miami, 25 de marzo
>
> Querido hermano Lucas:
>
> Te escribo para saber cómo estás; ¿todavía estás enfermo? Estoy un poco preocupada por ti. ¿No fuiste al doctor? Sé que él te va a decir que trabajas demasiado y que necesitas descansar. ¿Por qué no descansas aquí en Miami? Y ¿por qué no vienes con Rafael? Aquí puede practicar el inglés y conocer a los amigos de Carmen.
>
> Bueno, hermanito, te mando un gran abrazo y una sincera invitación a nuestra casa. Todos esperamos tu visita. Hasta entonces te manda un fuerte abrazo
>
> tu hermana que te quiere,
>
> Alicia

Actividades

A Tell about the person writing the letter and the person who will receive it by choosing the appropriate words in parentheses.

1. Alicia y Lucas son (hermanos / primos).
2. Alicia es de (la Argentina / Cuba) pero vive en (Miami / Buenos Aires).
3. Alicia cree que Lucas (está demasiado ocupado / es muy listo) y que debe (trabajar más / descansar).

B Give the sentence that Alicia uses to ask if Lucas went somewhere. Ask a classmate if he or she went somewhere (movies, game, mall, etc.) last Saturday.

354 CAPÍTULO 5

Estructura 2

How to Say Where People Went — **The preterit of** *ir*

1. To say where people went, use forms of the verb **ir** in the past (preterit) tense. Here are the forms of the verb you will need to talk about different people.

SINGULAR	PLURAL
fui	fuimos
fuiste	fuisteis*
fue	fueron

   *This form is rarely used in the Spanish-speaking world, except for Spain.

2. To ask where someone went, use **¿adónde?**

   ¿Adónde fueron ustedes anoche?   Fuimos al centro.

3. To say you went somewhere to do something, use **ir** + **a** + place + **a** + infinitive.

   ¿Fuiste a casa a descansar? No, fui a la piscina a nadar.

4. The following are words and phrases you can use to talk about various times in the past.

ayer	la semana pasada	el lunes (martes,
anoche	el año pasado	etc.) pasado

Actividades

A Lugares. Tell three places you went last week and three places you have to go next week.

Por ejemplo:

La semana pasada fui a _____.
La semana que viene tengo que ir a _____.

Lección 3 **355**

Actividad D Answers

1. El 24 de febrero fue a Disneyworld y Epcot Center con su familia.
2. El 5 de abril fue a una fiesta de cumpleaños con los compañeros de clase a las tres y media.
3. El 15 de mayo fue al concierto de Gloria Estefan con Jorge a las ocho.
4. El 12 de octubre fue al desfile del Día de la Raza con su mamá, papá y sus tíos a las doce y cuarto.
5. El 25 de noviembre fue a la casa de los abuelos.
6. El 30 de diciembre fue al concierto de Julio Iglesias con Carlos a las dos y media.

Additional Practice

After completing Actividades A, B, C, D, and E, you may wish to reinforce the lesson by doing the following activity.
Tell where you went, and with whom, during three school vacations last year.
Por ejemplo:
las vacaciones de noviembre
El año pasado en las vacaciones de noviembre, fui a casa de mis tíos con mi familia.

Reteaching

Have students tell a classmate three places that he or she went during three different years. The classmate will ask the year they went to each place. Then reverse roles.
Por ejemplo:
Estudiante A: Fui a Disneyworld.
Estudiante B: ¿En qué año fuiste?
Estudiante A: Fui en 1989.

B **¿Adónde fue el maestro?** With a classmate, make a list of five places you think your teacher went after school yesterday. Read your list to your teacher, who will say whether you're right or wrong.

Por ejemplo:

¿Fue usted anoche a una fiesta a bailar?

C **Mi compañero y yo.** Have a classmate tell you three places he or she went yesterday. Then report back to the class, comparing where you went to where your classmate went.

Por ejemplo:

ESTUDIANTE A	ESTUDIANTE B
(1) ¿Adónde fuiste ayer?	(2) Fui a un partido.
(3) ¿Y luego?	(4) Fui al centro comercial.

(A la clase:) Pam fue ayer a un partido y luego al centro comercial. Yo fui a casa y después a la piscina. Anoche los (las) dos fuimos al cine.

D **El diario de Carmen.** To the right are some of the headings of Carmen's diary last year. Tell the places she went, the things she did, and when she did them.

Por ejemplo:

El 22 de enero fue al Carnaval con Jorge a las siete.

E **Mi conjunto.** You are part of a rock group touring Latin America and the U.S. Give your group a name. Tell a classmate six places where you and your group went. Your classmate will report back to the class.

Por ejemplo:

Somos "Las Serpientes" y somos muy populares. El mes pasado fuimos a Buenos Aires, Santiago...

(A la clase:) El mes pasado "Las Serpientes" fueron a Buenos Aires, Santiago...

356 CAPÍTULO 5

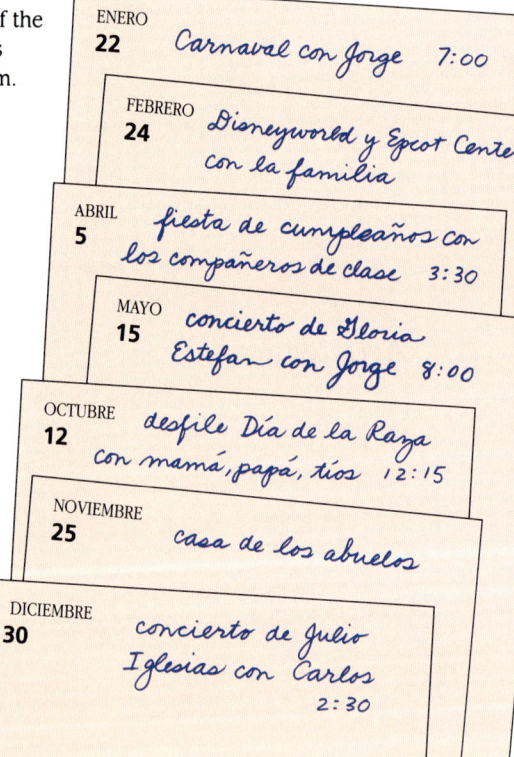

ENERO 22 — Carnaval con Jorge 7:00
FEBRERO 24 — Disneyworld y Epcot Center con la familia
ABRIL 5 — fiesta de cumpleaños con los compañeros de clase 3:30
MAYO 15 — concierto de Gloria Estefan con Jorge 8:00
OCTUBRE 12 — desfile Día de la Raza con mamá, papá, tíos 12:15
NOVIEMBRE 25 — casa de los abuelos
DICIEMBRE 30 — concierto de Julio Iglesias con Carlos 2:30

Finalmente

Situaciones

A conversar Converse with a classmate about a memorable trip you once took. Reverse roles.

1. Tell where you went, with whom, and give the month and year of the trip. Ask if your partner knows where the place is.
2. Tell your partner why he or she should go there.

A escribir Write a letter of application to a pen pal club; include the following information.

1. Tell what nationality the pen pal should be.
2. Tell where you live. Give your date of birth.
3. Describe your appearance and your personality.
4. Tell about the activities you like to do in your free time.

Repaso de vocabulario

TIEMPOS EN EL PASADO
anoche
el año pasado
ayer
el lunes (martes, etc.) pasado
el mes pasado
la semana pasada

NACIONALIDADES
alemán, alemana
argentino(a)
boliviano(a)
canadiense
colombiano(a)
costarricense
cubano(a)
chileno(a)
chino(a)
dominicano(a)
ecuatoriano(a)
español, española
estadounidense (norteamericano[a])
francés, francesa
guatemalteco(a)
hondureño(a)
inglés, inglesa
italiano(a)
japonés, japonesa
mexicano(a)
nicaragüense
panameño(a)
paraguayo(a)
peruano(a)
puertorriqueño(a)
ruso(a)
salvadoreño(a)
uruguayo(a)
venezolano(a)

IDIOMAS
el alemán
el chino
el italiano
el japonés
el ruso

OTRAS PALABRAS
desde
un millón de
nací

Lección 3 357

Finalmente

Situaciones

Lesson 3 Evaluation
The **A conversar** and **A escribir** situations on this page are designed to give students the opportunity to use as many language functions and as much vocabulary from this lesson as possible. The **A conversar** and **A escribir** are also intended to show how well students are able to meet the lesson objectives.

Presentation

Prior to doing the **A conversar** and **A escribir** on this page, you may wish to play the **Situaciones** listening activities on Cassette 5.3 as a means of helping students organize the material.

Note. Before administering Capítulo 5, Lecciones 1–3 Test, refer students to ¿Recuerdas? Lecciones 1–3, on page 400.

For the Native Speaker

Have native speakers make a list of twenty-five words in "Spanglish". Have them find out the correct Spanish for each term.

CAPÍTULO 5

Lección 4

Objectives

By the end of this lesson, students will be able to:

1. say with whom they do things
2. say what belongs to them and others

Lesson 4 Resources
1. Workbook, pp. 160–164
2. Vocabulario Transparencies
3. Pronunciation Transparency P-5.4.1
4. Audio Cassette 5.4 Compact Disc 8
5. Student Tape Manual, pp. 131–134
6. Bell Ringer Review Blackline Masters, p. 32
7. Computer Software: Practice & Test Generator
8. Video (cassette or disc)
9. Video Activities Booklet, pp. A71–A72
10. Estructura Masters, pp. 64–65
11. Diversiones Masters, pp. 61–62
12. Situation Cards
13. Lesson Quizzes, pp. 106–109
14. Testing Program

Bell Ringer Review

Directions to students: Copy the following countries on your paper. Beside each country write the language(s) spoken there.

Japón	China
Alemania	Italia
Inglaterra	Canadá
Rusia	Francia
los Estados Unidos	Perú
	España

CAPÍTULO 5

Lección 4

Nuestro idioma

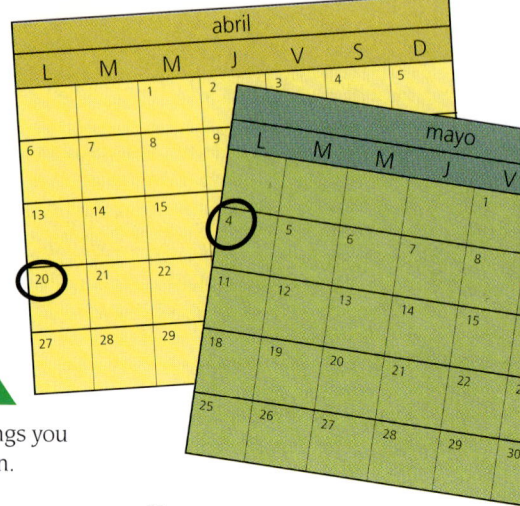

¡A comenzar!

The following are some of the things you will be learning to do in this lesson.

When you want to...	You use...
1. say "with me"	conmigo
2. say "with you" to a friend or family member	contigo
3. talk about what belongs to you and someone else ("our")	nuestro(a)

Now find examples of the above words and phrases in the following conversation.

358

Getting Ready for Lesson 4

You may wish to use of the following suggestions to prepare students for the lesson.

1. Talk about what you and your family do at the beach during your vacation. Use gestures or bring in photos or pictures from magazines to help illustrate your narration.
   Durante las vacaciones me gusta ir a la playa con mi familia pero no me gusta bucear. Prefiero practicar el esquí acuático con mi primo. A él no le gusta ir de pesca conmigo porque dice que es aburrido. También paseo en velero y tomo el sol. Nuestras vacaciones son muy divertidas.
2. Ask students where they can go to do the activities you mentioned above.

Carmen habla con su mamá.

CARMEN: Mamá, ¿me puedes explicar por qué papá está enojado conmigo?

MAMÁ: No está enojado contigo, Carmen. Es otra cosa. En nuestra casa todos tenemos que hablar español.

CARMEN: Claro, entiendo, pero...

MAMÁ: Y tienes que practicar porque tu tío y tu primo llegan de la Argentina el 20 de abril. Con ellos en casa, debes hablar nuestro idioma.

CARMEN: ¿Tío Lucas y mi primo Rafael? ¡Qué bueno! ¿Cuánto tiempo van a pasar con nosotros?

MAMÁ: Hasta el 4 de mayo — dos semanas. ¿No viste su carta?

Actividades preliminares

A Complete the following conversation between Carmen and her friend Carlos, using **conmigo** and **contigo**.

CARLOS: ¿Quieres ir al concierto el sábado?

CARMEN: Lo siento, no puedo ir _____ el sábado porque tengo que trabajar.

CARLOS: ¿Quieres ir al parque _____ el domingo a ver el partido?

CARMEN: Gracias por la invitacíon, pero tengo que estudiar para el examen de computadoras. No puedo ir _____ el domingo tampoco.

CARLOS: Carmen, ¿no quieres salir _____?

CARMEN: Ay, Carlos. Claro que quiero salir _____. ¿Por qué no vamos al cine el viernes?

B Complete this sentence to tell what people in your house have to do:

En nuestra casa todos tenemos que _____.

¡A comenzar!

Presentation

A. Lead students through each of the three functions given on page 358, progressing from the English to the Spanish for each function. Then have students find these words and phrases in the dialogue on page 359.

B. Introduce the Lesson 4 dialogue by reading it aloud or by playing the recorded version. Have students listen to the tape of the Lesson 4 dialogue to find out the following.
1. What advice does Carmen's mother give her?
2. What event is going to take place?

C. Now ask students to open their books and look at the dialogue as you lead them through what is said. For example:
1. Carmen quiere saber algo. ¿Qué dice?
2. La mamá de Carmen explica que Carmen está equivocada. ¿Qué dice?
3. En la casa de los Marín todos tienen que hacer algo. ¿Qué tienen que hacer?
4. ¿Por qué tiene que practicar español Carmen?
5. Su mamá dice: "En casa todos tenemos que hablar nuestro idioma". ¿Qué idioma?
6. ¿Cómo se llama el tío? ¿Y el primo?
7. ¿Dónde viven? ¿Cuándo llegan? ¿Cuándo regresan a Argentina? ¿Cuánto tiempo van a pasar en Miami?

Actividades preliminares

Actividad A Answers
1. contigo
2. conmigo
3. contigo
4. conmigo
5. contigo

Actividad B Answers
Answers will vary.

Vocabulario

Vocabulary Teaching Resources
1. Vocabulario Transparencies 5.4
2. Workbook, pp. 160–161
3. Cassette 5.4
4. Student Tape Manual, p. 131
5. Lesson Quizzes, pp. 106–107

Bell Ringer Review
Directions to students: Draw a large circle, rectangle, and square on your paper. Inside each shape write in Spanish the names of as many things as you can think of that have that shape.

Presentation
Have students open their books to page 360.
1. Model each new word and phrase on pages 360 and 361.
2. Ask individual students whether or not they like or know how to do the activities listed. For example: **¿Te gusta (Sabes) bucear?** Encourage students to give a complete response. For example: **Me gusta bucear.**

When Students Ask
The following additional vocabulary may be provided to allow students to talk about other beach-related activities.
la vela
la regata
la arena
el bote de motor
la barca
la loción
la tabla de velero
el castillo de arena

Vocabulario

Te invito a mi casa.

¿Vas a pasar dos semanas con nosotros? ¡Qué bueno!

Voy a planear una semana estupenda.

Vamos a ir a la playa y tomar el sol.

También podemos saltar las olas.

Total Physical Response

Getting Ready
For TPR 1 use pictures of the various locations and activities listed in the **Vocabulario** or sketch each one on a separate sheet of paper. Display them around the room.
For TPR 2 make a grid, dividing a sheet of paper into four columns and three rows (twelve squares) and labeling them **fila** and **columna**. Make copies and give one to every student.
Display the grids around the room. Working in teams, students will write down the activities they would like to to when they go to the beach.

TPR 1
Ve a la playa.
Saca fotos del concierto.

Te puedo enseñar a...

practicar el esquí acuático

También podemos ir de pesca en el mar.

bucear

pasear en velero

No necesitas gastar mucho dinero.

Podemos asistir a conciertos y a fiestas por la noche.

Regionalisms

You may wish to tell students that in some parts of the Spanish-speaking world, the following words or phrases are alternatives to those presented in the vocabulario.

pasear en velero (pasear en barco de vela)
practicar el esquí acuático (practicar el esquí naútico)

Actividades

Actividades A and B Answers
Answers will vary but should follow the model.

Actividad C Answers
Answers will vary but should include the following.
1. Vamos a planear...
2. Va a ser el... a la(s)... Va a ser en...
3. Vamos a pasar...
4. Necesitamos llevar...
5. Podemos...

Additional Practice
After completing Actividades A, B, and C, you may wish to reinforce the learning with the following. Invite a classmate to do one of the activities in the **Vocabulario**. Your classmate will either accept or reject your invitation and give an explanation.
Por ejemplo:

ESTUDIANTE A	ESTUDIANTE B
(1) ¿Te gusta ir a la playa?	(2) Sí, por qué?
(3) ¿Quieres ir el sábado?	(4) ¡Estupendo! (El sábado no puedo. Tengo que cuidar a mi hermano menor).

Reteaching

Have students open their books to page 360. Write two columns on the board: **Adentro podemos...** and **Afuera podemos...** Have students write each of the activities pictured under the appropriate column.

Actividades

A **Sé hacer muchas cosas.** Tell whether you know how to do the following activities. If you don't know how to do something, say whether you want to learn how.

Por ejemplo:
  jugar ajedrez

ESTUDIANTE A	ESTUDIANTE B
(1) ¿Sabes jugar ajedrez?	(2) No, no sé. ¿Y tú?
(3) Sí. Si quieres, te puedo enseñar.	(4) Gracias, quiero aprender. (No, gracias, no me gusta).

1. ir de pesca
2. practicar el esquí acuático
3. pasear en velero
4. bucear
5. saltar las olas
6. cuidar niños pequeños

B **¿Qué te gusta hacer?** Converse with a classmate about whether you like or dislike doing the following activities. If you dislike an activity, tell what you prefer to do. Reverse roles.

Por ejemplo:
  cantar

ESTUDIANTE A	ESTUDIANTE B
¿Te gusta cantar?	Sí, me gusta mucho. (No, no me gusta. Prefiero bailar).

1. ir al mar
2. asistir a conciertos
3. tomar el sol
4. pasar unos días con tus parientes
5. gastar dinero
6. planear fiestas

C **Un plan estupendo.** You and a classmate are in charge of planning one of the following activities at school: **una fiesta / una excursión / un baile / un viaje / un partido.** Write the details of the event by answering the questions below. Report to the class.

1. ¿Qué clase de actividad van a planear?
2. ¿Cuándo va a ser? ¿Dónde?
3. ¿Cuánto tiempo van a pasar allí tus compañeros?
4. ¿Qué necesitan llevar?
5. ¿Qué pueden hacer?

For the Native Speaker

Imagine that you have been shipwrecked on a desert island. Answer the following questions in Spanish.

1. Who is shipwrecked with you?
2. How long will both of you be there?
3. Who will rescue you?
4. What will you do on the island (for example: fish, sunbathe, swim)?

CULTURA VIVA 1

Cuba linda

Cuba es la más grande de las islas del Caribe. Es una isla tropical de gran belleza natural. Hay muchas playas bonitas como Varadero en la costa norte. También tiene valles y bahías preciosos y puertos excelentes.

La Habana, la capital, es la ciudad más grande del país. También es un puerto muy importante.

España gobernó a Cuba de 1492 a 1898. Los españoles llamaron a Cuba la "llave del Golfo". Durante la época colonial de Cuba salían barcos llenos de oro, plata, café, azúcar, especias y otros productos importantes de las Américas.

Actividades

A Which of the following could be said about where you live?

1. Tiene un clima tropical.
2. Hay playas bonitas.
3. Es una isla.
4. Tiene montañas y valles.
5. Hay puertos importantes.

B Which of the following words are *not* related to the ocean?

el puerto   la isla
el barco   la bahía
el azúcar   el golfo
la costa   el valle

C What does the phrase **"la llave del Golfo"** refer to?

a. Cuba's key location in the Caribbean
b. the wealth of the island
c. a beautiful bay

Lección 4   363

Pronunciation

1. Use Pronunciation Transparency P-5.4.1, or write the pronunciation activity on the chalkboard. Have students copy it into their notebooks.
   **Yo soy un hombre sincero
   de donde crece la palma,
   y antes de morirme quiero
   echar mis versos del alma.**
   ("Versos sencillos" by José Martí, poeta cubano, 1853–1895)
2. You may wish to play the recorded version of this activity, located at the end of Cassette 5.4.
3. Have students repeat words and phrases individually and in unison. You may also want to play the song "Guantanamera" by the Sandpipers, which features this verse.

Cultura viva 1

Reading Strategies

1. Have students locate Cuba on the map on page 1. Point out Cuba's close proximity to the U.S.
2. Read the **Cultura viva** on this page. Then do the **Actividades**.

Did You Know?

Often called the "Pearl of the Antilles," Cuba is located about 90 miles from the southern tip of Florida. Havana is the largest city and its commercial and industrial center. It is also the largest and one of the oldest cities in the the West Indies. About twenty percent of the Cuban population lives in Havana.

Critical Thinking Activity

Why is Cuba called the "Pearl of the Antilles?"

Actividades

Actividad A Answers
Answers will vary.

Actividad B Answers
el azúcar, la isla, el valle

Actividad C Answer
a

Learning from Photos and Maps

You may want to have students look at the photo and map on page 363. Have them tell what kinds of activities Cubans who go to **la playa de Varadero** can do. Have students look at the map and locate Florida. Also have them identify the other islands to the south, east, and northeast of Cuba (Jamaica; Haiti and the Dominican Republic; the Bahamas).

Estructura 1

Structure Teaching Resources
1. Workbook, p. 162
2. Cassette 5.4
3. Student Tape Manual, p. 132
4. Estructura Masters 5.4
5. Lesson Quizzes, p. 108

Bell Ringer Review

Directions to students: Make four columns on your paper: **mar, lago, río,** and **piscina.** Then list each of the following activities under the appropriate column, according to where you would be likely to do each activity. Some activities might appear in more than one column.
bucear
ir de pesca
pasear en velero
nadar
saltar las olas
tomar el sol
practicar el esquí acuático

Structure Focus

In this lesson **nuestro(s)/ nuestra(s)** will be presented. Students will learn how to say what they and others possess in common.

Learning from Realia

You may want to have students look at the realia on page 364. Have students guess at the meaning of "cariño." You may also have them write a brief message for the inside of the card.

Presentation

A. Lead students through the explanation on page 364.

B. Ask students for various items belonging to them. Add some that belong to you. Display items around the room. Ask questions such as: ¿Dónde están nuestros lápices? ¿Cómo es nuestro libro?

Estructura 1

How to Say What People Possess — **Nuestro(s)/Nuestra(s)**

You have learned to say what is yours, his, hers, and theirs, using **mi, tu,** and **su** to describe one possession and **mis, tus,** and **sus** to describe several.

> Mi papá está enfermo.
> ¿Cómo están tus padres?
> Señora, ¿cómo está su hija?

You have also indicated what belongs to someone else by using **de** + person.

> Es la camiseta de Fernando.
> Me gustan las clases del señor García.

When you want to talk about what you and someone else have, use **nuestro, nuestra, nuestros,** or **nuestras,** depending on what or whom you are describing.

> En nuestra casa debemos hablar español.
> Nuestros padres son cubanos.
> Nuestro maestro de inglés es del Canadá.

The following chart summarizes how to say what people possess.

SINGULAR	PLURAL
mi casa	mis padres
tu casa	tus cosas
su maestro	sus clases
nuestro tío	nuestros discos
nuestra tía	nuestras clases

En Tu Cumpleaños, Mamá
CON NUESTRO CARIÑO

364 CAPÍTULO 5

Actividades

A **Somos amigos.** Think of a friend whose likes are similar to yours. Write down your and your friend's favorite people and things, using the categories below.

Por ejemplo:

> un deporte
> *Nuestro deporte favorito es el béisbol.*

1. un programa de televisión
2. un equipo
3. una comida
4. una clase
5. una película
6. un disco
7. un conjunto musical
8. un/a cantante
9. un actor
10. una actriz

B **Un extranjero.** A visitor from Argentina comes to your class and asks all about your town, school, and Spanish class. Respond to the questions, either as a class or in groups.

Una fiesta de cumpleaños en Buenos Aires.
¿Cuántos años tiene el niño?

Por ejemplo:

> En su clase de español, ¿qué hacen?
> *En nuestra clase leemos, hablamos y estudiamos.*

1. En su ciudad, ¿qué hay?
2. En sus fiestas, ¿qué hacen?
3. En sus clubes, ¿qué hacen?
4. En su estado, ¿cuáles son las ciudades más grandes? ¿las ciudades más divertidas?
5. En su escuela, ¿cuántos estudiantes hay?

Actividades

Actividad A Answers
Answers will vary but should include the following.

1. Nuestro programa favorito...
2. Nuestro equipo favorito...
3. Nuestra comida favorita...
4. Nuestra clase favorita...
5. Nuestra película favorita...
6. Nuestro disco favorito...
7. Nuestro conjunto favorito...
8. Nuestro(a) cantante favorito(a)...
9. Nuestro actor favorito...
10. Nuestra actriz favorita...

Actividad B Answers
Answers will vary but should include the following.

1. En nuestra ciudad...
2. En nuestras fiestas...
3. En nuestros clubes...
4. En nuestro estado...
5. En nuestra escuela...

Learning from Photos

You may want to have students look at the photo on page 365. Have them tell who they think each of the people in the photo is in terms of family relations.

Reteaching

Have students imagine that a friend from out of town is visiting them. Have them tell him or her what things are found in their school and what there school is like. For example: **En nuestra escuela hay una biblioteca grande y moderna.**

Cultura viva 2

Reading Strategies
Read the **Cultura viva** on this page. If possible, bring in additional photos of Argentina from books, magazines or media sources.

Did You Know?
The **gaucho** was usually of mixed Spanish and Indian blood. He was an excellent horseman and spent most of his time on horseback. His costume consisted of baggy pants, silver belt, and a bright scarf. In the early days he made his living by selling the hides of wild horses. His weapon was the **bola,** a type of sling consisting of heavy balls tied to the ends of a cord. It was thrown to entangle and capture cattle or game. During the 1800s, the **gaucho** became a symbol of the Argentine nation and its values.

The **gaucho's** way of life ended with the invention of refrigerated ships, which facilitated the rapid development of the international meat industry. Today, day laborers have largely replaced the **gauchos** in Argentina.

Critical Thinking Activity
What are the differences and similarities between the American cowboy and the **gaucho**?

Actividades

Actividad A and B Answers
Answers will vary.

Actividad C Answers
Answers will vary but may include the following.
1. En Argentina hay muchos inmigrantes. En los Estados Unidos también hay muchos inmigrantes.
2. Como en Argentina, gran parte del territorio norteamericano es una extensa "pampa".

CULTURA VIVA 2

La Argentina

Los parientes de Carmen viven en la Argentina, en Sudamérica. La Argentina es el país más grande del mundo hispano. Tiene una población de unos 31 millones de habitantes y 14 o 15 millones de ellos viven en el área metropolitana de Buenos Aires, la capital del país.

Como los Estados Unidos, la Argentina es un país de inmigrantes. Los inmigrantes forman el 95 por ciento de la población nacional. Son principalmente de Europa: Italia, Alemania, Rusia, Polonia, Hungría, Inglaterra, Irlanda e Escocia.

Gran parte del territorio argentino es una extensa pampa, donde hay grandes haciendas, en que trabajan los gauchos —los vaqueros o "cowboys" argentinos.

Actividades

A Describe the region where you live: **una ciudad grande / la capital del estado (del país) / el campo / las afueras** (suburbs) **de una ciudad.**

B Which is the principal group of immigrants in your area?

Por ejemplo:
   Hay muchos _____ donde yo vivo.

C Tell one thing that Argentina has in common with the U.S.

Por ejemplo:
   En la Argentina _____. También en los Estados Unidos _____.

En Buenos Aires.

En la pampa.

366 CAPÍTULO 5

Estructura 2

How to Say with Whom You Do Things — **The preposition con**

1. To say with whom you do something, use the word **con** and the name of the person or the appropriate pronoun (him, her, you, them, us).

SINGULAR	PLURAL
conmigo	con nosotros(as)
contigo	con vosotros(as)*
con Juan (con él)	con mis amigos (con ellos)
con María (con ella)	con mis hermanas (con ellas)
con usted	con ustedes

*This form is rarely used in the Spanish-speaking world, except for Spain.

2. Notice that to say "with me" and "with you" (a friend), you use **conmigo** and **contigo**.

   ¿Quieres ir al cine conmigo?   Sí, gracias.
   ¿José va contigo al partido?   No, no puede.

3. To ask "with whom?", say **¿con quién?**

   ¿Con quién fuiste al cine anoche?   Fui con Marilú.

Actividades

A ¿Con los amigos o con la familia?
Name six places you like to go or things you like to do with others.

Por ejemplo:

>hablar por teléfono
>*Me gusta hablar por teléfono con mi amiga Eva.*

Una familia argentina que vive en el campo.

Lección 4 367

Actividad B Answers

Answers will vary but should include the following.

1. ... con ella...
2. ... con él....
3. ... con ella...
4. ... con ellos...
5. ... con ellos...
6. ... con él...

Actividad C Answers

1. ¿Por qué están enojados conmigo?
2. ¿Por qué tengo que ir al banco contigo?
3. ¿Por qué no puedo ir al centro contigo?
4. ¿Por qué no debo salir con él?
5. ¿Puedo ir al cine con ustedes?
6. Julia, ¿quieres ir conmigo al concierto?

Actividad D Answers

Answers will vary.

Learning from Photos

You may want to have students look at the photos on page 368. Have them describe several of the young people in the photos in terms of physical appearance and personality. For example: **En la foto de arriba, el muchacho a la izquierda es... Parece...**) You may also have them guess what each of the people likes to do in his or her free time.

Reteaching

Have students invite each other to do three things. They will either accept or reject the invitations.

B **¿Con quién?** Tell things you do with the following people and pets.

Por ejemplo:

tu hermano
Juego tenis con él los domingos.

1. tu amiga
2. tu amigo
3. tu mamá
4. tus padres
5. tus primos
6. tu perro (gato, caballo, etc.)

C **¿Qué dices?** What would you say in response to each of the following situations?

Por ejemplo:

Tu amigo te dice que no puede ir contigo a la fiesta.
(A tu amigo:) *¿Por qué no puedes ir conmigo a la fiesta?*

1. Tus padres están enojados contigo y no sabes por qué.
2. Tu mamá dice que tienes que ir al banco con ella pero no quieres.
3. Tu hermana mayor dice que no puedes ir al centro con ella.
4. No sabes por qué tus padres te dicen que no debes salir con Bruno.
5. Tus primos van a ver una película estupenda y quieres ir con ellos.
6. Quieres invitar a Julia a ir contigo al concierto.

D **¿Quieren ir conmigo?** Work in groups of three or four. One person in the group will invite the others to do something after school or on the weekend. Another person will report back to the class.

Por ejemplo:

ESTUDIANTE A	ESTUDIANTE B
¿Quieren ir al cine conmigo?	Sí, cómo no.

ESTUDIANTE C

No puedo ir contigo. Tengo que trabajar.
(A la clase:) Todd y Alicia van a ir al cine pero Julie dice que no puede ir con ellos porque tiene que trabajar.

Unos estudiantes argentinos.

Finalmente

Situaciones

A conversar

1. Your partner will invite you to go someplace with him or her.
2. If you've already gone there, tell when. If you haven't gone, ask what the place is like. Also find out what the two of you can do there.
3. Decide on a day and time for your visit.

A escribir Write a letter to a friend inviting him or her to go with you to the beach this summer (**este verano**).

1. Tell where you plan to go.
2. Tell when you will leave, how much time you will spend there, and when you will return.
3. Tell all the activities that the two of you can do at the beach.
4. Ask if your friend already knows how to do several water activities.
5. Tell what activities you can teach him or her to do, or that you both can learn to do.

Repaso de vocabulario

PREGUNTA
¿cuánto tiempo?

POSESIÓN
nuestro(a)

ACTIVIDADES
asistir a
bucear
enseñar a (to teach how to)
gastar (dinero)
invitar (a)
ir de pesca
pasar (tiempo)
pasear en velero
planear
practicar el esquí acuático
saltar las olas
tomar el sol

OTRAS PALABRAS Y EXPRESIONES
conmigo
contigo
estupendo(a)
el mar

Lección 4 369

Finalmente

Situaciones

Lesson 4 Evaluation
The A conversar and A escribir situations on this page are designed to give students the opportunity to use as many language functions and as much vocabulary in this lesson as possible. the A conversar and A escribir are also intended to show how well students are able to meet the lesson objectives.

Presentation

Prior to doing the A conversar and A escribir on this page, you may wish to play the Situaciones listening activities on Cassette 5.4 as a means of helping students organize the material.

For the Native Speaker

Have students make up invitations to a party they will give this weekend. They must come up with a theme and answer when, why, what, where, etc. You may wish to display invitations on a bulletin board.

CAPÍTULO 5

Lección 5

Objectives

By the end of this lesson, students will be able to:

1. say how long they and others have been doing something
2. correct themselves as they speak, using "**digo,...**"
3. say what they did at one point in the past
4. tell or ask a friend or relative what he or she did
5. report what someone says or hears
6. say what they and others request

Lesson 5 Resources

1. Workbook, pp. 165–169
2. Vocabulario Transparencies
3. Pronunciation Transparency P-5.5.1
4. Audio Cassette 5.5 Compact Disc 8
5. Student Tape Manual, pp. 135–139
6. Bell Ringer Review Blackline Masters, p. 33
7. Computer Software: Practice & Test Generator
8. Video (cassette or disc)
9. Video Activities Booklet, pp. A73–A74
10. Estructura Masters, pp. 66–68
11. Diversiones Masters, pp. 63–64
12. Situation Cards
13. Lesson Quizzes, pp. 110–113
14. Testing Program

¡A comenzar!

Presentation

A. Lead students through each of the four functions given on page *(continued)*

CAPÍTULO 5

Lección 5

Somos todos americanos

Los cubanos llegan de Cuba a Miami en

¡A comenzar!

The following are some of the things you will be learning to do in this lesson.

When you want to...	You use...
1. say how long someone has been doing something	**Hace** + time + **que** + activity.
2. correct yourself as you speak	**Digo**...
3. say what you did	**-í** on the end of **-er** and **-ir** verbs
4. tell a friend or relative what he or she did	**-iste** on the end of **-er** and **-ir** verbs

Now find examples of the above words and phrases in the following conversation.

370

Cooperative Learning

Carmen's intermingling of English and Spanish words is called "codeswitching." After completing Actividad preliminar B, have teams come up with other examples of codeswitching. Have teams cut up strips of paper. On one strip they write a Spanish word and on another its English equivalent. Then distribute the various strips around the room and have students match up the English and Spanish words. For example:

ESTUDIANTE A	ESTUDIANTE B
"Milk."	Digo, leche.

Carmen habla con su mamá.

CARMEN: Mamá, no me molesta practicar el español, ¿entiendes? Pero hace más de treinta años que ustedes están aquí. Tú saliste de Cuba en el sesenta y tres, y papá en el sesenta y cuatro.

MAMÁ: Sí, hija. Salí de Cuba en el sesenta y tres, pero nací en la isla y allí viví diez y seis años.

CARMEN: Pero yo nací aquí en la Florida y aquí aprendí a hablar inglés. Somos todos "Americans", digo, americanos. ¿Por qué es tan importante el español?

Actividades preliminares

A Complete the sentences below to tell how many days, months, or years you have been doing the following.

1. Hace _____ que vivo aquí.
2. Hace _____ que estudio español.
3. Hace _____ que me gusta la música de _____.

B Carmen continually mixes English with her Spanish. Help her correct herself in the following sentences.

Por ejemplo:

Somos todos "Americans".
Somos todos "Americans", digo, americanos.

1. Mira, papá, quiero comprar estas dos "T-shirts".
2. Son de puro "cotton".
3. Estamos aquí desde "nineteen sixty-three".
4. Me gusta mucho la clase de "computers".
5. ¿Me prestas la "magazine" nueva?

370, progressing from the English to the Spanish for each function. Then have students find these words and phrases in the dialogue on page 371.

B. Introduce the Lesson 5 dialogue by reading it aloud or by playing the recorded version. Have students listen to determine
   1. when Carmen's mother came to the U.S.
   2. why Carmen does not understand her mother's concern.

C. Have students open their books and look at the dialogue as you lead them through what is said. For example:
   1. ¿Cuándo tiempo hace que los Marín viven en los Estados Unidos?
   2. ¿Qué dice Carmen a su mamá?
   3. Su mamá está de acuerdo con Carmen. ¿Qué dice?
   4. Carmen, sin embargo, es de otro país. ¿Qué dice?
   5. Para Carmen, todos en la familia son americanos. Por eso, ¿qué le pregunta a su mamá?

D. Have students summarize what Carmen says, what her mother says, and what her father says.
   1. Carmen dice que...
   2. Su mamá dice que...
   3. Su papá dice que...

Actividades preliminares

Actividad A Answers
Answers will vary.

Actividad B Answers
1. ... digo, camisetas.
2. ... digo, algodón.
3. ... digo, mil novecientos sesenta y tres.
4. ... digo, computadoras.
5. ... digo, revista.

Getting Ready for Lesson 5

You may wish to use the following suggestion to prepare students for the lesson.
Think of some recent events or activities in your life. Give students a visual organizer such as a grid or list of events. For example:
1. el cine 2. el tenis 3. el viaje a México

Use a preponderance of **-er** and **-ir** verbs in describing the above activities so students can get accustomed to the sound of the stressed **-í** ending: **salir, ir, ver, aprender, correr, comer, abrir, escribir,** etc. Students will record the date of each event or place. For example:
En abril del año pasado fui con un grupo de estudiantes de la escuela a México.

Vocabulario

Vocabulary Teaching Resources
1. Vocabulario Transparencies 5.5
2. Workbook, p. 165
3. Cassette 5.5
4. Student Tape Manual, p. 135
5. Lesson Quizzes, p. 110

Bell Ringer Review

Directions to students: With whom did you go to the following places last year? Choose five and write a complete sentence about each one. Begin with **Fui**. Add a date if you wish.
Por ejemplo: el mar
Fui al mar con mi papá.
Fuimos en agosto.
un concierto
la piscina
un partido de baloncesto
la playa
un partido de fútbol americano
la biblioteca
el parque
la fiesta de tus amigos

Presentation

A. Have students open their books to page 372.
  1. Model each new phrase on pages 372 and 373. Have students repeat each phrase in unison.
  2. Ask individual students the following questions, allowing them to answer with just the time period **(dos meses, tres años, media hora, etc.)**.
     ¿Cuánto tiempo hace que...
     a. haces cola?
     b. juegas en el equipo de baloncesto (vóleibol, tenis, etc.)?

Vocabulario

¿Cuánto tiempo hace que...?

Hace catorce años que estamos aquí.
(de 1977 a 1991)

Hace tres días que estoy enferma.
(lunes, martes, miércoles)

Hace mucho tiempo que conozco* a Paco.

Hace poco tiempo que la señorita Chávez conoce a sus vecinos.
(del 2 de abril al 15 de abril)

Hace seis meses que estudio español.
(de septiembre a marzo)

Hace dos meses que pertenezco* al club de español. Las reuniones son muy divertidas.

Hace un mes que Anita pertenece al club de ajedrez.
(de septiembre a octubre)

(de noviembre a enero)

*Conocer and pertenecer are regular -er verbs, with the exception of the yo form: conozco and pertenezco.

372 CAPÍTULO 5

Total Physical Response

Getting Ready
Make copies of the vocabulary transparencies and give one to each student.

New Words
el corazón   la estrella
el globo   la cara
feliz   serio(a)

TPR 1

Hagan un círculo en la reunión del club de español.
Hagan un rectángulo en la chica que espera.
Dibujen un corazón en la muchacha con la gripe.
Dibujen una estrella en el chico que compra entradas.

c. tocas *(instrumento)*?
d. sabes *(hacer algo)*?
e. conoces a _____?
f. perteneces al club de _____?

3. Ask pairs of students how long they have been friends. **¿Cuánto tiempo hace que son amigos(as)?**

Regionalisms

You may wish to tell students that in some parts of the Spanish-speaking world, the following phrase is an alternative to the one presented in the Vocabulario.
hacer cola, (hacer fila)

Actividades

Actividad A Answers
The years of residence will vary.

1. Manuel es argentino. Hace... años que está en Miami.
2. Graciela es nicaragüense...
3. Margarita es costarricense...
4. La Srta. Camacho es cubana...
5. El Sr. Jiménez es dominicano...
6. La Sra. Costas es ecuatoriana...

Actividades

A **Una escuela internacional.** Many of Carmen's classmates and teachers are from Cuba as well as other countries. Below are their names, their countries of origin, and the years they left their countries. Tell each person's nationality and how long he or she has been in Miami.

Por ejemplo:

Rodrigo: Guatemala, 1988
Rodrigo es guatemalteco. Hace _____ años que está en Miami.

1. Manuel: la Argentina, 1980
2. Graciela: Nicaragua, 1982
3. Margarita: Costa Rica, 1990
4. la Srta. Camacho: Cuba, 1963
5. el Sr. Jiménez: la República Dominicana, 1975
6. la Sra. Costas: el Ecuador, 1969

Lección 5 **373**

Coloquen un cuadro en los nuevos vecinos.
Dibujen una cara feliz en la chica que está en el equipo de vóleibol.
Dibujen una cara seria en la chica que espera.
Dibujen una cara muy feliz en el chico que hace cola para las entradas.
(Interchange commands with other vocabulary. Use a transparency to check results.)

TPR 2
Escriban "¡Qué lástima!" en el globo de la chica enferma.
Escriban "¡Estupendo!" en el globo del chico que compra entradas.
Escriban "¡Caramba!" en la foto del club de ajedrez.
Escriban "Mucho gusto" en el globo de los nuevos vecinos.
(Check answers with a transparency.)

Actividades B, C, and D Answers
Answers will vary.

Extension
After completing Actividad D, you may wish to extend it by having students ask about the meetings of the organizations listed.
Por ejemplo:
el club de vídeo

ESTUDIANTE A	ESTUDIANTE B
¿Te gusta asistir a las reuniones del club de vídeo?	Sí, son muy divertidas.

B **¿Cuánto tiempo hace que los conoces?** Say how long you have known the following people.

Por ejemplo:
> tu amigo _____.
> *Hace varios meses que conozco a mi amigo Paco.*

1. tu amiga _____
2. tu amigo _____
3. tu maestro(a) de español
4. tu maestro(a) de educación física
5. un vecino
6. una vecina

C **¡Paciencia!** How long do you have to wait for the following people or things? Also tell whether or not you have to wait in line.

Por ejemplo:
> el autobús
> *A veces espero diez minutos. (No) Tengo que hacer cola.*

1. en la oficina del dentista
2. para comprar entradas en el cine
3. la nota después de un examen
4. en la cafetería a la hora de comer
5. a tu amigo(a) en el centro comercial
6. para comer en un restaurante
7. en el supermercado
8. en la tienda de vídeos

D **Somos miembros.** Ask a classmate if he or she belongs to the school clubs and teams below. Also find out how long he or she has been a member. Reverse roles.

Por ejemplo:
> el club de vídeo

ESTUDIANTE A	ESTUDIANTE B
(1) ¿Perteneces al club de vídeo?	(2) Sí.
(3) ¿Cuánto tiempo hace que perteneces al club?	(4) A ver... hace casi tres meses que pertenezco al club.

el club...
   de ajedrez
   de español
   de esquí
   internacional
   de agricultores
   de periodismo

el equipo de...
   baloncesto
   béisbol
   tenis
   fútbol
   fútbol americano
   vóleibol

For the Native Speaker
Write a 150-word composition telling how long your family has lived in the U.S. and what you like and dislike about living here.

CULTURA VIVA 1

Los cubanoamericanos

Aunque hoy día muchos cubanos son ciudadanos de los Estados Unidos, todavía son parte de dos culturas. Para los cubanoamericanos es muy importante mantener su idioma y cultura originales. También quieren mantener contacto con los amigos y familiares de su tierra. Muchos cubanoamericanos mandan dinero, ropa y medicinas a sus parientes y amigos que viven en la isla.

Carmen es parte de una nueva generación de cubanoamericanos que vive en dos culturas: la cubana (el idioma, la música, las costumbres, la comida, la familia) y la norteamericana (la escuela, las actitudes de sus compañeros de clase, las películas, la televisión).

Actividades

A In the first paragraph, to what place do the following phrases refer?

su tierra / la isla / la cultura original

B Cuban Americans live in two cultures. In the second paragraph, find as many things as you can that make up a "culture."

Cultura viva 1

Reading Strategies
1. Read the **Cultura viva** on this page. Then do the **Actividades**.
2. Discuss with your students the contributions of Cuban Americans to American society. Ask students to name individuals who are Cuban American (athletes, singers, politicians, etc.).

Did You Know?
Many other ethnic groups in the U.S. have maintained strong ties to their native culture and language. You may wish to have students identify those groups in your area.

Critical Thinking Activity
In groups, have students discuss the following questions.
1. If you had to leave your country, what would you miss the most?
2. What would be the most difficult thing to adjust to in your new country?
3. What do you think would be the most difficult thing about living in two cultures?

Actividades

Actividad A Answers
Cuba.

Actividad B Answers
El idioma, la música, las costumbres, la comida, la familia, la escuela, las actitudes de la gente, las películas, la televisión.

Pronunciation
1. Use Pronunciation Transparency P-5.5.1, or write the pronunciation activity on the chalkboard. Have students copy it into their notebooks.
   **Hace quince años
   nací en la Florida:
   chispa de cubana,
   lengua americana.**
2. You may wish to play the recorded version of this activity, located at the end of Cassette 5.5.
3. You may wish to focus on the elision of vowel sounds across word boundaries. For example:
   **"quinceaños"
   "nacíen"
   "lenguaamericana"**

Estructura 1

Structure Teaching Resources
1. Workbook, pp. 166–167
2. Cassette 5.5
3. Student Tape Manual, p. 136
4. Estructura Masters 5.5
5. Lesson Quizzes, p. 111

Bell Ringer Review
Directions to students: On your paper, draw a picture representing each of these new vocabulary words.
1. la entrada
2. la reunión
3. hacer cola
4. el ajedrez
5. el equipo

Structure Focus
In this lesson the **yo** and **tú** forms of the preterit of **-er** and **-ir** verbs are presented. The **yo** and **tú** forms of **-ar** verbs will be presented in Lesson 6.
Note: The following are infinitives students have used but whose preterit forms will not be introduced in Level 1.

decir	traer
querer	tener
poder	andar

Presentation
1. Before presenting the **yo** and **tú** **-er** and **-ir** forms of the preterit, remind students of the difference between the present and the past. For example: **Hoy voy a la biblioteca. Ayer fui al gimnasio. Hoy tú vas al cine. Ayer tú fuiste al estadio,** etc.
2. Now lead students through steps 1–5 on page 376.
3. After presenting the preterit you may wish to have students practice the stressed **-í** as a quick drill. Give them an infinitive and have them give you the first person form, clapping hands or tap-

---

Estructura 1

How to Say What You Did, What I Did

Yo and **tú** *forms of the preterit of* -er *and* -ir *verbs*

You have already learned to say where you went in the past. You have also learned to ask where a friend or family member went.

Anoche fui a casa de mi amiga Carmen.
¿Fuiste a la fiesta de Juan Carlos el sábado pasado?

1. To tell other things you did in the past using **-er** or **-ir** verbs, replace the **-er** or **-ir** with the ending of the past (preterit) tense: **-í**. You must write an accent mark over the letter **i** to indicate that it is stressed when you pronounce the word.

escribir	Ayer escribí una carta a mi prima.
salir	El domingo pasado salí con mis amigos.
comer	No comí en la cafetería ayer.

2. When you talk about people or things you saw (**ver**), there is no written accent over the **i**.

   Anoche vi una película fantástica. Y en el cine vi a mi primo Carlos.

3. To tell or ask a friend or relative what he or she did in the past using **-er** or **-ir** verbs, replace the **-er** or **-ir** with **-iste**.

escribir	¿Ya escribiste a tu abuela?
aprender	¿Aprendiste el vocabulario nuevo?
ver	¿Viste a Irene en la clase de inglés?

4. To ask a friend what he or she did, say **¿Qué hiciste?**

   ¿Qué hiciste cuando fuiste a California?

5. To say that you didn't do anything, say **No hice nada**.

   Anoche no salí. No hice nada.

These two forms (**hice, hiciste**) are the past tense (preterit) forms of the verb **hacer**.

Una clase de química en Buenos Aires.

376 CAPÍTULO 5

Cooperative Learning
Play the game of "Teléfono." The person sitting in the first seat of each row creates a "rumor" and passes it down the row. The last person writes it on the board. The person who started the "rumor" is asked to say **verdad** or **falso** to the "rumor". Remind students not to say anything that might be embarrassing or offensive.

Actividades

A ¿Qué viste? Tell three things or people you saw on your way to school this morning.

Por ejemplo:
> Vi a mi amiga Raquel.
> Vi un gato negro en la calle Oak.

B Te vi ayer. Tell three classmates that you saw each of them with someone yesterday and say where (even if it's not true). Each classmate will say whether it is possible or not.

Por ejemplo:

ESTUDIANTE A	ESTUDIANTE B
Sam, te vi ayer con Carmen en la reunión del club de español.	No me viste allí con ella. (Sí, es posible).

C ¿Qué viste? Ask two classmates how many hours they watch television during the week. Then ask what programs they saw last week.

Por ejemplo:

ESTUDIANTE A	ESTUDIANTE B
(1) ¿Cuántas horas a la semana ves la tele?	(2) Veo la tele seis horas a la semana.
(3) ¿Qué programas viste la semana pasada?	(4) Vi _____.

D ¿Qué hiciste ayer? Answer the following questions about what you did yesterday.

1. ¿Saliste anoche? ¿Con quién?
2. ¿Leíste un libro ayer? ¿Cuál?
3. ¿Viste a todos tus amigos ayer? ¿A quiénes? ¿Dónde?
4. ¿Comiste algo delicioso? ¿Qué comiste? ¿Dónde?
5. ¿Recibiste una carta? ¿De quién?
6. ¿Fuiste a una reunión? ¿Dónde? ¿Con quién?

El correo argentino.

Actividad E Answers
Answers will vary but should include the following.
1. ¿A qué hora saliste...?
2. ¿... hiciste...?
3. ¿... viste...?
4. ¿... fuiste...?
5. ¿... comiste...?

Actividad F Answers
Answers will vary.

Reteaching

Choose several **-er** and **-ir** infinitives and write them on the board. Ask individual students to tell you whether or not they did each of the activities yesterday. Then have them ask a classmate if he or she did any of the activities.

E **¿A qué hora?** Ask a classmate what time he or she did the following things yesterday. Then ask if he or she always does each thing at that time.

Por ejemplo:
> hacer la cama

ESTUDIANTE A	ESTUDIANTE B
(1) ¿A qué hora hiciste la cama ayer?	(2) A las siete.
(3) ¿Siempre haces la cama a las siete?	(4) Sí, siempre. (No, no siempre).

1. salir para la escuela
2. hacer la tarea de español
3. ver a tus amigos
4. ir a la clase de inglés
5. comer en la escuela

F **Chismes.** Make up a rumor about what three of your classmates have done. They will say whether the rumor is true (**"Es verdad"**) or false (**"No es verdad"**) and give an explanation. Use the verbs suggested below.

| leíste | saliste | perdiste | hiciste | recibiste |
| comiste | viste | fuiste | aprendiste | escribiste |

Por ejemplo:
> recibiste / escribiste

ESTUDIANTE A	ESTUDIANTE B
(1) Sandra, dicen que recibiste una "A" en el examen de álgebra.	(2) Es verdad. Siempre saco buenas notas en álgebra.
(3) Paul, dicen que escribiste en tu pupitre (desk).	(4) ¡No es verdad! Nunca escribo en mi pupitre.

Una compañera de clase.

378 CAPÍTULO 5

CULTURA VIVA 2

Una carta de la Argentina

Buenos Aires
6 de abril

Queridísima Alicia:

Muchas gracias por la invitación a Miami. Te llamé anoche para hablar del viaje, pero nadie contestó. Rafael va a ir conmigo a Miami. Está muy entusiasmado con la idea de visitar los Estados Unidos. Vamos a llegar el día 20 de abril a las 7:55 de la mañana, vuelo de Aerolíneas Argentinas número 445. Recibí el cheque que me mandaste. Gracias, hermanita.

Si no me llamas este domingo, te llamo el lunes por la noche.

¡Hasta pronto!

Un fuerte abrazo de tu hermano que te quiere,

Lucas

Actividad

From Lucas's list of things to do, tell which he did by answering **sí** or **no**.

1. escribir a Alicia
2. llamar a Alicia
3. hacer las reservaciones en Aerolíneas Argentinas
4. hacer las compras para Alicia
5. recibir el cheque de Alicia
6. hacer las maletas
7. mandar a Alicia la información sobre el vuelo

Lección 5

Estructura 2

Structure Teaching Resources

1. Workbook, pp. 168–169
2. Cassette 5.5
3. Student Tape Manual, p. 137
4. Estructura Masters 5.5
5. Lesson Quizzes, pp. 112–113

Bell Ringer Review

Directions to students: Tell how long you've been doing each of the following.

1. estudiar español
2. jugar _____
3. conocer a tu amigo(a) _____
4. escuchar la música de _____
5. vivir en tu casa (apartamento)

Structure Focus

The present tense of the verbs **decir, oír,** and **pedir** are presented in this lesson. Students will learn how to report what others say, hear, and request.

Presentation

A. Lead students through steps 1–3 on page 380.

B. To introduce **oír,** ask individual students simple questions. When they respond, pretend you didn't hear, gesturing and saying **¿Cómo? No te oigo.**
List on the board different noises you hear in the class. For example:
Oigo a Jane abrir un libro.
Oigo a Ralph hablar con su compañero, etc.
Summarize by saying, **Oímos muchas cosas.** Then lead them through step 4.

Estructura 2

How to Report What Someone Says or Hears — **The verbs decir and oír**

How to Request Things — **The verb pedir**

You have already seen some forms of the verb **decir**, which means "to say" or "to tell." For example, when you use the wrong word and want to correct yourself, you have said **digo**.

> **Todos somos "Americans", digo, americanos.**

To report or summarize what someone said, you have used **Dice(n) que**...

> **Miguel dice que Juanita está enferma hoy.**
> **Mis padres dicen que no puedo salir esta noche.**

1. The following are all the forms of **decir** in the present tense.

SINGULAR	PLURAL
digo	decimos
dices	decís*
dice	dicen

2. Use a form of **decir** when you want to quote directly what someone says to you.

> **Siempre me dice: "Eres muy guapa".**

3. Use a form of **decir** to summarize what someone says to you.

> **Siempre me dice que soy muy guapa.**

4. You use the verb **oír** to tell what you and others hear. The following are all the forms of **oír** in the present tense.

SINGULAR	PLURAL
oigo	oímos
oyes	oís*
oye	oyen

380 CAPÍTULO 5

5. The verb **pedir** ("to request, to ask for, or order something") changes from **e** to **i** in the same way **decir** does.

SINGULAR	PLURAL
pido	pedimos
pides	pedís*
pide	piden

Cuando vas a la cafetería, ¿qué bebida pides?
Para su cumpleaños mi hermana siempre pide ropa.

*This form is rarely used in the Spanish-speaking world, except for Spain.

Actividades

A **¿Qué me dices?** Ask a classmate what he or she says in the following situations.

Por ejemplo:

cuando salgo de clase

ESTUDIANTE A
¿Qué me dices cuando salgo de clase?

ESTUDIANTE B
Te digo ¡Adiós!

1. cuando te doy un regalo
2. cuando te digo gracias
3. cuando te llevo tu mochila
4. cuando no puedes salir conmigo
5. cuando te pido dinero
6. cuando te digo algo increíble

B **¿Qué dicen?** What do you and your friends say about the following?

Por ejemplo:

Los maestros dicen que ustedes van a tener clases los sábados.
Nosotros decimos que no queremos ir a la escuela los fines de semana.

1. Su maestro dice que ustedes deben tener muchos exámenes.
2. Dicen que la comida de la cafetería es excelente.
3. Los padres dicen que deben regresar a casa antes de las once de la noche.
4. Los dentistas dicen que los jóvenes no deben comer postres.

Lección 5

C. To introduce **pedir,** tell students something like the following: **Cuando voy a un restaurante, pido carne y legumbres. Mi esposo(a) pide pollo y una ensalada. Mis hijos piden hamburguesas y papas fritas. Todos pedimos helado. Y tú, ¿qué pides?**
Then lead them through step 5.

Actividades

Actividades A and B Answers
Answers will vary.

Actividad C Answers
Answers will vary but may include the following.

1. Oyen los camellos, los tigres, los osos, los elefantes, los monos, etc.
2. Oigo a mi hermano, a mis padres, un casete, un disco, la radio, etc.
3. Oímos un partido, música, las noticias, etc.
4. Oigo unos perros, unos gatos, etc.
5. Oye pájaros, un perro, un gato, un caballo, etc.
6. Oyen a la maestra (al maestro), a sus compañeros, una película, etc.

Actividades D and E Answers
Answers will vary.

Addtitional Practice
After completing Actividades A, B, C, D, and E, you may wish to reinforce the lesson by doing the following activity.

What do the people below say to you in the following situations?
Por ejemplo:
un amigo especial, cuando vas de vacaciones
Mi amigo me dice: ¿Me puedes escribir?

1. tus padres, cuando pides dinero
2. el maestro, cuando sacas malas notas
3. los amigos, cuando ganas un partido
4. tus padres, cuando trabajas demasiado
5. una amiga especial, el día de tu cumpleaños

Reteaching

Have students tell you where the following people probably are, based on the cues.

1. Mis amigos dicen que oyen música muy bonita.
2. Juan José dice que oye animales.
3. Elena y su prima dicen que oyen olas.
4. Digo que oigo una conversación en español.

C **¿Qué oyen?** Tell what or whom the people below might be hearing, according to where they are.

Por ejemplo:
　　Miguel está en una fiesta.
　　Oye música (un vídeo musical, una guitarra, a sus amigos).

1. Los turistas están en el parque zoológico.
2. Estás en tu habitación.
3. Tú y los compañeros están en tu casa. Escuchan la radio.
4. Estoy en la oficina del veterinario.
5. Maricarmen está en la casa de sus tíos en el campo.
6. Jorge y Elena están en la clase de español.

D **Todos me piden favores.** Tell one possession the following people frequently request from you.

Por ejemplo:
　　tu mamá
　　Mi mamá me pide la bicicleta.

1. tu compañero(a) de clase
2. tu papá
3. tus hermanos
4. tus maestros
5. tu abuelo(a)
6. tu amigo(a)

E **Los platos favoritos.** Working with a classmate, find out what each of you usually orders to eat in the following places or circumstances. Then report back to the class.

Por ejemplo:
　　en la cafetería de la escuela

ESTUDIANTE A	ESTUDIANTE B
(1) ¿Qué pides en la cafetería de la escuela?	(2) Pido hamburguesas. ¿Y tú?
(3) Yo también.	

(A la clase): Miguel y yo pedimos hamburguesas en la cafetería.

1. en un restaurante muy elegante
2. en un partido de béisbol
3. en un restaurante mexicano
4. en McDonald's
5. el día de tu cumpleaños

Finalmente

Situaciones

A conversar Converse with a classmate about birthday gifts.

1. Find out what gifts your partner asked for on a recent birthday.
2. Find out what gifts he or she actually received.
3. Ask which gift your partner likes best. Ask him or her to describe it.
4. Find out what your partner plans to ask for next year.
5. Reverse roles.

A escribir Write a note to a friend describing a memorable weekend. Include details about places you went, with whom, what you did and saw, what new friends you met **(Conocí a...)**, what new things you may have learned how to do, and special foods you ate.

Repaso de vocabulario

PREGUNTA
¿Cuánto tiempo hace que...?

ACTIVIDADES
conocer (-zco)
decir
esperar
hacer cola
oír
pedir
pertenecer (-zco)

PERSONA
el/la vecino(a)

COSAS
el club
la entrada
el equipo
la hora (hour)
el minuto
la reunión
el tiempo

OTRAS PALABRAS
casi
varios(as)

EXPRESIÓN
Hace... que...

Lección 5   383

For the Native Speaker

1. Explain in a composition your feelings about living in two cultures. Be sure to mention the advantages, disadvantages, as well as your likes and dislikes.
2. Write a 150-word composition describing the advantages of being bilingual.

CAPÍTULO 5

Lección 6

Objectives

By the end of this lesson, students will be able to:

1. say what they do for another person
2. say what they did at one point in the past
3. tell a friend or family member what he or she did at one point in the past
4. name common household chores
5. give a result of an action, using **por eso**

Lesson 6 Resources

1. Workbook, pp. 170–177
2. Vocabulario Transparencies
3. Pronunciation Transparency P-5.6.1
4. Audio Cassette 5.6 Compact Disc 8
5. Student Tape Manual, pp. 140–146
6. Bell Ringer Review Blackline Masters, pp. 34–35
7. Computer Software: Practice & Test Generator
8. Video (cassette or disc)
9. Video Activities Booklet, pp. A75–A79
10. Estructura Masters, pp. 69–72
11. Diversiones Masters, pp. 65–66
12. Situation Cards
13. Lesson Quizzes, pp. 114–116
14. Testing Program

¡A comenzar!

Presentation

A. Lead students through each of the five functions given on page 384, progressing from the English to the Spanish for each *(continued)*

CAPÍTULO 5

Lección 6

El idioma es muy importante

¡A comenzar!

The following are some of the things you will be learning to do in this lesson.

When you want to...	You use...
1. say what you do for another person	**Le** + activity + **a** + person.
2. say what you did at one point in the past	**-é** at the end of **-ar** verbs
3. tell a friend or family member what he or she did at one point in the past	**-aste** at the end of **-ar** verbs
4. tell a friend or family member what he or she gave	**diste** + object
5. give a result of an action ("therefore," "that's why")	**por eso**

Now find examples of the above words and phrases in the following conversation.

Getting Ready for Lesson 6

You may wish to use the following suggestion to prepare students for the lesson.

1. Give students a list of things you did and intended to do yesterday, using regular **-ar** verbs. For example:
   1. llamar a mamá
   2. firmar el formulario
   3. cortar el césped
   4. mandar cartas
   5. planchar la ropa
   6. lavar el coche
   7. limpiar la casa
   8. preparar una comida especial
2. Tell students about your day yesterday. Say that you just didn't get around to doing some things. Have students cross off of their lists the things you were able to accomplish.

Sigue la conversación entre Carmen y su mamá.

CARMEN: Mamá, no me escuchaste.
MAMÁ: Claro que te escuché, hijita.
CARMEN: Pues, entonces...
MAMÁ: Mira, Carmencita, tú puedes hablar inglés todo el día en la escuela, con tus amigos, por todas partes. Pero también somos cubanos y el idioma es muy importante para nosotros.
CARMEN: Pero, mamá...
MAMÁ: Escúchame, Carmen. Cuando le hablaste ayer a tu papá en inglés, cuando olvidaste las palabras en español, le diste la impresión de que no respetas ni el idioma ni nuestra cultura. Por eso le debes hablar en español.

Actividades preliminares

A Complete the following sentences to say what you do for the people indicated.

1. A mi maestro le doy _____ todos los días.
2. A mi hermano le doy _____ para su cumpleaños.
3. A mi hermano nunca le presto mi(s) _____.
4. A mi amigo le compro _____ porque le gusta(n) mucho.

B Give a result of the following actions, using **por eso**.

Por ejemplo:
> Enrique nunca estudia.
> *Por eso saca malas notas (no sabe contestar en clase, etc.).*

1. Mi papá no me puede llevar a la escuela hoy.
2. A Raúl no le gusta practicar la guitarra.
3. Hace tres días que Susana llega tarde a la clase de español.

3. Follow up by asking about each thing on your list. For each thing that you failed to do, students should respond with **No. ¿Por qué no _____ hoy?** For example:
   MAESTRO(A): ¿Llamé a mi mamá ayer?
   ESTUDIANTE: No. ¿Por qué no llama hoy?

le pido ayuda al (a la) maestro(a).

¡A comenzar!

Presentation

A. Lead students through each of the five functions given on page 384, progressing from the English to the Spanish for each function. Then have students find these words and phrases in the dialogue.

B. Introduce the Lesson 6 dialogue by reading it aloud or by playing the recorded version. Tell students that they will hear a conversation between Carmen and her mother about something Carmen has done that hurt her father's feelings. Have students listen to the tape of the Lesson 6 dialogue to find out how Carmen's father interprets her constant use of English in the home. This may require two listenings.

C. Ask students to open their books and look at the dialogue as you guide them with the following questions.
  1. Carmen cree que su mamá no escucha. ¿Qué dice?
  2. Su mamá le contesta. ¿Qué dice?
  3. Según la mamá, ¿cuándo puede hablar inglés Carmen?
  4. Según la mamá, ¿qué le molesta al papá? ¿Cómo lo explica la mamá?
  5. ¿Qué favor le pide la mamá a Carmen?

Actividades preliminares

Actividad A Answers
Answers will vary.

Actividad B Answers
Answers will vary but may include the following.

1. Por eso tengo que ir en bicicleta (llegar tarde).
2. Por eso no puede tocar bien.
3. Por eso el maestro está enojado.

Vocabulario

Vocabulary Teaching Resources
1. Vocabulario Transparencies 5.6
2. Workbook, pp. 170–171
3. Cassette 5.6
4. Student Tape Manual, p. 141
5. Lesson Quizzes, p. 114

Presentation

A. Have students open their books to page 386.
   1. Model each new word on page 386. Begin each phrase with **Tengo que...** Have students repeat each phrase in unison.
   2. Ask individual students whether or not they have to do the chores on pages 386 and 387. For example, **¿Tienes que poner la mesa?** Encourage students to give a complete response. For example, **Sí, tengo que poner la mesa.**

B. Ask students questions about chores they do at home. For example:
   1. ¿Cuándo cortas el césped? ¿En qué meses no lo tienes que cortar?
   2. ¿Quién plancha en tu casa?
   3. ¿En qué habitaciones pasas la aspiradora?
   4. En tu casa, ¿quién da de comer al gato?
   5. ¿Para qué pides permiso?
   6. ¿Quién saca la basura?

Note: Students will not be able to use the preterit of **poner**. The preterit of **poner** will be introduced in Level 2.

Vocabulario

A mi mamá le pido permiso para salir esta noche. Me permite salir si prometo hacer los quehaceres de la casa. Necesito...

cortar el césped

poner* la mesa

quitar los platos

lavar los platos

dar de comer al gato

sacar al perro

sacudir los muebles

sacar la basura

*The **yo** form of **poner** is **pongo**.

386 CAPÍTULO 5

Total Physical Response

Getting Ready
Bring to class real items or pictures of items for the underlined vocabulary in the activity. Arrange items or pictures on a table. Students will be using a combination of real items, pictures, and pantomime to perform the TPR.

TPR 1
(Call on pairs of students.)
Quiten <u>los platos</u> de la mesa.
Póngalos en la silla cerca de la puerta.
Saquen <u>la basura</u>.
Pongan la basura en el pasillo.
Sacudan los pupitres y mi escritorio.
Vayan a la silla donde están los platos.
Laven los platos. Póngalos en la mesa.
Corten el césped.

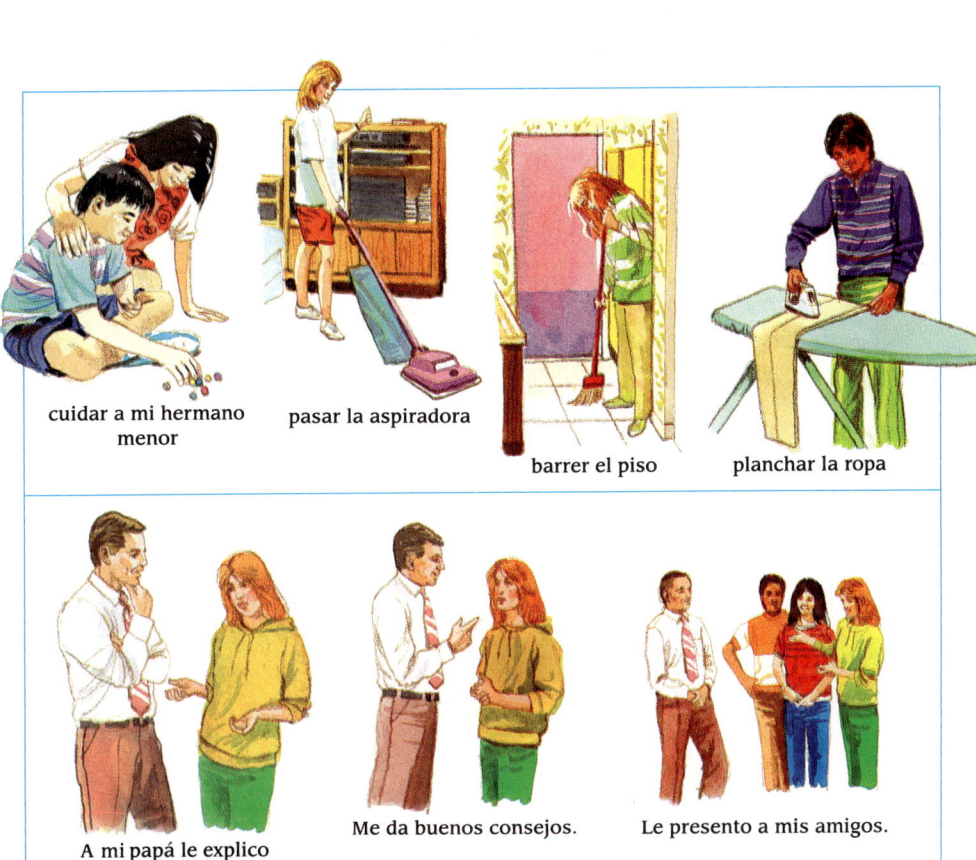

When Students Ask
You may wish to give students the following additional vocabulary to allow them to talk about chores.
lavar la ropa
hacer la cama
ordenar la habitación
colgar la ropa
recoger la ropa del suelo
secar los platos
regar las flores y las plantas

Regionalisms
You may wish to tell students that in some parts of the Spanish-speaking world the following words or phrases are alternatives to those presented in the vocabulario.
el césped (la grama) (el zacate) (Mex.) (la hierba) (los quehaceres) (las faenas)
quitar los platos (levantar la mesa)
lavar los platos (fregar los platos)
sacar al perro (pasear al perro)
sacudir los muebles (quitar el polvo)

Pasen la aspiradora por la alfombra.
Denle comida al gato.
Saquen el perro al pasillo.
Laven la ropa.
Sacudan el estéreo.

TPR 2
(Call on individual students.)
Pon la basura en la puerta.
Lava los platos cerca de la ventana.
Pasa la aspiradora por la alfombra.
Dale comida al gato.
Sacude tu pupitre.
Pon el perro en la ventana.
Lava la ropa.
Quita los platos de la mesa. Ponlos en tu pupitre.
Sacude el estéreo.
Corta el césped.

Actividades

Actividades A, B, C, D, and E Answers

Answers will vary but should follow the models.

Reteaching

Have students ask each other the same questions you asked in the vocabulary presentation.

Actividades

A **Le hago favores.** Tell whether or not you do the following favors for your best friend.

Por ejemplo:

> prestar dinero
> *Le presto dinero (No le presto dinero).*

1. mandar tarjetas postales cuando vas de vacaciones
2. dar regalos caros para su cumpleaños
3. explicar tus problemas
4. prometer decir la verdad (truth)
5. permitir usar tus cosas
6. presentar a tu familia
7. dar buenos consejos

B **¿Tienes que pedir permiso?** Tell whether or not you must ask permission at home to do the following things.

Por ejemplo:

> salir con tus amigos
> *(No) Tengo que pedir permiso para salir con mis amigos.*

1. escuchar música
2. invitar a un/a amigo(a) a casa
3. ver la tele
4. ir al cine por la tarde
5. salir por la noche
6. dormir en casa de un/a amigo(a)
7. comer en casa de un/a amigo(a)
8. dar una fiesta
9. ir a una fiesta
10. hablar por teléfono
11. regresar a casa después de las diez de la noche
12. vender tu radio o tu grabadora

En la cocina después de comer. ¿Qué hace el muchacho?

C **¿Estrictos o no?** Tell how often your mother or father allows you to do each of the things in activity **B**.

Por ejemplo:

> salir con tus amigos
> *Mi mamá siempre me permite salir con mis amigos.*

D **Los quehaceres de la casa.** Find out from a classmate if he or she does the following household chores. Reverse roles and report back to the class.

Por ejemplo:

limpiar la habitación

ESTUDIANTE A
En tu casa, ¿tienes que limpiar la habitación?

ESTUDIANTE B
Sí, todos los sábados. (No, es el quehacer de mi hermana mayor).

(A la clase): Elena tiene que limpiar la habitación todos los sábados. (En la casa de Elena su hermana mayor limpia la habitación).

1. dar de comer al perro (gato, conejo, etc.)
2. sacar la basura
3. cocinar
4. poner la mesa
5. quitar los platos
6. lavar los platos
7. sacar al perro
8. cuidar a los hermanos menores
9. pasar la aspiradora
10. sacudir los muebles
11. cortar el césped
12. lavar el coche
13. hacer la cama
14. planchar la ropa
15. barrer el piso

En un parque de Miami.

E **Buenos negocios.** Make a list of some of your possessions that you are willing to sell. Share the list with a classmate. Your classmate tells you what items he or she would like to buy. Come to an agreement on the price of each item. Choose from the items below or think of your own.

bicicleta	casetes	grabadora	muebles
cámara	colecciones	historietas	revistas
camisetas	discos	juegos de mesa	vídeos musicales
carteles	estéreo	libros	videojuegos

Por ejemplo:

ESTUDIANTE A
(1) ¿Me vendes tu cámara de marca Kodak?

(3) Bueno, te doy veinte dólares.

(5) No puedo pagar más.

ESTUDIANTE B
(2) Depende. ¿Cuánto me pagas?

(4) Es muy poco. La cámara es casi nueva.

(6) Bueno, está bien.

Lección 6

Cultura viva 1

Reading Strategies
Read the **Cultura viva** on this page. Then do the **Actividad**.

Did You Know?
Other diminutive suffixes are -(e)cito(a), -ico(a), and -illo(a).

When diminutive suffixes are added to the name of an animal, they are not terms of endearment, but rather an indication of age or size. For example, **el perrito** is a puppy.

Generally speaking, diminutives are not used as frequently by Spaniards as they are by Hispanic Americans.

Critical Thinking Activities
In groups, have students write a list of diminutives in English. For example: John (Johnny), Thomas (Tom, Tommy), dog (doggy), etc. How are these words formed? How are they different from diminutives in Spanish?

Actividad Answers
1. mi hermanito
2. mi primita
3. mi perrito
4. mi gatito
5. mi conejito

Learning from Photos
You may want to have students look at the photos on page 390. Have them guess what the relationship between the girl and the woman might be. Also have students tell what the girl is doing.

CULTURA VIVA 1

Los diminutivos

Cuando Carmen habla con su mamá, su mamá le dice "hijita" y "Carmencita". Cuando el tío Lucas le escribe a la mamá de Carmen, le dice "hermanita". Cuando la mamá le contesta sus cartas, le dice "hermanito".

Los hispanos usan *-ito* e *-ita* al final de los nombres de las personas para indicar que sienten cariño por esas personas.

Actividad

How would you refer to the following to show affection?

Por ejemplo:
> tu abuela
> *mi abuelita*

1. tu hermano
2. tu prima
3. tu perro
4. tu gato
5. tu conejo

Pronunciation
1. Use Pronunciation Transparency P-5.6.1, or write the pronunciation activity on the chalkboard. Have students copy it into their notebooks.
   Mamacita, cómprame un regalito.
   Papacito, ayúdame un poquito.
   Hermanita, hazme un favorcito.
   Abuelito, préstame un dinerito.
2. You may wish to play the recorded version of this activity, located at the end of Cassette 5.6.
3. Have students repeat words and phrases individually and in unison. You may wish to focus on the /t/ sound: mamacita, papacito, poquito, hermanita, etc.

Estructura 1

How to Say What You Do to or for Another Person — **Indirect object pronoun le**

You have used **me** to request a favor for yourself or to describe favors done for you.

¿Me puedes prestar un sello?

You have used **te** to offer a favor to a friend or a family member or to describe what you do for him or her.

Te puedo dar cinco dólares.

1. To say that someone is doing something to or for another person, use **le** + activity.

   Pobre Miguel está enfermo. Sus amigos le hacen muchos favores.

2. Also use **le** to say what you do to or for someone you address formally **(usted)**.

   Señorita, le doy mi tarea esta tarde.

3. The words **me, te,** and **le** go before the verb form that indicates who is doing the action. Word groups such as **voy a decir, puedo dar,** and **quieres prestar** cannot be broken up. The words **me, te** and **le** go before them.

   Te puedo dar mi tarea de inglés.
   ¿Me quieres prestar tu bolígrafo?

4. If you use the word **no**, it goes before the **me, te,** or **le**.

   No le voy a decir mis secretos.

5. Since **le** can refer to him, her, or you **(usted),** you will sometimes need to clarify who the **le** is. You do this by adding **a** + the name of the person.

   Todos los meses Ron le manda cartas *a Raquel*, pero Raquel no le escribe *a Ron* porque ella no sabe inglés.
   Señora, le voy a prestar cinco dólares *a usted,* pero no le puedo prestar nada *a Miguel.*

Lección 6

Actividades

Actividad A Answers
Answers will vary.

Actividad B Answers
1. sé
2. contigo
3. te
4. me
5. estoy
6. me
7. dices
8. tu
9. me
10. permites
11. te
12. traigo

Actividad C Answers
1. ¿Por qué no le escribes una carta?
2. ¿... le haces un favor?
3. ¿... le das un regalo?
4. ¿... le dices "perdón"?

Actividades

A **¿A quién?** Name one person to whom or for whom you do each of the following things.

1. Le digo mis secretos a _____.
2. Le presto dinero a _____.
3. Le mando cartas a _____.
4. Le doy regalos especiales a _____.
5. Le hago muchos favores a _____.

B **Pobre Alfredo.** Read the story below; then complete the paragraph following it as if you were Alfredo's father.

Nadie sabe qué pasa con Alfredo. Cuando su papá le habla, Alfredo no le contesta. Está muy triste estos días y el papá está preocupado. No le dice nada a su papá. Prefiere estar en su habitación y tampoco le permite entrar cuando él le trae su comida.

(El papá de Alfredo le dice): Alfredo, yo no _____ qué pasa _____. Cuando _____ hablo, no _____ contestas. Veo que estás muy triste estos días. Francamente, _____ preocupado. No _____ _____ nada. Prefieres estar en _____ habitación y tampoco _____ _____ entrar cuando _____ _____ tu comida.

C **Están peleados.** Carmen had a fight with her friend Jorge. Use the ideas below to suggest things she can do for him to make up; then think of one idea of your own.

Por ejemplo:
> hablar
> ¿Por qué no le hablas?

1. escribir una carta
2. hacer un favor
3. dar un regalo
4. pedir perdón

La mamá le prepara el desayuno a su hija.

392 CAPÍTULO 5

D Hoy y mañana. Name two things you do for someone else during the course of the day. Then name two things you are going to do for someone tomorrow.

Por ejemplo:

Todos los días le hablo a mi amiga Eva por teléfono...
Mañana le voy a comprar un regalo a mi hermano...

E Le quiero presentar a mis amigos. Tomorrow a local Hispanic businesswoman will come to your Spanish class. Practice introducing four of your classmates to her. Also say something about each one.

Por ejemplo:

Señora, le quiero presentar a Tony. Tony pertenece al equipo de baloncesto. Juega muy bien.

Unos amigos en Miami.

F ¿Qué le dices? In the situations below, what would you say to or ask each person?

Por ejemplo:

a tu prima cuando te visita
Le pregunto si quiere escuchar mi disco nuevo.

1. a tu mamá o a tu papá cuando te pide sacar la basura
2. a tu amigo cuando no puedes ir a una fiesta porque tienes que cuidar a tu hermano menor
3. a tu maestro cuando no haces la tarea
4. a tu amigo cuando te pide consejos
5. a tu mamá o a tu papá cuando te pide poner la mesa
6. a tu abuela cuando le dices que necesitas cinco dólares
7. a tu compañero de clase cuando le dices que sacaste una "A" en el examen

Lección 6 393

Cultura viva 2

Reading Strategies
Read the **Cultura viva** on this page. Then do the **Actividades**.

> #### Did You Know?
> In many areas where there is a large Hispanic population, bilingual education is offered to school children. Besides learning basic subjects in Spanish and in English, the children also study their cultural heritage.

Critical Thinking Activity
In teams, have students discuss the following quote from a Cuban American living in Miami.
"Para nosotros, la cuestión no es una de *reemplazar* el inglés con el español, sino de *añadir* el inglés al español".
What does the quote mean? Do you agree with it?
Have one member from each team report to the class on the team's conclusions.

Actividades

Actividad A Answers
Recordar: mantener, usar, practicar
No recordar: abandonar, perder, olvidar

Actividad B Answers
Answers will vary.

Learning from Photos and Realia
You may want to have students look at the photos on page 394. Have them look at the top photo and imagine what a bilingual science class is like. Ask how they would feel if next year their science class were taught partially in English and partially in Spanish. Have students look at the lower photo and guess what **"librería"** means.

CULTURA VIVA 2

El lenguaje: algo muy frágil

Para los inmigrantes hay, en realidad, dos problemas enormes. El primero es adaptarse rápidamente y aprender el idioma del nuevo país. El segundo es mantener el idioma materno —el idioma de los padres, los abuelos y los bisabuelos.

Parece increíble, pero puedes perder tu idioma. Tu idioma es muy frágil y si no lo usas, lo puedes olvidar. Los extranjeros que vienen a los Estados Unidos dicen que después de sólo dos años de no usar su idioma, empiezan a tener problemas con el vocabulario.

Actividades

A The following are some words used to describe what can happen to our language. Decide which of these words relate to remembering the language **(recordar)** and which relate to not remembering **(no recordar)**. List them in the appropriate category.

1. abandonar
2. mantener
3. perder
4. olvidar
5. usar
6. practicar

B What two pieces of advice can you give a classmate about what he or she should do over summer vacation so as not to forget the Spanish he or she has learned this year?

Por ejemplo:
   Debes hablar español con los amigos por teléfono.

¡VÍDEO! ¡APRENDA INGLÉS!
Ahora **SÍ** puede, en su casa y en sus momentos libres. Ud. aprenderá inglés con nuestro moderno sistema en video cassettes. Es fácil, rápido y divertido.

llámenos al: **940-9441**

AMERICAN VIDEO LANGUAGE INSTITUTE, INC.
3909 N. E. 163rd St. • Suite 308 • N. Miami Beach, FL 33160

CAPÍTULO 5

Estructura 2

How to Say What You Did and Ask What a Friend Did *Yo and tú forms of the preterit of -ar verbs*

You have learned to say what you did and to ask a friend what he or she did in the past using **-er** and **-ir** verbs.

    ¿Qué hiciste anoche?   Fui al cine.
    ¿Viste a Julia allí?   Claro, ¡salí con ella!

1. To talk about what you did in the past using **-ar** verbs, use **-é** to replace the **-ar**.

    Estudié mucho anoche. Terminé mi composición a las diez y media.

2. To ask what a friend did in the past using **-ar** verbs, use **-aste** to replace the **-ar**.

    ¿Le hablaste a tu papá anoche? ¿Le enseñaste tus notas?

3. The verb **dar** is irregular in the preterit tense. Although it is an **-ar** verb, it uses endings of **-er** and **-ir** verbs: **di, diste**.

    ¿Qué le diste a Sara?   **Le di una camiseta.**

Actividades

A **Favores que le hice yo.** Tell for whom you did each of the following favors recently. If you didn't do one of the favors, use the sentence *No le (activity) a nadie*.

Por ejemplo:

    mandar una carta
    Le mandé una carta a mi abuelo (No le mandé una carta a nadie).

1. enseñar unas fotos
2. comprar un regalo
3. ayudar
4. presentar a tus amigos(as)
5. prestar discos
6. dar dinero

Lección 6   **395**

Actividad B Answers
Answers will vary but should include the following.

1. ¿Escuchaste música ayer?
2. ¿Cuidaste niños ayer?
3. ¿Practicaste deportes ayer?
4. ¿Ayudaste a tus padres ayer?
5. ¿Limpiaste la habitación ayer?
6. ¿Estudiaste mucho ayer?
7. ¿Llamaste a tus amigos ayer?

Actividad C Answers
Answers will vary but should include the following.

1. Este año estudio... pero el año pasado estudié...
2. ... voy... fui...
3. ... leo... leí...
4. ... hago... hice...
5. ... salgo... salí...

Actividad D Answers
Answers will vary.

Additional Practice
After completing Actividades A, B, C, and D, you may wish to reinforce the lesson by doing the following activities.

1. The following are some things Carmen says she didn't do on certain days last week. Tell her she must do them.
   Por ejemplo:
   No fui a la reunión ayer.
   Tienes que ir a las reuniones.
   a. el lunes: No fui a mi clase de computadoras.
   b. el martes: No limpié mi habitación.
   c. el miércoles: No estudié para mis exámenes.
   d. el jueves: No ayudé a mi mamá.

Reteaching

Answer the following questions about things you did recently.

1. Cuando compraste tus "jeans," ¿cuánto pagaste?
2. Anoche, ¿cuánto tiempo estudiaste?
3. Cuando fuiste de vacaciones, ¿viajaste a un lugar (place) interesante? ¿Adónde?
4. Cuando saliste por la noche, ¿a qué hora regresate a casa?

B **Para mí, es muy fácil.** Ask a classmate if he or she did the activities below yesterday. Your classmate will answer and tell his or her opinion of that activity, choosing from the following words.

    interesante   fácil   difícil   aburrido   divertido

Por ejemplo:
    gastar mucho dinero

ESTUDIANTE A	ESTUDIANTE B
¿Gastaste mucho dinero ayer?	Sí, para mí es fácil gastar dinero.

1. escuchar música
2. cuidar niños
3. practicar deportes
4. ayudar a tus padres
5. limpiar la habitación
6. estudiar mucho
7. llamar a tus amigos

C **Este año y el año pasado.** Compare this school year to last year, considering the following questions.

Por ejemplo:
    ¿Vas a muchos partidos?
    Este año voy a muchos partidos pero el año pasado fui a dos partidos.

1. ¿Qué estudias?
2. ¿Vas a muchas reuniones?
3. ¿Lees muchos libros?
4. ¿Haces muchas tareas?
5. ¿Sales con muchos amigos?

D **Lugares.** What would you say you did in the following places?

Por ejemplo:
    en la tienda
    Vi camisetas bonitas pero no compré nada.

1. en la biblioteca
2. en la escuela
3. en el parque
4. en casa
5. en la playa
6. en el trabajo
7. en casa de los abuelos
8. en la fiesta
9. en las vacaciones

Unos compañeros de clase.

Cooperative Learning

Do a team word-web. Have students write the word "CULTURA" in the middle of a paper and write key ideas around it. Team members will link ideas and add family members they associate with each idea. At the bottom of the paper team members must come up with a sentence of what culture means to them.

Finalmente

Situaciones

A conversar Converse with a classmate about your activities last weekend.

1. Ask your partner what he or she did at various times during the weekend. Find out where your partner went, what he or she did, and with whom. Give your reactions.
2. Reverse roles.

A escribir There's a special meeting you want to attend next week in school, but it's at the same time as Spanish class. You must get your teacher's permission to attend the meeting. Write your teacher a note of explanation.

1. Ask for permission to go to the meeting.
2. Give the date you will not be in class.
3. Promise to do the homework for that day.
4. Tell what favor you will do for your teacher if he or she allows you to go to the meeting.

Repaso de vocabulario

ACTIVIDADES
barrer
cortar el césped
dar consejos a
dar de comer (al gato, al perro, etc.)
explicar
hacer los quehaceres
pagar
pasar la aspiradora
pedir permiso (para)
permitir
planchar
poner la mesa
presentar
prometer
quitar los platos
sacar la basura
sacudir los muebles
vender

OTRA PALABRA
el problema

Finalmente

Situaciones

Lesson 6 Evaluation
The **A conversar** and **A escribir** situations on this page are designed to give students the opportunity to use as many language functions and as much vocabulary from this lesson as possible. The **A conversar** and **A escribir** are also intended to show how well students are able to meet the lesson objectives.

Presentation

Prior to doing the **A conversar** and **A escribir** on this page, you may wish to play the **Situaciones** listening activities on Cassette 5.6 as a means of helping students organize the material.

For the Native Speaker

Have students write a 150–word composition about what they did during their last vacation.

Lectura

You will be able to figure out many of the words in the following reading from the context in which they appear or because they look like English words that have similar meanings. First, look over the article below and complete activities **A** and **B**. Then, after reading the article more carefully, complete activities **C** and **D**.

DANZA

Los ritmos de la danza afrocubana clásica invaden la Plaza España de Madrid

La llegada de nuevos inmigrantes cubanos a Europa en estos últimos años ha despertado el interés por los ritmos afrocubanos, especialmente en España, donde el número de exiliados es mayor. En numerosas escuelas de ballet y danza madrileñas se puede escuchar, junto al tradicional sonido de palmas y castañuelas, los ritmos sensuales del trópico expresados con exquisito lirismo por bailarines clásicos, verdaderos maestros en su género, como María Elena García, que baila en todas partes, "¡hasta en la mismísima Plaza España, y Olé!".

Actividades

A List the words you know or think you recognize in the above reading.

Por ejemplo:
> nuevos, inmigrantes, cubanos...

B The following look like Spanish words you've learned. Can you identify the root word?

Por ejemplo:
> llegada
> *(looks like)* llegar

1. madrileñas
2. numerosas
3. expresados
4. verdaderos

C Which of the following could be an appropriate title for this article?

1. Cubanos de vacaciones en Madrid
2. La música del trópico llega a España
3. La Plaza España —sitio de muchos conciertos

D Answer the following questions about the above article.

1. Según la primera frase de este artículo, ¿qué país europeo tiene más cubanos exiliados?
2. ¿Cómo describe el artículo la música tradicional de España? ¿Cómo describe la música de Cuba?
3. Según el artículo, ¿por qué es tan popular en España la danza afrocubana?

El Ballet Folklórico de Cuba.

Actividades

Actividad A Answers
Answers will vary but may include the following:
Europa, años, interés, especialmente, España, donde, número, numerosas, escuelas, ballet, danza, escuchar, tradicional, sensuales, trópico, expresados, exquisito, bailarines, clásicos, verdaderos, maestros, baila, todas, hasta.

Actividad B Answers
1. Madrid
2. número
3. expresar
4. verdad

Actividad C Answers
2

Actividad D Answers
1. España.
2. La música de España: el sonido de palmas y castañuelas; la música de Cuba: los ritmos sensuales del trópico.
3. Hay muchos nuevos inmigrantes cubanos en España.

Capítulo de Repaso

Bell Ringer Review
Tell three places you went last week and with whom.

Repaso Resources
1. Workbook, pp. 176–177
2. Cassette 5.6
3. Student Tape Manual, pp. 145–146
4. Video Cassette

¿Recuerdas?

Presentation

To review Chapter 5, call on individual students to give an example for each communicative function listed for Lecciones 1–3; and Lecciones 4–6, p. 400. The numbers in parentheses on page 400 refer to the actual page(s) in Chapter 5 where each function was presented and practiced. You may wish to have your students go back to these pages for additional review and practice before going on to the Actividades, pages 401-403

Lecciones 1–3 Answers

The following words and phrases are examples for each of the eleven functions lister under Lecciones 1–3. These words and phrases should be included in the students response to each function listed.

1. ¿Me puedes... ?
2. Te puedo...
3. la cosa, el aparato...
4. Se dice...
5. Mi(s) amigo(s) me...
6. alemán(ana), boliviano(a), cubano(a), español(ola), etc.
7. Mi novecientos noventa y dos, etc.
8. Vivo aquí desde 1991, etc.
9. Dos mil, cuatro mil quinientos, un millón etc.
10. fui, fuiste, fue, fuimos, fueron
11. ayer, la semana pasada, anoche, etc.

Capítulo 5 Repaso

¿Recuerdas?

Do you remember how to do the following things, which you learned in **Capítulo 5**?

LECCIONES 1–3

1. ask favors of others (p. 328)
2. offer favors to a friend or family member (p. 331)
3. describe things you don't know the name for in terms of size, shape, material, and use (p. 340)
4. give the meaning of a word in Spanish (p. 340)
5. ask or say what others do to or for you (p. 343)
6. give nationalities and tell what languages people speak (pp. 348–349)
7. give the year an event occurred (p. 352)
8. say that something has been going on since a certain date (p. 352)
9. give numbers to the millions (p. 352)
10. say where you and others went (p. 355)
11. tell when you and others went places (p. 355)

LECCIONES 4–6

1. say what belongs to you and others (p. 364)
2. talk about activities you do with others (p. 367)
3. say or ask how long someone has been doing something (pp. 372–373)
4. tell what you did at one point in the past (pp. 376, 395)
5. ask or tell a friend what he or she did in the past (pp. 376, 395)
6. report what you and others say and hear (p. 380)
7. tell what you and others request or ask for (p. 380)
8. say what you do for others (p. 391)

Actividades

A **Regalos de cumpleaños.**

1. List the things your relatives or friends typically give you for your birthday.

Por ejemplo:
> Mis abuelos me dan ropa.

2. List three items you are going to ask your parents for on your next birthday.

Por ejemplo:
> Les voy a pedir un estéreo...

Un padre con su hija.

3. Now list the things you are going to give to the following people on their birthdays. Describe the gift completely, including color, what it is made of, etc.
   a. a tu amigo(a)
   b. a tu maestro(a)
   c. a tu abuelo, tía, hermano, madre, etc.

B **Persuasión.** You want permission from your mother or father to do something. Offer to do something for him or her in exchange.

Por ejemplo:
> Mamá, si me haces un cheque para comprar _____, yo te lavo la ropa.

C **Amigos otra vez.** List three or four things that you would do to make up with a friend after an argument.

Por ejemplo:
> Le puedo decir que _____. También le puedo mandar _____ o le puedo ayudar con _____.

Repaso **401**

Lecciones 4–6 Answers

The following words and phrases are examples for each of the eight functions listed under Lecciones 4–6. These words an phrases should be included in the students' response to each function listed.

1. nuestro(a)/nuestros(as)
2. contigo, con él, ellos, ella(s), usted(es)
3. Hace que
4. Escribí, comí, escuché, etc.
5. escribiste, comiste, escuchaste, etc.
6. digo, dices, dice, decimos, dicen; oigo, oyes, oye, oímos, oyen
7. pido, pides, pide, pedimos, piden
8. Le...

Actividades

Presentation

Each practice activity in this Repaso of Chapter 5 reviews several of the language functions listed on page 400. Students are asked to use the language they have learned at a higher, more integrated level, compared to the individual practice activities in Lessons 1–6 of Chapter 5.

Actividades A, B, and C Answers
Answers will vary.

Actividad D Answers

1. *El Universal es un periódico venezolano.*
2. *El Miami Herald*... estadounidense (norteamericano)
3. *El Espectador*... colombiano.
4. *El Día*... uruguayo.
5. *El Heraldo de México*... mexicano.
6. *El País*... español.
7. *El Diario/La Prensa*... estadounidense (norteamericano).

Actividad E Answers

1. Answers will vary.
2. ¿Cómo te llamas? / ¿Cuándo empezaste a estudiar aquí? (¿Cuándo llegaste?) / ¿Cuándo naciste? / ¿Cuántos años tienes? / ¿Cómo se llama tu papá? ¿tu mamá? / ¿Con quién vives? / ¿Cuál es tu dirección? ¿tu número de teléfono? / ¿Dónde viviste antes? / ¿En qué escuela estudiaste? / Answers will vary
3. Les quiero presentar a...

D Periódicos de todo el mundo. Identify by nationality each of the following newspapers sold in Miami.

Por ejemplo:
Ya es un periódico español.

E El nuevo estudiante. A new student who speaks only Spanish has enrolled in your school.

1. List five things you would like to ask him or her.
2. Help the new student fill out the enrollment form.
   A classmate will play the role of the new student. Ask him or her questions to get information for the form.
3. Introduce the new student to another classmate and describe him or her, based on the information in the form.

F Diccionario moderno. Make a list of four or five special words you use with friends that might not be understood by persons from a different generation or region. Give a definition in Spanish for each word or expression. Share the list of definitions with the class and see if they agree.

Por ejemplo:
"dude"
Es un muchacho.

G Bienvenido. List five or six things you could do to welcome a new student.

Por ejemplo:
Le puedo enseñar dónde está la cafetería.

H Un viaje. You have just come back from an exciting trip and try to persuade a classmate to take a trip to the same place, telling all the places one can visit, the things one must see, and what one should do there. Your classmate will ask you what you did there, where you went, and what you saw.

Por ejemplo:

ESTUDIANTE A	ESTUDIANTE B
Fui a _____. Es fantástico.	Ah, ¿sí? ¿Cuándo fuiste?

I El sospechoso. Alicia wasn't home last night when Bruno called. He asks her where she went, with whom, and then makes accusations, which she denies. Play the roles of Bruno and Alicia with a partner. End up as friends again—somehow.

Por ejemplo:

ESTUDIANTE A	ESTUDIANTE B
¿Adónde fuiste anoche?	...
¿Con quién?	...
¿Qué hiciste?	...
¡Qué va! Yo sé que...	...

Actividades F, G, H, and I Answers
Answers will vary.

Chapter Overview

Cultural setting

This chapter continues with Carmen Marín and her family in Miami. We also meet Carmen's uncle Lucas and her cousin Rafael, from Buenos Aires, Argentina, who come to spend several weeks with the Marín family. The major cultural issues deal with

- the confusion that can arise over the disparity between the metric system and the system used in the U.S. for measuring height, weight, distances, and clothing;
- the difference in seasons between the Northern and Southern hemispheres.

Rationale

A The presentation of the preterit is completed in this chapter: first person plural endings are introduced in Lesson 1, third person singular endings in Lesson 3, and third person plural endings in Lesson 4. A summary and practice of all preterit forms is given in Lesson 6.

B Presentation of indirect object pronouns is also completed here. The functions of **me, te,** and **le** should be solidly rooted by now. Students should not have trouble grasping the functions of the plural forms **les** and **nos**.

C The third person direct object pronouns **lo, la, los,** and **las** are presented in Lesson 4. No attempt is made to contrast the use of indirect and direct object pronouns. This distinction will be made and practiced in Level 2.

D Finally, to enable students to compare and contrast persons and things, the functions of **tanto como, tanto(a)... como, más (menos)... que** are introduced.

We hope you enjoy the remainder of your stay in Miami!

CAPÍTULO 6

Estructura

This chapter focuses on the following:
- identification of articles of clothing and accessories;
- use of **les** to tell what you do for others;
- use of **nos** to tell what people do for you and others;
- giving and getting directions;
- telling what you and others did;
- referring to people and things already mentioned;
- describing the weather;
- describing and asking how you and others feel;
- comparing and contrasting people and things;
- giving weights, measurements, and distances;
- distinguishing one thing from another.

De visita en Miami

Video
The video is an optional component, intended to reinforce the vocabulary, structures, and cultural content in each lesson. Please refer to the Video Activities Booklet for suggestions on how to use this resource.

Lección 1 (2207)

Lección 2 (2415)

Lección 3 (2554)

Lección 4 (2643)

Lección 5 (2757)

Lección 6 (2919)

Enfoque cultural (3128)

¡Te toca a ti! (3316)

Pacing
The video is an optional component, intended to reinforce the vocabulary, structures, and cultural content in each lesson. Please refer to the Video Activities Booklet for suggestions on how to use this resource.

Student Portfolio
Writing assignments include the following:

Lesson 1: p. 417, A escribir; Workbook, p. 179, Act. D
Lesson 2: p. 428, Act. B
Lesson 3: p. 443, A escribir; Workbook, p. 190, Act. D
Leson 4: p. 457, A escribir
Lesson 5: p. 469, A escribir; Workbook, p. 202
Lesson 6: p. 483, A escribir

CAPÍTULO 6

Lección 1

Objectives

By the end of this lesson, students will be able to:
1. talk about doing something for others
2. tell what they and others did in the past
3. name articles of clothing

Lesson 1 Resources
1. Workbook, pp. 178–182
2. Vocabulario Transparencies
3. Pronunciation Transparency P-6.1.1
4. Audio Cassette 6.1 Compact Disc 9
5. Student Tape Manual, pp. 147–152
6. Bell Ringer Review Blackline Masters, p. 36
7. Computer Software: Practice & Test Generator
8. Video (cassette or disc)
9. Video Activities Booklet, pp. A81–A82
10. Estructura Masters, pp. 73–74
11. Diversiones Masters, pp. 67–68
12. Situation Cards
13. Lesson Quizzes, pp. 117–120
14. Testing Program

Bell Ringer Review

Directions to students: Write as many expressions as you can using: **dar, pedir, hacer, pasar,** and **sacar.**

¡A comenzar!

Presentation

A. Lead students through each of the two functions given on page 406, progressing from the English to the Spanish for each function.

CAPÍTULO 6

Lección 1

¡Liquidación de temporada!

¡A comenzar!

The following are some of the things you will be learning to do in this lesson.

When you want to...	You use...
1. talk about doing something for others (ustedes)	**Les** + activity.
2. tell what you and others did in the past	**-amos** on the end of **-ar** verbs; **-imos** on the end of **-er** and **-ir** verbs

Now find examples of the above words and phrases in the following advertisement.

406

Getting Ready for Lesson 1

You may wish to use one or more of the following suggestions to prepare students for the lesson:

1. Ask for three or four volunteers to take part in a fashion show. As students walk across the front of the classroom, describe what they are wearing (**llevar**), including colors and other adjectives, for example: **elegante, sensacional, fenomenal,** etc.

2. Borrow the lost-and-found box from the school office. Screen out any objectionable items. Then go through the contents with the class, naming and describing articles of clothing and having students speculate on **¿De quién es?**

Carmen lee con mucho interés un anuncio en el periódico.

¡Liquidación de temporada en Levy!

¡Ya rebajamos ropa de primavera un 50 por ciento o más! Todo para ustedes, nuestros clientes. Camisas, pantalones, chaquetas. Ropa elegante para toda la familia. Sensacional liquidación total. Descuentos increíbles.

¡Grandes rebajas!

➤ Camisas y blusas	Antes: $23.99	Ahora: sólo $11.99
➤ Pantalones de moda	Antes: $36.50	Ahora: sólo $17.50
➤ Jeans para damas o caballeros	Antes: $37.25	Ahora: sólo $18.99

Y para su comodidad, abrimos una nueva sucursal en el centro comercial Bayside. Abierto los domingos y días de fiesta de las 12 a las 5:30. Todas las tiendas abren de las 9 de la mañana a las 9 de la noche. Cerrado los domingos.

Almacenes LEVY, donde lo bueno cuesta barato. **¡Siempre les ofrecemos lo mejor!**

Actividades preliminares

A Find out the following about what your classmates are wearing (llevar) today.

1. ¿Cuántos llevan chaqueta hoy?
2. ¿Cuántos llevan camisa? ¿Y un suéter?
3. ¿Cuántos llevan "jeans"?

B Complete the following about shopping in your area.

1. Las mejores liquidaciones en las tiendas de mi ciudad son en los meses de _____.
2. Me gusta comprar ropa cuando hay descuentos de un _____ por ciento.

C Offer something to your classmates.

Por ejemplo:

Les doy (presto, compro, vendo) mi _____.

Vocabulario

Vocabulary Teaching Resources
1. Vocabulario Transparencies 6.1
2. Workbook, pp. 178–179
3. Cassette 6.1
4. Student Tape Manual, p. 148
5. Lesson Quizzes, pp. 117–118

Bell Ringer Review

Directions to students: Draw the appropriate number of circles on your paper to represent the members of your immediate family. Draw lines out from each circle and list the chores that each member is responsible for doing. Don't forget shopping, cooking, etc. Are the chores divided evenly or not?

Presentation

A. Have students open their books to the Vocabulario on pages 408 and 409. Lead students through the Vocabulario, beginning with the phrase **Quisiera comprar...** Have students repeat each phrase in unison.

B. You may wish to ask individual students whether they want to buy the articles of clothing or jewelry on pages 408 and 409. For example, **Daniela, ¿quieres comprar un vestido?**

C. You may wish to stand in the back of the classroom and describe students individually in terms of what they're wearing. The person being described will raise his or her hand. If students are unable to identify themselves based on the clothing description, provide more details such as hair color, etc.

Vocabulario

Quisiera comprar...
- unos pantalones
- una corbata
- un traje de caballero
- una chaqueta
- una camisa
- un cinturón de cuero
- unos calcetines

Ayer compré...
- un vestido
- una blusa de algodón
- un traje de dama
- un traje de baño
- unas pantimedias
- unos shorts
- una bolsa grande
- unas sandalias
- una falda
- unos anteojos de sol
- unos tenis

408 CAPÍTULO 6

Total Physical Response

Getting Ready
Collect two sets of the articles of clothing taught in the Vocabulario. Bring in a large stuffed animal, or a dummy to dress.

New Words
denle   denles
ponte   pónganse
póngale   póngales

TPR 1

(Call on pairs of students.)
Denle las camisas a ____.
Denles las faldas a dos muchachas rubias.
Denle los guantes a un muchacho alto.
Pónganse los anteojos de sol.
Pónganle el abrigo a ____.
Pónganle el vestido de baño y las medias al mono.
Pónganse las corbatas.

Actividades

A **En la tienda.** Organize the words and phrases in the **Vocabulario** according to the following categories.

Por ejemplo:

ropa para hombres
pantalones, camisas, corbatas...

1. ropa para mujeres
2. ropa para jóvenes
3. artículos para mujeres
4. artículos para hombres
5. joyas

Lección 1 409

Actividad B Answers

Answers will vary but may include the following:

1. blusas, camisas, vestidos
2. cinturones, bolsas, guantes
3. botas, tenis
4. pulseras, aretes, bolsas
5. anillos, pulseras, collares
6. abrigos, trajes de caballero, faldas

Actividades C, D, and E Answers

Answers will vary.

Addititional Practice

After completing Actividades A, B, C, D, and E, you may wish to reinforce the learning with the following activities:

1. Using the words in the Vocabulario, list all the clothes you need to buy and tell why.
   Por ejemplo:
   Necesito comprar unos tenis para la escuela. También necesito comprar un traje de baño para nadar en la piscina.
2. Have students help you coordinate your clothing by suggesting articles that match with the following. For example:
   a. ¿Qué debo llevar con jeans?
   b. ¿Qué debo llevar con un vestido elegante?
   c. ¿Qué debo llevar con una falda roja?
   d. ¿Qué debo llevar con shorts?

Reteaching

Using the Vocabulario on pages 408 and 409, ask students to tell where they went last weekend and what they wore, including colors.

B **¿De qué es?** List articles of clothing and accessories according to what they are made of.

Por ejemplo:

artículos de plata
un collar, unos aretes, un anillo...

1. artículos de algodón
2. artículos de cuero
3. artículos de goma
4. artículos de plástico
5. artículos de oro
6. artículos de lana (wool)

C **¿Qué ropa llevan?** Tell what you and your classmates wear during the following months.

1. En enero llevamos _____.
2. En abril llevamos _____.
3. En julio llevamos _____.
4. En octubre llevamos _____.

D **¿Elegante o informal?** Converse with a classmate about what you wear when you go to the following places.

Por ejemplo:

el centro comercial

ESTUDIANTE A
(1) ¿Qué ropa llevas cuando vas al centro comercial?
(3) Yo prefiero llevar pantalones, una camisa y un suéter.

ESTUDIANTE B
(2) A veces llevo "jeans" y una camiseta. ¿Y tú?

1. un partido de fútbol americano
2. una fiesta
3. un restaurante
4. la escuela

E **Las compras.** Tell where you went shopping last and what clothes or other items you bought.

Por ejemplo:

El sábado pasado fui al centro comercial y compré un cinturón. (Anoche fui al centro, pero no compré ropa. Compré un casete).

For the Native Speaker

Describe in detail the clothing you would use to participate in three of your favorite activities.

Cooperative Learning

Have each team make a collage of clothing. It should include items that students can describe in terms of article of clothing, material, and price. Then have the members of each team describe their collage to the class.

CULTURA VIVA 1

Los anuncios

En Miami, como en otras grandes ciudades bilingües, puedes ver anuncios en inglés y español.

Actividades

A What number would you call in the above ads to check prices on the following items?

1. comida
2. un coche
3. anteojos nuevos
4. ropa para jóvenes
5. un conejo o un gato

B List as many things as you can think of that would be sold in each of the stores above.

Por ejemplo:

En ____ venden ____.

Lección 1   411

Pronunciation

1. Use Pronunciation Transparency P-6.1.1, or write the pronunciation activity on the chalkboard. Have students copy it into their notebooks.
   **Venga a Almacenes Levy donde lo bueno cuesta barato.
   Levy, la tienda de la oferta barata.
   Todo por poca plata.**

2. You may wish to play the recorded version of this activity, located at the end of Cassette 6.1.
3. Have students repeat words and phrases individually and in unison. You may wish to focus on the /v/ sound: **venga, bueno, barato,** Levy.

Cultura viva 1

Reading Strategies
1. Lead students through each of the advertisements on page 411. Ask them what is being advertised. Ask students to guess the meaning of any new words.
2. Now do the **Actividades** on this page.

Did You Know?
Major American companies have done a great deal of market research about the Hispanic population in the U.S. because the buying power of Hispanics in this country is in the millions of dollars. Many major U.S. companies advertise in Spanish. Hispanics tend to be loyal to brands. Also, a greater percentage of advertisements in Spanish are designed to appeal to the family.

Critical Thinking Activities
1. Have students think of several reasons why many American companies advertise in Spanish for the Hispanic population in the U.S.
2. If Spanish-language newspapers are available in your area, you may want to ask each student to cut out ads, paste them on a poster board, and explain the ads to the class.

Actividades

Actividad A Answers
1. 225–0056
2. 585–1400
3. 626–2717
4. 393–3918
5. 863–1966

Actividad B Answers
Answers will vary.

411

Estructura 1

Structure Teaching Resources
1. Workbook, pp. 180–181
2. Cassette 6.1
3. Student Tape Manual, p. 148
4. Estructura Masters 6.1
5. Lesson Quizzes, p. 119

Bell Ringer Review
Directions to students: On a Saturday afternoon, you come home to find your older brother dressed for the beach, your mother dressed for the theater, and your younger sister dressed for the tennis championship. Draw a sketch of each person and label their clothing.

Structure Focus
The indirect object pronoun **les** is presented in this lesson. Students have used the indirect object pronoun **les** with the verb **gustar** in Chapter 4, Lessons 1 and 3. The indirect object pronoun **le** was presented in Chapter 5, Lesson 6.

Presentation
A. Lead students through steps 1–2 on page 412.
B. You may wish to review the uses of the indirect object pronoun **le** in Chapter 5, Lesson 6.

Actividades

Actividad A Answers
Answers will vary but should include the following:

1. A mis padres les...
2. A mi maestro le...
3. A mi mejor amigo le...
4. A todos mis amigos les...
5. A mis parientes les...

Estructura 1

How to Say What You Do for Others — **Indirect object pronoun les**

You have used **le** to tell what you do to or for someone else.

> A Miguel le voy a dar una billetera para su cumpleaños.
> A Susana le voy a dar unos aretes.

1. To say what you do to or for more than one person, use **les**.

   > ¿Conoces a mis amigos Paco y Raúl? Siempre les tengo que explicar las tareas. Les digo que deben estudiar más.

2. Notice that **les** can refer to "you" (plural) or "them." If it is not clear to whom you are referring, add **a** + the name of the group. For example, **a ustedes, a ellos, a ellas, a mis padres, a mis amigos, a Roberto y a Julia**.

   > A ustedes les voy a decir la verdad. Si visitan mi pueblo, no les puedo enseñar nada. A mis padres siempre les digo que es un pueblo aburrido.

Actividades

A **¿Siempre o no siempre?** Tell how often you do favors for the following people.

Por ejemplo:
> a tus hermanos
> *A mis hermanos siempre les hago favores.*

1. a tus padres
2. a tu maestro de inglés
3. a tu mejor amigo
4. a todos tus amigos
5. a tus parientes

B Un millón de dólares. You have just won a million dollars! Tell what you will buy or do for the following people.

Por ejemplo:

tus amigos
A mis amigos Mark y Paula les voy a comprar un Porsche.

1. a tus padres
2. a tus hermanos
3. a tus amigos
4. a tus maestros
5. a tus abuelos
6. a tus primos

C ¿Qué les diste? You still had money left over, so you gave all your old possessions away to friends and family and bought everything new. Tell to whom you gave five of your possessions.

Por ejemplo:

A mis primos les di mi estéreo.
A Laura y a Ken les di mis discos.

D ¿Eres generoso? Tell what you can do for the following people.

Por ejemplo:

dos compañeros de clase
Les voy a (puedo, quiero, etc.) ayudar con la tarea.

1. dos amigos
2. dos maestros
3. tus padres
4. tus hermanos
5. tus abuelos

Lección 1 **413**

Cultura viva 2

Reading Strategies
1. Read Rafael's letter aloud. Then read the letter again, calling on students to read one line each.
2. Now do the **Actividad** on this page.

Did You Know?
Baseball has always been a favorite pastime of Cubans. It is also Cuba's national sport. Before Fidel Castro became dictator of Cuba, the country had a team, the Cuban Sugar Kings, which played in the minor leagues in the U.S. In recent years the Dominican Republic is the nation that has contributed the greatest number of players to American baseball teams, including Pedro Guerrero, and Ramoncito Martínez. Baseball is not played in Argentina; soccer is Argentina's national sport.

Critical Thinking Activity
Read Rafael's letter to his mother once more, paying particular attention to the opening and closing portions. How is his letter different from one you might write to your mother?

Actividad Answers
1. Sí.
2. No.
3. No.
4. Sí.
5. Sí.
6. Sí.

Learning from Photos
You may want to have students look at the photos on page 414. Have them guess what Carmen might be saying to her cousin Rafael in the top photo. In the bottom photo, what might Rafael and his companion be talking about? Have students describe the clothing each person is wearing in both photos.

CULTURA VIVA 2

¡Tío Lucas y Rafael ya están en Miami!

Desde Miami, Rafael le escribe una carta a su mamá, que está en Buenos Aires.

Miami, 27 de abril

Querida mamita:

Papá y yo llegamos bien el jueves pasado y pasamos la primera semana aquí bastante ocupados. Estamos bien. Y tú, ¿cómo estás? ¿Muy solita?

Ayer Carmen y yo tomamos el tren (el "Metrorail") y visitamos varias partes de la cuidad, incluso la "Pequeña Habana". ¡Hasta jugué béisbol con unos chicos en el parque! Y saqué un montón de fotos. Anoche fui con Carmen a una fiesta en casa de una de sus compañeras. Practiqué el inglés con todos sus amigos. Dicen que hablo bastante bien. ¿Qué te parece?

Bueno, mamá, el domingo te escribo. Los tíos te mandan un abrazo y yo, un beso grande.

Tu hijo que te quiere mucho,
Rafael

Actividad

The following are some of the things Rafael wanted to do during his stay in Florida. Tell which of the following happened, according to his letter to his mother, by responding **sí** or **no**.

1. llegar sin problemas
2. ir a la playa
3. visitar Tampa
4. sacar muchas fotos
5. practicar el inglés
6. conocer a jóvenes

Estructura 2

How to Say What You and Others Did in the Past — **Preterit nosotros** *forms*

You have learned to say what you did in the past (preterit) by using the following verb endings.

- for **-ar** verbs: **-é**
- for **-er** and **-ir** verbs: **-í**

Llamé a Carmen anoche a las seis. A las siete salí con ella.

You have learned to tell or ask a friend or family member what he or she did using the following verb endings.

- for **-ar** verbs: **-aste**
- for **-er** and **-ir** verbs: **-iste**

¿Cuándo llegaste a Miami? ¿Ya viste muchas cosas?

1. To say what you and another person ("we") did in the past, use the following verb endings.

    - for **-ar** verbs: **-amos**
    - for **-er** and **-ir** verbs: **-imos**

    En el picnic jugamos béisbol y después comimos.

   Notice that for **-ar** and **-ir** verbs, these are the same endings you use to form the present tense.

2. The following verbs are exceptions to the above rules.

ir	fuimos	El sábado pasado fuimos al cine.
dar	dimos	Ayer por la tarde dimos un paseo por la playa.
hacer	hicimos	Anoche no hicimos nada.

For the Native Speaker

Imagine that you have a part-time job in a record/tape store. In writing, describe a recent day at work. What kind of customers did you have? What type of records/tapes did you sell? What else did you have to do?

Estructura 2

Structure Teaching Resources
1. Workbook, p. 182
2. Cassette 6.1
3. Student Tape Manual, p. 149
4. Estructura Masters 6.1
5. Lesson Quizzes, p. 120

Bell Ringer Review
Directions to students: Which of the following items would you tell Rafael to take with him to Miami? Which should he not take?
Por ejemplo: las maletas
Debes llevar las maletas.

1. la cámara
2. el diccionario
3. el pasaporte
4. los discos
5. el mapa
6. el libro de matemáticas
7. la calculadora
8. el teléfono
9. ropa cómoda
10. los cheques de viajero

Structure Focus
In this lesson, the presentation of the preterit is limited to **nosotros** forms. The **yo** and **tú** forms of the preterit were presented in Chapter 5, Lessons 5 and 6. The third person singular and plural preterit forms will be presented in Chapter 6, Lessons 3 and 4. A summary of preterit forms is presented in Chapter 6, Lesson 6.

Presentation
A. Lead students through steps 1–2 on page 415. You may wish to refer students to the verb charts in the back of their textbook, or write several paradigms on the chalkboard. Remind students they have already learned the **yo** and **tú** preterit forms, and that in

this lesson they will be using the **nosotros** form.

B. You may wish to practice **yo** and **tú** forms of the preterit by reviewing some of the activities in Chapter 5, Lessons 5 and 6.
Note. Oímos and **leímos** take an accent on the **i**.

Actividades

Actividad A Answers
Answers will vary but should include:

1. (No) Visitamos...
2. (No) Hablamos...
3. (No) Jugamos...
4. (No) Salimos...
5. (No) Comimos...
6. (No) Dimos...
7. (No) Hicimos...
8. (No) Recibimos...

Actividades B and C Answers
Answers will vary.

Reteaching

Ask students how they would say they and their friends did each of the following activities yesterday: **ir a la escuela; comprar ropa; jugar tenis; comer hamburguesas; hacer la tarea; recibir regalos; salir temprano; dormir mucho; escribir cartas.**

Actividades

A ¿Y ustedes? Tell whether or not you and your family or friends did the following activities in the past few months.

Por ejemplo:

ir al zoológico
(No) Fuimos al zoológico.

1. visitar Miami
2. hablar español
3. jugar béisbol
4. salir a la playa
5. comer comida cubana
6. dar un paseo por la ciudad
7. hacer un picnic
8. recibir invitaciones a una fiesta

B Mi compañero y yo. Ask a classmate the following questions about things the two of you did. Report to the class those things the two of you have in common.

Por ejemplo:

¿Saliste anoche?

ESTUDIANTE A
(1) ¿Saliste anoche?
(3) Yo también.

ESTUDIANTE B
(2) Sí, salí con mis amigos.

(A la clase:) Victoria y yo salimos anoche.

1. ¿En qué año naciste?
2. ¿Practicaste un deporte ayer?
3. ¿Qué programas viste anoche?
4. ¿Adónde fuiste ayer después de las clases?
5. ¿Qué estudiaste anoche? ¿Dónde estudiaste?
6. ¿Qué hiciste el fin de semana pasado?
7. ¿A qué hora llegaste a la escuela esta mañana? (Llegué...)

C ¡Muchas gracias, maestros! Your teachers have agreed to give less homework. You and your classmates have thanked them by giving each a present. Tell what gifts you have given to four of your teachers and tell why you selected each gift.

Por ejemplo:

A la maestra de español le dimos un diccionario grande porque le gustan las palabras raras.

Finalmente

Situaciones

A conversar You've saved enough money to buy some new clothes. Your partner will play the role of the department store salesperson.

1. Ask the salesperson to show you certain articles of clothing.
2. Ask about prices and alternate colors.
3. Inquire about matching accessories.
4. Make your selections. The salesperson will tell you the total cost.

A escribir Think of an exciting place you went to once with family or friends. Write a letter to a classmate telling about your trip.

1. Describe the activities that you and others did during the day.
2. Tell what you did in the evening. Tell with whom you did each activity.
3. Describe any souvenirs or other items you bought for yourself or others.

Repaso de vocabulario

ROPA
el abrigo
la blusa
las botas
la bufanda
los calcetines
la camisa
la corbata
la chaqueta
la falda
el gorro
los guantes
el impermeable
los pantalones
las pantimedias
las sandalias
los "shorts"
el suéter
los tenis
el traje de baño
el traje de caballero
el traje de dama
el vestido

JOYAS
el anillo
el arete
el collar
la pulsera

ARTÍCULOS
los anteojos
   de sol
la bolsa
el cinturón
el paraguas

ACTIVIDAD
llevar (to wear)

Finalmente

Situaciones

Lesson 1 Evaluation
The A conversar and A escribir situations on this page are designed to give students the opportunity to use as many language functions and as much vocabulary from this lesson as possible. The A conversar and A escribir are also intended to show how well students are able to meet the lesson objectives.

Presentation

Prior to doing the A conversar and A escribir on this page, you may wish to play the Situaciones listening activities on Cassette 6.1 as a means of helping students organize the material.

Learning from Realia

You may want to have students look at the realia on page 417. If they were to buy the following items during this sale, how much would they pay for each with the 10% discount?

1. zapatos: $40
2. chaqueta: $50
3. abrigo: $77

CAPÍTULO 6

Lección 2

Objectives

By the end of this lesson, students will be able to:
1. say what people do for them and others
2. say that they did certain activities in the past
3. describe clothing and accessories

Lesson 2 Resources
1. Workbook, pp. 183–188
2. Vocabulario Transparencies
3. Pronunciation Transparency P-6.2.1
4. Audio Cassette 6.2 Compact Disc 9
5. Student Tape Manual, pp. 153–158
6. Bell Ringer Review Blackline Masters, p. 37
7. Computer Software: Practice & Test Generator
8. Video (cassette or disc)
9. Video Activities Booklet, pp. A83–A84
10. Estructura Masters, pp. 75–76
11. Diversiones Masters, pp. 69–70
12. Situation Cards
13. Lesson Quizzes, pp. 121–124
14. Testing Program

Bell Ringer Review

Directions to students: What would you suggest your father, mother, and little brother wear on these occasions?
papá — para el trabajo
mamá — para el trabajo
hermanito — para la playa

¡A comenzar!

Presentation

A. Lead students through each of

418

CAPÍTULO 6

Lección 2

¿Vamos al centro comercial?

¡A comenzar!

The following are some of the things you will be learning to do in this lesson.

When you want to...	You use...
1. say what people do for you and others	**Nos** + activity.
2. say that you did certain activities in the past	**-cé** or **-qué** on certain **-ar** verbs

Now find examples of the above words and phrases in the following conversation.

418

Getting Ready for Lesson 2

You may wish to use one or more of the following suggestions to prepare students for the lesson:

1. Cut out illustrations from magazines to present various types of clothing. Describe the illustrations. For example: **Este hombre lleva una camisa de manga larga y pantalones de rayas. Esta mujer lleva un traje elegante de seda... un vestido de flores de manga corta... un traje de invierno... una camiseta y pantalones deportivos, etc.**

2. Describe the clothing worn by students in the class. After your descriptions, ask questions about what the students are wearing. For example: **¿Lleva Eric una camiseta de rayas? ¿Lleva Janet una blusa de manga larga? ¿Lleva Tom**

Carmen está en casa con su primo Rafael y su tío Lucas.

RAFAEL: Carmen, ya empecé a estudiar las palabras que me enseñaste en inglés. Y ayer practiqué mucho pero no entiendo qué dice aquí en el periódico.
CARMEN: A ver... Dice que hay una liquidación de temporada.
RAFAEL: Bueno, quisiera comprar unos regalos antes de regresar a Buenos Aires.
TÍO LUCAS: Oye, Carmencita, ¿por qué no llevas a tu primo al centro comercial? Le puedes enseñar las tiendas y también le puedes presentar a tus amigos.
RAFAEL: ¿Vamos a la calle Ocho?
CARMEN: No, Rafael. Voy a ver si mamá nos da permiso para ir al centro comercial Bayside.
RAFAEL: ¡Qué bueno! Oye, papá, ¿nos puedes prestar dinero?

Actividades preliminares

A Tell where the following are located.

Por ejemplo:

Argentina
Está en la América del Sur.

1. Florida
2. Buenos Aires
3. la calle Ocho
4. Miami

B Complete the following sentences about what you did recently.

1. Compré _____. Pagué _____.
2. Saqué una buena nota en la clase de _____.
3. Llegué tarde a la clase de _____.
4. Jugué _____ con mis amigos.
5. Practiqué _____.

---

the two functions given on page 418, progressing from the English to the Spanish for each function. Then have students find these words and phrases in the dialogue on page 419.

B. Introduce the Lesson 2 dialogue by reading it aloud or by playing the recorded version. Tell students they are going to hear a conversation between Carmen, her Uncle Lucas, and her cousin Rafael. Have them listen to find out:

1. ¿Qué quiere hacer Rafael?
2. ¿Adónde quieren ir Carmen y Rafael?

C. Now ask students to open their books and look at the dialogue as you lead them through what is said. For example:

1. ¿Qué no entiende Rafael? ¿Qué dice el periódico?
2. ¿Qué quiere hacer Rafael?
3. Lucas le recomienda algo a Carmen. ¿Qué dice?
4. Rafael quiere saber si van a cierto lugar. ¿Dónde? ¿Adónde van a ir?
5. ¿Qué le pregunta Rafael a su papá?

D. After reading the dialogue with your students, you may wish to follow up with these questions:

1. Cuando vas al centro comercial, ¿te prestan dinero tus padres?
2. Si quieres comprar pantalones deportivos, ¿adónde vas ?(¿a qué tienda vas?)
3. Si quieres comprar un vestido elegante, ¿adónde vas?
4. Si quieres comprar camisetas de moda, ¿adónde vas?, etc.

Actividades preliminares

Actividad A Answers
1. Está en los Estados Unidos (la América del Norte).
2. Está en Argentina.
3. Está en Miami.
4. Está en Florida.

Actividad B Answers
Answers will vary.

---

pantalones de lunares?, etc. Students may respond with **Sí** or **No**.
3. Using the magazine pictures and any other available illustrations, ask individual students either/or questions about their clothing preferences. For example:
John, ¿qué te gustan más, los pantalones de cuadros o de un sólo color?
Angela, ¿qué te gusta más, un vestido de lunares o un vestido de flores?
Michael, ¿qué te gusta más, una camisa de manga corta o de manga larga?
Amy, ¿qué te gusta más, una falda de rayas o de un sólo color?, etc.

Vocabulario

Vocabulary Teaching Resources
1. Vocabulario Transparencies 6.2
2. Workbook, pp. 183–185
3. Cassette 6.2
4. Student Tape Manual, p. 154
5. Lesson Quizzes, pp. 121–122

Bell Ringer Review

Directions to students: Sometimes when we hear a word we immediately think of an image we associate with it. Copy down these words and beside each write the first word or expression you associate with it. Be spontaneous!

**los aretes de oro
un anillo
un paraguas
un gorro
botas
guantes
el béisbol
diciembre**

Presentation

A. Have students open their books to the Vocabulario on pages 420 and 421. Model the question at the top of page 420, **¿Qué clase de ropa buscas?** Then introduce each phrase in the Vocabulario, beginning each time with **Busco...** Have students repeat after you each time. Then introduce each word or phrase on page 421, beginning with the questions **¿Qué diseño te gusta?** and **¿Qué tela prefieres?**

B. You may wish to ask students personalized questions such as, **¿Te gusta la blusa de seda? ¿Les gustan los pantalones de lana? ¿Necesitas un vestido de un solo color? ¿Cuándo llevas un abrigo de lana?**, etc.

Vocabulario

¿Qué clase de ropa buscas? Busco...

una blusa... sin mangas
de manga larga
de manga corta
un vestido elegante
unos pantalones de moda
una camisa deportiva

ropa para damas
ropa para caballeros

un traje de...
primavera
verano
otoño
invierno

420 CAPÍTULO 6

Total Physical Response

Getting Ready
Bring to class the articles of clothing mentioned in the TPR activities below. Display the clothing on hangers and add prices to each item. Have fake paper money in $5 and $10 bills.

New Words
pruébate   pruébense
escoge   escojan
págale   páguenle

TPR 1

Toquen la blusa de lunares.
Apunten al vestido elegante.
Escojan tres artículos de ropa para mujeres.
Escojan tres artículos de ropa para hombres.

¿Qué diseño te gusta? Quiero una camisa...
de cuadros, de lunares, de rayas, de un solo color, de flores

¿Qué tela prefieres? Prefiero ropa de...
seda, lana

Actividades

A Ropa adecuada. Make four columns, one for each season of the year. Under each season, list two articles of clothing you would typically wear.

Por ejemplo:
> verano
> *ropa de algodón, sandalias...*

B Inventario. List three articles of clothing that you wear in summer and three you wear in winter. Describe each article in detail.

Por ejemplo:
> En verano llevo pantalones grises. Son de algodón. Son viejos. En invierno llevo botas negras de cuero. Me gustan mucho.

Lección 2   421

C. Have students compliment each other on one article of clothing they are wearing. For example: **¡Qué vestido más lindo! Me gusta mucho tu camisa de lunares,** etc.

When Students Ask

You may wish to give students the following additional vocabulary to allow them to talk about clothing.
el encaje
el lino
la piel
el nilón
el probador
las rebajas
la talla
el estampado
me/te queda(n)
pasado(a) de moda
bordado(a)
la camisa de vestir
apretado(a)
ancho(a)
no me queda
no hace juego con

Actividades

Actividad A Answers
Answers may vary but might include the following:
verano: una camisa de manga corta, unos shorts
otoño: una camisa de manga larga, un suéter
invierno: ropa de lana; un abrigo
primavera: ropa de algodón, una chaqueta

Actividad B Answers
Answers will vary.

Pruébense las blusas de flores.
Pruébense las blusas de algodón.
Páguenle a la maestra (al maestro) $20 por la camisa deportiva.
Páguenle a la maestra (al maestro) $100 por el vestido elegante.
(Continue interchanging commands and clothing.)

TPR 2

(Call on pairs of students to respond. Alternate your commands between them.)
1. Dale el vestido elegante a _____.
2. Pruébate el vestido elegante.
1. Dile que es bonito.
2. Pregúntale el precio y págale.
(Interchange clothing, prices, and descriptions.)

Actividades C and D Answers
Answers will vary.

Class Management
You may wish to model Actividad C with several of your better students initially. The teacher may play the role of Student A. After modeling in this way, have students do Actividad C in pairs according to the directions.

Actividad E Answers
Sonia: Lleva una falda amarilla de lunares.
Yolanda: Lleva una blusa de seda, una falda blanca, sandalias, joyas de plástico de muchos colores.
Paco: Lleva una camisa de cuadros anaranjados, negros y blancos, "jeans", zapatos de cuero, anteojos de sol.
Cristina: Lleva un traje de baño de rayas azules y rojas, anteojos de sol, sandalias.
Héctor: Lleva un traje de baño de flores, una camiseta amarilla.
David: Lleva una camisa de flores verdes, amarillas y rojas, "shorts" blancos, calcetines blancos, tenis.

Additional Practice
After completing Actividades A, B, C, D, and E, you may wish to reinforce the learning with the following activity:
Create and describe a situation in which someone was inappropriately dressed for an event. **Por ejemplo:**

ESTUDIANTE A	ESTUDIANTE B
Mi amiga fue a la iglesia. Llevó un traje de baño.	¡Qué horror!

Reteaching
Tell students where you went yesterday, last weekend, etc. Describe what you wore. Have students write down the clothing you describe.

C Lo que buscas. Write down five items of clothing you need to buy for winter or summer. Describe each item.

Por ejemplo:

> Para el verano necesito una camiseta de rayas. Prefiero una blanca y azul.

D ¿Me compras algo, por favor? A classmate will play the role of a parent. Ask him or her for each of the items you listed in activity C. He or she says no to each request, but gives a good reason. Student A then reports back to the class.

Por ejemplo:

ESTUDIANTE A	ESTUDIANTE B
Mamá (Papá), ¿me compras una camiseta de rayas?	No, ya tienes muchas camisetas.

(A la clase:) Mi mamá (papá) no me quiere comprar una camiseta porque dice que ya tengo muchas camisetas.

E En la fiesta. Describe to a classmate with as much detail as possible what each person is wearing in the picture below. Your classmate will identify whom you are describing.

Por ejemplo:

ESTUDIANTE A	ESTUDIANTE B
Una muchacha lleva una falda amarilla de lunares.	Hablas de Sonia, ¿no?

422 CAPÍTULO 6

For the Native Speaker
Write an advertisement for a clothing store. Describe in detail the articles of clothing featured in the ad.

Cooperative Learning
After completing Actividad A, page 421, do a Four Corners activity. Each corner will represent a season. Students will select the season they like best and go to that corner. They pair up and and tell each other why they like the season. The teacher monitors and calls on some students from each corner. If desired, have students move to the season (corner) they like least, and tell why.

CULTURA VIVA 1

La Pequeña Habana

La Pequeña Habana es un barrio de Miami. En este barrio puedes ver muchos cafés, bodegas, tiendas y puntos de reunión donde la cultura cubana está en todas partes. Allí puedes comprar cosas que no hay en muchas otras ciudades de los Estados Unidos, como, por ejemplo, frutas y verduras tropicales, guayaberas, piñatas, churros y helados de frutas tropicales.

Las fiestas más importantes del año son el Desfile del Día de la Herencia Hispánica y el "Carnaval Miami". Dicen que el carnaval atrae más gente que todas las otras festividades hispanas de los Estados Unidos.

Actividad

Tell what a visitor to **La Pequeña Habana** could do, based on the photos.

Por ejemplo:
  Puede comer comida nicaragüense.

Lección 2 423

Cultura viva 1

Reading Strategies
1. If possible, show a map of Miami, including the Pequeña Habana section.
2. Read the **Cultura viva** on this page. Then do the **Actividad**.
3. Have students list in Spanish all the things they might see in **La Pequeña Habana**.

Did You Know?
La Pequeña Habana is a neighborhood in Miami between Flagler and Eighth Street, west of the downtown area. Since the early 1960's it has been the center of Cuban immigrants' economic and social life. Walking in La Pequeña Habana gives you the feeling you're in Cuba. Most businesses are owned by Cubans and most customers are Cubans. Since the fall of Anastasio Somoza, the former dictator of Nicaragua, in 1979 there has been a large influx of Nicaraguan immigrants to this area.

Critical Thinking Activity
Based on the reading, how do you think La Pequeña Habana will change over the next twenty years? Do you think there will be more evidence of the Cuban culture or less?
Note. A guayabera is a type of shirt. Usually it is embroidered, or has small tucks as decorations. Churros are sticks of fried pastry. They are usually served with hot chocolate.

Actividad Answers
Puede leer revistas en español; comer churros y helados de frutas tropicales; comer en restaurantes nicaragüenses, salvadoreños y cubanos; comprar flores y piñatas.

Pronunciation
1. Use Pronunciation Transparency P-6.2.1, or write the pronunciation activity on the chalkboard. Have students copy it into their notebooks.
   Me encanta la comida cubana: frijoles negros, plátanos fritos. Si quieren comer en la Pequeña Habana, Pues vengan con nosotros, Paco y Ana.
2. You may wish to play the recorded version of this activity, located at the end of Cassette 6.2.
3. Have students repeat words and phrases individually and in unison. You may wish to focus on the /a/ sound, as in **encanta, comida, cubana, Habana, Ana.**

Estructura 1

Structure Teaching Resources
1. Workbook, p. 186
4. Estructura Masters 6.2
2. Cassette 6.2
3. Student Tape Manual, p. 155
5. Lesson Quizzes, p. 123

Bell Ringer Review
Directions to students: In Spanish, write the name of each season on your paper. Then beside each season, write the three months that belong to it.

Structure Focus
In this lesson the object pronoun **nos** is presented. The indirect object pronoun **le** was presented in Chapter 5, Lesson 6. The indirect object pronoun **les** was presented in Chapter 6, Lesson 1.

Presentation
A. Lead students through steps 1–2 on page 424. In step 1, you may wish to have students read the illustrated dialogue. As review, you may also ask various students to read the dialogue, pretending that Diana is not there.
B. You may wish to review earlier exercises that practice the use of **gustar**, this time substituting **nos** as the indirect object pronoun. See Chapter 1, Lessons 4 and 6; Chapter 4, Lessons 1 and 3.

Estructura 1

How to Say What People Do for You and Others
How to Talk about What You and Others Like and Dislike

Object pronoun nos

You have used **me, te, le,** and **les** to talk about what people do to or for you and others.

    Si me ayudas con la tarea, te compro un casete.

    Todos me piden favores. Ayer le presté mi libro de inglés a Jaime. También les presté cinco dólares a Raquel y a Yolanda.

1. To say that someone does something for you and others ("for us"), use **nos** + activity.

Papá, Diana y yo queremos saber si nos puedes prestar el coche.

Entonces, ¿nos das el dinero para tomar un taxi?

No les puedo prestar el coche porque tengo que ir al centro.

2. To say what you and others like or dislike, use **(no) nos** + **gusta(n)**.

    Nos gusta la clase de arte porque nos gusta dibujar.
    No nos gustan mucho los partidos de tenis.

Actividades

A **El maestro ideal.** Tell whether or not the ideal teacher does the following for you and your classmates.

Por ejemplo:

> hacer exámenes fáciles
> *Sí, nos hace exámenes fáciles.*

1. escuchar
2. dar dos horas de tarea
3. explicar bien las lecciones
4. criticar mucho
5. enseñar cosas interesantes
6. hacer exámenes todos los días
7. dar buenos consejos

B **Maestro, ¡por favor!** Work with a classmate to make five unusual requests of your teacher. Then report your requests to the class.

Por ejemplo:

> **Señorita, ¿nos puede dar tareas muy fáciles? (Señor, ¿nos permite comer en clase?)**

C **Durante todo el año.** Tell two things that you and your family or friends like about each of the four seasons.

Por ejemplo:

> en verano
> *En verano nos gusta ir a la playa. También nos gustan los partidos de béisbol.*

1. en verano
2. en otoño
3. en invierno
4. en primavera

Lección 2   425

Cultura viva 2

Reading Strategies
1. Read the **Cultura viva** on this page. Then do the **Actividad**.
2. If there is a Cuban restaurant in your area, ask for a menu to share with your students.
3. Invite a Cuban American to speak to your class about the foods described in the reading.

Did You Know?
Although there are similarities between Cuban food and that of other Latin American countries, Cuban food is more like that of Spain. What gives Cuban cooking its distinctive character are the seasonings: lime or lemon juice, onions, sweet peppers, and garlic. The hot spices found in Mexican cooking are rarely used. The main staples of a Cuban meal are beans and rice. These are always eaten together. Roast pork is also a favorite. Many desserts such as guava paste and **dulce de coco** (grated coconut cooked in syrup) are made from tropical fruits.

Critical Thinking Activity
After rereading the **Cultura viva**, compare and contrast Cuban and Mexican food, as described on page 136. How are they alike and how are they different?

Actividad Answers
Arroz frito:
Fried rice...
Chicharrones de pollo:
Fried chicken chunks...
Bistec al queso:
Cheese melt steak...
Arroz con pollo:
Chicken and rice...
Bistec empanizado:
Breaded steak...
Carne de res con vegetales:
Beef vegetable stew...

CULTURA VIVA 2

La comida cubana

En la Florida y en otras partes de los Estados Unidos, puedes comer comida cubana. Algunos de los ingredientes básicos son: el arroz, frijoles de distintos colores, varias verduras y frutas tropicales (como los plátanos y las guanábanas), papas, pescado, carne de puerco y pollo. La comida cubana no es tan picante como la mexicana. Para terminar, el café cubano es muy rico y los helados de frutas tropicales son deliciosos.

arroz blanco con frijoles negros

plátanos fritos

naranjas, guayabas, chirimoyas y mangos

Actividad

This is a portion of the bilingual menu from a restaurant on **la calle Ocho**. The chef mixed up the English translations. Can you match the items on the menu with their correct English translations?

Especialidades	Today's Specials
ARROZ FRITO Plátanos Maduros	Beef vegetable stew, with yellow rice and fried bananas
CHICHARRONES DE POLLO Con Arroz Blanco	Cheese melt steak, with mashed potatoes
BISTEC AL QUESO Con Puré de Papas	Breaded steak, with french fries
ARROZ CON POLLO Con Plátanos Maduros	Fried rice, with fried bananas
BISTEC EMPANIZADO Con Papas Fritas	Fried chicken chunks, with white rice
CARNE DE RES CON VEGETALES Con Arroz Amarillo y Plátanos Maduros	Chicken and rice, with fried plantains

Learning from Photos
You may want to have students look at the photos on page 426. Have individual students tell if they have ever eaten each of the foods shown. Ask which foods they would like to eat.

Estructura 2

How to Write about the Past

Irregular yo forms of certain -ar verbs in the preterit

You have learned to say what you did in the past using **-ar** verbs.

> Anoche llamé a mi amigo Tomás.
> Después hablé con mi amiga Inés.

1. In Rafael's letter to his mother on p. 414, he used the past tense forms **jugué, saqué,** and **practiqué.**

> Jugué béisbol. Saqué muchas fotos. Practiqué el inglés.

If you pronounce these words aloud, you can hear the sound of the past tense. When you write certain verbs using the **yo** form in the past tense, you must change the spelling.

2. The following verbs ending in **-car, -gar,** and **-zar** will make these changes.

-qué	tocar	Anoche toqué la guitarra.
	sacar	Saqué una "A" en el examen.
	practicar	Practiqué el español con Eva.
	explicar	Le expliqué la tarea a José.
	buscar	En el centro le busqué un regalo a mi primo.
-gué	llegar	El lunes llegué tarde a la escuela.
	jugar	Jugué béisbol con los amigos.
	pagar	Compré un traje de baño. No pagué mucho.
-cé	empezar	Anoche empecé la composición. Voy a terminar hoy.

These changes affect the way you spell the words, not how you pronounce them.

Actividades

Actividad A Answers
1. empecé
2. Llegué
3. expliqué
4. pagué
5. busqué
6. empecé
7. Saqué

Actividad B Answers
Answers will vary but should include the following:
1. Este año saco... pero el año pasado saqué...
2. ... estudio... estudié...
3. ... leo... leí...
4. ... hago... hice...
5. ... practico... practiqué...

Reteaching
How would you say you did the following things yesterday?
buscar tu número de teléfono, practicar la guitarra, empezar la tarea, explicarle el problema de química a Jorge, llegar temprano, pagar cinco dólares, sacar muchas fotos.

Actividades

A **Notas.** Carmen wrote the following notes to her friend Jorge on the days she was taking her computer class. Complete them, using the **yo** form of the preterit of the following verbs.

| buscar | explicar | pagar | sacar |
| empezar | llegar | practicar | |

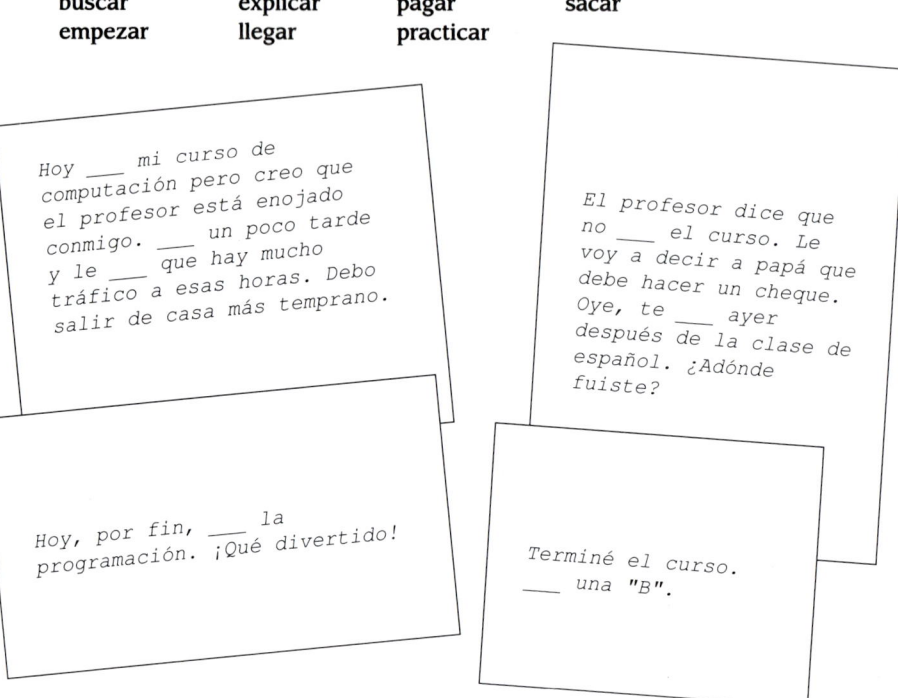

B **Este año y el año pasado.** Compare this school year to last year in terms of the following topics.

Por ejemplo:
  los deportes que practicas
  Este año juego tenis pero el año pasado jugué baloncesto.

1. las notas que sacas
2. las materias (subjects) que estudias
3. los libros que lees
4. las tareas que haces
5. los deportes que practicas

Cooperative Learning
Divide teams into pairs. Give each pair the infinitive of the verbs presented in Actividad B, page 428. Have students write the past tense of the verbs. Then as a team, they should complete the sentences in Actividad B.

Finalmente

Situaciones

A conversar A classmate will play the role of a new Spanish-speaking exchange student whose first day of school is tomorrow. You call him or her and make plans to meet tomorrow before classes start.

1. Say hello, introduce yourself, and ask where he or she is from.
2. Find out when he or she arrived in the U.S.
3. Say that you'd like to show him or her around school tomorrow and introduce him or her to your friends. Your partner accepts the invitation and thanks you.
4. Tell your partner what time you will arrive at school and where you will be.
5. Describe yourself so your partner will know who you are. Tell what you look like and what you will be wearing. Your partner does the same. Say good-bye.

A escribir Identify who, in your opinion, is the best-dressed and worst-dressed celebrity today. Write a review, describing each person's clothing and appearance in general, making reference to photos in magazines, an album cover, a poster, or a live concert or TV appearance. To make your review seem more lively, write in the present tense.

Repaso de vocabulario

CLASES DE ROPA
de manga corta
de manga larga
de moda
deportivo(a)
para caballeros
para damas
sin mangas

TELAS
la lana
la seda

DISEÑOS
de cuadros
de flores
de lunares (m.)
de rayas
de un solo color

ESTACIONES
la primavera
el verano
el otoño
el invierno

Lección 2

CAPÍTULO 6

Lección 3

Objectives

By the end of this lesson, students will be able to:

1. give directions
2. identify modes of transportation
3. say what someone did at one point in the past
4. say that someone is coming

Lesson 3 Resources
1. Workbook, pp. 189–194
2. Vocabulario Transparencies
3. Pronunciation Transparency P-6.3.1
4. Audio Cassette 6.3 Compact Disc 9
5. Student Tape Manual, pp. 159–164
6. Bell Ringer Review Blackline Masters, p. 38
7. Computer Software: Practice & Test Generator
8. Video (cassette or disc)
9. Video Activities Booklet, pp. A85–A86
10. Estructura Masters, pp. 77–78
11. Diversiones Masters, pp. 71–72
12. Situation Cards
13. Lesson Quizzes, pp. 125–128
14. Testing Program

Bell Ringer Review

Directions to students: Write the names of the four seasons across the top of your paper and list each of the following activities in the appropriate column.

esquiar, bucear, saltar las olas, patinar sobre hielo, montar en bicicleta, nadar en la piscina, pasear en velero, jugar béisbol, jugar tenis, jugar fútbol americano, ir de pesca, practicar el esquí acuático

---

CAPÍTULO 6

Lección 3

Aquí se dice "guagua"

¡A comenzar!

The following are some of the things you will be learning to do in this lesson.

When you want to...	You use...
1. say something is far / near	Está lejos / Está cerca.
2. say what someone did in the past	-ó at the end of -ar verbs
3. say that something or someone is approaching	Ya viene.

Now find examples of the above words and phrases in the following conversation.

430

Getting Ready for Lesson 3

You may wish to use one or more of the following suggestions to prepare students for the lesson:

1. Sketch a map of your own town or area on a transparency and fill in places such as the library, a museum, the post office, hospital, hotel, school, church, synagogue, park, streets, and department stores as well as some students' houses. Use this map to describe the locations of various places and houses in relation to each other. For example: **El hospital está lejos de nuestra escuela pero el museo está cerca. La casa de Julia está en la esquina de las calles Vine y Elm. Al lado de su casa está la biblioteca. A dos cuadras de la casa de Don hay un restaurante, etc.**

Carmen y Rafael salen de compras.

RAFAEL: ¿Está muy lejos el centro comercial?
CARMEN: No, está bastante cerca.
RAFAEL: ¿A cuántos kilómetros?
CARMEN: Pues, en kilómetros, no sé. Pero no hay problema. Tomamos la guagua.
RAFAEL: ¿Tomamos *qué*?
CARMEN: Digo, el autobús. Aquí se dice "guagua". Oye, ¿cuánto dinero te prestó tu papá?
RAFAEL: Me prestó veinte dólares. Vamos, ya viene el autobús.

Actividades preliminares

A Tell whether the following are close to or far from school.

Por ejemplo:

un restaurante
Un restaurante está cerca (lejos).

1. un centro comercial
2. una tienda de computadoras
3. tu casa
4. el trabajo de tu papá (mamá)
5. un cine

B Tell what three people lent you recently.

Por ejemplo:

Mi papá me prestó su coche.

Vocabulario

Vocabulary Teaching Resources
1. Vocabulario Transparencies 6.3
2. Workbook, pp. 189–190
3. Cassette 6.3
4. Student Tape Manual, p. 159
5. Lesson Quizzes, pp. 125–126

Bell Ringer Review

Directions to students: What a weird circus! Draw the following animals according to their descriptions.

1. El elefante lleva un traje de caballero, una camisa de lunares, una corbata de flores, un sombrero y unos zapatos de tenis.
2. El gorila lleva un vestido de cuadros, sandalias y una bufanda.
3. El león lleva una camisa de rayas, unos shorts, sandalias y un gorro de béisbol.

Presentation

A. Have students open their books to the Vocabulario on pages 432 and 433. Model each new phrase. Have students repeat each phrase in unison.

B. You may want to use Vocabulario Transparencies 6.3 or the one you made of your area in "Getting Ready for Lesson 3" to direct students to various locations. They will tell you where they end up. For example: **Están en la esquina de ____ y ____. Siguen derecho dos cuadras. ¿Dónde están?**

C. Have students name places according to your questions. For example: **¿Qué hay al lado de ____/enfrente de ____/a la izquierda de ____/a tres cuadras de ____?**, etc.

Vocabulario

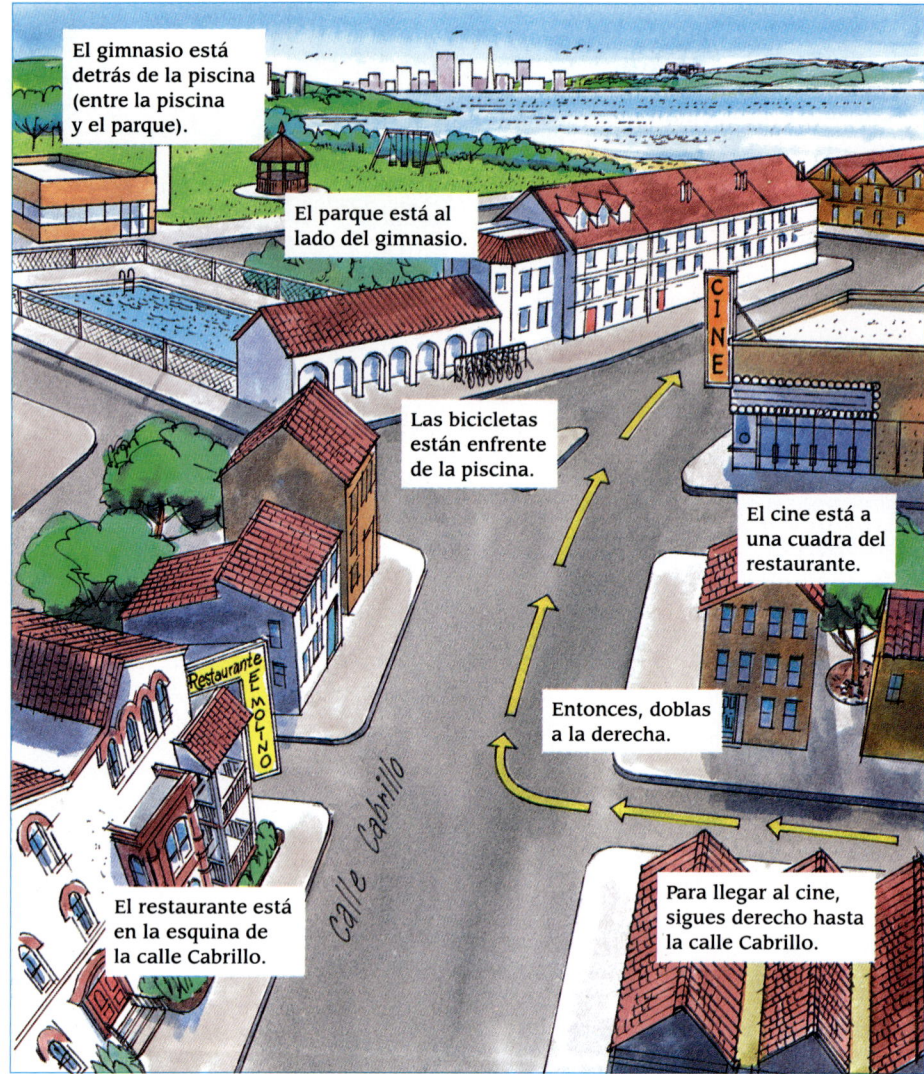

432 CAPÍTULO 6

Total Physical Response

Getting Ready
Use Vocabulario Transparencies 6.3, filling in appropriate places for the TPR commands. Or sketch a map of your own town or area on a transparency and fill in with the appropriate places for the TPR commands. Then make photocopies of the modes of transportation on page 433 and cut up into individual pieces.

New Words
estaciona   mueve   cielo

TPR 1

(Call individual students to the overhead projector.)
Pon el autobús enfrente del cine.
Pon el tren entre la piscina y el parque.
Estaciona la camioneta a la derecha del gimnasio.

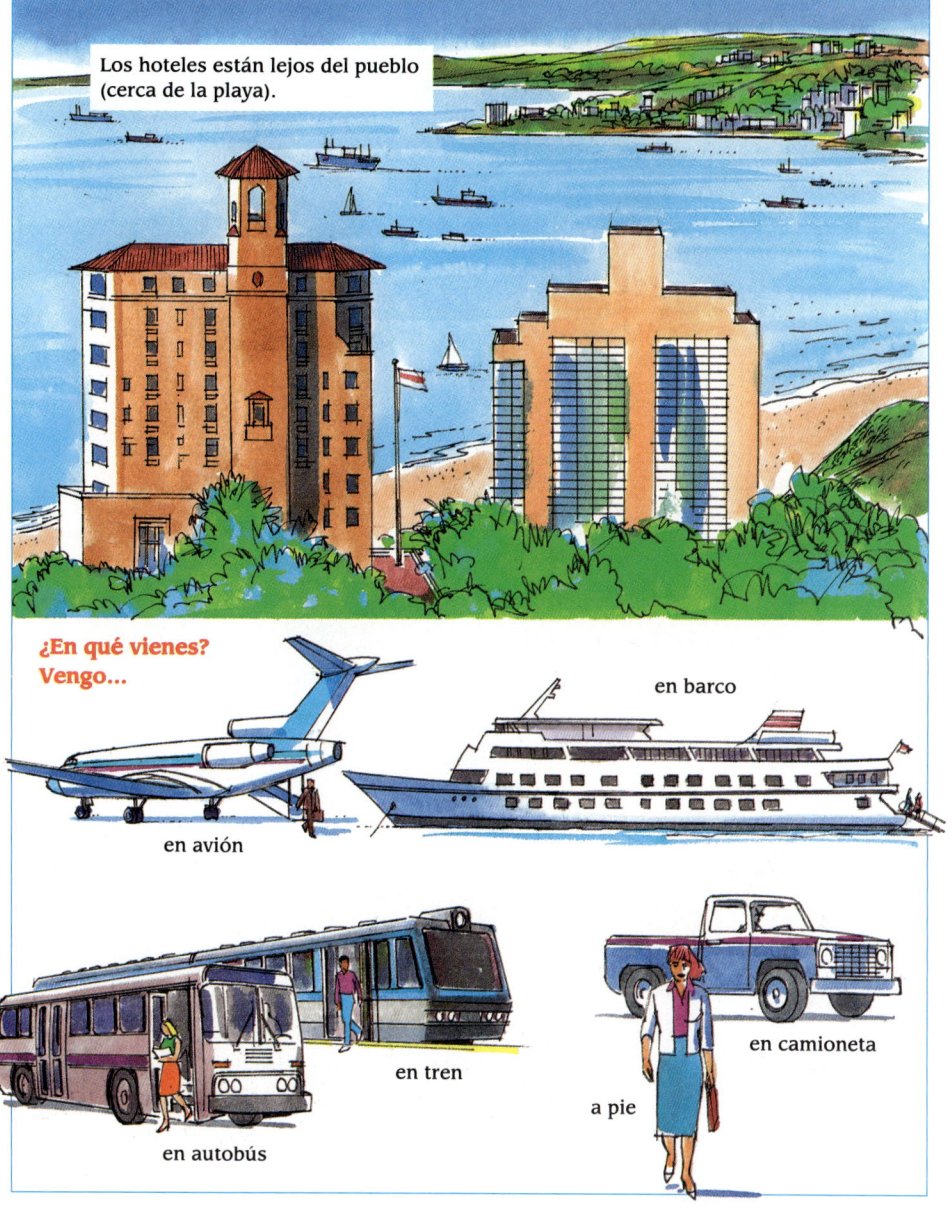

Los hoteles están lejos del pueblo (cerca de la playa).

¿En qué vienes? Vengo...

en avión
en barco
en tren
en camioneta
a pie
en autobús

D. Have students tell places they went recently and how they got there. For example: **El sábado pasado fui a ___ en ___.** Have them talk about other people as well. For example: **Mis padres fueron a ___ en ___. (Mi amiga y yo fuimos... /José fue..., etc.)**

Regionalisms

You may wish to tell students that in some parts of the Spanish-speaking world the following words or phrases are alternatives to those presented in the Vocabulario.
el autobús (el camión) (México), **(la guagua)** (Cuba), **(el colectivo)** (Argentina), **(el ómnibus)** (Uruguay, Perú), **(el micro)** (Chile), **(la camioneta)** (Guatemala); **el barco (el navío); la camioneta (la furgoneta)**

Estaciona el tren a la izquierda del gimnasio.
Estaciona la camioneta al lado del restaurante.
Pon el avión en el cielo sobre la piscina.
Pon el barco en el océano.
Ve a pie al parque.
Ve en autobús al restaurante.
Mueve la camioneta a la esquina de la calle Cabrillo.
Mueve el tren al lado del restaurante.
Mueve el autobús al lado del cine.
Ve en camioneta al parque.
Ve a pie a la piscina.
Ve en tren al hotel.
Ve en avión a la piscina.
Regresa al hotel a pie.
Regresa al restaurante a pie.
(Interchange commands, locations, and modes of transportation.)

Actividades

Actividad A Answers

Answers will vary but may include the following:

1. Está en la esquina de la calle ocho y la avenida diez y seis.
2. ... y la avenida diez y siete.
3. ... y la avenida quince.
4. ... y la avenida diez y nueve.
5. ... y la avenida diez y nueve, cerca de la heladería.
6. ... y la avenida diez y ochco.

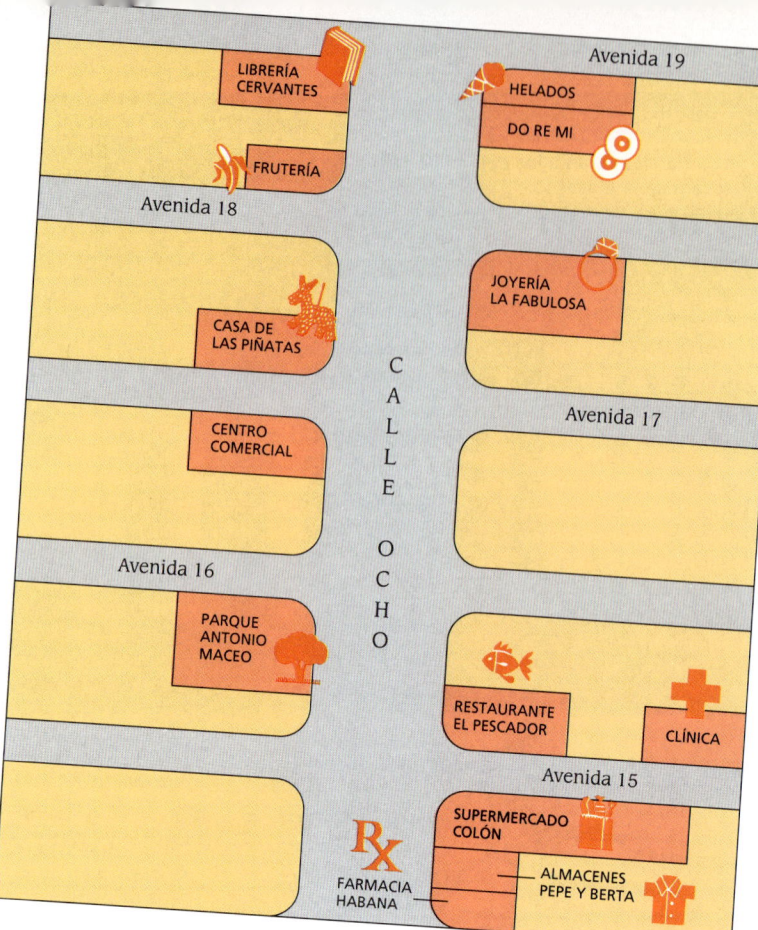

Actividades

A **El plano de la ciudad.** Using the map of **La Pequeña Habana**, describe where each of the following is.

Por ejemplo:

el supermercado Colón
Está en la esquina de la calle Ocho y la avenida Quince.
(Está al lado de los Almacenes Pepe y Berta, etc.).

1. el parque Antonio Maceo
2. el centro comercial
3. el restaurante El Pescador
4. la heladería
5. la librería Cervantes
6. la frutería

For the Native Speaker

Students will write down on separate slips of paper several places they like to go in their town or city. Put the slips of paper in a bag. Working in pairs, each student will draw a slip from the bag and will tell his or her partner how to get to that destination without telling the actual name of the destination. Each partner will guess the place he or she has been directed to go.

Cooperative Learning

Using the map on page 434, make two sets of maps of La Pequeña Habana. Include the names of six stores on one map and the names of six different stores on the other map. Teams will divide up in pairs. Each partner will ask the other for the missing store names on their map by giving the street location of each unlabeled store. To identify the missing names, stu-

B En mi ciudad. Where would you tell a new student to go in your town or city to do the following things?

Por ejemplo:

para comprar una tarjeta de cumpleaños
Debes ir a la tienda "Marie's". Cuando sales de la escuela, doblas a la izquierda. Sigues tres cuadras y doblas a la derecha. La tienda está al lado del cine.

1. para comprar revistas
2. para comprar un videojuego
3. para comer hamburguesas
4. para ver una película nueva
5. para nadar
6. para sacar una novela de la biblioteca

C ¿En qué vienes? Ask three classmates how they get to school.

Por ejemplo:

ESTUDIANTE A	ESTUDIANTE B
John, ¿en qué vienes a la escuela?	A veces vengo a pie pero casi siempre vengo en autobús.

D ¿Adónde vamos? In pairs or small groups, think of a place in your area where you want another group to go, but don't tell them their destination. Give them detailed directions. Have them tell you where they are.

Por ejemplo:

GRUPO A
(1) **Uds. salen de la escuela, doblan a la izquierda y siguen diez cuadras. Van al edificio al lado de la tienda de discos.**

GRUPO B
(2) **Estamos en** "Wendy's", **¿verdad?**

(3) **¡Sí!** (¿"Wendy's"? **No,** "Wendy's" **está muy lejos. Están en el cine**).

Lección 3   435

Cultura viva 1

Reading Strategies
1. Read the **Cultura viva** on this page. Use the maps on pages xv, xvi, and 1 to illustrate the different geographical references in the reading.
2. Now do the **Actividad** on this page.

Did You Know?
Just as some terms in the Spanish language vary considerably from one country or region to another, the same happens in the English language.
Have students notice the difference between the British and U.S. expressions, just in talking about cars.

British	U.S.
bonnet	hood
lorry	truck
boot	trunk
estate car	station wagon
wing	fender

Even within the U.S. people speak differently. For example, any one of the following expressions may be used to refer to a carbonated drink: "pop," "soda pop," "soda," "soft drink," "tonic."

Critical Thinking Activity
Can you give some examples of different words that are used to say the same thing in English? Where might you look for examples?

Actividad Answers
1. coche
2. habitación
3. anteojos
4. piscina
5. cinturón

CULTURA VIVA 1

Los dialectos de un idioma

En su conversación con Rafael, Carmen usó la palabra "guagua" en vez de "autobús". La gente de diferentes regiones muchas veces dice cosas de una manera diferente aunque habla el mismo idioma. El español que se habla en México es un poco diferente del que se habla en el Caribe, en España, en los países de la región andina, y en Chile o la Argentina.

Por ejemplo, aquí tienes tres palabras diferentes para una misma cosa.

Así se dice generalmente:	un autobús.
Pero se dice así en el Caribe:	una guagua.
Y se dice así en México:	un camión.

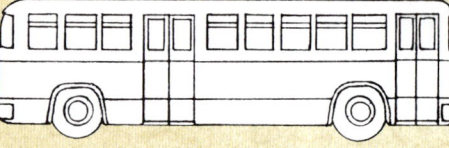

Actividad

Each of the following groups of words contains different ways of saying the same thing. Choose the general term for each, which you have learned in this book.

1. carro   coche   auto   máquina
2. habitación cuarto   dormitorio recámara
3. gafas   anteojos   lentes   espejuelos
4. alberca   piscina   pileta
5. cinturón   cinto   correa

Pronunciation
A. You may wish to play the recorded version of this pronunciation activity, located at the end of Cassette 6.3. You may also wish to write these lines on the chalkboard and have students copy them into their notebooks:

Para ti es durazno
para mí es melocotón.
Yo tomo la guagua
y tú, el camión.
Un idioma, una herencia.
Digo yo: ¡Viva la diferencia!

B. Have students repeat words and phrases individually and in unison. You may wish to focus on the /t/ sound as in **ti; melocotón; tomo; tú.**

Estructura 1

How to Say That Someone Is Coming   *The verb* **venir**

1. To ask what mode of transportation a friend uses to arrive somewhere, ask **¿En qué vienes?**

    ¿En qué vienes a la escuela?   **A veces vengo en coche.**

2. Here are all the present tense forms of the verb **venir**.

SINGULAR	PLURAL
vengo	venimos
vienes	venís*
viene	vienen

    *This form is rarely used in the Spanish-speaking world, except for Spain.

    ¿Vienes a mi fiesta?
    Sí, vengo con mi primo José. Venimos con los discos y los tacos. Creo que Miguel no viene; está enfermo.

Actividades

A ¿En qué vienen? Tell how the following people or things get to the places below.

Por ejemplo:

    tu amigo(a) / a tu casa
    Viene a pie (en bicicleta, en coche).

1. tu abuelo(a) / a tu casa
2. tu mamá (papá) / del trabajo a tu casa
3. tu hermano(a) / de la escuela a tu casa
4. tu tío(a) / a tu casa
5. un coche importado / del Japón a los Estados Unidos
6. un hombre (una mujer) de negocios / de Nueva York a Los Ángeles
7. una carta / de la Argentina a los Estados Unidos

Lección 3 437

Estructura 1

Structure Teaching Resources
1. Workbook, p. 191
2. Cassette 6.3
3. Student Tape Manual, p. 160
4. Estructura Masters 6.3
5. Lesson Quizzes, p. 127

Bell Ringer Review

Directions to students: Imagine you will be taking several trips (both near and far) in the future. Write down what method of transportation you will use to get to the places listed.
Por ejemplo: a Francia
Voy a ir a Francia en avión.

1. a Canadá
2. a Puerto Rico
3. al banco
4. a tu restaurante favorito
5. a la casa de tus abuelos
6. a Nueva York
7. al cine

Presentation

Lead students through steps 1–2 on page 437. You may want to ask students the following questions using **venir**. For example: **¿Cómo vienes a la escuela? ¿Cómo vienen a... y... ? ¿Quién viene en moto? ¿Cuántos vienen en autobús?**, etc.

Actividades

Actividad A Answers
Answers 1–4 will vary.

5. Viene en barco.
6. Viene en avión.
7. Viene en avión.

437

Actividad B Answers
Answers will vary but should include **vengo**.

Actividad C Answers
Answers regarding modes of transportation will vary but may include the following:

1. Los canadienses vienen de Canadá en avión, en coche, a pie o en tren.
2. Los portugueses... Portugal en avión o en barco.
3. Los japoneses... de Japón en avión o en barco.
4. Los dominicanos... la República Dominicana en avión o en barco.
5. Los mexicanos... México en avión, en coche, a pie o en tren.
6. Los argentinos... Argentina en avión.
7. Los ecuatorianos... de Ecuador en avión.

Actividad D Answers
Answers will vary but should follow the model.

Reteaching
Have students tell you on what day of the week the following people are coming to visit them.

1. los abuelos / el domingo
2. tu amiga / el miércoles
3. yo / el sábado
4. nosotros / el jueves
5. tú / el martes

Learning from Photos
You may want to have students look at the photo on page 438. Have students describe what the girls in the photo are wearing on their way to class. Ask students to guess what month it might be.

438

B **Estás invitado.** You have been invited to a party at 8:00 at a friend's house. Your friend calls you to make sure you're coming. Answer his or her questions.

Por ejemplo:

¿De dónde vienes?
Vengo de mi casa (del partido, del centro, etc.).

1. ¿En qué vienes?
2. ¿Con quién vienes?
3. ¿Con qué ropa vienes?
4. ¿A qué hora vienes?

C **¿De dónde vienen?** The U.S. has become home to many people from other countries. Tell where the following groups come from and how they arrive.

Por ejemplo:

los cubanos
Los cubanos vienen de Cuba en avión o en barco.

1. los canadienses
2. los portugueses
3. los japoneses
4. los dominicanos
5. los mexicanos
6. los argentinos
7. los ecuatorianos

D **Los meses del año.** Tell how you and your classmates are dressed when you come to school in the following months.

Por ejemplo:

en abril
En abril venimos con pantalones de algodón, camisas o blusas...

1. en septiembre
2. en enero
3. en mayo
4. en noviembre

438 CAPÍTULO 6

CULTURA VIVA 2

Una carta a los abuelos

Carmen les escribe una carta a sus abuelitos, que viven en Nueva York.

Miami, 27 de abril

Queridos abuelitos:

Gracias por su carta tan bonita. Mi tío Lucas llegó con mi primo Rafael de la Argentina la semana pasada. Fuimos anoche a un restaurante en La Pequeña Habana donde comimos comida típica cubana. Rafael comió arroz con pollo y de postre comió helado de mamey. Un día, mi tío Lucas nos preparó un plato al estilo argentino. ¡Qué rico!

El sábado pasado mi compañera Julia dio una fiesta y nos invitó a Rafael y a mí. Rafael tocó la guitarra, bailó mucho y habló inglés toda la noche.

Bueno, abuelitos, termino mi carta ahora. Les prometo escribir otra la semana que viene.

Un abrazo de su nieta que los quiere mucho,

Actividad

Which of the following statements about what Rafael or tío Lucas did in Florida are correct, based on Carmen's letter? If the statement is correct, write **Sí, es cierto.** If the statement is incorrect, correct it as in the example.

Por ejemplo:

> Rafael tocó el saxofón en la fiesta.
> *No. Tocó la guitarra.*

1. Rafael llegó a la Florida con su papá.
2. Rafael habló español en la fiesta.
3. Rafael comió pescado en el restaurante cubano.
4. El tío Lucas preparó comida mexicana una noche.

Lección 3

Cultura viva 2

Reading Strategies
1. Read the **Cultura viva** aloud to the class. Then have individual students take turns reading one or two sentences.
2. Now have students do the **Actividad** on this page.
3. Using Carmen's letter as a model, have students write a second letter to the grandparents. This time Carmen will describe going to an "American" restaurant.

Did You Know?
Some popular Argentine dishes are **asado con cuero,** beef roasted in its hide over an open fire; **pucheros,** stews of chicken or other meat with vegetables; **empanadas,** pastries stuffed with meat or seafood; and **matahambre,** stuffed roast. The Argentine diet includes a considerable amount of meat, since a large area of the pampa, which covers about one fifth of Argentina, is a grazing area for cattle.

Like the U.S., Argentina is a country of immigrants: the Italians introduced spaghetti and other pastas into the Argentine diet, and the English introduced tea time—a custom many Argentines still observe.

Critical Thinking Activity
Compare the letter Carmen wrote to her grandparents to a letter you might write to your grandparents. How would your letter be different? How might it be similar?

Actividad Answers
1. Sí.
2. No. Habló inglés.
3. No. Comió arroz con pollo.
4. No. Preparó un plato al estilo argentino.

For the Native Speaker
Have students interview an immigrant who is now living in your area. They should ask him or her about final preparations for the trip to the U.S., buying tickets, the trip itself, first impressions, etc. Have students read their interviews to the class.

Estructura 2

Structure Teaching Resources
1. Workbook, pp. 192–194
2. Cassette 6.3
3. Student Tape Manual, p. 160
4. Estructura Masters 6.3
5. Lesson Quizzes, p. 128

Bell Ringer Review
Directions to students: Draw a map of your school. Write out directions to go to three of your classes. Then exchange papers with a classmate and see whether or not you can follow each other's directions.

Structure Focus
In this lesson, the presentation of the preterit is limited to the third person singular. The third person plural preterit forms will be presented in Chapter 6, Lesson 4. A summary of preterit forms is presented in Chapter 6, Lesson 6.

Presentation
A. Lead students through steps 1–2 on page 440. You may wish to review forms of the preterit students have studied earlier by going over selected exercises in the lessons cited in the Structure Focus above.

B. You may wish to narrate the following, emphasizing the preterit forms of the verbs: **Ayer Carmen fue al centro. Antes de ir le pidió dinero a su papá para comprar discos. Su papá le dio veinte dólares. En el centro Carmen vio a su amiga Julia. Julia invitó a Carmen a una fiesta en su casa el sábado. Car-**

Estructura 2

How To Say What Someone Did in the Past **Third person singular forms of the preterit**

You have already practiced asking or telling a friend what he or she did in the past.

¿Qué hiciste ayer? ¿Jugaste béisbol o fuiste al cine?

You have also learned to say what you did in the past.

El invierno pasado aprendí a esquiar. Esquié con mis amigos.

In addition, you have learned to say what you and someone else ("we") did in the past.

Carmen y yo fuimos a la fiesta de Ana. Comimos mucho.

1. To describe the past actions of another person or thing (he, she, it) or to talk to a person formally **(usted)**, use these endings for the preterit tense.
   - for **-ar** verbs: **-ó**
   - for **-er** and **-ir** verbs: **-ió**

The written accent over the **-ó** tells you to stress that vowel sound. It is very important to write the accent and pronounce the vowel.

Carmen no compró nada en el centro comercial. Su primo compró un suéter y algunos discos. Después, en una cafetería, Carmen comió helado y su primo comió pizza.

Señor Marín, ¿vivió usted muchos años en Cuba?
Y usted, señora, ¿cuándo llegó a los Estados Unidos?

2. The following verbs are formed differently.

ir	fue	El tío Lucas no fue al centro comercial con Rafael.
dar	dio	Pero le dio dinero.
ver	vio	El tío Lucas vio un programa en la tele.
hacer	hizo	También le hizo un favor a su hermana.
leer	leyó	Carmen le leyó el anuncio a Rafael.
oír	oyó	Creo que tu papá no te oyó.
pedir	pidió	Y pidió permiso para dar una fiesta.

440   CAPÍTULO 6

Cooperative Learning
Have students pair up within their teams. One student in each pair will be a reporter. The other student will be a "famous person," for example, someone who is admired in your community, a celebrity, or a historical figure. The reporter will decide what questions he or she will ask the "famous person." Have students practice the interview and then role-play in front of the class using the mannerisms and the clothing of the "famous person."

Actividades

A Favores. Name someone who did each of the following favors for you recently. If no one did the favor, use the word **nadie**.

Por ejemplo:

ayudar
La maestra de inglés me ayudó con mi composición. (Nadie me ayudó).

1. prestar dinero
2. mandar una carta
3. llamar por teléfono
4. dar buenos consejos
5. comprar algo bonito
6. enseñar a hacer algo nuevo

B Muchos planes. Using the verb phrases below, write a short paragraph telling what Carmen's mother did at the following times: (a) prior to Lucas and Rafael's visit, (b) the day they arrived, and (c) during their visit.

Por ejemplo:

antes / invitar a Lucas y a Rafael
Antes invitó a Lucas y a Rafael...

ANTES

llamar a la Argentina
escribir una carta
dar instrucciones
buscar otra cama para la habitación
hacer la cama

EL DÍA DE SU LLEGADA

oír las noticias en la radio
ver a su hermano
llevar a sus parientes a casa

DURANTE LA VISITA

preparar una comida cubana
llevar a sus parientes a Orlando

Medios EN ESPAÑOL

Medios de Comunicación en Español que Prestan Servicio Diariamente a la Comunidad Hispana...

RADIO

WCMQ   1220 AM   92.1 FM
1411 Coral Way.................... 854-1830

WOCN   1450 AM
1779 W. Flagler..................... 649-1450

WRHC   1550 AM
2260 S.W. 8th Street............. 541-3300

WQBA   1140 AM
2828 Coral Way.................... 447-1144

WSUA   1160 AM

Actividades C, D, and E Answers
Answers will vary.

Class Management
You may wish to do Actividades D and E in pairs rather than as a whole class activity. Each student in the pair can take notes on what their partner says. Then have students read their notes to the class.

Actividad F Answers
1. a
2. a, b, or c
3. a or b
4. c
5. a or b

Reteaching
Ask students how they would say their best friend did the following things:

1. trabajar en casa
2. comer en la cafetería
3. ver la tele
4. hacer ejercicio
5. leer el periódico
6. ir a la playa
7. dar un paseo
8. pedir dinero a su papá

C ¿Qué hizo tu compañero? Find out from a classmate three things that he or she did last week. Report back to the class.

Por ejemplo:

ESTUDIANTE A	ESTUDIANTE B
¿Qué hiciste la semana pasada, Debra?	Gané el partido de tenis. Salí con mis amigas el sábado por la noche...

(A la clase:) **Debra ganó el partido de tenis, salió con sus amigas el sábado por la noche...**

D Gustos. Do you always eat the same things as your friends? Tell when you ate with your friends last and what each of you ate.

Por ejemplo:
> Joe y yo fuimos a comer en la cafetería ayer. Yo pedí una hamburguesa, Joe pidió un sandwich de queso. Los dos pedimos ensaladas.

E Regalos. Tell what gifts you have exchanged with five friends or family members during the last year.

Por ejemplo:
> **Para mi cumpleaños mi papá me dio entradas a un partido de béisbol. Yo le di una corbata.**

F Lecturas. Carmen is reading more in Spanish to improve her vocabulary. Tell whether she probably read the following items in (a) **el periódico,** (b) **una revista,** or (c) **una carta.**

Por ejemplo:
> las noticias
> *Leyó las noticias en el periódico.*

1. un anuncio de una liquidación de faldas
2. una receta para arroz con pollo
3. instrucciones para hacer una falda
4. los planes de los abuelos para viajar a México
5. su horóscopo

Fútbol:

Brasil se enfrenta a Chile en Santiago

SANTIAGO, (AFP) - Las Selecciones de Brasil y Chile protagonizarán un "difícil" partido el próximo miércoles, en el Estadio Nacional, pronosticó el técnico brasileño Pablo Roberto Falcao al arribar a Santiago junto al nuevo plantel brasileño.

"Si bien es cierto que es un amistoso, Chile cuenta con la base de Colo Colo y Universidad Católica, los líderes de la Primera División. Será un juego muy difícil", expresó Falcao al referirse al primero de los dos encuentros de la Copa Expedito Texeira, programado para las 20H00 locales (23H00 Gmt).

Ese partido -dijo Falcao- "me servirá para observar lo que podemos ir elaborando para nuestro futuro futbolístico" y señaló que, lamentablemente, sus jugadores sólo podrán realizar dos prácticas muy suaves en Santiago.

Falcao, quien dirigió al equipo de Brasil, que sufrió un revés por 3/0 ante España, observó atentamente a sus futbolistas en el entrenamiento que hicieron en el césped del estadio San Carlos de Apoquindo

Finalmente

Situaciones

A conversar Imagine you are a new student at your school. Converse with a classmate to find out the following information.

1. Ask how to get to your next class.
2. Find out where the gym is.
3. Ask about two other places that you have to go within the school.
4. Ask about a good place to get something to eat after school. Find out what mode of transportation you need to take and ask directions.

A escribir Write a brief composition about someone you admire a great deal, such as someone in your family, community, a celebrity, or a historical figure. Tell when and where the person was born and list several of his or her accomplishments.

Repaso de vocabulario

INSTRUCCIONES
al lado de
cerca de
detrás de
enfrente de
entre
lejos de

ACTIVIDADES
doblar
venir

TRANSPORTE
a pie
el autobús
el avión
el barco
la camioneta
el tren

OTRAS PALABRAS
la cuadra
la esquina
hasta (as far as, up to)
el lado

EXPRESIÓN
Está a + distance + de + place.
Sigue(s) derecho.

CAPÍTULO 6

Lección 4

Objectives

By the end of this lesson, students will be able to:
1. describe weather conditions
2. refer back to someone or something already mentioned
3. say what others did in the past

Lesson 4 Resources
1. Workbook, pp. 195–199
2. Vocabulario Transparencies
3. Pronunciation Transparency P-6.4.1
4. Audio Cassette 6.4 Compact Disc 9
5. Student Tape Manual, pp. 165–169
6. Bell Ringer Review Blackline Masters, pp. 39–40
7. Computer Software: Practice & Test Generator
8. Video (cassette or disc)
9. Video Activities Booklet, pp. A87–A88
10. Estructura Masters, pp. 79–82
11. Diversiones Masters, pp. 73–74
12. Situation Cards
13. Lesson Quizzes, pp. 129–131

Bell Ringer Review

Directions to students: Villabonita is a small but pretty town. See whether you can draw a plan of the town from the instructions given.
En el centro hay un parque en la Plaza Mayor. Al lado del parque hay varias tiendas — de ropa, de discos, etc. Enfrente de las tiendas hay un cine y un banco. Entre el cine y el banco hay un pequeño mercado. Al lado del cine hay un hotel de diez pisos. Cerca del hotel grande hay un restaurante.

CAPÍTULO 6

Lección 4

Un regalo especial

¡A comenzar!

The following are some of the things you will be learning to do in this lesson.

When you want to...	You use...
1. say that it's hot or cool out	**Hace calor / Hace fresco.**
2. refer back to someone or something already mentioned	**la** (feminine words) **lo** (masculine words)
3. say what others did in the past	**-aron** at the end of **-ar** verbs; **-ieron** at the end of regular **-er** or **-ir** verbs

Now find examples of the above words and phrases in the following conversation.

Getting Ready for Lesson 4

You may wish to use one or more of the following suggestions to prepare students for the lesson:
1. Use the weather map on page 448, or your daily newspaper's weather report (international listing, if possible). Distribute to students a list of cities such as those below and sketch or write beside each city the following articles of clothing: **abrigo, chaqueta, traje de baño.** Use gestures as you describe the weather in these cities. For example: **Hoy en nuestra ciudad hace fresco pero el periódico dice que en Tucson hace calor, con la temperatura máxima cerca de 95 grados. ¡Qué calor!**
As you describe the weather for these cities, have students circle the article of

Carmen y Rafael conversan en el autobús.

CARMEN: ¿Qué regalos necesitas comprar, Rafael?
RAFAEL: Bueno, primero le quiero comprar algo muy bonito a mi mamá.
CARMEN: No la conozco. Mis padres la conocieron cuando visitaron la Argentina el año pasado. Bueno, ¿qué le piensas comprar a tu mamá?
RAFAEL: Pues, sé que le gusta la ropa. Le puedo comprar un suéter de lana.
CARMEN: Pero, ¿de lana, en abril? ¡Hace mucho calor!
RAFAEL: Pero, Carmen, cuando aquí es primavera, en la Argentina es otoño y hace fresco.
CARMEN: Ah, sí, claro. Pues, vi un bonito suéter de lana en el centro comercial la semana pasada. ¿Por qué no lo compramos?

Actividades preliminares

A Complete the following sentences about the weather in your area.

1. Hace calor en los meses de _____.
2. Hace fresco en los meses de _____.
3. Cuando hace calor me gusta _____.
4. Cuando hace fresco me gusta _____.

B Complete the following sentences about what some of your friends did recently.

1. Fueron a _____.
2. Vieron _____.
3. Comieron _____.
4. Compraron _____.
5. Jugaron _____.

¡A comenzar!

Presentation

A. Lead students through each of the three functions given on page 444, progressing from the English to the Spanish for each function. Then have students find these words and phrases in the dialogue on page 445.

B. Introduce the Lesson 4 dialogue by reading it aloud or by playing the recorded version. Have students listen to determine what the difference is between the weather in Miami and in Buenos Aires.

C. Now ask students to open their books and look at the dialogue as you lead them through the following questions:
  1. ¿A quién quiere comprar un regalo Rafael?
  2. ¿Conoce Carmen a la mamá de Rafael? ¿La conocen sus padres? ¿Cuándo la conocieron?
  3. ¿Qué le piensa comprar?
  4. ¿Qué tiempo hace en Miami en abril? ¿Qué tiempo hace en Buenos Aires?
  5. ¿Dónde vio Carmen un bonito suéter de lana? ¿Cuándo?

Actividades preliminares

Actividad A Answers
Answers may vary.

Actividad B Answers
Answers will vary.

Additional Practice
Tell how often you see the following people.
Por ejemplo: tu hermana
La veo todos los días.

1. tu abuela
2. el director de la escuela
3. tu amigo _____
4. tu amiga _____
5. el dentista

---

clothing they would wear there. Be sure to use the temperature as this will key the meanings of **calor, fresco, frío,** etc. Use only extremes for comparison.

2. Ask individual students in the class if they know other students: **Jack, ¿conoces a Lisa?** After the student responds affirmatively, say: **Sí, la conoces.** Repeat this several times with different students, male and female. Then use **¿Ves a _____ mucho?** and repeat.

Vocabulario

Vocabulary Teaching Resources
1. Vocabulario Transparencies 6.4
2. Workbook, p. 195
3. Cassette 6.4
4. Student Tape Manual, p. 166
5. Lesson Quizzes, p. 129

Bell Ringer Review
Directions to students: Reread the letter that Carmen wrote to her grandparents (page 439). Close your book. Then complete the following sentences from the letter by filling in the blanks. See how much you can remember.

1. Mi tío Lucas llegó con mi primo ____ de la ____ la semana pasada.
2. Fuimos anoche a un restaurante en La Pequeña ____ donde comimos comida típica ____.
3. Rafael comió arroz con ____ y de postre comió helado de ____.
4. Mi compañera Julia dio una ____ y nos invitó a Rafael y a ____.
5. Rafael ____ la guitarra, bailó mucho y habló ____ toda la noche.

Presentation
A. Have students open their books to the Vocabulario on pages 446 and 447. Model each new word on page 446, beginning with the question, **¿Qué tiempo hace?** Have students repeat each phrase or word in unison.

B. You may wish to ask students where they go and what they do in the following situations:
   1. cuando hace sol
   2. cuando hace frío
   3. cuando llueve

Vocabulario

¿Qué tiempo hace?

Hace buen tiempo.
Hace sol.
Hace calor.
Hace un tiempo regular.
Hace fresco.
Hace frío.
Nieva.
Está nublado.
Hace mal tiempo.
Hace viento.
Llueve.

Total Physical Response

Getting Ready
For TPR1 use Vocabulario Transparencies 6.4. Call students to the projector. For TPR 2, make photocopies of pages 446 and 447 on standard size paper. Make one copy per student.

TPR 1
(Pairs of students.)
Apunten al cuadro donde hace calor.
Apunten al cuadro donde llueve.
Toquen el cuadro donde hay montañas.
Toquen el cuadro donde está el desierto.
Cubran el bosque con el papel.
Señalen al cuadro donde nieva.
Señalen al cuadro donde hace viento.
(Interchange commands and vocabulary.)

¿Por qué no vamos...?
- al desierto
- al lago
- al bosque
- al río
- a las montañas

Podemos...
- dar una caminata
- dormir al aire libre

Actividades

A **De viaje.** Name three places in the U.S, or elsewhere, that you would like to visit because of the weather. Then name three places you would not like to visit.

Por ejemplo:

Quisiera visitar ____ porque siempre ____. No quisiera visitar ____ porque ____.

Now tell one or two things that you could do in each of the places you listed.

Por ejemplo:

En ____ puedo ____.

Lección 4

Actividad B Answers
1. En Lima hace fresco y está soleado.
2. En México hace fresco y está nublado.
3. En San Juan hace calor y llueve.
4. En Bogotá hace fresco y llueve.
5. En Santiago hace calor y está soleado.
6. En Caracas hace calor y está nublado.

Comparisons and contrasts will vary.

Extension
After doing Actividad B, you may wish to extend the learning by asking students to describe the weather in the remaining cities listed in the weather chart, i.e., **Nueva York, Los Ángeles, Montreal.**

Actividades C and D Answers
Answers will vary.

B **¿Qué tiempo hace?** Describe the weather in each of the following Latin American cities, based on the weather map. Then select two cities to compare or contrast. Compare weather conditions using **y**; contrast conditions using **pero**.

Por ejemplo:

Buenos Aires
En Buenos Aires hace calor y está nublado.
Buenos Aires / La Habana
En Buenos Aires hace calor y está nublado pero en La Habana hace fresco.

1. Lima
2. México
3. San Juan
4. Bogotá
5. Santiago
6. Caracas

C **Cosas de cada estación.** Working in small groups, each student tells what he or she does during each season. One student records all the activities mentioned. Another student uses this list to report back to the class on the group's activities.

Por ejemplo:

en verano

ESTUDIANTE A
En verano nado y juego béisbol.

ESTUDIANTE B
(Escribe:) nadar, jugar béisbol

ESTUDIANTE C
En verano nadamos y jugamos béisbol.

D **Diversiones.** Write down at least three activities to do in each of the places listed on p. 449.

Por ejemplo:

la playa
En la playa puedes practicar el esquí acuático, bucear, tomar el sol...

448 CAPÍTULO 6

TEMPERATURAS EN OTRAS CIUDADES

CIUDAD	MIN	MAX	CONDICIONES
Nueva York	10	18	soleado
Los Angeles	51	74	soleado
Bogotá	45	64	lluvia
Buenos Aires	67	89	nublado
Caracas	57	81	nublado
La Habana	57	66	nublado
Lima	63	77	soleado
México	36	75	nublado
Montreal	-12	13	nieve
Nassau	53	66	nublado
San Juan	71	90	lluvia
Santiago	57	88	soleado

Cooperative Learning
Assign each team one of the places mentioned in Actividad D. Each team will decide on three or four activities that can be done in the place assigned to them. They must be activities that can be acted out in front of the class. When each team presents its activities in front of the class, team members should take turns miming their activities.

For the Native Speaker
Have native speakers write a short weather report. Then have each student present his or her weather report to the class. Students will indicate comprehension by telling what kind of clothing they will wear for the day.

1. el lago
2. el desierto
3. las montañas
4. el bosque
5. el río
6. el campo
7. la ciudad

E Todo depende del tiempo. Answer the following questions for each of these weather reports for Miami.

- ¿Qué ropa vas a llevar?
- ¿Qué piensas hacer?

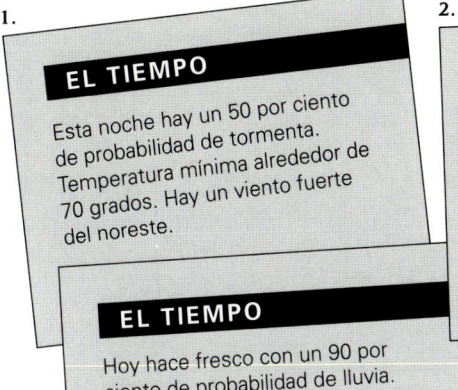

1. **EL TIEMPO**
Esta noche hay un 50 por ciento de probabilidad de tormenta. Temperatura mínima alrededor de 70 grados. Hay un viento fuerte del noreste.

2. **EL TIEMPO**
Hace un día estupendo; soleado, claro, con una temperatura media de 75 grados.

3. **EL TIEMPO**
Hoy hace fresco con un 90 por ciento de probabilidad de lluvia. Temperatura máxima cerca de 58 grados; temperatura mínima alrededor de 45 grados. Hace mucho viento.

4. **EL TIEMPO**
Hoy hace calor con un 80 por ciento de probabilidad de lluvia. Temperatura máxima cerca de 90 grados; temperatura mínima alrededor de 75 grados. Hay un viento ligero del sur.

F De vacaciones. The suitcase below was left behind by a forgetful traveler. Answer the following questions about this person by looking at the luggage.

1. ¿Cómo viaja?
2. ¿De dónde es?
3. ¿Qué le gusta hacer?
4. ¿Adónde va?
5. ¿Qué lleva?
6. ¿Va muy lejos de donde vive?
7. ¿Qué tiempo hace allí?

Lección 4   449

Cultura viva 1

Reading Strategies
1. Read the **Cultura viva** on this page. Use the map to illustrate the Northern and Southern hemispheres described in the reading.
2. Now do the **Actividad** on this page.

Did You Know?
The closer one gets to the equator, the less extreme the seasonal changes are. Altitude and ocean currents also play a role. For example, in Ecuador one can follow the equator through three climate zones: coastal, mountain, and tropical jungle.

In the southern hemisphere the school year begins in March and ends in December.

Critical Thinking Activity
Ask students the following questions:
1. If you lived in Argentina, during which months would you be most likely to do each of the following activities?
   a. ir a la playa
   b. esquiar
   c. acampar
2. During which months would you have your summer vacation?
3. In what season would you celebrate Christmas (Chanukah)?

Actividad Answers
Answers will vary.

Extension
After doing the Actividad, you may wish to extend the learning by reviewing months and seasons.

Learning from Maps
You may want to have students look at the map on page 450 and locate the equator. Have them name the South American countries that are fully or partially below the equator.

CULTURA VIVA 1

Las estaciones del año

Las estaciones del año, el frío y el calor, dependen del hemisferio. Los Estados Unidos están en el hemisferio boreal (norte), pero la Argentina está en el hemisferio austral (sur). Cuando aquí estamos en invierno, en la Argentina están en verano.

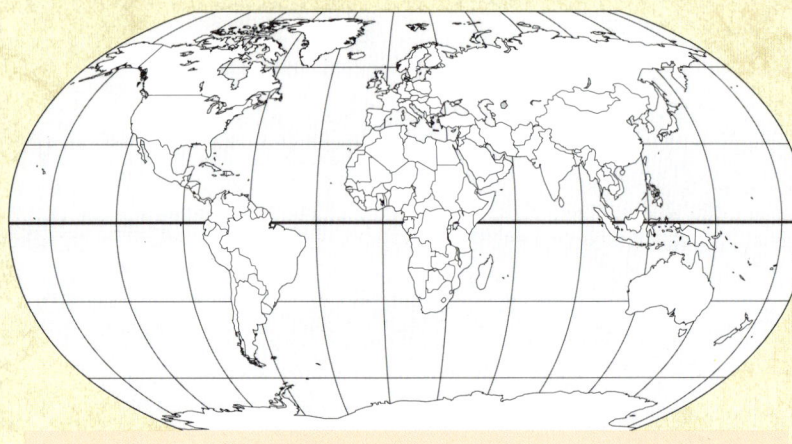

LA ESTACIÓN	EN LOS ESTADOS UNIDOS	EN LA ARGENTINA
el verano	junio, julio, agosto	diciembre, enero, febrero
el otoño	septiembre, octubre, noviembre	marzo, abril, mayo
el invierno	diciembre, enero, febrero	junio, julio, agosto
la primavera	marzo, abril, mayo	septiembre, octubre, noviembre

Actividad
List the things students are probably doing right now in the Southern Hemisphere. What clothes are they probably wearing?

450 CAPÍTULO 6

Pronunciation
1. Use Pronunciation Transparency P-6.4.1, or write the pronunciation activity on the chalkboard. Have students copy it into their notebooks.
   En enero hace frío,
   en febrero también;
   en marzo hace viento,
   en abril está bien.
2. You may wish to play the recorded version of this activity, located at the end of Cassette 6.4.
3. Have students repeat words and phrases individually and in unison. You may wish to focus on the /b,v/ sound as in **febrero, también, viento, abril.**

Estructura 1

How to Talk about What Others Did — *Third person plural forms of the preterit*

You have learned to tell what someone did in the past using **-ar**, **-er**, and **-ir** verbs. You used the same form to tell or ask what someone whom you address formally **(usted)** did in the past.

- Regular **-ar** verbs: **-ó**

  Andrés terminó su tarea de álgebra y luego empezó su composición.

- Regular **-er** and **-ir** verbs: **-ió**

  Escribió dos páginas y luego aprendió el vocabulario nuevo para la clase de español.

1. To tell what more than one person **(ellos, ellas)** did in the past or to talk to more than one person **(ustedes)** about their past actions, use the following forms of the preterit tense.

   - **-ar** verbs: **-aron**
   - **-er** and **-ir** verbs: **-ieron**

   Carmen y Rafael tomaron el autobús para ir al centro comercial. Allí vieron muchas cosas bonitas y buscaron suéteres. Después comieron algo en la cafetería. Cuando regresaron a casa, los padres de Carmen les preguntaron: —¿Compraron algo bonito?

2. As you have seen, the following verbs are formed differently.

ir	Mis tíos *fueron* a Puerto Rico el mes pasado.
dar	Allí *dieron* muchos paseos por la playa.
hacer	*Hicieron* muchas cosas en San Juan.
leer	*Leyeron* libros sobre Puerto Rico antes de viajar.
oír	*Oyeron* música puertorriqueña.
ver	*Vieron* playas bonitas.
pedir	En los restaurantes siempre *pidieron* comida puertorriqueña.

Lección 4   451

studied earlier by going over selected exercises in the lessons cited in the Structure Focus above.

You may also wish to refer students to the preterit verb charts at the back of their textbook, or write several verb paradigms on the chalkboard, pointing out the preterit forms students have already learned, and those they will learn in this lesson.

Actividades

Actividad A Answers
1. Practicaron el inglés.
2. Compraron regalos.
3. Mandaron tarjetas postales.
4. Comieron comida...
5. Dieron paseos...
6. Hicieron amigos nuevos.
7. Vieron programas...
8. Fueron al cine.
9. Leyeron el periódico.
10. Oyeron música cubana.

Actividad B Answers
Answers will vary.

Actividad C Answers
Answers will vary, however students should use the third person preterit in each question.

Additional Practice
After completing Actividades A, B, and C, you may wish to reinforce the learning with the following activity: The school newspaper is asking you to interview two exchange students from Honduras. Make a list of five questions you will ask them about their first week in the U.S. Two classmates will play the roles of the exchange students. **Por ejemplo: ¿Cuándo llegaron? ¿Cuándo aprendieron a hablar inglés?**

Reteaching

How would you say your friends did the following things last week: **trabajar en casa, comer en la cafetería, ver la tele, hacer ejercicio, leer el periódico, ir a la playa, dar un paseo, pedir dinero a su papá**

452

Actividades

A En los Estados Unidos. Below is a list of some of the things that Tío Lucas and Rafael did during their visit to the U.S. Say what they did.

Por ejemplo:

visitar el Epcot Center / vivir en casa de Carmen
Visitaron el Epcot Center. Vivieron en casa de Carmen.

1. practicar el inglés
2. comprar regalos
3. mandar tarjetas postales
4. comer comida americana y cubana
5. dar paseos por la ciudad
6. hacer amigos nuevos
7. ver programas interesantes
8. ir al cine
9. leer el periódico
10. oír música cubana

B ¿Qué hicieron? Tell a classmate five things that you and your friends did between your last Spanish class and this one. Your classmate will make a note of them and report to the class.

Por ejemplo:

Jugamos "frisbee" y comimos hamburguesas.

(A la clase:) David y sus amigos jugaron "frisbee" y comieron hamburguesas.

C Mis compañeros. Interview two of your classmates about recent activities, using the topics below. Use the following question words in your interview: **qué, cuándo, a qué hora, dónde, adónde, por qué, cómo, quién.** Take notes and report back to the class the things your classmates have in common.

Por ejemplo:

programas de televisión
¿Qué programas vieron ustedes? (Juan, ¿a qué hora viste...?)

(A la clase:) Los dos vieron un partido de béisbol...

1. viajes
2. notas
3. comida
4. películas
5. fiestas
6. música
7. deportes
8. compras
9. quehaceres
10. ropa

452   CAPÍTULO 6

CULTURA VIVA 2

La temperatura

Sólo en los Estados Unidos se usa el sistema Fahrenheit para medir la temperatura. En el resto del mundo se usa la escala de Celsius, o los "grados centígrados", para medir el frío y el calor. Para estimar la temperatura, usa estas fórmulas:

grados Fahrenheit − 32 × 0,55 = grados centígrados
grados centígrados × 1,8 + 32 = grados Fahrenheit

35° C

18° C

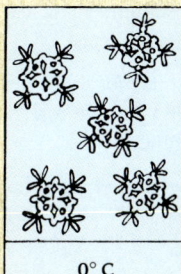
0° C

-12° C

Actividades

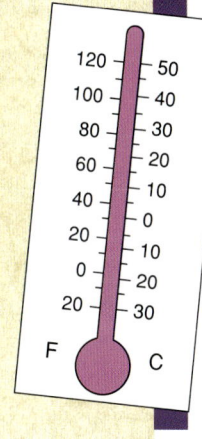

A In the above reading, can you find the word that means "to measure"?

B What temperature, in Fahrenheit, is it in the following cities?

1. Buenos Aires   15°C
2. Ciudad de México   30°C
3. París   17°C
4. Madrid   19°C
5. Moscú   10°C

C Tell what the weather is like in the cities in activity **B**. Imagine yourself in each of these cities. What are you wearing?

Lección 4   453

Cooperative Learning

Have each team do Actividad B on page 453. After each team completes the activity, the reporter will give the answers, using a map to point out where the cities mentioned in Actividad B are located.

For the Native Speaker

Have native speakers bring in world weather reports from a newspaper from the school library or some other source. Ask students to choose four different countries from the weather report, and write short paragraphs describing the weather in each of those countries and comparing it to what the weather is like in other countries. Have students present their weather reports to the class in a television news format.

Cultura viva 2

Reading Strategies

1. Read the **Cultura viva** on this page. Write the formula for converting from Fahrenheit to Centigrade on the chalkboard.
2. Now do the **Actividades** on this page.

Did You Know?

The Celsius scale has 100 degrees between the freezing and boiling temperatures of water. Water freezes at 0°C and boils at 100°C. In a Fahrenheit temperature scale the freezing point of water is at 32 degrees and the boiling point is at 212 degrees. In a Celsius scale normal body temperature of human beings is 37°C. In a Fahrenheit scale it is 98.6 degrees.

Critical Thinking Activity

Make copies of the weather report for several cities in the U.S. or Latin America, including the temperature for a particular day. Give one copy to each student. Have students convert the temperature to Celsius. Then have them write a weather report for one city on the weather map.

Actividades

Actividad A Answers
Medir

Actividad B Answers
1. 59
2. 86
3. 63 (62.6)
4. 66 (66.2)
5. 50

Actividad C Answers
Answers will vary.

Estructura 2

Structure Teaching Resources
1. Workbook, pp. 198–199
2. Cassette 6.4
3. Student Tape Manual, p. 167
4. Estructura Masters 6.4
5. Lesson Quizzes, p. 130

Bell Ringer Review

Directions to students: Copy each of the following weather expressions and draw beside each one an appropriate outfit to wear. Label your outfit in Spanish.
Llueve.
Hace frío y nieva.
Hace mucho calor en la playa.
Hace fresco con viento.

Presentation
Lead students through steps 1–4 on pages 454 and 455. You may wish to give students additional examples of the use of direct object pronouns, both in English and in Spanish, writing these additional examples on the chalkboard.

Reteaching

Place several classroom objects in a paper bag (pen, pencil, paper, book, etc.). Pass the bag around the classroom. Have each student take one item out of the bag. Then ask the class, **¿Quién tiene mi lápiz?** The students who has the pencil answers, **Yo lo tengo.** Etc.

Estructura 2

How to Talk about Things or People Already Mentioned — Direct object pronouns

1. If you have already mentioned a person or thing, there is really no need to keep repeating the name of the person or thing.

   Jan received a wallet for her birthday. The wallet is black leather. Her sister gave her the wallet. Yesterday she couldn't find the wallet. She thinks she lost the wallet at the movies.

   In English, we substitute words such as "it, her, him," and "them" (called pronouns) so we don't have to keep repeating the same word. In the above sentences, we can say "it" once we know we're talking about a wallet.

2. In Spanish, the words you use for these pronouns depend on whether the person or thing you are referring to is singular or plural, masculine or feminine.

MASCULINE		FEMININE	
SINGULAR	PLURAL	SINGULAR	PLURAL
lo	**los**	**la**	**las**

3. Notice where these words are placed.

   ENRIQUE: **Si buscas la revista de historia, la puedes encontrar en la biblioteca. Pero, ¿por qué la quieres?**
   JOSÉ: **No la quiero. La necesita mi papá. A él le gustan las revistas de historia. Siempre las lee.**

   ANA: **¿Viste a Rafael? Lo necesito ver, es muy importante.**
   CARMEN: **Pues, está en el gimnasio con sus amigos. Los vi durante el almuerzo.**

   As you can see, **la/las** and **lo/los** in the above examples are placed immediately before the verb that tells who is doing the action. If the sentence has **"no"** in it, the **"no"** is placed before **la/las** or **lo/los**.

454 CAPÍTULO 6

Cooperative Learning

Ask each team to select one or two individuals to describe. The individuals may be other classmates, or someone else known to the class. After rehearsal, the team reporter will describe one of these individuals to the class. The class must then guess who this person is.

Finalmente

Situaciones

A conversar Invite a classmate to do something with you this weekend.

1. Find out what your partner wants to do if the weather is good. Make alternate plans if the weather is bad.
2. Decide how much money you will need.
3. Talk about what you will probably wear in each case.
4. Decide on how you will get there.

A escribir A group of your friends went out last night, but you couldn't go with them. You tried to call them to find out what happened but you couldn't reach them. Write them a note to find out details such as where they went, what they wore, what they did, whom they saw, where they ate, and what time they returned home.

Repaso de vocabulario

PREGUNTA
¿Qué tiempo hace?

LUGARES
el bosque
el desierto
el lago
la montaña
el río

ACTIVIDADES
dormir al aire libre
dar una caminata

EXPRESIONES
Está nublado.
Hace...
   buen tiempo.
   calor.
   fresco.
   frío.
   mal tiempo.
   sol.
   un tiempo regular.
   viento.
Llueve.
Nieva.

Saludos de Santiago de Chile

CAPÍTULO 6

Lección 5

Objectives

By the end of this lesson, students will be able to:
1. describe physical sensations
2. compare people and things

Lesson 5 Resources
1. Workbook, pp. 200–204
2. Vocabulario Transparency
3. Audio Cassette 6.5 Compact Disc 10
4. Student Tape Manual, pp. 170–173
5. Bell Ringer Review Blackline Masters, p. 41
6. Computer Software: Practice & Test Generator
7. Video (cassette or disc)
8. Video Activities Booklet, pp. A89–A90
9. Estructura Masters, pp. 83–86
10. Diversiones Masters, pp. 75–76
11. Situation Cards
12. Lesson Quizzes, pp. 132–134
13. Testing Program

Bell Ringer Review

Directions to students: Carmen and Rafael are discussing what they do at different times of the year. Since Rafael lives in the southern hemisphere, everything is reversed. Follow the model as Rafael contrasts his activities with Carmen's.

Por ejemplo:

Carmen: **En junio voy a la playa.**
You write for Rafael: **En junio esquío en las montañas.**

1. En julio nado en la piscina.
2. En septiembre juego fútbol.
3. En enero y en febrero patino sobre hielo.
4. En mayo juego tenis.
5. En octubre hago caminatas.

CAPÍTULO 6

Lección 5

En el centro comercial

¡A comenzar!

The following are some of the things you will be learning to do in this lesson.

When you want to...	You use...
1. say someone is like someone else	**Es como** + person.
2. compare two people	**Es más** + description + **que** + person.
3. say you're hungry	**Tengo hambre.**

Now find examples of the above words and phrases in the following conversation.

458

Getting Ready for Lesson 5

You may wish to use one or more of the following suggestions to prepare students for the lesson:

1. Use the weather reports from the previous lesson and make comparisons between cities. Give students the list of cities. Have them write today's temperature for your area at the top of the sheet. For each city you mention, have them write (+) if the temperature is higher there than in your city, (-) if it's lower, and (=) if it's the same. For example:

En St. Louis hace tanto calor como aquí en nuestra ciudad. Las dos ciudades tienen una temperatura de 76 grados. Pero en Dallas hace más calor. Allí la temperatura es 84 grados. Y en Boston hace menos calor con

En el centro comercial, Carmen y Rafael hablan del regalo.

CARMEN: ¿Sabes la talla de tu mamá? ¿Y los colores que le gustan?
RAFAEL: Bueno, a decir la verdad, no.
CARMEN: ¿Sabes, por ejemplo, si le gusta el verde?
RAFAEL: Bueno, no. En realidad, prefiere el rojo.
CARMEN: Ah, es como yo. ¿Es alta?
RAFAEL: Pues, es más baja que tú.
CARMEN: Ajá, más baja. ¿Y más delgada?
RAFAEL: No, mamá es más gorda que tú. Pero es rubia como tú. Oye, compramos el suéter después. Tengo hambre. ¿No quieres comer algo?
CARMEN: Ay, Rafael, ¡eres imposible!

Actividad preliminar

Compare the following pairs of items using the words in parentheses.

Por ejemplo:

los idiomas / las matemáticas (fácil)
Los idiomas son más fáciles que las matemáticas.
(Las matemáticas son más fáciles que los idiomas.)

1. el fútbol / el béisbol (interesante)
2. los zapatos deportivos / las camisetas (popular)
3. la ropa deportiva / la ropa elegante (bonito)
4. la comida italiana / la comida mexicana (delicioso)

Vocabulario

Vocabulary Teaching Resources
1. Vocabulario Transparency 6.5
2. Workbook, p. 200
3. Cassette 6.5
4. Student Tape Manual, p. 170
5. Lesson Quizzes, p. 132

Bell Ringer Review
Directions to students: Draw a picture representing these weather conditions.
1. Está nublado.
2. Hace sol.
3. Llueve hoy.
4. Hace mucho frío.
5. Nieva mucho.
6. Hace calor.
7. Hace fresco.
8. Hace mucho viento.

Presentation
A. Have students open their books to the Vocabulario on page 460. Model each new phrase. Have students repeat each phrase in unison.
B. Ask individual students how they feel. For example: ¿Tienes frío? ¿Tienes sed? Ask students to look at the Vocabulario on page 460 before they answer.

Vocabulario

Tengo mucha sed. ¿Quieres tomar algo?

Tengo mucha hambre. ¿Quieres comer algo?

Tengo mucho frío. ¿Me puedes traer mi suéter?

Tengo mucho sueño, mamá. Voy a dormir.

Tengo mucha prisa. No quiero llegar tarde.

Tengo mucho miedo. Quiero regresar a casa.

Tengo mucho calor. ¿Por qué no vamos a la piscina?

460 CAPÍTULO 6

Total Physical Response

Getting Ready
Use Vocabulario Transparency 6.5 and felt pens.
Apunta a la persona que tiene frío.
Apunta al muchacho que tiene hambre.
Señala al muchacho que tiene calor.
Señala a la muchacha que tiene miedo.
Haz un círculo en el muchacho que tiene prisa.
Haz un rectángulo en la muchacha que tiene sed.
Haz un triángulo en el muchacho que tiene sueño.
Levanten la mano derecha si tienen frío en el invierno.
Levanten la mano izquierda si tienen calor en el verano.
Pongan la cabeza en el pupitre si tienen sueño a las doce de la noche.

Actividades

A **¿Cómo estás?** Tell how you feel in the following situations.

Por ejemplo:

Es un día de agosto a las tres de la tarde.
Tengo (mucho) calor.

1. Hace doce horas que no comes.
2. Corriste cuarenta y cinco minutos y hace dos horas que no tomas agua.
3. Estudiaste hasta las dos de la noche y saliste para la escuela a las siete de la mañana.
4. La temperatura está a cinco grados bajo cero y hace mucho viento.
5. La temperatura está a cuarenta grados.
6. Das un paseo por el campo y ves una serpiente muy grande.
7. Estás en casa a las ocho de la mañana y tu primera clase es a las ocho y veinte.

B **¿Cuándo?** Complete the sentences below to tell when you feel the following.

1. Tengo hambre cuando...
2. Tengo sed cuando...
3. Tengo prisa cuando...
4. Tengo miedo cuando...
5. Tengo frío cuando...
6. Tengo calor cuando...
7. Tengo sueño cuando...

En una cafetería cubana de la calle Ocho.

Lección 5 461

Actividades

Actividad A Answers
Answers will vary but may include the following:

1. Tengo (mucha) hambre.
2. Tengo (mucha) sed.
3. Tengo (mucho) sueño.
4. Tengo mucho frío.
5. Tengo frío.
6. Tengo (mucho) miedo.
7. Tengo (mucha) prisa.

Actividad B
Answers will vary.

Additional Practice
After completing Actividades A and B, you may wish to reinforce the learning with the following activity: Ask students how they would respond to the following. For example:
Tu amiga dice: No me gustan las películas de terror.
Tú le dices: Tienes miedo.

1. Tu maestra dice: ¿Puedes cerrar la ventana, por favor?
2. Tu hermano dice: Quiero tomar agua.
3. Tus amigos dicen: Vamos a dormir.
4. Tu maestro dice: No quiero llegar tarde a clase.
5. Tu mamá dice: Quiero comer pizza.

Reteaching

Show illustrations, or act out situations, that will elicit one of the expressions in the Vocabulario on page 460. For example, pretend you are drinking from a glass. Ask students, **¿Tengo hambre o tengo sed?**

Learning from Photos

You may want to have students look at the photo on page 461. Have them imagine they're in this restaurant. They should greet the employee and order a meal.

Cooperative Learning

A. Working in groups, have one member at a time act out an expression from the Vocabulario on page 460. The other members of the group will guess the action.

B. Assign one expression on page 460 to each group. The group will act it out in front of the class. The class tries to guess what each group is trying to mime.

461

Cultura viva 1

Reading Strategies
1. Read the **Cultura viva** on this page. After reading it once, have students guess the meaning of the words **talla** and **tabla**.
2. Now have students read the selection again, including the chart, before asking them to do the **Actividad** on this page.

Did You Know?
Shoe and clothing sizes in most Hispanic countries are different from sizes used in the U.S.
Note. Talla refers to clothing size; **número** refers to shoe and glove size.

Critical Thinking Activity
Using the chart on page 462, ask students to write down their European size for each of the appropriate categories shown.

Actividad Answers
Answers will vary.

Learning From Realia
You may want to ask students to look again at the chart on page 462.
1. What is the European equivalent of American half sizes?
2. How many articles of clothing are missing from this chart? Give the names in Spanish.

CULTURA VIVA 1

Las tallas

Las tallas de la ropa varían de un país a otro. La tabla que sigue tiene las equivalencias entre el sistema de tallas europeo y el americano. Para comprar ropa, dices "Mi talla es..."

TALLAS EN ESTADOS UNIDOS Y EN EUROPA							
BLUSAS Y SUÉTERES							
Estados Unidos	32	34	36	38	40	42	44
Inglaterra	34	36	38	40	42	44	46
Europa	40	42	44	46	48	50	52
VESTIDOS Y TRAJES DE SEÑORA							
Estados Unidos		10	12	14	16	18	20
Inglaterra		32	33	35	36	38	39
Europa		38	40	42	44	46	48
TRAJES Y ABRIGOS DE CABALLERO							
Estados Unidos		36	38	40	42	44	46
Europa e Inglaterra		46	48	50	52	54	56
CAMISAS							
Estados Unidos	14	14½	15	15½	15¾	16	16½	17
Europa	36	37	38	39	40	41	42	43
CALCETINES							
Estados Unidos			9½	10	10½	11	11½
Europa			38-39	39-40	40-41	41-42	42-43
ZAPATOS DE SEÑORA							
Estados Unidos	4	5	6	7	8	9	10	11
Inglaterra	2	3	4	5	6	7	8	9
Francia	36	37	38	39	40	41	42	43
Italia y España	32	34	36	38	40	42	44	46
MEDIAS							
Estados Unidos e Inglaterra		8	8½	9	9½	10	10½
Europa		0	1	2	3	4	5

Actividad

Give the size you will buy for yourself for the following items in the countries named.

Por ejemplo:

> Estás en Francia y buscas un suéter.
> *Voy a comprar zapatos de la talla cuarenta y cuatro.*

1. Estás en España y quieres un traje.
2. Estás en Inglaterra y quieres una camisa/una blusa.
3. Estás en Italia y buscas un suéter.
4. Estás en Alemania y necesitas calcetines.

Estructura 1

How to Make Comparisons of Numbers and Amounts

Más / menos... que...
Tanto... como....

1. To say that there is or are more of one than of another, use **más... que...**
    Hay más muchachos que muchachas aquí.
    Mi padre gana más dinero que mi tío.

2. To say that there is or are less or fewer of one than the other, use **menos... que...**
    Hay menos amarillo que rojo en la camisa.
    Mi prima tiene menos vestidos que mi hermana.

3. To say that there is as much or as many of one as the other, use **tanto(a, os, as)... como...**
    Necesito ahorrar tanto dinero como tú.
    Miguel tiene tanta hambre como yo.
    Mi hermano tiene tantos carteles como mi primo.
    Tengo tantas clases como mis amigos.

4. To say that there isn't as much of one as the other, use **"no"** before the above examples.
    No tengo tanto dinero como tú.
    No tengo tantas clases como mis amigos.

5. To say that someone does something as much as someone else, use **tanto como**.
    En la clase de historia, yo estudio tanto como tú. Silvia puede ahorrar tanto como María.

Notice that when **tanto como** is used this way, the ending (-o) of **tanto** never changes.

Lección 5 463

Estructura 1

Structure Teaching Resources
1. Workbook, pp. 201–202
2. Cassette 6.5
3. Student Tape Manual, p. 171
4. Estructura Masters 6.5
5. Lesson Quizzes, p. 133

Bell Ringer Review
Directions to students: What would be the solutions to the following problems? Copy each word and then draw a picture depicting a cure.
1. Tengo mucha sed.
2. Tenemos calor.
3. Tienen hambre.
4. Tengo miedo.
5. Tenemos frío.
6. Tienes mucha prisa.
7. Tengo sueño.

Structure Focus
The presentation in this lesson is limited to comparisons of numbers and amounts: **más/menos... que...** and **tanto... como...** Comparisons based on characteristics will be presented in Estructura 2 of this lesson.

Presentation
Lead students through steps 1–5 on page 463. You may wish to give additional examples, such as: **Hay más estudiantes en esta clase que en la clase a las diez; Hay menos páginas en este libro que en el libro de historia;** etc.

Actividades

A En la clase. Tell what your Spanish classmates are like by comparing the categories below.

Por ejemplo:

muchachos o muchachas
Hay más muchachas que muchachos en la clase.
deportistas o artistas
Hay más deportistas que artistas.

1. cantantes o deportistas
2. rubios o pelirrojos
3. personas con anteojos o sin anteojos
4. personas con frenos o sin frenos en los dientes
5. estudiantes aplicados o estudiantes perezosos
6. muchachas de pelo largo o de pelo corto
7. estudiantes con "jeans" o con pantalones
8. muchachas con pantalones o con faldas

B A decir la verdad. Tell whether the following statements about you and your best friend are true or not.

Por ejemplo:

Estudias tanto como él/ella.
Sí, estudio tanto como él. (No, estudio menos que él).

1. En la clase de español sabes menos que él/ella.
2. Escuchas los problemas de los amigos tanto como él/ella.
3. Trabajas tanto como él/ella.
4. Sabes tanto como él/ella.
5. El mes pasado saliste por la noche más que él/ella.
6. Ayer estudiaste tanto como él/ella.
7. Anoche hablaste por teléfono menos que él/ella.
8. En la cafetería comiste menos que él/ella.

464 CAPÍTULO 6

Cooperative Learning

You may wish to do Actividad A as a cooperative learning activity. Do an oral round robin, with all the team members taking turns and contributing answers:

For the Native Speaker

Write a 150-word comparison of two of your classes. Mention the quantity of work required, the teacher, activities that you like or dislike, etc.

Actividades

Actividad A Answers
1. Hay más cantantes (deportistas) que...
2. Hay más rubios (pelirrojos) que...
3. Hay más personas con anteojos (sin anteojos) que...
4. Hay más personas con frenos (sin frenos) en los dientes que...
5. Hay más estudiantes aplicados (perezosos) que...
6. Hay más muchachas de pelo largo (de pelo corto) que...
7. Hay más estudiante con "jeans" (pantalones) que...
8. Hay más muchachas con pantalones (faldas) que...

Actividad B Answers
Answers will vary.

C **No soy como él.** Compare yourself to a friend or family member in terms of the following topics.

Por ejemplo:

tener tarea
Yo tengo más (menos) tarea que mi amiga Mónica. (Yo tengo tanta tarea como mi amiga Mónica).

1. ir a bailes
2. practicar deportes
3. leer libros
4. ver películas
5. ahorrar dinero
6. tener problemas
7. hacer ejercicio

D **Mi compañero y yo.** Compare yourself to a classmate, answering the following questions.

Por ejemplo:

¿Tienes tantas clases como él/ella?
No tengo tantas clases como ella. Ella tiene más clases que yo.

1. ¿Tienes tantos discos como él/ella?
2. ¿Ahorras tanto dinero?
3. ¿Ganas tantos partidos?
4. ¿Vas a tantos restaurantes?
5. ¿Ves tantas películas?
6. ¿Haces tanto ejercicio?

Lección 5 465

Cultura viva 2

Reading Strategies
1. Ask students to name which birthdays are special in the U.S.
2. Now read the **Cultura viva** on this page and do the **Actividades**.

Did You Know?
Most **quinceañera** celebrations include a church service, the purpose of which is to give thanks for having reached this important age. During the celebration, **la quinceañera** wears a formal dress, like a prom dress. Her father accompanies her to the altar where she remains for the entire ceremony. She may give a speech. Her court of honor, fourteen girls with their partners, go to the church with her. Following the religious ceremony, there may be a party, including a formal dance.
Quinceañera celebrations are common in Mexico, the Caribbean, and certain Central American nations.

Critical Thinking Activity
Is there any other celebration that is similar to the **quinceañera** in the U.S.? What do you think is the importance and meaning of a **quinceañera** for the girl's family?

Actividades

Actividad A Answers
Special U.S. birthdays: 16, 18, 21.
Special birthday for Hispanic girls: 15; it is called the quinceañera.

Actividad B Answers
1. culta, encantadora
2. un matrimonio muy apreciado
3. grata
4. conocido

Actividad C Answers
Answers will vary.

CULTURA VIVA 2

La quinceañera

En algunos países hispanos, el cumpleaños de los quince años es muy importante para las muchachas. Los padres dan una gran fiesta con baile para presentar a la muchacha en sociedad.

> Hoy cumple sus ansiados quince la culta y encantadora señorita Carmen Marín Revueltas, hija de un matrimonio muy apreciado, el abogado Luís Marín Armas y la señora Alicia Revueltas de Marín Armas. Con motivo de esta grata ocasión, la quinceañera celebrará un baile en un conocido club de esta ciudad. ¡Muchas felicidades!

Éste es el anuncio que apareció en un periódico de Miami cuando Carmen cumplió sus quince años.

Para una Amiga Especial

*Porque eres una amiga
En quien me gusta pensar,
Cuando viene tu cumpleaños
No te puedo olvidar.

Feliz Cumpleaños*

Y aquí está la tarjeta que Jorge, un compañero de clase de Carmen, le mandó para su cumpleaños.

Actividades

A Which birthdays are special in the U.S.? In the above reading, find out which birthday is special for many Hispanic girls. What is this celebration called?

B In the newspaper article what words are used to describe:
1. Carmen
2. los Marín
3. la ocasión
4. el club

C Tell the things you did or plan to do for your fifteenth birthday. Tell the things you received or asked for (or are going to ask for).

For the Native Speaker
Imagine that you are a newspaper reporter. Write an article about a **quinceañera** that you recently attended. Include information about the food, music, gifts, guests, other entertainment, etc.

Estructura 2

How to Make Comparisons   Tan... como...
Based on Characteristics   Más / menos... que...

1. You may want to compare people and things on the basis of their qualities or characteristics; for example, smaller, taller, prettier, cheaper. To say that someone or something is the same as another person or thing, use **tan... como**.

   Soy tan alto como tú.
   Eva es tan guapa como Inés.

2. If the persons or things are not the same, use **"no"** with the above examples.

   No soy tan alta como Mariví.
   Jorge no es tan guapo como su hermano.

3. To say that someone or something is more than another person or thing, use **más... que**.

   Soy más aplicado que mi hermana.
   Teresa es más simpática que su prima.

4. To say that someone or something is less than another, use **menos... que**.

   Soy menos puntual que tú.

5. To compare people's ages, use **menor que** (younger than) and **mayor que** (older than).

   Mi hermana es menor que yo.
   Mi amigo es mayor que yo.

6. To say that something is better than something else, use **mejor que**. To say it is worse than something else, use **peor que**.

   El libro es mejor que la película.
   La cantante es peor que la bailarina.

Lección 5   467

For the Native Speaker

Who is your favorite athlete? Why? Compare your favorite with another famous athlete. Mention their training, past record, playing style, potential, etc.

Actividades

Actividad A Answers
Answers will vary.

Actividad B Answers
Answers will vary but may include the following:
1. No es tan independiente como yo. Es más tímida que yo.
2. No es tan responsable como yo. Soy más responsable que ella.
3. No es tan antipática como yo. Es más simpática que yo.
4. No es tan alta como yo. Es más baja que yo.

Actividad C Answers
Answers will vary.

Reteaching

Ask individual students to compare the following. Tell which is better and why.
1. la clase de álgebra o la clase de inglés
2. el fútbol americano o el baloncesto
3. la música clásica o la música rock
4. las motos o los coches
5. un perro o un gato

Actividades

A Comparaciones. Think of two items for each of the categories below and compare them in terms of better or worse.

Por ejemplo:
> días de la semana
> *Los sábados son mejores que los lunes. (Los martes son peores que los viernes, etc.).*

1. películas
2. equipos de béisbol
3. equipos de baloncesto
4. coches

B Elena y yo. Carmen Marín is comparing herself to her friend Elena. For each statement she makes, give two other ways she could have said it.

Por ejemplo:
> Elena es menos gorda que yo.
> *No es tan gorda como yo. Es más delgada que yo.*

1. Es menos independiente que yo.
2. Es menos responsable que yo.
3. Es menos antipática que yo.
4. Es menos alta que yo.

C Este año y el año pasado. Compared to last year, give your opinion of what the following people and things are like this year (este año). Tell why.

Por ejemplo:
> la escuela
> *La escuela es más interesante este año porque...*

1. tus amigos
2. los equipos de la escuela
3. la música más popular
4. la ropa de moda
5. los programas de la tele
6. la comida de la cafetería
7. las tareas

Finalmente

Situaciones

A conversar Converse with a classmate about one of your favorite celebrities.

1. Decide on a category (such as athlete, musician, or movie star) that you both want to talk about.
2. Compare your favorite with your classmate's favorite in terms of appearance, abilities, and achievements.

A escribir Rate your school, comparing it to a rival school. Write about why your school is better than the rival school. Compare sports teams, equipment, facilities, the students, faculties, libraries, school colors, mascots, and so on.

Repaso de vocabulario

COMPARACIONES
como
más (... que)
mejor (que)
menos (... que)
peor (que)
tan... como
tanto(a, os, as)... como
tanto como

EXPRESIONES
tener
  calor (m.)
  frío
  hambre (f.)
  miedo
  prisa
  sed (f.)
  sueño

CAPÍTULO 6

Lección 6

Objectives

By the end of this lesson, students will be able to:

1. ask or tell how much someone or something weighs
2. ask or tell how tall someone is
3. distinguish "this one" from "that one"
4. talk about past events

Lesson 6 Resources
1. Workbook, pp. 205–214
2. Vocabulario Transparencies
3. Pronunciation Transparency P-6.6.1
4. Audio Cassette 6.6 Compact Disc 10
5. Student Tape Manual, pp. 174–180
6. Bell Ringer Review Blackline Masters, pp. 42–43
7. Computer Software: Practice & Test Generator
8. Video (cassette or disc)
9. Video Activities Booklet, pp. A91–A95
10. Estructura Masters, pp. 87–89
11. Diversiones Masters, pp. 77–78
12. Situation Cards
13. Lesson Quizzes, pp. 135–137
14. Testing Program

Bell Ringer Review

Display pictures of two well-known personalities. Directions to students: Look at the pictures on the board. Think about the characteristics and interests of each person. Then write five sentences comparing the two people.

CAPÍTULO 6

Lección 6

¿Qué talla, por favor?

¡A comenzar!

The following are some of the things you will be learning to do in this lesson.

When you want to...	You use...
1. distinguish "this..." from "that..."	Este(a)... ese(a)...
2. ask how much someone weighs	¿Cuánto pesa?
3. ask how tall someone is	¿Cuánto mide?

Now find examples of the above words and phrases in the following conversation.

470

Getting Ready for Lesson

You may wish to use one or more of the following suggestions to prepare students for the lesson:

1. Select judiciously two or three students to come to the front of the classroom and help you estimate their heights (using the U.S. system of measurement: **pies** and **pulgadas**). For example: Jim, ¿cuánto mides? Yo mido ____ y veo que tú eres más alto que yo. ¿Mides cinco pies y cuántas pulgadas? ¿cuatro? ¿cinco? Estimate the heights of a few other individuals; then have students do the same for three or four volunteers. See who can give the closest estimate.

2. Have two volunteers come to the front of the classroom. Have them stand several feet apart. Stand next to one stu-

Carmen y Rafael hablan con la empleada de una tienda.

EMPLEADA: Buenas tardes. ¿Qué buscan?
CARMEN: Buenas tardes, señorita. Quisiéramos ver ese suéter rojo, por favor.
EMPLEADA: Sí, cómo no, señorita. Este suéter es muy popular este año. ¿Qué talla?
CARMEN: Diez.
RAFAEL: No, Carmen, tiene que ser cuarenta y cuatro o cuarenta y seis.
CARMEN: No, Rafael. Si tu mamá es como yo, esa talla es muy grande. A ver... ¿cuánto pesa?
RAFAEL: No sé... sesenta, más o menos.
CARMEN: ¿Sesenta? ¡No lo puedo creer! ¿Cuánto mide?
RAFAEL: ¿Uno sesenta?
CARMEN: ¿C-ó-m-o?

Actividad preliminar

Say one thing about each of the following times or places.

Por ejemplo:
> esta tarde
> *Esta tarde voy a salir con mis amigos.*

1. este año
2. esta escuela
3. esta ciudad (este pueblo)
4. este mes
5. esta estación
6. este fin de semana

Vocabulario

Vocabulary Teaching Resources
1. Vocabulario Transparencies 6.6
2. Workbook, pp. 205–206
3. Cassette 6.6
4. Student Tape Manual, p. 174
5. Lesson Quizzes, p. 135

Bell Ringer Review

Directions to students: Help Luisa straighten out her sentences by copying them on your paper and correcting the underlined words.

1. En el verano siempre tengo <u>frío</u> después de jugar tenis. Por eso tomo mucha agua.
2. Mi familia y yo tenemos <u>sueño</u> para llegar al cine a tiempo.
3. Cuando no como, tengo <u>calor</u>.
4. Tengo <u>sed</u> después de ver la tele hasta la medianoche.
5. Me gustan las películas de terror pero siempre tengo <u>prisa</u> cuando las veo.
6. Cuando hacen 35 centígrados, tengo mucha <u>hambre</u>.
7. Tengo <u>miedo</u> cuando nieva y hace mucho viento.

Presentation

A. Have students open their books to the Vocabulario on pages 472 and 473.
 1. Model each new phrase on page 472. Have students repeat each phrase in unison.
 2. Be sensitive in choosing certain students to ask how much they weigh and how tall they are. For example: ¿Cuánto pesas tú? ¿Cuánto mides tú? Encourage students to give a complete response. For example: Yo peso... , Yo mido...

Vocabulario

472 CAPÍTULO 6

Total Physical Response

Getting Ready
Use the following items for TPR 1 and display them in front of the class.
un libro
una regla
un lápiz
un borrador
un bolígrafo
un saco de 5 libras de azúcar
un paquetito de espaguetis
una lata grande de frutas
unos platos de cartón
unos cubiertos de metal y de plástico
For TPR 2, borrow a scale and measuring tape.

New Words
coge   cojan

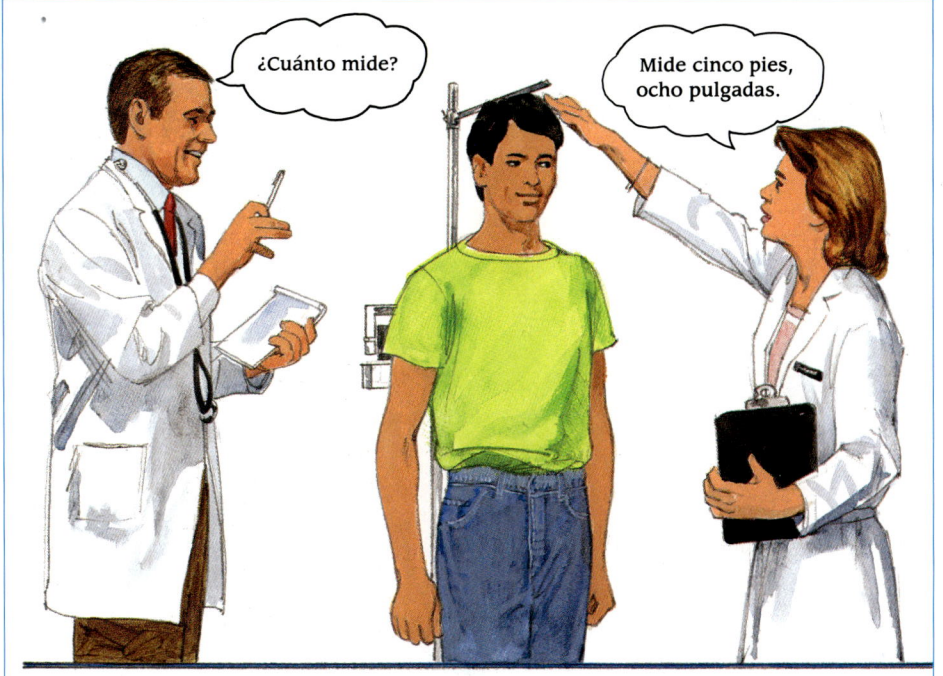

Actividades

A **¿Está muy lejos?** Take turns with a classmate estimating the distance from your school to each of the following places in miles or city blocks. Then give directions on how to get to each place.

Por ejemplo:

la biblioteca
La biblioteca no está muy lejos. Está a dos millas de aquí, más o menos. Sales de la escuela, doblas a la derecha, sigues doce cuadras, entonces doblas a la izquierda y está en la esquina.

1. la casa de tu amigo
2. un restaurante popular
3. el centro comercial
4. tu casa
5. un banco
6. el hospital

Actividad B Answers
Answers will vary.

Actividad C Answers
1. El cuadrado mide ocho pies.
2. El rombo mide veinte y cuatro pulgadas (dos pies).
3. El triángulo mide catorce pies.
4. El rectángulo mide treinta y cuatro pies.

Reteaching

On one piece of paper draw geometric figures of various dimensions. Indicate whether the dimensions are in inches or feet. On another piece of paper draw cans, packages, and other items and include the weight of each one. Make enough copies for each student. Students figure out the perimeter of each geometric figure and the weight of each item. Have them write in complete sentences.

B Vamos a viajar. Tell whether the following places are near or far from where you live. Also tell how you would get to each place. Estimate how long a trip each would be.

Por ejemplo:
> la playa
> *La playa está muy lejos de aquí. Si quiero ir, tengo que viajar en coche (avión, etc.). Voy a tardar más o menos cinco horas.*

1. el desierto
2. un lago grande
3. un río
4. las montañas
5. el bosque
6. un parque

C La tarea de matemáticas. Carmen is babysitting for Miguelito and helping him with his math homework. He has to give the perimeters of the following shapes. What are the correct answers?

Por ejemplo:
> el rectángulo
> *El rectángulo mide 26 pulgadas.*

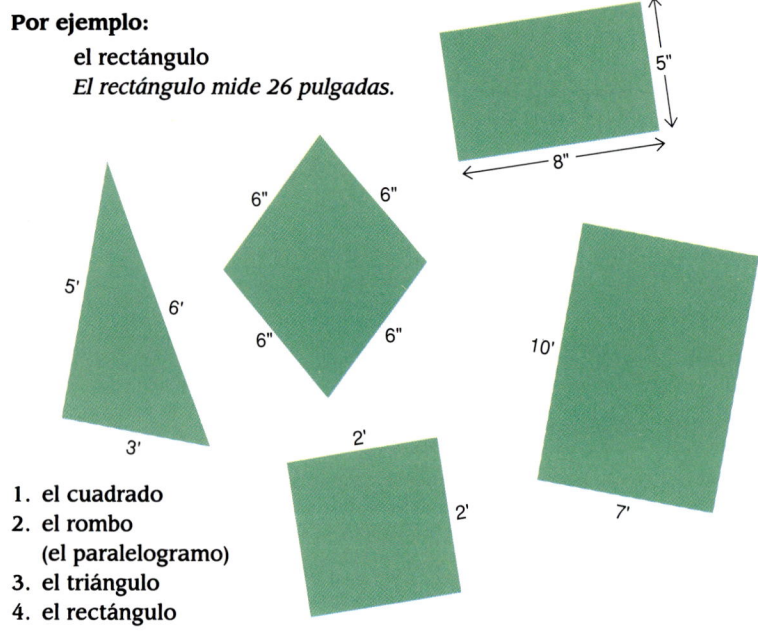

1. el cuadrado
2. el rombo
   (el paralelogramo)
3. el triángulo
4. el rectángulo

474 CAPÍTULO 6

D Comparaciones. Compare the following pairs of persons or things and answer the questions.

Por ejemplo:
> ¿Quién es más alta?
> Andrea, 5 pies / Julia, 4 pies, 8 pulgadas
> *Andrea es más alta.*

1. ¿Quién pesa más?
   Julio Panza, 160 libras / David Winer, 126 libras

2. ¿Quién es más alta?
   Angélica Morán, 6 pies / Ann Darcey, 5 pies, 8 pulgadas

3. ¿Dónde hace más frío?
   Buenos Aires, 38 grados / Filadelfia, 53 grados

4. ¿Cuál café es más barato?
   Café Bustelo, 8 onzas, $3.29 / Nescafé, 12 onzas, $3.29

5. ¿Cuál es más pesado?
   azúcar, 5 libras / papas, 10 libras

6. ¿Cuál es más liviana?
   una tarjeta postal / una carta

For the Native Speaker

Make a map of the United States that includes the following cities: Los Angeles, San Francisco, New York, Chicago, Philadelphia, Washington D. C., Seattle, Boston, Miami, Dallas, Bismarck, New Orleans, Springfield. Using kilometers, indicate the distance between New York and all the other cities.
Make a chart that shows your findings.

Actividad D Answers
1. Julio Panza pesa más.
2. Angélica Morán es más alta.
3. En Buenos Aires hace más frío.
4. El Nescafé es más barato.
5. Las papas son más pesadas.
6. La tarjeta postal es más liviana.

Learning from Realia
You may want to have students look at the realia on page 475 and identify as many items as they can.

Cultura viva 1

Reading Strategies
Read the **Cultura viva** on this page. Then do the **Actividad**.

> **Interdisciplinary Connection**
>
> The metric system is the accepted standard of measurement throughout the world. It is based on the decimal system. The U.S. uses a dual system, the metric and the English system.

Critical Thinking Activity
1. Have students estimate the length of the following in centimeters.
   - your thumb
   - a new pencil
   - your elbow to your fingertips
   - the distance between the pupils of a classmate's eyes

   Then give students rulers marked off in centimeters and have them measure the above items. How well did they estimate?
2. What are the advantages and disadvantages of using the metric system and the English system?

Actividad Answers
1. kilómetros
2. centímetros
3. gramos
4. litros

Additional Practice
After completing the **Actividad** on this page, you may want to do the following activity:

How would the following things be measured: **gramos, litros, metros, kilómetros, kilos, centímetros?**

1. chocolates
2. refrescos o agua
3. tela para un traje
4. la distancia entre dos ciudades
5. azúcar
6. frijoles

Answers
1. gramos
2. litros
3. metros
4. kilómetros
5. kilos
6. kilos

CULTURA VIVA 1

El sistema métrico

Como ya sabes, en otros países usan el sistema métrico. Por ejemplo, usan grados centígrados para la temperatura, kilos y gramos para el peso, litros para los líquidos, y kilómetros y metros para la altura y la distancia.

Aquí tienes algunas maneras de estimar medidas con el sistema métrico.

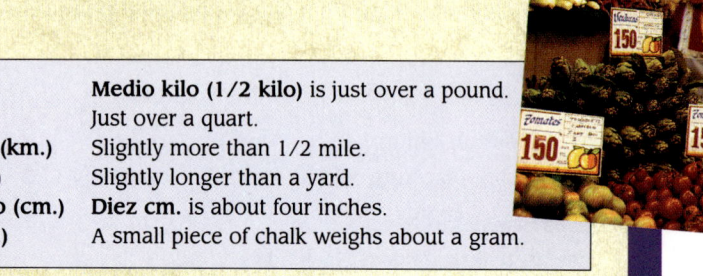

un kilo (k.)	Medio kilo (1/2 kilo) is just over a pound.
un litro (l.)	Just over a quart.
un kilómetro (km.)	Slightly more than 1/2 mile.
un metro (m.)	Slightly longer than a yard.
un centímetro (cm.)	Diez cm. is about four inches.
un gramo (gr.)	A small piece of chalk weighs about a gram.

Actividad

What metric units of measurement would you use to respond to the following questions?

Por ejemplo:
> ¿Cuánto pesa Miguel?
> *kilos*

1. ¿Está muy lejos su casa?
2. ¿Cuánto mide Paco?
3. ¿Cuánto pesa la carta?
4. ¿Cuánta leche debo comprar?

CAPÍTULO 6

Pronunciation
1. Use Pronunciation Transparency P-6.6.1, or write the pronunciation activity on the chalkboard. Have students copy it into their notebooks.
   ¿Un jugador de baloncesto? Dos metros.
   ¿Un tenista? Un metro ochenta.
   ¿Un futbolista? Un metro setenta.
   ¿Y una bailarina? Uno cincuenta.
2. You may wish to play the recorded version of this activity, located at the end of Cassette 6.6.
3. Have students repeat words and phrases individually and in unison. You may wish to focus on the /t/ sound: **baloncesto; metros; tenista; ochenta; futbolista; setenta; cinquenta.**

Estructura 1

How to Distinguish One Thing from Another — Este / ese

1. When you want to describe or point out someone or something that is nearby or close in time ("this class, these books"), use the following descriptive words.

MASCULINE		FEMININE	
SINGULAR	PLURAL	SINGULAR	PLURAL
este	estos	esta	estas

En esta tienda hay ropa bonita. Por ejemplo, me gustan estos pantalones y este suéter. ¿No te gustan estas camisas? Dicen que esta semana hay descuentos increíbles.

2. When you want to describe or point out something that is farther away from you or more remote in time ("that place, those years"), use the following descriptive words.

MASCULINE		FEMININE	
SINGULAR	PLURAL	SINGULAR	PLURAL
ese	esos	esa	esas

Pablo llegó en 1989. En ese año, jugó en el equipo de fútbol. ¡Siempre recuerda esos partidos, y esas fiestas, y esa muchacha rubia!

Notice that these words come before the word they describe.

477

Actividades

Actividad A Answers
Answers will vary.

Actividad B Answers
1. No me gusta este televisor, ni este sofá, ni esta habitación.
2. ...gustan estas clases, ni estos libros, ni estos exámenes.
3. ...estas papas fritas, ni este pescado, ni este refresco.
4. ...estas tiendas, ni estos empleados, ni estos autobuses.

Actividad C Answers
Answers should include the following phrases:
1. esa/esta billetera
2. ese/este paraguas
3. esa/esta bolsa
4. ese/este reloj
5. esos/estos anteojos de sol
6. ese/este collar

Reteaching
Display some items students know the Spanish words for on your desk and on another desk not near yours. Have students tell which item(s) they prefer. For example: **Prefiero esos (estos) casetes.**

Learning from Realia
You may want to have students look at the realia on page 477 and explain the significance of **Nuestra gente no necesita usar este libro** in relation to the dictionary.

Actividades

A **Ese año.** Think of a school vacation you had one year. Make five statements, comparing where you went and what you did that year with what you're going to do this year.

Por ejemplo:

> Recuerdo las vacaciones de verano de 1990. Ese año fui a _____. Pero este año voy a _____.

B **De mal humor.** One day Bruno was in a bad mood all day long. He hated everything he saw. How would he complain about the following?

Por ejemplo:

> en el desayuno: el jugo / el café / los huevos
> *No me gusta este jugo, ni este café, ni estos huevos.*

1. en casa: el televisor / el sofá / la habitación
2. en la escuela: las clases / los libros / los exámenes
3. en la cafetería: las papas fritas / el pescado / el refresco
4. en la ciudad: las tiendas / los empleados / los autobuses

C **En la tienda.** Ask the salesclerk in a store to show you each of the items in the display case where he or she is standing. The salesclerk wants to confirm which item you want to see. Play the roles with a classmate.

Por ejemplo:

ESTUDIANTE A
(1) Señor (Señorita), quisiera ver ese anillo, por favor.
(3) Sí, gracias. Es muy bonito.

ESTUDIANTE B
(2) ¿Este anillo?

478 CAPÍTULO 6

CULTURA VIVA 2

José Martí

José Martí (1853-1895) es uno de los poetas más famosos de Cuba. Es también el héroe más importante para los cubanos porque trabajó mucho por la independencia cubana de España.

Aquí tienes un ejemplo de su poesía.

> Si dicen que del joyero
> tome la joya mejor,
> tomo a un amigo sincero
> y pongo a un lado el amor.
>
> Todo es hermoso y constante,
> todo es música y razón.
> Y todo, como un diamante,
> antes que luz es carbón.

("Versos sencillos")

Actividades

A ¿Quiénes son algunos de nuestros héroes en los Estados Unidos?

B Para ti, ¿son héroes...?

1. ¿los científicos?
2. ¿los escritores?
3. ¿los músicos?
4. ¿los políticos?
5. ¿los cantantes?
6. ¿los maestros?
7. ¿los deportistas?

Estructura 2

Estructura 2

How to Talk about the Past   Summary of the preterit

1. To talk about people's actions in the past, you have learned to put the following endings on verbs.

-ar verbs		-er and -ir verbs	
-é	-amos	-í	-imos
-aste	-asteis*	-iste	-isteis*
-ó	-aron	-ió	-ieron

2. You have also learned to spell the **yo** form of certain **-ar** verbs.

llegar	llegué	buscar	busqué
jugar	jugué	practicar	practiqué
pagar	pagué	explicar	expliqué
sacar	saqué	empezar	empecé
tocar	toqué		

3. You have learned the special forms of **ir, ver, dar, hacer, pedir, leer,** and **oír** in the past.

ir	
fui	fuimos
fuiste	fuisteis*
fue	fueron

ver	
vi	vimos
viste	visteis*
vio	vieron

dar	
di	dimos
diste	disteis*
dio	dieron

hacer	
hice	hicimos
hiciste	hicisteis*
hizo	hicieron

pedir	
pedí	pedimos
pediste	pedisteis*
pidió	pidieron

Structure Teaching Resources
1. Workbook, pp. 209–210
2. Cassette 6.6
3. Student Tape Manual, p. 176
4. Estructura Masters 6.6
5. Lesson Quizzes, p. 137

Bell Ringer Review

Directions to students: Draw three circles on your paper. In each circle draw one of the following: a sumo wrestler, a parakeet, and a giant sequoia tree. Now write descriptive phrases about each one, focusing on height, weight, and other physical characteristics. Be prepared to compare your pictures orally.

Structure Focus
This section summarizes all forms of the preterit taught in the text.

Presentation
A. Lead students through steps 1–3 on pages 480 and 481.
B. Ask students questions using the preterit.

Reteaching
Have students brainstorm endings for this sentence.
El verano pasado yo...

Cooperative Learning
In pairs have students write a letter in which they describe what they did on their last vacation. Students exchange letters and answer them.

leer	
leí	leímos
leíste	leísteis*
leyó	leyeron

oír	
oí	oímos
oíste	oísteis*
oyó	oyeron

* This form is rarely used in the Spanish-speaking world, except for Spain.

Actividades

A **¡Qué desastre!** Señor Ramírez's students had spring fever and didn't do the things they were supposed to. Say that no one (**nadie**) did the following things.

Por ejemplo:

No escucharon al maestro.
Nadie lo escuchó.

1. No hicieron las tareas.
2. No estudiaron la lección.
3. No leyeron el capítulo.
4. No comieron la comida en la cafetería.
5. No vieron la película en la clase de historia.
6. No oyeron las instrucciones.

B **¿Qué hiciste?** Using the cues below, interview a classmate about things he or she did recently. Then ask one additional question of your own for each. Take notes and report back to the class.

Por ejemplo:

ir al cine

ESTUDIANTE A
(1) ¿Fuiste al cine la semana pasada?

ESTUDIANTE B
(2) Sí.

(3) ¿Qué viste? (¿Con quién fuiste? ¿Qué hiciste después?)

(A la clase:) Elisa fue al cine. Vio... (Fue con..., Después...).

1. salir con los amigos
2. leer algo interesante
3. practicar deportes
4. comprar algo
5. comer en un restaurante
6. ver un programa bueno
7. ir a un partido
8. escuchar música
9. sacar una buena nota
10. viajar

Lección 6   481

Actividades

Actividad A Answers
1. Nadie las hizo.
2. ... la estudió.
3. ... lo leyó.
4. ... la comió.
5. ... la vio.
6. ... las oyó.

Actividad B Answers
Answers will vary but should include the following verb forms:

1. saliste, salí, salió
2. leíste, leí, leyó
3. practicaste, practiqué, practicó (jugó)
4. compraste, compré, compró
5. comiste, comí, comió
6. viste, vi, vio
7. fuiste, fui, fue
8. escuchaste, escuché, escuchó
9. sacaste, saqué, sacó
10. viajaste, viajé, viajó

Actividades C and D Answers
Answers will vary.

C **La semana pasada.** List five things you did last week under a column labeled **"Yo."** Then ask two classmates what they did last week. List their activities under columns labeled by each student's name.

Por ejemplo:

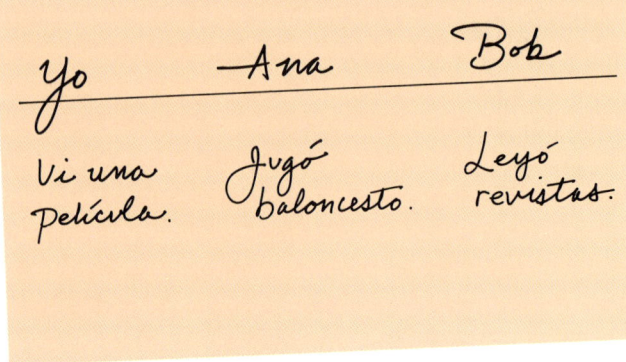

D **¿Qué hicieron ustedes?** Using the list you made in activity **C**, tell the following.

1. Is there something similar that all of you did? Report on this, using the **nosotros** form of the verbs.
2. Is there something that your two classmates did that you didn't? Report on this using the **ellos** or **ellas** form of the verbs.
3. Then report on the other things that you did **(yo)** and the other things that each of your two classmates did **(él** or **ella)**.

482 CAPÍTULO 6

Finalmente

Situaciones

A conversar You are a customer in a clothing store. A classmate will play the role of a salesclerk.

1. Greet the salesclerk and tell him or her what you would like to see.
2. The salesclerk asks your preference of: (a) color, (b) fabric (cotton, wool, silk, etc.), and (c) style (sporty, dress, short sleeves, etc.). Respond with as much detail as possible.
3. The salesclerk tries to persuade you to buy the item, saying two nice things about it.
4. Ask the price. Then decide whether to buy it.

A escribir Yesterday your Spanish class had an end-of-year outing at a local park. Write a note to a friend who couldn't attend, telling about all the activities you, your classmates, and your teacher did or didn't do. Include details related to food, games, sports, music, and dancing.

Repaso de vocabulario

PREGUNTAS
¿Cuánto mide(s)?
¿Cuánto pesa(s)?

MEDIDAS
la libra
la milla
la onza
el pie
la pulgada

DESCRIPCIONES
liviano(a)
pesado(a)

OTRAS PALABRAS
ese, esa, esos, esas
este, esta, estos, estas

EXPRESIONES
más o menos
tardar + *tiempo* + en llegar

Lectura

For the Native Speaker

Write a short composition about an imaginary shopping trip to your favorite mall. Include the stores you visited, a description and cost of the items you bought, how you got to the mall, and what you liked best and least about your shopping trip.

Lectura

Getting Students Ready for Reading

A. You may want to stress the following points to your students:
   1. Read for general meaning without stopping to look up the words you don't understand.
   2. Look for cognates. For example: **emoción, fantástico, casino**
   3. Read a second time looking for specific detail.
   4. Underline the words you didn't understand and try to guess their meaning by their context.
   5. If you still don't know the meaning of the words, look them up in the dictionary.

B. Before reading the Lectura, you may wish to have students discuss in groups the following questions:
   1. What are the advantages of traveling in a cruise ship?
   2. If you were planning a cruise, where would you go and why?

Lectura

You will be able to figure out many of the words in the following reading from the context in which they appear or because they look like English words that have similar meanings.

The following is an ad for a trip Carmen's family took. Look at the pictures—what kind of trip is it? What might the word **"crucero"** mean?

Permita que el SeaEscape le lleve en un crucero por un día.

Toda la emoción de un crucero por más días en un día fantástico.

Disfrute de 3 deliciosas comidas (incluidas en el precio). Baile al compás de música en vivo. Tome baños de sol junto a la piscina. Diviértase con la revista musical estilo cabaret del SeaEscape. Y todos los lunes es la noche de Grandes Conjuntos Musicales.

Navegue desde Miami hasta Freeport-Lucaya y regrese por sólo $99. Desde Tampa navegue por el Golfo de México por sólo $79. O, desde Puerto Cañaveral, navegue por el Atlántico por sólo $79.

Tarifas especiales para personas mayores, adolescentes y niños. En el precio se incluye transportación por autobús de ida y regreso desde algunos hoteles hasta el muelle.

Para reservaciones e información, vea a su agente de viajes o al conserje de su hotel, o llame a las oficinas del SeaEscape cualquier día de la semana hasta las 11:00 p.m. desde cualquier lugar en los Estados Unidos al 1-800-555-0900 o desde la Florida al 555-6753.

SeaEscape

Actividades

A What kinds of information would you expect to find in an ad like this?

B Skim the ad to find out what types of information are included. Is there anything you did not list in question **A?**

C Scan the ad for the information needed in the following activities.
1. List the words that indicate the activities you could participate in.
2. List the words that indicate the duration of the trip.
3. What are the prices for the following?
   a. round-trip from Miami to Freeport
   b. Gulf of Mexico cruise
   c. Atlantic cruise
4. Which of the following people would be eligible for special rates?
   a. Carmen
   b. el tío Lucas
   c. la abuela de Carmen
   d. tú
   e. tus compañeros de clase
   f. tus padres o hermanos
5. From where you live, what number would you call to make reservations?
6. What words are used to describe the following?
   a. the food
   b. the musical revue
   c. the cruise itself

D Now look more closely at the ad and choose the most likely definition of the following words and expressions.
1. ida y regreso
   a. rápido
   b. ir y regresar
   c. a todas horas
2. tarifas especiales
   a. descuentos
   b. reservas
   c. actividades

E Write a note to a classmate inviting him or her to go with you. Tell him or her all the things you two can do on the cruise. Your classmate will write back either accepting or rejecting your invitation and give reasons.

Lectura 485

Actividades

Actividad A Answers
Answers will vary but may include the following:
price and length of trip, available activities, points of departure.

Actividad B Answers
Answers will vary.

Actividad C Answers
1. Disfrute de 3 deliciosas comidas, baile, tome baños de sol, diviértase con la revista musical.
2. Un crucero por un día, un día fantástico.
3. a. $99.
   b. $79
   c. $79.
4. a,c,d,e (f depends on age of student's family members)
5. Answers will vary.
6. a. deliciosas
   b. estilo cabaret
   c. Toda la emoción de un crucero por más días en un día fantástico.

Actividad D Answers
1. b
2. a

Actividad E Answers
Answers will vary.

Capítulo de repaso

Bell Ringer Review

Directions to students: Rita saw two very strange animals at the zoo today. Draw them, using the following directions:

1. In the bottom left corner draw a fairly large elephant.
2. In the upper right corner draw a smaller gorilla, showing the perspective that distance creates.

Now, add each of the following items to the correct animal, depending on whether it is the closer one (**este**) or the one farther away (**ese**).

este gorro
esos anteojos de sol
este monopatín
este traje de baño
esos esquís acuáticos
esta bufanda
esos tenis
esos shorts
estas sandalias
esa revista romántica

Repaso Resources
1. Workbook, p. 211–214
2. Cassette 6.6
3. Student Tape Manual, pp. 179–181
4. Video Cassette
5. Cumulative Test, p. 117–125

¿Recuerdas?

Presentation

To review Chapter 6, call on individual students to give an example for each communicative function listed for Lecciones 1–3 and Lecciones 4–6, page 486. The number in parentheses on page 486 refers to the actual page(s) in Chapter 6 where each function was presented and practiced. You may wish to have

---

Capítulo 6 Repaso

¿Recuerdas?

Do you remember how to do the following things, which you learned in **Capítulo 6**?

LECCIONES 1-3
1. identify articles of clothing (pp. 408–409)
2. say what you do for others (p. 412)
3. tell what you and someone else did at one point in the past (p. 415)
4. describe articles of clothing (pp. 420–421)
5. describe what people do for you and others ("us") (p. 424)
6. tell what you and others like and dislike (p. 424)
7. write about the past (p. 427)
8. tell what means of transportation you and others use (p. 433)
9. give and get directions (pp. 432–433)
10. tell how far away something is (p. 432)
11. say that someone is coming (p. 437)
12. tell what someone did in the past (p. 440)

LECCIONES 4-6
1. describe the weather (pp. 446–447)
2. tell what others did in the past (p. 451)
3. refer to people and things already mentioned (p. 454)
4. describe how you feel (p. 460)
5. compare and contrast people and things (pp. 463, 467)
6. give weights, measurements, and distances (pp. 472–473)
7. distinguish one thing from another (p. 477)

Actividades

A **Lo bueno y lo malo.** Tell three good things and three bad things about the season you are in now.

Por ejemplo:

> verano
> Lo bueno: *Puedo ir a la playa.*
> Lo malo: *Hace mucho calor.*

B **Por teléfono.** Carmen is speaking to her friend Bárbara on the phone. You can hear only Carmen's side of the conversation. What do you think Bárbara is saying in each case?

BÁRBARA	CARMEN
1. _____	Bien, bien, ¿y tú?
2. _____	Son casi las tres. Voy a ver mi telenovela favorita.
3. _____	Sí que me permite, pero dice que uso demasiado el teléfono.
4. _____	Mi mamá no está. Fue de compras con mi primo.
5. _____	Sí, mi primo nos visita.
6. _____	De Buenos Aires.
7. _____	En la Argentina, chica. ¿No estudias geografía?
8. _____	Dos semanas. Está aquí con su papá desde el 20 de abril.
9. _____	Muy simpático pero no habla mucho inglés.
10. _____	Sí, pero no me molesta. Me gusta el español pero necesito practicar más. Ya viene mi mamá. Te llamo más tarde.

---

your students go back to these pages for additional review and practice before continuing on to the Actividades, pages 487–489.

Lecciones 1–3 Answers

The following words and phrase are examples for each of the 12 functions listed under Lecciones 1–3. These words and phrases should be included in the students' response to each function listed.

1. El abrigo, la blusa, las botas, etc.
2. Les...
3. Jugamos, comimos, etc.
4. Ropa de invierno, ropa de manga corta, etc.
5. Nos...
6. Nos gusta, no nos gusta
7. Toqué, saqué, practiqué, expliqué, busqué, llegué, jugué, pagué, empecé
8. A pie, el autobús, el avión, el barco, la camioneta, el tren
9. Al lado de, cerca de, derecho, detrás de, enfrente de, entre, lejos de
10. Está a...
11. Vengo, vienes, viene, venimos, vienen
12. Compró, fue, dio, vio, hizo, etc.

Lecciones 4–6 Answers

The following words and phrases are examples for each of the seven functions listed under Lecciones 4–6. These words and phrases should be included in the students' response to each function listed.

1. Está nublado, hace buen tiempo, frío, etc.
2. Terminaron, fueron, dieron, etc.
3. Lo, los, la, las
4. Tengo calor, frío, hambre, miedo, prisa, sed, sueño.
5. Más/menos... que, tanto... como, tan... como
6. La libra, la milla, la onza, el pie, la pulgada
7. Este/ese

Actividades

Presentation

Each practice activity in this Chapter 6 review combines several of the language functions listed on page 486. Students are asked to use the language they have learned at a higher, more integrated level, compared to the individual practice activities in Lecciones 1–6 of Chapter 6.

Actividad A Answers
Answers will vary.

Actividad B Answers
Answers will vary but may include the following:

1. ¿Cómo estás?
2. ¿Qué piensas hacer? (¿Qué haces?)
3. ¿Tú mamá te permite ver las telenovelas?
4. ¿Por qué lo puedes usar ahora?
5. ¿Dices, tu primo?
6. ¿De dónde es?
7. ¿Dónde está Buenos Aires?
8. ¿Cuántos días va a estar con ustedes?
9. ¿Cómo es?
10. ¿Tienes que hablar (en) español con él?

Actividad C Answers
Answers will vary but may include the following:

1. El tío Samuel dice que vienen pero no pueden llegar hasta el sábado por la noche.
2. El doctor Sotelo dice que no viene porque tiene que trabajar.
3. Jorge dice que no viene porque sus padres no le permiten salir.
4. La tía Ana dice que no viene porque el niño está enfermo.
5. La tía Lourdes dice que viene y trae el postre.
6. Victoria dice que no viene porque tiene que estudiar.
7. Los abuelos dicen que vienen el sábado a las cinco y cuarto.

Actividad D Answers
Answers will vary.

Actividad E Answers
Answer will vary but may include the following:

C **¿Vienen o no vienen?** Carmen's family is having a party on Saturday afternoon to welcome Tío Lucas and Rafael. Carmen calls everyone to see if he or she is planning to come. Based on the responses below, tell whether each person is coming and summarize any other messages.

Por ejemplo:

Tío Juan: Sí, cómo no. ¿Me das la dirección?
El tío Juan dice que viene pero necesita la dirección.

1. Tío Samuel: Sí, pero no podemos venir hasta el sábado por la noche.
2. el doctor Sotelo: Tengo que trabajar todo el fin de semana.
3. Jorge: No puedo. Mis padres están enojados conmigo. No me permiten salir.
4. Tía Ana: No puedo porque el niño está enfermo.
5. Tía Lourdes: Sí, les llevamos el postre.
6. Victoria: Ay, qué pena! Tengo exámenes.
7. los abuelos: Llegamos el sábado a las cinco y cuarto.

D **El detective.** Bring an unusual object to class in a paper bag. In groups of three or four, try to guess what's in each person's bag by asking questions such as those below. Think of other helpful questions of your own.

Por ejemplo:

¿De qué es? ¿Cómo es? ¿Para qué sirve? ¿De qué color es? ¿Cuánto pesa?

E **¡Qué horror!** Tell what you did—or didn't do—in the following situations.

Por ejemplo:

En el restaurante cuando te sirvieron el plato que pediste, ¡viste insectos en la comida! ¿Qué hiciste?
Pedí otro plato. No pagué.

1. Cuando saliste del restaurante, recordaste que dejaste (you left) tu billetera en la mesa. ¿Qué hiciste?
2. Tú y tus amigos fueron al cine pero parece que todos dejaron las billeteras en casa. ¿Qué hicieron?
3. Cuando pediste permiso para salir con tus amigos el viernes por la noche, tu mamá te contestó: "Si no limpias tu habitación y haces todas tus tareas, no puedes salir". ¿Qué hiciste?
4. Nadie estudió para el examen de biología. Cuando tú y los compañeros llegaron a clase, ¿qué hicieron?

F **Los quehaceres de la casa.** The members of Carmen's family take turns doing the chores. Below is last week's schedule. How would Carmen describe everyone's chores for each day last week?

Por ejemplo:

El lunes pasado, mi papá _____. Mi mamá _____. Yo_____.

lunes	martes	miércoles	jueves	viernes	sábado	domingo
preparar la comida						
m	p	C	m	C	p	m
limpiar los baños						
C					m	
dar de comer al conejo						
C	C	C	m	m	p	p
barrer la terraza						
m	m	m	p	p	C	C
cuidar al gato del vecino						
C	C	C	C	p	p	m

1. Regresé al restaurante. Busqué mi billetera.
2. Regresamos a casa. No fuimos al cine.
3. Limpié mi habitación y después hice mis tareas.
4. Tomamos el examen pero sacamos malas notas.

Actividad F Answers
1. El lunes pasado, mi mamá preparó la comida y barrió la terraza. Yo limpié los baños, di de comer al conejo y cuidé al gato del vecino.
2. El martes pasado, mi papá preparó... , mi mamá barrió... y yo di... y cuidé...
3. El miércoles pasado, mi mamá barrió... y yo preparé... y cuidé...
4. El jueves pasado, mi mamá preparó... y dio... , mi papá barrió... y yo cuidé...
5. El viernes pasado, mi mamá dio... , mi papá barrió... y cuidó... , y yo preparé...
6. El sábado pasado, mi papá preparó... , dio y cuidó... Mi mamá limpió... y yo barrí...
7. El domingo pasado, mi mamá preparó... y cuidó... Mi papá dio... y yo barrí...

Verb Charts

Present Tense

REGULAR VERBS

-ar		-er		-ir	
hablar		comer		escribir	
hablo	hablamos	como	comemos	escribo	escribimos
hablas	habláis*	comes	coméis*	escribes	escribís*
habla	hablan	come	comen	escribe	escriben

STEM-CHANGING VERBS

e—ie		o—ue; u—ue		e—i	
querer		poder		pedir	
quiero	queremos	puedo	podemos	pido	pedimos
quieres	queréis*	puedes	podéis*	pides	pedís*
quiere	quieren	puede	pueden	pide	piden

Other stem-changing verbs like querer: empezar, entender, pensar, perder, preferir.

Other stem-changing verbs like poder: dormir, jugar, recordar.

IRREGULAR VERBS

decir		estar		ir		oír	
digo	decimos	estoy	estamos	voy	vamos	oigo	oímos
dices	decís*	estás	estáis*	vas	vais*	oyes	oís*
dice	dicen	está	están	va	van	oye	oyen

ser		tener		venir	
soy	somos	tengo	tenemos	vengo	venimos
eres	sois*	tienes	tenéis*	vienes	venís*
es	son	tiene	tienen	viene	vienen

THE FOLLOWING VERBS ARE FORMED REGULARLY WITH THE EXCEPTION OF THE YO FORM.

conocer	conozco	pertenecer	pertenezco	salir	salgo
dar	doy	poner	pongo	traer	traigo
hacer	hago	saber	sé	ver	veo

*This form is rarely used, except for Spain.

Preterit Tense

REGULAR VERBS

-ar

hablar

hablé	hablamos
hablaste	hablasteis*
habló	hablaron

-er, -ir

comer

comí	comimos
comiste	comisteis*
comió	comieron

escribir

escribí	escribimos
escribiste	escribisteis*
escribió	escribieron

IRREGULAR VERBS

dar

di	dimos
diste	disteis*
dio	dieron

hacer

hice	hicimos
hiciste	hicisteis*
hizo	hicieron

ir

fui	fuimos
fuiste	fuisteis*
fue	fueron

leer

leí	leímos
leíste	leísteis*
leyó	leyeron

oír

oí	oímos
oíste	oísteis*
oyó	oyeron

pedir

pedí	pedimos
pediste	pedisteis*
pidió	pidieron

ver

vi	vimos
viste	visteis*
vio	vieron

VERBS ENDING IN -AR WITH SPELLING CHANGES IN THE YO FORM

buscar	busqué	jugar	jugué
explicar	expliqué	llegar	llegué
practicar	practiqué	pagar	pagué
sacar	saqué		
tocar	toqué	empezar	empecé

*This form is rarely used, except for Spain.

Vocabulario Español-Inglés

The **Vocabulario Español-Inglés** contains all productive and receptive vocabulary from the text.

The numbers following each productive entry indicate the chapter and lesson in which the word is introduced.

The following are abbreviations used in this glossary.

adv.	adverb
com.	command
f.	feminine
fam.	familiar
inf.	infinitive
m.	masculine
pers.	personal
pl.	plural
prep.	preposition; prepositional
pron.	pronoun
sing.	singular
subj.	subjunctive

A

a at, 1.3; to, 1.5
a causa de due to
¡a comenzar! Let's begin!
a la izquierda to the left, 3.3
a la una at one o'clock, 1.3
a las (dos) at (two) o'clock, 1.3
a medida made-to-order
a menudo often
a mí me gusta I like, 4.1
a pie on foot, 6.3
¿A qué hora es . . . ? At what time is . . . ?, 1.3
a ti te gusta you like, 4.1
a veces sometimes, 2.4
a ver let's see, 1.6
abajo downstairs, 3.3
el / la **abogado(a)** lawyer, 4.2
el **abrazo** embrace, hug
un abrazo fuerte a strong embrace
abreviado(a) abbreviated
el **abrigo** overcoat, 6.1
abril April, 4.6
abrir to open, 5.2
la **abuela** grandmother, 4.1
el **abuelo** grandfather, 4.1
los **abuelos** grandparents, 4.1
aburrido(a) boring, 2.2; bored, 3.4
¡Qué aburrido! How boring!, 1.6
las **aceitunas** olives
acompañado(a) accompanied
acompañar to accompany
la **actitud** attitude
la **actividad** activity
el **actor** actor, 2.1
la **actriz** actress, 2.1
el **acueducto** aqueduct
el **Acueducto Romano** Roman Aqueduct (Spain)
adaptarse to adapt oneself
adecuado(a) adequate
los **ademanes** gestures
adentro indoors; inside, 3.3
adiós good-bye, 1.4
adivinar to guess
el / la **adivinador / a** guesser
¿adónde? (to) where?, 1.5
¿Adónde quieres ir? Where do you want to go?, 1.5
¿Adónde vas? Where are you going?, 2.3
las **aerolíneas** airlines
el **aeropuerto** airport
afectar to affect
afectuoso(a) affectionate
los **aficionados** fans
africano(a) African
afuera outside, 3.3
las **afueras** outskirts
la **agencia** agency
la **agencia de servicios sociales** social service agency
la **agencia de viajes** travel agency
el / la **agente** agent
el **agente de propiedades** real estate agent
agosto August, 4.6
el / la **agricultor / a** farmer, 4.2
el **agua** (f.) water, 2.5
ahora now, 2.3
ahorrar to save, 3.1
el **aire** air
al aire libre outdoors
el **ajedrez** chess, 4.5
el **ají** bell pepper
al (a + el) to the, 1.5
al aire libre outdoors, 6.4
al final at / in the end
al lado de next to, beside, 6.3
al máximo to the maximum
al sur to the south
alarmarse: se alarman they become alarmed
la **alberca** swimming pool (Mexico)
el **álbum** album
el **alemán** German (language), 5.3
alemán(ana) German, 5.3
Alemania Germany
la **alfombra** rug, 3.6
el **álgebra** algebra, 1.4
algo something, 1.2
el **algodón** cotton, 5.2
algunos(as) some
los **alimentos** food
allí there, 3.3
el **almacén** department store
el **almuerzo** lunch, 2.5
alrededor around
alto(a) tall, 2.2
el / la **alumno(a)** student
el **ama de casa** (f.) homemaker, 4.2
amable kind, 2.1
amarillo(a) yellow, 3.6
la **América Central** Central America
la **América del Norte** North America
la **América del Sur** South America
las **Américas** the Americas
el / la **amigo(a)** friend, 2.3
anaranjado(a) orange, 3.6
andar: andar en monopatín to skateboard, 1.2

Vocabulario español-inglés

los **Andes**   Andes (Mountains)
el **anillo**   ring, 6.1
el **animal**   animal, 4.3
anoche   last night, 5.3
ante   before, in front of (prep.)
anteayer   the day before yesterday, 5.3
los **anteojos**   eyeglasses, 4.4
los **anteojos de sol**   sunglasses, 6.1
antes   before (adv.)
antes de   before (time), 3.1
antiguo(a)   old (object), 3.5
antipático(a)   unpleasant (person), 2.2
el **anuncio**   advertisement, 5.1
el **anuncio comercial**   commercial
el **año**   year, 4.6
el **año pasado**   last year, 5.3
el **año que viene**   next year, 4.6
¿En qué año naciste?   What year were you born?, 5.3
el **aparato**   gadget, machine, 5.2
la **apariencia**   appearance
el **apartamento**   apartment, 3.2
el **apellido**   last name
la **apendicitis**   appendicitis
aplicado(a)   industrious, studious, 2.2
aprender   to learn, 1.4
aprender a   + inf. to learn (how) to, 4.5
aprobado   passing
no aprobado   failing
aprovechar   to take advantage (of)
aquí   here, 1.1
árabe   Arab
el **área**   (f.) area

el **arete**   earring, 6.1
argentino(a)   Argentinian, 5.3
el **armario**   dresser, 3.6
la **armería**   armory, gunsmith
el / la **arquitecto(a)**   arquitect, 4.2
arreglar   to arrange, organize
arriba   up, upstairs, 3.3
arrogante   arrogant, 2.1
el **arroz**   rice, 2.5
el **arte**   art, 1.4
las **artes marciales**   martial arts
las **artesanías**   crafts
los **artículos**   articles
los **artículos de viajes**   travel needs
el / la **artista**   artist, 2.1
artístico(a)   artistic
el **ascensor**   elevator, 3.3
así   so; this way
así como   just like
asistir a   to attend, 5.4
la **asociación**   association
la **aspiradora**   vacuum cleaner, 5.6
atraer   to attract
los **audífonos**   headphones
auditivo: el sistema auditivo   hearing
el **auditorio**   auditorium
aunque   although
austral   southern
el **auto**   automobile, car
la **autobiografía**   autobiography
el **autobús**   bus, 6.3
autorizado(a)   authorized
avanzado(a)   advanced
la **avenida**   avenue, 3.2
la **aventura**   adventure, 4.5
el **programa de aventuras**   adventure program, 4.5

la **aviación**   aviation
la **compañía de aviación**   aviation (airline) company
el **avión**   airplane, 6.3
ayer   yesterday, 5.3
el **ayudante**   aide, assistant
ayudar   to help, 5.1
el **ayuntamiento**   city hall
azul   blue, 3.6

B

la **bahía**   bay
bailar   to dance, 1.2
el / la **bailarín(ina)**   dancer, 2.1
el **baile**   dance, 1.5
bajar   to go down
bajo(a)   short (person), 2.2
el **baloncesto**   basketball, 1.2
el **banco**   bank, 2.6
el **baño**   bathroom, 3.6
barato(a)   inexpensive, cheap, 3.5
la **barba**   beard, 4.4
el **barco**   boat, ship, 6.3
barrer   to sweep, 5.6
el **barrio**   neighborhood
la **base**   base, foundation
básico(a)   basic
basta   it's enough
bastante   fairly; enough, 2.2
la **basura**   trash, 3.3
la **bebida**   beverage, 2.5
el **béisbol**   baseball, 1.2
la **belleza**   beauty
el **beso**   kiss
la **biblioteca**   library, 1.5
la **bicicleta**   bicycle, 1.2
montar en bicicleta   to ride a bicycle, 1.2
bien   fine, well, 1.1
bienvenido(a)   welcome
el **bigote**   mustache, 4.4
bilingüe   bilingual
el **billete**   ticket

Vocabulario español-inglés

la **billetera** billfold, wallet, 5.2
la **biografía** biography
la **biología** biology, 1.4
los **bisabuelos** great-grandparents
la **bisutería** costume jewelry
blanco(a) white, 3.6
la **blusa** blouse, 6.1
la **bodega** grocery store
las **boleadoras** hunting slings (Argentina)
el **boletín de evaluación** report card
el **boliche** bowling, 2.6
   jugar boliche to bowl, 2.6
el **bolígrafo** ballpoint pen, 1.4
boliviano(a) Bolivian, 5.3
la **bolsa** handbag, 6.1
el **bolsillo** pocket, 5.2
el **bolso** handbag
el / la **bombero(a)** firefighter, 4.2
la **bombonería** candy and chocolate shop
bonito(a) pretty, 3.5
boreal northern
el **bosque** forest, woods, 6.4
las **botas** boots, 6.1
el **bouffett** buffet
las **boutiques** boutiques
bucear to skin-dive, 5.4
buen: ¡Buen viaje! Have a good trip!
bueno(a) good, 1.6
   buenas noches good evening, good night, 1.3
   buenas tardes good afternoon, 1.3
   buenos días good morning, 1.3
   ¡Qué bueno! That's great!, 1.6

bueno: lo bueno the good thing
la **bufanda** scarf, 6.1
buscar to look for, 2.3

C

el **caballero** gentleman, man, 6.2
   la **ropa de caballeros** men's clothing, 6.2
el **caballo** horse, 4.3
   montar a caballo to ride horseback, 1.5
la **cabeza** head
cada each
   cada uno(a) each one
   cada vez más more and more
el **café** coffee, 2.5; coffee shop
café brown, 4.4
la **cafetería** cafeteria, 1.5
los **calcetines** socks, 6.1
la **calculadora** calculator, 1.4
el **calendario** calendar
la **calle** street, 3.1
el **calor** heat, 6.5
   hace calor it's hot, 6.4
   tener calor to be hot, 6.5
la **cama** bed, 3.6
la **cámara** camera, 3.1
cambiar to change, 3.1
el **camello** camel, 4.3
la **caminata** hike, 6.4
   hacer una caminata to take a hike, 6.4
el **camión** bus (Mexico)
la **camioneta** pick-up truck, 6.3
la **camisa** shirt, 6.1
la **camiseta** T-shirt, 3.5
el **campo** countryside, 1.5
canadiense Canadian, 5.3
el **canal** channel (TV)
el **canario** canary, 4.3
cansado(a) tired, 3.4

el / la **cantante** singer, 2.1
   cantar to sing, 1.5
la **cantidad** quantity
la **capital** capital
el **capítulo** chapter
el **Caribe** the Caribbean (Sea)
el **cariño** affection
   cariños (with) love
el **carnaval** carnival
la **carne** meat, 2.5
caro(a) expensive, 3.5
el / la **carpintero(a)** carpenter, 4.2
el **carro** car
la **carta** letter, 3.1
   la **carta de presentación** letter of introduction
las **cartas** playing cards, 4.5
   jugar cartas to play cards, 4.5
el **cartel** poster, 3.5
el **cartucho** cartridge
la **casa** house, home, 2.6
   la **casa de cambio** money exchange office
   ir a casa to go home, 1.2
casado(a) married
el **casete** cassette, 3.5
casi almost, 5.5
el **catálogo** catalogue
la **catedral** cathedral
católico(a) Catholic
catorce fourteen, 1.3
la **caza** hunting
   ir de caza to go hunting
la **celebración** celebration
celebrar to celebrate
celeste sky-blue
la **cena** supper, dinner, 2.5
cenar to eat supper
centígrado(a) centigrade (degrees)
el **centro** downtown, 2.3
   el **centro comercial** shopping center, 1.5

Vocabulario español-inglés **497**

cerca de near, 6.3
el cereal cereal, 2.5
cero zero, 1.3
cerrado(a) closed
el césped lawn, 5.6
el ciclismo cycling
los ciegos blind persons
cien one hundred, 3.3
ciento one hundred, 4.2
ciento uno (dos) one hundred one (two), 4.2
la ciencia ficción science fiction, 4.5
el programa de ciencia ficción science fiction program, 4.5
las ciencias science(s), 1.4
las ciencias domésticas home economics
cierto true; certain
cinco five, 1.3
cincuenta fifty, 3.3
el cine movie theater, 1.5
el cinto belt
el cinturón belt, 6.1
el circo circus
la cita appointment
la ciudad city, 1.5
el / la ciudadano(a) citizen
claro(a) light, bright
la clase class, 1.4; kind, 4.5
¿Qué clase de . . .? What kind of . . . ?, 4.5
el / la cliente client
el clima climate
la clínica clinic
el club club, 5.5
cobrar to charge
el coche car, 1.5
el cochinillo asado roast suckling pig
la cocina kitchen, 3.6; cuisine
cocinar to cook, 1.5

la cola line, 5.5
hacer cola to stand in line, 5.5
la colección collection, 3.5
el / la coleccionista collector
el collar necklace, 6.1
colombiano(a) Colombian, 5.3
colonial colonial
la combinación combination
el comedor dining room, 3.6
comer to eat, 1.2
dar de comer to feed, 5.6
comercial commercial
el comercio commerce, business
cómico(a) funny, 4.5
el programa cómico comedy (program), 4.5
la comida food, 2.5; meal
la comisión commission
como as, like, 6.5
así como just like
como siempre as always
tan . . . como as . . . as, 6.5
¿cómo? what?; how?, 1.4
¿Cómo es . . .? What is he / she / it like?; What are you (formal) like?, 2.1
¿Cómo está usted? How are you (formal)?, 1.3
¿Cómo estás? How are you (fam.)?, 1.3
¿Cómo se dice . . .? How do you say . . .?, 5.2
¿Cómo son? What are they like?, 2.1
¿Cómo te llamas? What is your name (fam.)?, 1.1

¡cómo!: ¡Cómo no! Of course!, 1.2
la comodidad comfort
cómodo(a) comfortable, 3.1
el / la compañero(a) de clase classmate, 2.1
la compañía company, 4.2
la compañía de aviación aviation (airline) company
los complementos accessories
completamente completely
la composición composition, 1.4
los compradores buyers
comprar to buy, 1.2
las compras the shopping
ir de compras to go shopping
comprender to understand
la computación computer class
la computadora computer, 1.5
usar la computadora to use the computer, 1.5
común common
con with, 1.2
con el tiempo eventually
con permiso excuse me, 2.3
conmigo with me, 5.4
contigo with you (fam.), 5.4
el concierto concert, 2.3
el concurso game show, 4.5
el condominio condominium
el conejillo de Indias guinea pig
el conejo rabbit, 4.3
la confección sewing

498 Vocabulario español-inglés

la **confección deportiva** athletic wear
la **confusión** confusion
la **conga** popular Cuban music and dance
el **conjunto** musical group, 2.3
conocer (zco) to know, be familiar with a person or place, 5.5
el **consejo** piece of advice, 5.6
   dar consejos a to give advice to, 5.6
construido(a) built
el **consulado** consulate
el **contacto** contact
contar (ue) to count
contemplar to look at
contemporáneo(a) contemporary
contento(a) happy, 3.4
contestar to answer, 1.4
contener to contain
contra against
las **contribuciones** contributions
el **control** control
controlar to control
la **conversación** conversation
conversar to talk, chat
el **corazón** heart
la **corbata** necktie, 6.1
la **correa** belt
el **correo** post office, 5.1
   el **correo aéreo** air mail
correr to run, to jog, 1.2
la **corsetería** corset shop
cortar to cut, 5.6
las **cortes** courts (of law)
corto(a) short (object), 4.4
la **cosa** thing, 5.2
la **cosmética** cosmetics
la **costa** coast
costarricense Costa Rican, 5.3
la **costumbre** custom

creo: creo que I think that, 4.2
cruzar to cross
el **cuaderno** notebook, 1.4
la **cuadra** city block, 6.3
cuadrado(a) square, 5.2
el **cuadro: de cuadros** plaid, 6.2
¿cuál? which (one); what?, 4.5
   ¿Cuál es tu número de teléfono? What is your telephone number? (fam.), 3.3
¿cuándo? when?, 2.4
¿cuánto(a)? how much?, 3.3
   ¿Cuánto mide(s)? How tall are you (is he / she / it)?, 6.6
   ¿Cuánto pesa(s)? How much do you (does he / she / it) weigh?, 6.6
   ¿Cuánto tiempo? How long?, How much time?, 5.4
   ¿Cuánto tiempo hace que . . . ? How long has (have) . . . ?, 5.5
   ¿Cuánto vale? How much does it cost?, 4.2
¿cuántos(as)? how many?, 3.3
   ¿Cuántos años tiene(s)? How old are you (is he / she / it)?, 4.2
cuarenta forty, 3.3
el **cuarto** room (of a house), 3.6
cuarto(a) fourth, 3.2
cuatrocientos(as) four hundred, 4.2
cubano(a) Cuban, 5.3
el **cuero** leather, 5.2
cuesta it costs
cuidar to take care of, 4.3
la **cultura** culture

el **cumpleaños** birthday, 4.6
la **curiosidad** curiosity
el **curso** course

CH

el **chachachá** popular Latin American dance
la **chaqueta** jacket, 6.1
el **cheque** check, 5.1
   el **cheque de viajero** traveler's check, 3.1
   hacer un cheque to write a check, 5.1
chileno(a) Chilean, 5.3
el **chino** Chinese (language), 5.3
chino(a) Chinese, 5.3
el **choclo** ear of corn (Andes)
el **chorizo** Spanish sausage
los **churros** fritters, crullers

D

las **damas** ladies, 6.2
   para damas for ladies, 6.2
dar to give, 5.1
   dar consejos a to give advice to, 5.6
   dar de comer a to feed, 5.6
   dar un paseo to go for a walk, 1.2
de of, from, 2.3
   de acuerdo OK, 2.6
   de antigüedad of antiquity
   de compras shopping
   de cuadros plaid, 6.2
   de flores flowered (print), 6.2
   de habla española Spanish-speaking
   de invierno winter (clothes), 6.2
   de la mañana in the morning, 1.3

Vocabulario español-inglés

de la noche in the evening, at night, 1.3
de la tarde in the afternoon, 1.3
de lunares polka-dotted, 6.2
de manga corta short-sleeved, 6.2
de manga larga long-sleeved, 6.2
de medicina medical
de moda in fashion, 6.2
de nada you're welcome, 2.1
de otoño autumn (clothes), 6.2
de primavera spring (clothes), 6.2
¿De qué es? What's it made of?, 5.2
¿De qué marca es? What's the brand name?, 3.5
¿De quién es / son? Whose is it / are they?, 2.3
de rayas striped, 6.2
de un solo color solid (color), 6.2
de verano summer (clothes), 6.2
debe he / she / it / you (formal) must (probability)
deber should, ought, 3.1
décimo(a) tenth, 3.2
decir to say, to tell, 5.5
la **decisión** decision
los **defensores** defenders
del (de + el) from the, of the, 2.3
delgado(a) thin, 2.2
delicioso(a) delicious
demasiado(a) too, too much, 2.2
el / la **dentista** dentist, 4.2
depender to depend
dependiente dependent
el **deporte** sport, 1.2

el / la **deportista** athlete, 2.1
deportivo(a) casual, sports, 6.2
el programa deportivo sports program, 4.5
deprimente depressing, 2.1
deprimido(a) depressed, 3.4
la **derecha** right, 3.3
a la derecha to the right, 3.3
derecho(a) straight ahead, 6.3
sigue derecho go straight ahead (fam. sing. com.), 6.3
el **desastre: ¡Qué desastre!** What a disaster!, 1.6
el **desayuno** breakfast, 2.5
descansar to rest, 1.2
el **descuento** discount
desde since, 5.3
el **desfile** parade
el **desierto** desert, 6.4
despacio slow
las **despedidas** farewells
después afterwards, 2.3
después de after, 3.1
detrás de behind, 6.3
el **día** day, 2.6
buenos días good morning, 1.3
el **día de fiesta** holiday
el **Día de la Raza** Hispanic Pride Day
el **dialecto** dialect
diariamente daily
el **diario** diary
dibujar to draw, 1.5
el **dibujo** drawing
el **dibujo técnico** drafting
el **diccionario** dictionary
dice he / she / it says, you (formal) say, 4.5
dices you (fam.) say, 5.5
diciembre December, 4.6

los **dientes** teeth, 4.4
los **frenos en los dientes** (dental) braces, 4.4
diez ten, 1.3
diez y nueve nineteen, 1.3
diez y ocho eighteen, 1.3
diez y seis sixteen, 1.3
diez y siete seventeen, 1.3
la **diferencia** difference
diferente different, 2.1
difícil difficult, 1.6
digo I say; I mean, 5.5
los **diminutivos** diminutives
el **dinero** money, 2.3
la **dirección** address, 3.2
el / la **director / a** director
el **disco** record, 1.2
las **discotecas** discotheques
la **distancia** distance
la **larga distancia** long distance
distinguido excellent
divertido(a) fun, 2.2
¡Qué divertido! What fun!, 1.6
doblar to turn, 6.3
doce twelve, 1.3
el / la **doctor / a** doctor, 4.2
el **dólar** dollar, 1.3
el **domingo** Sunday, 2.6
dominicano(a) Dominican, 5.3
el **dominó** dominoes (game)
don title of respect used with a man's first name
donde where
¿dónde?: ¿Dónde está? Where is it?, 3.2
doña title of respect used with a woman's first name
dormir (ue) to sleep, 3.1
el **dormitorio** bedroom
dos two, 1.3

doscientos(as) two hundred, 4.2
doy I give
el **drama** drama (class)
el / la **dueño(a)** owner, 4.2
durante during

E

la **economía** economy
ecuatoriano(a) Ecuadorian, 5.3
la **edad** age
el **edificio** building, 3.2
la **educación física** physical education, 1.4
educativo(a) educational, 4.5
el **programa educativo** educational program, 4.5
el **efecto** effect, result
el **ejercicio** exercise, 2.3
hacer ejercicio to exercise, 2.3
el the (m.), 1.4
él he, 3.1
el / la **electricista** electrician, 4.2
el **elefante** elephant, 4.3
elegante elegant, 2.1
ella she, her, 3.1
ellas they, them (f.), 3.1
ellos they, them (m.), 3.1
el **elote** ear of corn (Mexico)
emocionado(a) excited, 3.4
emocionante exciting, 2.1
empezar (ie) to start, 4.5
el / la **empleado(a)** employee, 4.2
en at; in; on, 3.2
en fin in all
en punto on the dot, 2.6

¿En qué año naciste? What year were you (fam.) born?, 5.3
¿En qué piso está? What floor is it on?, 3.2
en realidad in reality
en vez de instead of
enamorado(a) in love, 3.4
encanta: le encanta he / she / it loves, you (formal) love
encontrar (ue) to find
la **encuesta** survey
enero January, 4.6
la **enfermería** infirmary, hospital
el / la **enfermero(a)** nurse, 4.2
enfermo(a) sick, 3.4
enfrente de in front of, 6.3
enojado(a) mad, angry, 3.4
enorme enormous
la **ensalada** salad, 2.5
enseñar to show, 5.1
enseñar a to teach how to, 5.4
entender (ie) to understand, 2.6
entero(a) whole
entiendes you (fam.) understand, 2.6
entiendo I understand, 2.6
entonces then, 2.3
la **entrada** admission ticket, 5.5
entrar to enter
entre between, 6.3
la **época** period
el **equipo** team, 5.5; equipment
equivocado(a) mistaken, 3.4
eres you are, 2.1
¿Eres de aquí? Are you from here?, 1.1

es he / she / it is, you (formal) are, 2.1
es controlado(a) is controlled
es decir that is to say
es formado(a) is formed
¿Es usted . . .? Are you (formal) . . . ?, 2.1
esa that (f.), 6.6
esas those (f.), 6.6
la **escala** scale
la **escalera** stairs, 3.3
escribir to write, 1.4
el / la **escritor / a** writer, 2.1
el **escritorio** desk, 3.6
escúchame listen to me (fam. sing. com.)
escuchar to listen to, 1.2
la **escuela** school, 1.5
ese that (m.), 6.6
eso that
esos those (m.), 6.6
España Spain
el **español** Spanish (language), 1.4
español / a Spanish, 5.3
especial special
especialmente especially
las **especias** spices
el **espejo** mirror
los **espejuelos** eyeglasses
esperar to await
esperar to wait for, 5.5
el **esquí acuático** water skiing, 5.4
practicar el esquí acuático to water-ski, 5.4
esquiar to ski, 1.5
la **esquina** street corner, 6.3
esta this (f.), 6.6
esta mañana this morning, 2.4
esta noche tonight, 2.4

Vocabulario español-inglés

esta tarde this afternoon, **2.4**
estacionar to park
la **estación** season, **6.2**; radio station
el **estadio** stadium, **1.5**
el **estado** state
los **Estados Unidos** the United States
estadounidense from the United States, **5.3**
estar to be, **3.2**
  está nublado it's cloudy, **6.4**
  estar a + distance to be + distance from, **6.3**
  estar casado(a) to be married
  estar en to be in (at, on), **3.2**
  estás en tu casa make yourself at home
estas these (f.), **6.6**
este this (m.), **6.6**
el **estéreo** stereo, **3.5**
estimado(a) dear
estimar to estimate
estos these (m.), **6.6**
estricto(a) strict
estridente noisy
la **estructura** structure (grammar)
el / la **estudiante** student, **2.1**
  estudiar to study, **1.2**
  estudiar para to study to be a, **4.2**
  estudiar para un examen to study for an exam, **1.4**
la **estufa** stove, **3.6**
estupendo(a) terrific, **5.4**
Europa Europe
evidente evident
exacto correct, right
el **examen** exam, test, **1.4**
excelente excellent, **2.1**
el **exceso** excess
la **excusa** excuse

la **exhibición** exhibition
exigente demanding
existían they existed
el **éxito** success
la **experiencia** experience
experimentado(a) experienced
el / la **experto(a)** expert
explicar to explain, **5.6**
expresar to express
el **expreso** express (train)
exquisito(a) exquisite
extranjero(a) foreign, **4.5**
la **película extranjera** foreign film, **4.5**

F

la **fábrica** factory, **4.2**
fácil easy, **1.6**
la **falda** skirt, **6.1**
la **familia** family, **3.1**
los **familiares** relatives
famoso(a) famous
fantástico(a) fantastic
el **favor** favor, **5.1**
  favor de please
favorito(a) favorite, **2.3**
febrero February, **4.6**
la **fecha** date
  la **fecha de vencimiento** expiration date
fenomenal phenomenal, terrific
feo(a) ugly, **2.2**
la **feria** fair
el **festival** festival
la **fiesta** party, **1.5**
fíjate look (fam. sing. com.)
fijo(a) fixed
el **fin** end
  el **fin de semana** weekend, **2.6**
  en fin in all
  por fin finally
final: al final at / in the end
finalmente finally

financiero(a) finance
la **revista financiera** finance magazine
la **firma** signature
formado(a) formed
  es formado is formed
formal formal
formar to form
formidable terrific, great, **2.1**
la **fórmula** formula
el **formulario** form (document), **2.1**
la **fotografía** photography
el / la **fotógrafo(a)** photographer
la **foto** picture, photograph
  sacar fotos to take pictures, **1.5**
frágil fragile
el **francés** French (language), **1.4**
francés(esa) French, **5.3**
los **frenos: los frenos en los dientes** dental braces, **4.4**
el **fresco** coolness, **6.4**
  hace fresco it's cool, **6.4**
los **frijoles** beans, **2.5**
el **frío** cold, **6.5**
  hace frío it's cold, **6.4**
  tener frío to be cold, **6.5**
la **fruta** fruit, **2.5**
fuerte strong
  un fuerte abrazo a strong embrace
el / la **fumador / a** smoker, one who smokes
fumar to smoke
el **fútbol** soccer, **1.2**
el **fútbol americano** football, **1.2**
el **futuro** future
futuro(a): la futura mamá future mom

G

las **gambas** shrimp (Spain)
el / la **ganador(a)** winner
las **ganancias** revenues
ganar to earn money, 2.3; to win, 4.5
la **gaseosa** soft drink, soda, 2.5
la **gasolinera** gasoline station
gastar to spend money, 5.4
el **gato** cat, 4.3
los **gauchos** Argentinian cowboys
la **gaveta** locker, 1.4
los **gemelos** twins
la **generación** generation
general: por lo general in general
generalmente generally
generoso(a) generous, 2.2
la **gente** people
la **geometría** geometry, 1.4
el **gimnasio** gymnasium, 2.3
el **giro postal** money order
el **gobernador** governor
gobernar to rule
el **gobierno** government
el **golfo** gulf
la **goma** rubber, 5.2
gordo(a) fat, 2.2
el **gorila** gorilla, 4.3
el **gorro** cap, 6.1
el **gourmet** gourmet
la **grabadora** tape recorder, 3.5
gracias thank you, thanks, 1.2
gracias por . . . thank you for . . . , 2.1
el **grado** grade
los **grados** degrees
gran great
grande big, 2.2
gris gray, 3.6

el **grupo** group
la **guagua** bus (Caribbean)
la **guanábana** soursop, tropical fruit
los **guantes** gloves, 6.1
guapo(a) good-looking, 2.2
guardar to keep, store, 5.2
guatemalteco(a) Guatemalan, 5.3
la **guayabera** loose-fitting men's shirt
la **guerra** war
la **guitarra** guitar, 5.3
tocar la guitarra to play the guitar, 1.5
el / la **guitarrista** guitar player, 2.1
gusta: ¿Le gusta . . . ? Do you (formal) / does he / she / it like . . . ?, 4.1
me gusta I like, 1.4
¿Qué te gusta más? What do you (fam.) like best?, 1.4
te gusta you like, 1.4
¿Te gusta . . . ? Do you like . . . ?, 1.6
gustan: ¿Les gustan . . . ? Do you (pl.)/ they like . . . ?, 4.1
te gustan you like (pl.), 1.4
¿Te gustan . . . ? Do you (fam.) like (pl.) . . . ?, 1.6
el **gusto** taste

H

la **habitación** bedroom, 2.3
hablar to speak, talk, 1.2
hablar con to speak with, talk to, 1.2
hablar por teléfono to talk on the telephone, 1.2

hace: hace buen tiempo the weather is nice, 6.4
hace calor it's hot, 6.4
hace fresco it's cool, 6.4
hace frío it's cold, 6.4
hace mal tiempo the weather is bad, 6.4
hace . . . que it has been . . . since, 5.5
hace sol it's sunny, 6.4
hace un tiempo regular the weather is so-so, 6.4
hace viento it's windy, 6.4
hacer to do, 1.2
hacer cola to stand in line, 5.5
hacer ejercicio to exercise, 2.3
hacer la tarea to do homework, 1.2
hacer las maletas to pack (suitcases), 3.1
hacer un cheque to write a check, 5.1
hacer un favor to do a favor, 5.1
hacer una caminata to hike, 6.4
hacer una pregunta to ask a question, 1.4
las **haciendas** ranches
el **hambre** (f.) hunger, 6.5
tener hambre to be hungry, 6.5
la **hamburguesa** hamburger, 2.5
hasta until, 2.6; as far as, 6.3; even
hasta entonces until then
hasta luego see you later, 1.4
hasta pronto see you soon

Vocabulario español-inglés **503**

hay there is, there are, **3.3**
hebreo(a) Hebrew
hecho(a) made
el **helado** ice cream, **2.5**
el **hemisferio** hemisphere
la **herencia** heritage
la **hermana** sister, **4.1**
el **hermano** brother, **4.1**
los **hermanos** siblings (brothers and sisters), **4.1**
el **hielo** ice, **1.5**
la **hija** daughter, **4.1**
el **hijo** son, **4.1**
los **hijos** children (sons and daughters), **4.1**
hispano(a) Hispanic
los **hispanohablantes** Spanish-speakers
los **hispanos** Hispanics
la **historia** history, **1.4**
histórica historic; historical
la **historieta** comic strip, **4.5**
hola hi, hello, **1.1**
el **hombre** man, **4.2**
el **hombre de negocios** businessman, **4.2**
hondureño(a) Honduran, **5.3**
la **hora** hour, **5.5**
a toda hora at all hours
el **horario** schedule
horrible horrible, awful, **2.1**
el **horror: ¡Qué horror!** How horrible!, **1.6**
el **hospital** hospital
el **hostal** hostel
hoy today, **2.4**
hoy día nowadays
el **huevo** egg, **2.5**

I

la **idea** idea
ideal ideal

el **idioma** language, **1.4**
la **iglesia** church, **2.6**
la **imagen** image
impaciente impatient, **2.1**
el **impermeable** raincoat, **6.1**
importa: no importa it doesn't matter, **2.4**
importante important
imposible impossible
la **impresión** impression
incluir to include
incluso including
incluyo I include
increíble incredible, **2.1**
la **independencia** independence
independiente independent
indicar to indicate
indio(a) Indian
la **información** information
informal casual (clothes)
el / la **ingeniero(a)** engineer, **4.2**
el **inglés** English (language), **1.4**
inglés(esa) English, **5.3**
el **ingrediente** ingredient
el **inmigrante** immigrant
la **institución** institution
el **instrumento** instrument
inteligente intelligent, **2.1**
intercambio exchange
interesante interesting, **2.1**
los **intereses** interests
internacional international
el **invierno** winter, **6.2**
la **invitación** invitation
los **invitados** guests
invitar to invite, **5.1**
ir to go, **1.2**
ir a casa to go home, **1.2**
ir a pie to go on foot, walk, **6.3**

ir de pesca to go fishing, **5.4**
ir de vacaciones to go on vacation, **2.3**
la **isla** island
el **italiano** Italian (language), **5.3**
italiano(a) Italian, **5.3**
la **izquierda** left, **3.3**
a la izquierda to (on) the left, **3.3**

J

el **jamón** ham, **2.5**
el **japonés** Japanese (language), **5.3**
japonés(esa) Japanese, **5.3**
joven young, **2.2**
los **jóvenes** young people, **4.3**
la **joya** jewel, pl. jewelry, **6.1**
la **joyería** jewelry store
juegas you (fam.) play, **2.4**
juego I play, **2.4**
el **juego** game, **4.5**
el **juego de mesa** board game, **4.5**
el **jueves** Thursday, **2.6**
jugar (ue) to play, **1.2**
el **jugo** juice, **2.5**
julio July, **4.6**
justo(a) fair
la **juventud** young people; youth

L

la the (f.), **1.4**
el **laboratorio** laboratory
lacio straight (hair), **4.4**
el **lado** side, **6.3**
al lado de next to; beside, **6.3**
el **lago** lake, **6.4**
la **lámpara** lamp, **3.6**
la **lana** wool, **6.2**

504 *Vocabulario español-inglés*

el **lápiz** pencil, **1.4**
los **lápices:** los **lápices de colores** colored pencils
largo(a) long, **4.4**
  la **larga distancia** long distance
el **latín** Latin (language)
latino(a) Latin
lavar to wash, **2.6**
la **lección** lesson
la **leche** milk, **2.5**
la **lechuga** lettuce, **2.5**
la **lectura** reading
leer to read, **1.2**
legal legal
las **legumbres** vegetables, **2.5**
lejos far, **6.3**
  lejos de far from, **6.3**
la **lencería** linen shop
la **lengua** language
el **lenguaje** language
los **lentes** lenses, eyeglasses
  los **lentes de contacto** contact lenses, **4.4**
el **león** lion, **4.3**
la **libra** pound, **6.6**
libre free, **4.5**
  al aire libre outdoors, **6.4**
  los **ratos libres** free time, **4.5**
la **librería** bookstore
el **libro** book, **1.2**
ligero(a) light (wind)
limpiar to clean, **2.3**
lindo(a) pretty
la **línea** line
la **línea del ecuador** equator
el **lío: ¡Qué lío!** What a mess!
la **liquidación** clearance (sale), **6.1**
listo(a) smart, **2.2**
liviano(a) light (weight), **6.6**
local local
la **lotería** lottery
luego later, **2.3**
el **lugar** place, **1.5**

el **lunes** Monday, **2.6**

LL

la **llama** llama, **4.3**
llamar to call, **3.1**
llamo: me llamo . . . my name is . . . , **1.1**
la **llave** key, **5.2**
llegar to arrive, **2.4**
  llegar a to arrive at, **2.4**
llenar to fill
lleno(a) full
llevar to take, **3.1**; to carry, **5.2**; to wear, **6.1**
llueve it's raining, **6.4**
la **lluvia** rain

M

la **madera** wood, **5.2**
la **madre** mother, **4.1**
el / la **madrileño(a)** native of Madrid
el / la **maestro(a)** teacher, **1.2**
la **maleta** suitcase, **3.1**
  hacer las maletas to pack (suitcases), **3.1**
malo(a) bad, **2.2**
la **mamá** mom, **4.1**
el **mamey** mamey, tropical fruit
mandar to send, **5.1**
manejar to drive, **1.5**
la **manera** manner, way
la **manga** sleeve, **6.2**
  de manga corta short-sleeved, **6.2**
  de manga larga long-sleeved, **6.2**
  sin mangas sleeveless, **6.2**
mantener (ie) to maintain, to support
la **mantequilla** butter, **2.5**
la **mañana** morning, **2.4**
  de la mañana in the morning, **1.3**
  esta mañana this morning, **2.4**

  por la mañana in the morning, **2.4**
mañana tomorrow, **2.3**
el **mapa** map, **3.1**
la **máquina** car (Caribbean)
el **mar** sea, **5.4**
maravillarse: se maravillan they marvel (at)
maravilloso(a) marvelous, wonderful
la **marca** brand name, **3.5**
las **marcas: marcas internacionales** international brands
marcar to dial
el **marido** husband
la **marroquinería** Moroccan leatherwork
el **martes** Tuesday, **2.6**
marzo March, **4.6**
más more, **6.5**
  más o menos more or less, **6.6**
  más que more than, **6.5**
las **matemáticas** mathematics, **1.4**
las **materias** subjects
materno(a) maternal
máximo(a) maximum
  al máximo to the maximum
mayo May, **4.6**
mayor older, **4.1**
el / la **mayor** the oldest
los **mayores** older people; adults
la **mayoría** majority
la **mazorca** ear of corn
la **mecánica** mechanics
el / la **mecánico(a)** mechanic, **4.2**
la **media** half, **1.3**
mediano(a) medium
las **medias** stockings, **6.1**
medievales medieval
medir(i) to measure
mejor better, **6.5**
la **memoria** memory

Vocabulario español-inglés **505**

  menor younger, 4.1
el / la **menor** the youngest
  menos less, 6.5
   menos que less than, 6.5
el **mensaje** message
el **mercado** market
la **mermelada** jam, preserves, 2.5
el **mes** month, 4.6
 el **mes pasado** last month, 5.3
 el **mes que viene** next month, 4.6
la **mesa** table, 3.6
el **metal** metal, 5.2
el **metro** subway
 metropolitano(a) metropolitan
 mexicano(a) Mexican, 5.3
 mi my, 3.6
 mí me (prep. pron.)
  a mí me gusta I like, 4.1
  para mí for me
la **microinformática** computerware
el **miedo: tener miedo** to be scared, 6.5
el **miembro** member
 mientras while
el **miércoles** Wednesday, 2.6
 mil one thousand, 4.3
la **milla** mile, 6.6
el **millón (de)** million, 5.3
 mimado(a) spoiled
 mínimo(a) minimum
el **minuto** minute, 5.5
 mira look (fam. sing. com.)
la **misión** mission
el / la **mismo(a)** the same
 lo mismo the same thing
 misterioso(a) mysterious
la **mochila** bookbag, knapsack, 1.4

la **moda** fashion, 4.5
 de moda in fashion, 6.2
el **modelo** model
 moderno(a) modern, 3.5
el **monasterio** monastery
la **moneda** coin, 3.5
el **mono** monkey, 4.3
el **monopatín** skateboard, 1.2
 andar en monopatín to skateboard, 1.2
la **montaña** mountain, 6.4
 montar to ride, 1.2
 montar a caballo to ride horseback, 1.5
 montar en bicicleta to ride a bicycle, 1.2
 morado(a) purple, 3.6
 moreno(a) dark (hair, complexion), 4.4
los **moros** Moors
el **mostrador** counter (in a shop)
la **moto** motorcycle, 3.5
la **motocicleta** motorcycle
el **motor** engine
la **muchacha** girl, 2.2
el **muchacho** boy, 2.2
 muchísimos(as) many
 mucho a lot, 1.4; a lot (of), many, 4.2
 mucho gusto nice to meet you, 1.1
 muchos(as) a lot, many, 4.2
los **muebles** furniture, 3.6
la **mujer** woman, 4.2
 la **mujer de negocios** businesswoman, 4.2
 la **mujer policía** police officer, 4.2
el **mundo** world
 todo el mundo everybody, everyone
la **muralla** city wall
el **museo** museum
la **música** music, 1.4
el / la **músico(a)** musician, 2.1

 muy very, 1.1
  muy bien very well, 1.1

N

 nací I was born, 5.3
el **nacimiento** birth
 nacional national
 el **sistema nacional** national system
 nada nothing, 1.2
 nadar to swim, 1.2
 natural natural
la **naturaleza** nature
la **Navidad** Christmas
 necesario(a) necessary
 necesitar to need, 1.4
los **negocios** business(es)
 negro(a) black, 3.6
 nervioso(a) nervous, 3.4
 ni nor
  ni . . . ni neither . . . nor
 nicaragüense Nicaraguan, 5.3
los **nietos** grandchildren
 nieva it's snowing, 6.4
 ningún(una) not any, any, 1.5
  no quiero ir a ningún lugar I don't want to go anywhere, 1.5
el / la **niño(a)** child, 4.3
 no no, not, 1.2
  ¿no? no?, 1.4
  no aprobado failing
  no importa it doesn't matter, 2.4
  ¡No me digas! You don't say!, 1.6
  no muy bien not too well, 1.1
  no sólo not only
la **noche** night, 2.4
  de la noche at night, 1.3
  esta noche tonight, 2.4

    por la noche at night, 2.4
el **nombre** name, 5.1
el **norte** North
    norteamericano(a) North American, 5.3
    nosotros(as) we, us, 3.1
la **nota** grade, 1.4; note
    sacar buenas notas to get good grades, 1.4
las **noticias** news, 4.5
el **noticiero** newscast
    novecientos(as) nine hundred, 4.3
la **novela** novel, 4.5
    noveno(a) ninth, 3.2
    noventa ninety, 3.3
    noviembre November, 4.6
    nuestro(a) our, 5.4
    nueve nine, 1.3
    nuevo(a) new, 3.5
el **número** number, 3.1
el **número de teléfono** telephone number, 3.1
    nunca never, 2.4

O

    o or, 1.4
el **objeto** object
la **obra** work (artistic)
    ochenta eighty, 3.3
    ocho eight, 1.3
    ochocientos(as) eight hundred, 4.3
    octavo(a) eighth, 3.2
    octubre October, 4.6
la **ocupación** occupation
    ocupado(a) busy, 3.4
    ocurre it occurs, it happens
la **oferta** offer
la **oficina** office, 3.3
    ofrecer to offer
    oír to hear, 5.5
el **ojo** eye, 4.4
las **olas** waves (ocean), 5.4
    correr las olas to surf, 5.4
    olvidar to forget, 3.1
    once eleven, 1.3
la **onza** ounce, 6.6
la **opinión** opinion
    la **opinión pública** public opinion
la **oportunidad** opportunity
la **óptica** optical store
el **origen** origin
    original original
el **oro** gold, 5.2
el **oso** bear, 4.3
el **otoño** autumn, 6.2
    otro(a) another, other, 4.5
    oye: ¡oye! hey!, listen!, 2.4
    oyes you (fam.) hear, 5.5

P

la **paciencia** patience
    paciente patient
los **pacientes** patients
el **padre** father, 4.1
los **padres** parents, 4.1
la **paella** Spanish rice dish with chicken, seafood, etc., seasoned with saffron
    pagar to pay, 5.6
la **página** page, 1.4
el **país** country
la **palabra** word, 1.4
la **pampa** extensive plain in Argentina
el **pan** bread, 2.5
    el **pan tostado** toast, 2.5
    panameño(a) Panamanian, 5.3
los **pantalones** pants, 6.1
el **papá** dad, 4.1
los **papás** mom and dad, 4.1
las **papas fritas** french fries, 2.5
el **papel** paper, 1.4
la **papelería** stationery store
    para for, 2.5; to; in order to, 5.2
    para caballeros for gentlemen, 6.2
    para damas for ladies, 6.2
    para el desayuno (el almuerzo, la cena) for breakfast (lunch, dinner), 2.5
    para mí for me
    ¿Para qué sirve? What is it used for?, 5.2
    para ti for you
    para todos for all
la **parada** bus stop
el **paraguas** umbrella, 6.1
    paraguayo(a) Paraguayan, 5.3
    parece seems, looks like, 4.1
    parece que . . . it seems that . . . , 4.3
la **pared** wall, 3.6
el / la **pariente(ta)** relative, 4.1
el **parque** park, 1.5
    el **parque zoológico** zoo, 4.3
la **parte** place; part
    particulares private
el **partido** game, match, 1.2
    pasado(a) last, 5.3
    el **año pasado** last year, 5.3
    pasado mañana the day after tomorrow, 4.6
    la **semana pasada** last week, 5.3
el **pasaporte** passport, 3.1
    pasar to spend (time), 5.4
    pasar la aspiradora to vacuum, 5.6
    pasar to pass
    pasa come in (fam. sing. com.)
    pasa: ¿Qué pasa? What's wrong?, What's going on?, 2.5

Vocabulario español-inglés **507**

pasar por to pass by, stop by
pasear to go for a ride
pasear en bote to go for a boat ride
pasear en velero to go sailing, 5.4
el **paseo** stroll, walk, 1.2; boulevard, promenade, 3.2
dar un paseo to go for a walk, 1.2
el **pastel** pie, pastry, 2.5
los **pastores** shepherds
patinar to skate, 1.5
patinar sobre hielo to ice-skate, 1.5
pedir (i) to ask for, 5.6
pedir permiso to ask for permission, 5.6
peleados: están peleados they are not on speaking terms
la **peletería** fur shop
la **película** movie, film, 1.2
la **película extranjera** foreign film, 4.5
la **película policial** detective movie, 4.5
la **película de terror** horror movie, 4.5
pelirrojo(a) red-headed, 4.4
el **pelo** hair, 4.4
la **pena: ¡Qué pena!** What a shame!, 1.6
pensar (ie) to intend, to plan, 2.2
peor worse, 6.5
el / la **pequeñito(a)** little one
pequeño(a) small, 2.2
la **percusión** percussion
perder (ie) to lose, 4.5
perdón excuse me, 1.4
perezoso(a) lazy, 2.2
perfectamente perfectly
la **perfumería** perfumery
el **periódico** newspaper, 2.3
el / la **periodista** journalist, 4.2

el **periquito** parakeet, 4.3
el **permiso** permission, 5.6
con permiso excuse me, 2.3
pedir permiso to ask for permission, 5.6
permitir to allow, permit, 5.6
pero but, 1.6
el **perro** dog, 4.3
las **personas** persons
pertenecer (zco) a to belong to, 5.5
peruano(a) Peruvian, 5.3
pesado(a) heavy, 6.6
la **pesca** fishing, 5.4
ir de pesca to go fishing, 5.4
el **pescado** fish, 2.5
la **peseta** monetary unit of Spain
el **pez** fish, 4.3
el **pez dorado** goldfish, 4.3
picante spicy
el **picnic** picnic
el **pie** foot (measurement), 6.6
ir a pie to go on foot, to walk, 6.3
la **piel** leather; fur
piensan they think
piensas you (fam.) plan, intend, 2.2
pienso I plan, intend, 2.2
la **pileta** swimming pool (Argentina)
el **pingüino** penguin, 4.3
pintar to paint
el / la **pintor(a)** painter
la **pintura** painting
la **piñata** hanging papier-mâché figure filled with candy and gifts
la **piscina** swimming pool, 1.5
el **piso** story, floor (of a building), 3.2; floor, 3.6

la **pizzería** pizzeria
planchar to iron, 5.6
planear to plan, 5.4
el **plano** plan; map
la **planta** floor
la planta baja ground floor
el **plástico** plastic, 5.2
la **plata** silver, 5.2
el **plátano** banana
el **plato** dish, 5.6
la **playa** beach, 1.5
la **plaza** plaza, (public) square, 3.2
la **población** population
pobre poor
poco(a) little, 4.2
un poco a little, 2.2
pocos(as) few, 4.2
poder (ue) to be able, 4.6
el **policía** police officer, 4.2
la **policía** police (department)
policial: la película policial detective movie, 4.5
la **política** politics
político(a) political
el / la **político(a)** politician, 2.1
el **pollo** chicken, 2.5
poner: poner la mesa to set the table, 5.6
popular popular, 2.1
por for; by
por ciento percent
¡Por Dios! For goodness sake!
por ejemplo for example
por eso therefore, that's why, 5.6
por favor please, 5.1
por fin finally
por la mañana in the morning, 2.4
por la noche at night, 2.4
por la tarde in the afternoon, 2.4

508 *Vocabulario español-inglés*

por lo general in general
¿por qué? why, 2.5
¿Por qué no . . . ? Why not . . . ?, 2.5
por todas partes everywhere
porque because, 1.5
portátil portable
la **portería** custodian's quarters or office
el / la **portero(a)** custodian
posible possible
la **postal** postcard
el **postre** dessert, 2.5
practicar to play, to practice, 1.2
  practicar deportes to play sports, 1.2
  practicar el esquí acuático to water-ski, 5.4
el **precio** price
precioso(a) beautiful
la **preferencia** preference
preferible preferable
preferir (ie) to prefer, 4.5
la **pregunta** question, 1.4
  hacer una pregunta to ask a question, 1.4
preliminar preliminary
preocupado(a) worried, 3.4
preparado(a) prepared, ready
preparar to prepare, to get ready, 2.5
la **presentación** introduction
  la **carta de presentación** letter of introduction
presentar to introduce, 5.6
el **presente** present
el **préstamo** loan
prestar to lend, 5.1
la **primavera** spring, 6.4
primero(a) first, 2.3

el / la **primo(a)** cousin, 4.1
principales main
principalmente mainly
la **prisa: tener prisa** to be in a hurry, 6.5
privado(a) private
la **probabilidad** probability
el **problema** problem, 5.6
el **producto** product
profesional professional
el / la **profesor / a** teacher, professor, 4.2
el **programa** program, 4.5
  el **programa de aventuras** adventure program, 4.5
  el **programa de ciencia ficción** science fiction program, 4.5
  el **programa de terror** horror program, 4.5
  el **programa deportivo** sports program, 4.5
  el **programa educativo** educational program, 4.5
  el **programa extranjero** foreign program, 4.5
  el **programa policial** detective program, 4.5
  el **programa romántico** love story, 4.5
la **programación** programming
prohibido(a) prohibited
prohibir to prohibit
prometer to promise, 5.6
propio(a) one's own
la **protección** protection
el **proyecto** project
público(a) public
  la **opinión pública** public opinion
el **pueblo** town, 2.3
puedes you (fam.) can, 4.6
puedo I can, 4.6
el **puente de observación** observation deck

el **puerco** pork
la **puerta** door, 3.6
el **puerto** port
puertorriqueño(a) Puerto Rican, 5.3
pues well, 1.6; because
la **pulgada** inch, 6.6
la **pulsera** bracelet, 6.1
el **punto: los puntos de reunión** gathering places
puntual punctual, 2.1

Q

que that
  que le dé that it goes to
qué what, 1.2; how, 1.6
  ¡Qué aburrido! How boring!, 1.6
  ¿Qué clase de . . . ? What kind of . . . ?, 4.5
  ¡Qué divertido! What fun!, 1.6
  ¡Qué horror! How horrible!, 1.6
  ¡Qué lío! What a mess!
  ¡Qué maravilla! How wonderful!
  ¡Qué raro! How strange!, 1.6
  ¡Qué suerte! What luck!, 1.6
  ¿Qué tal? How are you?, 1.1
  ¿Qué tiempo hace? What's the weather like?, 6.4
  ¡Qué va! No way!, 1.6
el **quehacer** chore, task, 5.6
querer (ie) to want
querido(a) dear
el **queso** cheese, 2.5
quién who, 2.2
quiere: te quiere he / she loves you

quieres you (fam.) want, **1.2**
quiero I want, **1.2**
la **química** chemistry, **1.4**
quince fifteen, **1.3**
quinientos(as) five hundred, **4.2**
quinto(a) fifth, **3.2**
quisiera I would like, **3.4**
quitar to remove, **5.6**

R

el **radio** radio (instrument, set), **3.5**
la **radio** radio (broadcasting, as a medium), **1.4**
rápidamente rapidly
rápido fast
la **raqueta:** la **raqueta de tenis** tennis racket
raro: ¡Qué raro! How strange!, **1.6**
el **ratoncito** mouse, **4.3**
el **rato:** los **ratos libres** free time, **4.5**
la **razón** reason
la **reacción** reaction
la **realidad: en realidad** in reality
rebajar to lower (the price)
la **rebaja** (price) reduction
la **recámara** bedroom (Mexico)
recibir to receive, **3.1**
la **recomendación** recommendation
recordar (ue) to remember, **3.1**
rectangular rectangular, **5.2**
recuerdas you (fam.) remember, **3.1**
recuerdo I remember, **3.1**
el **recuerdo** souvenir, **3.5**
los **recuerdos** memories
la **red** network
redondo(a) round, **5.2**

el **refresco** noncarbonated soft drink, **2.5**
el **refrigerador** refrigerator, **3.6**
el **regalo** gift, **2.3**
regatear to bargain
la **región** region
regresar to return, **4.6**
regular so-so, fair, **1.1**
el **reloj** clock, **5.2**
la **relojería** watch and clock store
el **repaso** review
el **reportero(a)** reporter
representar to represent
la **República Dominicana** the Dominican Republic
la **reservación** reservation
la **resolución** resolution
respetar to respect
responsable responsible
el **restaurante** restaurant, **1.5**
el **resto** the rest
la **reunión** meeting, reunion, **5.5**
la **revista** magazine, **1.2**
rico(a) tasty
el **río** river, **6.4**
riquísimo(a) very tasty
el **ritmo** rhythm
rizado(a) curly, **4.4**
rodeado(a) surrounded
rojo(a) red, **3.6**
romano(a) Roman
romántico(a) romantic, **4.5**
el **programa romántico** love story, **4.5**
la **ropa** clothes, clothing, **3.1**
la **ropa para caballeros** men's clothing, **6.2**
la **ropa para damas** ladies' clothing, **6.2**
la **ropa interior** underwear
rosado(a) pink, **3.6**
rubio(a) blonde, **4.4**

la **rumba** Cuban dance
el **ruso** Russian (language), **5.3**
ruso(a) Russian, **5.3**

S

S.A. abbreviation of **Sociedad Anónima,** Incorporated
el **sábado** Saturday, **2.6**
saber to know, **1.5**
sacar to take out, **5.6**
sacar buenas notas to get good grades, **1.4**
sacar fotos to take pictures, **1.5**
sacudir (los muebles) to dust, **5.6**
la **sala** living room, **3.6**
el **salario** salary
salgo I go out, **3.1**
la **salida** departure
salir to go out, **3.1**
la **salsa** Caribbean rhythm and dance
saltar las olas to jump, ride the waves, **5.4**
los **saludos** greetings; regards
salvadoreño(a) Salvadoran, **5.3**
las **sandalias** sandals, **6.1**
el **sandwich** sandwich, **2.5**
Santo Tomás Saint Thomas
las **sardinas** sardines
la **sastrería** tailor's shop
se: Se dice . . . It's said . . . , **5.2**
se solicita is wanted, is requested
sé I know, **1.5**
la **sed** thirst, **6.5**
tener sed to be thirsty, **6.5**
la **seda** silk, **6.2**
según according (to)
segundo(a) second, **3.2**
seguro(a) sure, certain, **3.4**

510 *Vocabulario español-inglés*

seis six, 1.3
seiscientos(as) six hundred, 4.3
el **sello** stamp, 3.5
la **semana** week, 2.6
   la **semana pasada** last week, 5.3
   la **semana que viene** next week, 4.6
sensacional sensational
el **señor** Mr., sir, 1.3
la **señora** Mrs., ma'am, 1.3
las **señoras** women
la **señorita** Miss, 1.3
septiembre September, 4.6
séptimo(a) seventh, 3.2
ser to be, 2.1
la **serpiente** snake, 4.3
el **servicio** restroom, 3.3; service
servir (i) to serve
sesenta sixty, 3.3
setecientos(as) seven hundred, 4.3
setenta seventy, 3.3
sexto(a) sixth, 3.2
los **shorts** shorts (pants), 6.1
si if, 3.1
sí yes, 1.1
siempre always, 2.4
sienten they feel
siete seven, 1.3
sigue go on, continue (fam. sing. com.), 6.3; he / she / it continues; you (formal) continue
   sigue derecho go straight (fam. sing. com.), 6.3
siguen you (pl.) go on, 6.3
sigues you (fam.) go on, 6.3
el **silencio** silence
la **silla** chair, 3.6
similar similar
simpático(a) nice, pleasant, 2.2

sin without, 6.2
   sin embargo nevertheless
   sin mangas sleeveless, 6.2
la **sinagoga** synagogue, 2.6
sincero(a) sincere
sino que but also
sirve: sirve para . . . it's used for . . . , 5.2
   ¿Para qué sirve? What is it used for?, 5.2
el **sistema** system
   el **sistema auditivo** hearing
   el **sistema nacional** national system
la **situación** situation
sobre about
el **sobre** envelope, 5.1
sobresaliente outstanding
sociable sociable, friendly
el **sofá** sofa, 3.6
el **sol** sun, 6.4
solicita: se solicita is wanted, is requested
solicito I want
solo(a) alone
sólo only
somos we are, 2.1
son they are, 2.1
el **sonido** sound
la **sopa** soup, 2.5
el / la **sospechoso(a)** suspect
el **sótano** basement (of a house), 3.3
soy I am, 2.1
   soy de . . . I'm from . . . , 1.1
su(s) his, her, your (formal), their, 4.1
la **sucursal** branch of a department store
Sudamérica South America

el **sueño** sleep, 6.5; dream
   tener sueño to be sleepy, 6.5
la **suerte** luck, 1.6
   ¡Qué suerte! What luck!, 1.6
el **suéter** sweater, 6.1
suficiente sufficient
el **supermercado** supermarket, 2.6
supervisar to supervise
el / la **supervisor / a** supervisor, 4.2
el **sur** South
   al sur to the south
el **suroeste** Southwest

T

tacaño(a) stingy, 2.2
la **talla** size (of clothing)
   las **tallas especiales** special (clothing) sizes
el **tamaño** size
también also, too, 1.6
tampoco neither
tan: tan . . . como as . . . as, 6.5
tanto: tanto como . . . as much as . . . , 6.5
tantos(as): tantos(as) como . . . as many as . . . , 6.5
las **tapas** hors d'oeuvres (Spain)
tardar: tardar en . . . to take time . . . , 6.6
la **tarde** afternoon, 2.4
   de la tarde in the afternoon, 1.3
   esta tarde this afternoon, 2.4
   por la tarde in the afternoon, 2.4
tarde late, 2.4
la **tarea** homework, 1.2

Vocabulario español-inglés **511**

la **tarjeta** card, **5.1**
la **tarjeta de crédito** credit card, **5.1**
　la **tarjeta joven** special student card for Spain's train system
　la **tarjeta postal** postcard, **3.5**
el **té** tea, **2.5**
el **teatro** theater
la **tele** TV, **1.2**
　ver la tele to watch TV, **1.2**
el **teléfono** telephone, **3.1**
　hablar por teléfono to talk on the phone, **1.2**
　el **número de teléfono** telephone number, **3.1**
la **telenovela** soap opera, **4.5**
el **televisor** television (set), **3.5**
la **temperatura** temperature
la **temporada** season
temprano early, **2.4**
tener to have, **3.5**
　tener calor to be hot, **6.5**
　tener frío to be cold, **6.5**
　tener hambre to be hungry, **6.5**
　tener miedo to be scared, **6.5**
　tener prisa to be in a hurry, **6.5**
　tener que + inf. to have to, **4.4**
　tener sed to be thirsty, **6.5**
　tener sueño to be sleepy, **6.5**
tengo I have, **3.5**
el **tenis** tennis, **1.2**
los **tenis** sneakers, **6.1**
tercero(a) third, **3.2**

terminar to end, finish, **4.5**
el **territorio** territory
el **terror** horror, **4.5**
　la **película de terror** horror movie, **4.5**
el **tesoro** treasure
ti you, yourself (prep. pron.)
　a ti te gusta you like, **4.1**
　para ti for you
la **tía** aunt, **4.1**
el **tiempo** time, **5.5**; weather, **6.4**
　con el tiempo eventually
la **tienda** store, **1.5**
　la **tienda vaquera** jeans store
tienden they tend to
tienes you (fam.) have, **3.5**
la **tierra** land, country
el **tigre** tiger, **4.3**
tímido(a) timid, shy
el **tío** uncle, **4.1**
los **tíos** aunt(s) and uncle(s), **4.1**
típicamente typically
típico(a) typical
tirar to throw
los **títulos** titles
tocar to play (an instrument), **1.5**; to touch
todavía still
　todavía no not yet
todo everything
　todo lo que... everything that...
todo(a) every, all, **4.2**; whole
　para todos for all
　todas las horas all the time
　todo el mundo everybody, everyone
　todos los días every day, **2.6**

tomar to take, **3.2**
　tomar algo to drink something, **1.2**
　tomar sol to sunbathe, **5.4**
el **tomate** tomato, **2.5**
tonto(a) silly, foolish, **2.2**
la **torre** tower
la **tortilla** omelet (Spain)
la **tortuga** turtle, **4.3**
el **total** total
trabajar to work, **1.4**
el **trabajo** work, job, **2.3**
traer to bring, **5.1**
el **tráfico** traffic
traigo I bring, **5.2**
el **traje: el traje de baño** bathing suit, **6.1**
el **traje para caballero** gentleman's suit, **6.1**
el **traje para dama** lady's suit, **6.1**
tranquilo(a) calm, relaxed, **3.4**
transmitir to transmit, to broadcast
el **transporte** transportation
el **tranvía** local train (Spain)
trece thirteen, **1.3**
treinta thirty, **3.3**
el **tren** train, **6.3**
tres three, **1.3**
triste sad, **3.4**
el **trofeo** trophy, **3.5**
tropical tropical
tu your, **3.6**
tú you, **3.1**
el **turismo** tourism
el / la **turista** tourist

U

un a, **3.5**
una a, **3.5**
la **universidad** university
uno one, **1.3**

512 Vocabulario español-inglés

la **urgencia médica** medical emergency
uruguayo(a) Uruguayan, 5.3
usado(a) used
usar to use, 1.4
usted you (formal), 1.3
ustedes you (pl.), 3.1
utilizar to use

V

va he / she / it goes, you (formal) go, 2.3
las **vacaciones** vacation, 2.3
ir de vacaciones to go on vacation, 2.3
vale(n) it (they) cost(s), 4.2
el **valle** valley
vamos we go, 2.3
¡Vamos! Let's go! (pl. com)
van they go, 2.3
el **vaquero** cowboy
las **variedades** varieties
el **programable variedades** variety show
varios(as) various, 5.5
los **varones** boys
vas you (faml) go, 2.3
las **veces** times
a veces sometimes, 2.4
el / la **vecino(a)** neighbor, 5.5
veinte twenty, 1.3
el **velero** sailboat, 5.4
pasear en velero to go sailing, 5.4

los **vendedores** salespeople, vendors
vender to sell, 5.6
venezolano(a) Venezuelan, 5.3
vengo I come, 6.3
venir (ie) to come, 6.3
la **ventana** window, 3.6
ver to watch, to see, 1.2
ver la tele to watch TV, 1.2
el **verano** summer, 6.2
verdad: ¿verdad? right?, 2.5
verde green, 4.4
las **verduras** vegetables
el **vestíbulo** entryway
el **vestido** dress, 6.1
vestido(a) dressed
los **veteranos** veterans
el / la **veterinario(a)** veterinarian, 4.2
viajar to travel, 3.1
el **viaje** trip
la **vida** life
el **vídeo** video, 3.5
el **vídeo musical** music video
la **videocasetera** videocassette player
el **videojuego** video game, 2.1
el **vidrio** glass (material), 5.2
viejo(a) old, 2.2
vienes you (fam.) come, 6.3
el **viento** wind, 6.4
hace viento it's windy, 6.4
el **viernes** Friday, 2.6

vino he / she / it / you (formal) came
la **visita** visit
los **visitantes** visitors
visitar to visit, 1.2
la **vista** view
la **viuda** widow
vivir to live, 3.1
vivo(a) alive; live
el **vocabulario** vocabulary
el **volumen** volume
a todo volumen at its loudest (volume)
vosotros(as) you (fam. pl.), 3.1
voy I go, 2.3
el **vuelo** flight

Y

y and, 1.6
y media half past the hour, 1.3
ya already, 1.5
ya no no longer
yo I, 3.1

Z

la **zapatería** shoe store
la **zapatería deportiva** sport shoe store
los **zapatos** shoes, 3.5
la **zoología** zoology

Vocabulario español-inglés

Vocabulario Inglés-Español

The **Vocabulario Inglés-Español** contains all productive vocabulary from the text.

The numbers following each productive entry indicate the chapter and lesson in which the word is first introduced.

The following are abbreviations used in this glossary.

adv.	adverb
com.	command
dir. obj.	direct object
f.	feminine
fam.	familiar
ind. obj.	indirect object
inf.	infinitive
m.	masculine
obj. of prep.	object of the preposition
pers.	personal
pl.	plural
prep.	preposition; prepositional
pron.	pronoun
sing.	singular
subj.	subjunctive

A

a un(una), 3.5
  a lot mucho, 1.4
  a lot of mucho(a), 4.2
actor el actor, 2.1
actress la actriz, 2.1
address la dirección, 3.2
admission: admission ticket la entrada, 5.5
adventure la aventura, 4.5
  adventure program el programa de aventuras, 4.5
advertisement el anuncio, 5.1
advice el consejo, 5.6
to **advise** dar consejos a, 5.6
after después de, 3.1
afternoon la tarde, 2.4
  in the afternoon de la tarde, 1.3; por la tarde, 2.4
  this afternoon esta tarde, 2.4
afterwards después, 2.3
airplane el avión, 6.3
algebra el álgebra, 1.4
all todo(a), 4.2
to **allow** permitir, 5.6
almost casi, 5.5
already ya, 1.5
also también, 1.6
always siempre, 2.4
and y, 1.6
angry enojado(a), 3.4
animal el animal, 4.3
another otro(a), 4.5
to **answer** contestar, 1.4
anything: I don't want to do anything no quiero hacer nada, 1.2
anywhere: I don't want to go anywhere no quiero ir a ningún lugar, 1.5
apartment el apartamento, 3.2
April abril, 4.6
architect el/la arquitecto(a), 4.2
Argentinian argentino(a), 5.3
to **arrive** llegar, 2.4
  to arrive at llegar a, 2.4
arrogant arrogante, 2.1
art el arte, 1.4
artist el/la artista, 2.1
as . . . as tan . . . como, 6.5
  as far as hasta, 6.3
  as many as . . . tantos(as) como . . . , 6.5
  as much as . . . tanto(a) como . . . , 6.5
to **ask for** pedir (i), 5.6
  to ask for permission pedir permiso, 5.6
  to ask a question hacer una pregunta, 1.4
at a, 1.3; en, 3.2
athlete el/la deportista, 2.1
to **attend** asistir a, 5.4
August agosto, 4.6
aunt la tía, 4.1
  aunt(s) and uncle(s) los tíos, 4.1
autumn el otoño, 6.2
avenue la avenida, 3.2

B

bad malo(a), 2.2; mal, 6.4
  the weather is bad hace mal tiempo, 6.4
ballpoint pen el bolígrafo, 1.4
bank el banco, 2.6
baseball el béisbol, 1.2
basement (of a house) el sótano, 3.3
basketball el baloncesto, 1.2
bathing suit el traje de baño, 6.1
bathroom el baño, 3.6
to **be** estar, 3.2; ser, 2.1
  to be in/at/on estar en, 3.2
to **be able to** poder (ue), 4.6
beach la playa, 1.5
beans los frijoles, 2.5
bear el oso, 4.3
beard la barba, 4.4
because porque, 1.5
bed la cama, 3.6
bedroom la habitación, 2.3
been: it has been . . . since hace . . . que, 5.5
before antes de, 3.1
behind detrás de, 6.3
to **belong to** pertenecer (zco) a, 5.5
below abajo, 3.3
belt el cinturón, 6.1
best: What do you [fam.] like best? ¿Qué te gusta más?, 1.4
better mejor, 6.5
between entre, 6.3
beverage la bebida, 2.5
bicycle la bicicleta, 1.2
  to ride a bicycle montar en bicicleta, 1.2
big grande, 2.2
biology la biología, 1.4
birthday el cumpleaños, 4.6
black negro(a), 3.6
block: city block la cuadra, 6.3
blond rubio(a), 4.4
blouse la blusa, 6.1
blue azul, 3.6
board: board game el juego de mesa, 4.5
boat el barco, 6.3

Vocabulario inglés-español

Bolivian boliviano(a), 5.3
book el libro, 1.2
boots las botas, 6.1
bored aburrido(a), 3.4
boring aburrido(a), 2.2
   How boring! ¡Qué aburrido!, 1.6
born: I was born nací (nacer), 5.3
boulevard el paseo, 3.2
to **bowl** jugar boliche (m.), 2.6
boy el muchacho, 2.2
bracelet la pulsera, 6.1
braces (dental) los frenos de los dientes, 4.4
brand: brand name la marca, 3.5
   What's the brand name? ¿De qué marca es?, 2.3
bread el pan, 2.5
breakfast el desayuno, 2.5
to **bring** traer, 5.1
   I bring traigo, 5.2
brother el hermano, 4.1
   brother(s) and sister(s) los hermanos, 4.1
brown de color café, 4.4
building el edificio, 3.2
bus el autobús, 6.3
businessman el hombre de negocios, 4.2
businesswoman la mujer de negocios, 4.2
busy ocupado(a), 3.4
but pero, 1.6
butter la mantequilla, 2.5
to **buy** comprar, 1.2

C

cafeteria la cafetería, 1.5
calculator la calculadora, 1.4
to **call** llamar, 3.1
calm tranquilo(a), 3.4
camel el camello, 4.3
camera la cámara, 3.1
Canadian canadiense, 5.3
canary el canario, 4.3
cap el gorro, 6.1
car el coche, 1.5
card tarjeta, 5.1
   credit card la tarjeta de crédito, 5.1
carpenter el carpintero(a), 4.2
to **carry** llevar, 5.2
cassette el casete, 3.5
cat el gato, 4.3
cereal el cereal, 2.5
chair la silla, 3.6
to **change** cambiar, 3.1
check el cheque, 5.1
   traveler's check el cheque de viajero, 3.1
cheese el queso, 2.5
chess el ajedrez, 4.5
chicken el pollo, 2.5
child el / la niño(a), 4.3
children (sons and daughters) los hijos, 4.1
Chilean chileno(a), 5.3
Chinese chino(a), 5.3; (language) el chino, 5.3
chore el quehacer, 5.6
church la iglesia, 2.6
city la ciudad, 1.5
class la clase, 1.4
classmate el / la compañero(a) de clase, 2.1
to **clean** limpiar, 2.3
clearance (sale) la liquidación, 6.1
clock el reloj, 5.2
clothing la ropa, 3.1
cloudy: it's cloudy está nublado, 6.4

club el club, 5.5
coffee el café, 2.5
coin la moneda, 3.5
cold el frío, 6.5
   it's cold hace frío, 6.4
   to be cold tener frío, 6.5
collection la colección, 3.5
Colombian colombiano(a), 5.3
to **come** venir (ie), 6.3
   I come vengo, 6.3
comedy (program) el programa cómico, 4.5
comfortable cómodo(a), 3.1
comic (strip) la historieta, 4.5
company la compañía, 4.2
composition la composición, 1.4
computer la computadora, 1.5
concert el concierto, 2.3
to **continue:**
   you [fam.] **continue** sigues, 6.3
   you [pl.] **continue** siguen, 6.3
to **cook** cocinar, 1.5
cool: it's cool hace fresco, 6.4
corner: street corner la esquina, 6.3
to **cost** valer, 4.2
Costa Rican costarricense, 5.3
cotton el algodón, 5.2
countryside el campo, 1.5
course: Of course! ¡Cómo no!, 1.2
cousin el / la primo(a), 4.1
credit card la tarjeta de crédito, 5.1
Cuban cubano(a), 5.3

516 *Vocabulario inglés-español*

curly (hair) rizado(a), 4.4
to **cut** cortar, 5.6

D

dad el papá, 4.1
to **dance** bailar, 1.2
dance el baile, 1.5
dancer el / la bailarín(ina), 2.1
dark (hair, complexion) moreno(a), 4.4
daughter la hija, 4.1
December diciembre, 4.6
dentist el / la dentista, 4.2
depressed deprimido(a), 3.4
depressing deprimente, 2.1
desert el desierto, 6.4
desk el escritorio, 3.6
dessert el postre, 2.5
detective: detective movie la película policial, 4.5
different diferente, 2.1
difficult difícil, 1.6
disaster: What a disaster! ¡Qué desastre!, 1.6
dish el plato, 5.6
to **do** hacer, 1.2
doctor el / la doctor / a, 4.2
dog el perro, 4.3
dollar el dólar, 1.3
Dominican dominicano(a), 5.3
door la puerta, 3.6
dot: on the dot en punto, 2.6
downtown el centro, 2.3
to **draw** dibujar, 1.5
dress el vestido, 6.1
dresser el armario, 3.6
to **drink** tomar, 1.2
to **drive** manejar, 1.5

E

early temprano, 2.4
to **earn (money)** ganar, 2.3
earring el arete, 6.1
easy fácil, 1.6
to **eat** comer, 1.2
Ecuadorian ecuatoriano(a), 5.3
education: physical education la educación física, 1.4
educational educativo(a), 4.5
egg el huevo, 2.5
eight ocho, 1.2
eight hundred ochocientos(as), 4.3
eighteen diez y ocho, 1.3
eighth octavo(a), 3.2
eighty ochenta, 3.3
electrician el / la electricista, 4.2
elegant elegante, 2.1
elephant el elefante, 4.3
elevator el ascensor, 3.3
eleven once, 1.3
employee el / la empleado(a), 4.2
engineer el / la ingeniero(a), 4.2
English inglés(esa), 5.3; **(language)** el inglés, 1.4
enough bastante, 2.2
envelope el sobre, 5.1
evening noche, 1.3
  in the evening de la noche, 1.3; por la noche, 2.4
every todo(a), 4.2
  every day todos los días, 2.6
exam el examen, 1.4
  to study for an exam estudiar para un examen, 1.4
excellent excelente, 2.1

excited emocionado(a), 3.4
exciting emocionante, 2.1
excuse: excuse me con permiso, 1.4; perdón, 1.4
to **exercise** hacer ejercicio, 2.3
expensive caro(a), 3.5
to **explain** explicar, 5.6
eye el ojo, 4.4
eyeglasses los anteojos, 4.4

F

factory la fábrica, 4.2
family la familia, 3.1
far: far from lejos de, 6.3
farmer el / la agricultor / a, 4.2
fashion la moda, 4.5
  in fashion de moda, 6.2
fat gordo(a), 2.2
father el padre, 4.1
favor el favor, 5.1
  to do a favor hacer un favor, 5.1
favorite favorito(a), 2.3
fear el miedo, 3.6
February febrero, 4.6
to **feed** dar de comer a, 5.6
few pocos(as), 4.2
fifteen quince, 1.3
fifth quinto(a), 3.2
fifty cincuenta, 3.3
film la película, 1.2
to **finish** terminar, 4.5
firefighter el / la bombero(a), 4.2
first primero(a), 2.3
fish el pescado, 2.5; el pez, 4.3
fishing la pesca, 5.4
  to go fishing ir de pesca, 5.4

Vocabulario inglés-español

five cinco, 1.3
  five hundred quinientos(as), 4.2
floor el piso, 3.6
  What floor is it on? ¿En qué piso está?, 3.2
flowered (print) de flores, 6.2
food la comida, 2.5
foot (measurement) el pie, 6.6
  on foot a pie, 6.3
football el fútbol americano, 1.2
for para, 5.2
  What is it used for? ¿Para qué sirve?, 5.2
foreign extranjero(a), 4.5
  foreign film la película extranjera, 4.5
forest el bosque, 6.4
to **forget** olvidar, 3.1
form (document) el formulario, 2.1
forty cuarenta, 3.3
  four hundred cuatrocientos(as), 4.2
fourteen catorce, 1.3
fourth cuarto(a), 3.2
free libre, 4.5
  free time los ratos libres, 4.5
French francés(esa), 5.3; **(language)** el francés, 1.4
french fries las papas fritas, 2.5
Friday el viernes, 2.6
friend el / la amigo(a), 2.3
from de, 2.3
  Are you [fam.] **from here?** ¿Eres de aquí?, 1.1
  from the del (de + el), de la, 2.3
  I'm from . . . soy de . . . , 1.1

front: in front of enfrente de, 6.3
fruit la fruta, 2.5
fun divertido(a), 2.2
  What fun! ¡Qué divertido!, 1.6
funny cómico(a), 4.5

G

gadget el aparato, 5.2
game el partido, 1.2
  game show el concurso, 4.5
garbage la basura, 3.3
generous generoso(a), 2.2
gentleman el caballero, 6.2
  for gentlemen para caballeros, 6.2
geometry la geometría, 1.4
German alemán(ana), 5.3; **(language)** el alemán, 5.3
to **get: to get good grades** sacar buenas notas, 1.4
gift el regalo, 2.3
girl la muchacha, 2.2
to **give** dar, 5.1
  to give advice to dar consejos a, 5.6
  I give doy, 5.2
glass (material) el vidrio, 5.2
gloves los guantes, 6.1
to **go** ir, 1.2
  he / she / it goes, you [formal] **go** va, 2.3
  I go voy, 2.3
  they go van, 2.3
  we go vamos, 2.3
  you [fam.] **go** vas, 2.3
to **go out** salir, 3.1
  I go out salgo, 3.1
gold el oro, 5.2
goldfish el pez dorado, 4.3
good bueno, 1.6

good afternoon buenas tardes, 1.3
good evening buenas noches, 1.3
good morning buenos días, 1.3
good night buenas noches, 1.3
good-looking guapo(a), 2.2
good-bye adiós, 1.4
gorilla el gorila, 4.3
grade la nota, 1.4
grandfather el abuelo, 4.1
grandmother la abuela, 4.1
grandparents los abuelos, 4.1
gray gris, 3.6
great: That's great! ¡Qué bueno!, 1.6
green verde, 4.4
group: musical group el conjunto, 2.3
Guatemalan guatemalteco(a), 5.3
guitar la guitarra, 5.3
  guitar player el / la guitarrista, 2.1
  to play the guitar tocar la guitarra, 1.5
gymnasium el gimnasio, 2.3

H

hair el pelo, 4.4
half: half an hour la media hora, 1.3
  half past the hour y media, 1.3
ham el jamón, 2.5
hamburger la hamburguesa, 2.5
handbag la bolsa, 6.1
happy contento(a), 3.4
to **have** tener (ie), 3.5
  to have to tener que + inf., 4.4

518 *Vocabulario inglés-español*

I have tengo, 3.5
he él, 3.1
to **hear** oír, 5.5
heat el calor, 6.5
heavy pesado(a), 6.6
hello hola, 1.1
to **help** ayudar, 5.1
her su(s) [poss.], 4.1
her ella [obj. of prep.], 3.1; la [dir. obj.], 6.4; le [ind. obj.], 4.1
here aquí, 1.1
to **hike** dar una caminata, 6.4
him le [ind. obj.], 4.1; lo [dir. object], 6.4
his su(s), 4.1; de él, 2.3
history la historia, 1.4
home casa, 1.2
 to go home ir a casa, 1.2
homemaker el ama (f.) de casa, 4.2
homework la tarea, 1.2
 to do homework hacer la tarea, 1.2
Honduran hondureño(a), 5.3
horrible horrible, 2.1
 How horrible! ¡Qué horrible!, 1.6
horror el terror, 4.5
 horror program el programa de terror, 4.5
horse el caballo, 4.3
horseback: to ride horseback montar a caballo, 1.5
hot: it's hot hace calor, 6.4
hour la hora, 5.5
house la casa, 2.6
How . . . ! ¡Qué . . . !, 1.6
how? ¿cómo?, 1.4
 How are you [fam.]? ¿Cómo estás?, 1.3; ¿Qué tal?, 1.1

How are you [formal]? ¿Cómo está usted?, 1.3
How do you say . . . ? ¿Cómo se dice . . . ?, 5.2
How long? ¿Cuánto tiempo?, 5.4
How long has it been since . . . ? ¿Cuánto tiempo hace que . . . ?, 5.5
how many? ¿cuántos(as)?, 3.3
how much? ¿cuánto(a)?, 3.3
How much do you (does he / she) weigh? ¿Cuánto pesa(s)?, 6.6
How much does it cost? ¿Cuánto vale?, 4.2
How old are you (is he / she)? ¿Cuántos años tiene(s)?, 4.2
How tall are you (is he / she)? ¿Cuánto mide(s)?, 6.6
hundred: one hundred cien, 3.3; ciento, 4.2
one hundred one (two) ciento uno (dos), 4.2
hungry: to be hungry tener hambre(f.), 6.5
hurry: to be in a hurry tener prisa, 6.5

I

I yo, 3.1
ice el hielo, 1.5
ice cream el helado, 2.5
to **ice-skate** patinar sobre hielo, 1.5
if si, 3.1
impatient impaciente, 2.1

in en, 3.2
 in love enamorado(a), 3.4
inch la pulgada, 6.6
incredible increíble, 2.1
industrious aplicado(a), 2.2
inexpensive barato(a), 3.5
inside adentro, 3.3
intelligent inteligente, 2.1
interesting interesante, 2.1
to **introduce** presentar, 5.6
to **iron** planchar, 5.6
it lo [dir. obj. pron.], 6.4
 it is + distance **from** está a + distance, 6.3
its su(s), 4.1
Italian italiano(a), 5.3; **(language)** el italiano, 5.3

J

jacket la chaqueta, 6.1
jam la mermelada, 2.5
January enero, 4.6
Japanese japonés(esa), 5.3; **(language)** el japonés, 5.3
jewel la joya, 6.1
job el trabajo, 2.3
journalist el / la periodista, 4.2
juice el jugo, 2.5
July julio, 4.6
jump saltar, 5.4
jump the waves saltar las olas

K

to **keep** guardar, 5.2
key la llave, 5.2
kind amable, 2.1; la clase, 4.5

Vocabulario inglés-español 519

What kind of . . . ? ¿Qué clase de . . . ?, 4.5
kitchen la cocina, 3.6
knapsack la mochila, 1.4
to **know** saber, 1.5; **(a person or place)** conocer (zco), 5.5
  I know sé, 1.5

L

ladies las damas, 6.2
  for ladies para damas, 6.2
  ladies' clothing ropa para damas, 6.2
lake el lago, 6.4
lamp la lámpara, 3.6
language el idioma, 1.4
last pasado(a), 5.3
  last month el mes pasado, 5.3
  last night anoche, 5.3
  last week la semana pasada, 5.3
  last year el año pasado, 5.3
late tarde, 2.4
later luego, 2.3
  see you later hasta luego, 1.4
lawn el césped, 5.6
lawyer el / la abogado(a), 4.2
lazy perezoso(a), 2.2
to **learn** aprender, 1.4
  to learn how to aprender a + inf., 4.5
leather el cuero, 5.2
left la izquierda, 3.3
  (on) to the left a la izquierda, 3.3
to **lend** prestar, 5.1
lenses: contact lenses los lentes de contacto, 4.4
less menos, 6.5

less than menos que, 6.5
more or less más o menos, 6.6
letter la carta, 3.1
lettuce la lechuga, 2.5
library la biblioteca, 1.5
light (weight) liviano(a), 6.6
like como, 6.5
to **like: Do you like . . . ?** ¿Te gusta . . . ?, 1.6
  Do you [fam.] **like** [pl.] **. . . ?** ¿Te gustan . . . ?, 1.6
  Do you [formal] **(does he / she) like . . . ?** ¿Le gusta . . . ?, 4.1
  Do you [pl.] **(do they) like . . . ?** ¿Les gustan . . . ?, 4.1
  I like me gusta, 1.4; a mí me gusta, 4.1
  I would like quisiera, 3.4
  What do you [fam.] **like best?** ¿Qué te gusta más?, 1.4
  you like te gusta, 1.4; a ti te gusta, 4.1
  you like [pl.] te gustan, 1.4
line la cola, 5.5
  to stand in line hacer cola,
lion el león, 4.3
to **listen (to)** escuchar, 1.2
  Listen! ¡Oye!, 2.4
little: a little un poco, 2.2
to **live** vivir, 3.1
llama la llama, 4.3
locker la gaveta, 1.4
long largo(a), 4.4
  long-sleeved de manga larga, 6.2
to **look for** buscar, 2.3
to **lose** perder (ie), 4.5
love: in love enamorado(a), 3.4

love story el programa romántico, 4.5
luck la suerte, 1.6
  What luck! ¡Qué suerte!, 1.6
lunch el almuerzo, 2.5

M

ma'am señora (abbreviation Sra.), 1.3
magazine la revista, 1.2
man el hombre, 4.2
many muchos(as), 4.2
map el mapa, 3.1
March marzo, 4.6
mathematics las matemáticas, 1.4
matter: it doesn't matter no importa, 2.4
May mayo, 4.6
me me [obj. pron.], 5.1
meat la carne, 2.5
mechanic el / la mecánico(a), 4.2
meeting la reunión, 5.5
men los caballeros, 6.2
  men's clothing ropa para caballeros, 6.2
metal el metal, 5.2
Mexican mexicano(a), 5.3
mile la milla, 6.6
milk la leche, 2.5
million el millón (de), 5.3
minute el minuto, 5.5
mirror el espejo, 3.6
Miss señorita (abbreviation Srta.), 1.3
mistaken equivocado(a), 3.4
modern moderno(a), 3.5
mom la mamá, 4.1
  mom and dad los papás, 4.1
Monday el lunes, 2.6
money el dinero, 2.3
monkey el mono, 4.3

Vocabulario inglés-español

month el mes, 4.6
  last month el mes pasado, 5.3
more más, 6.5
  more or less más o menos, 6.6
  more than más que, 6.5
morning la mañana, 2.4
  in the morning por la mañana, 2.4; de la mañana, 6.2
  this morning esta mañana, 2.4
mother la madre, 4.1
motorcycle la moto, 3.5
mountain la montaña, 6.4
mouse el ratoncito, 4.3
movie la película, 1.2
movies el cine, 1.5
Mr. señor (abbreviation Sr.), 1.3
Mrs. señora (abbreviation Sra.), 1.3
music la música, 1.4
musician el / la músico(a), 2.1
mustache el bigote, 4.4
my mi(s), 3.6

N

name el nombre, 5.1
  my name is . . . me llamo . . . , 1.1
  What is your name [fam.]? ¿Cómo te llamas?, 1.1
near cerca de, 6.3
necklace el collar, 6.1
necktie la corbata, 6.1
to **need** necesitar, 1.4
neighbor el / la vecino(a), 5.5
nervous nervioso(a), 3.4
never nunca, 2.4
new nuevo(a), 3.5
news las noticias, 4.5
newspaper el periódico, 2.3
next que viene, 4.6
  next month el mes que viene, 4.6
  next year el año que viene, 4.6
  next to al lado de, 6.3
Nicaraguan nicaragüense, 5.3
nice simpático(a), 2.2
  nice to meet you mucho gusto, 1.1
  the weather is nice hace buen tiempo, 6.4
night la noche, 2.4
  at night de la noche, 1.3; por la noche, 2.4
  last night anoche, 5.3
nine nueve, 1.3
  nine hundred novecientos(as), 4.3
nineteen diez y nueve, 1.3
ninety noventa, 3.3
ninth noveno(a), 3.2
no no, 1.2
North American norteamericano(a), 5.3
not no, 1.2
notebook el cuaderno, 1.4
nothing nada, 1.2
November noviembre, 4.6
now ahora, 2.3
number número, 3.1
  telephone number el número de teléfono, 3.1
nurse el / la enfermero(a), 4.2

O

o'clock: at one o'clock a la una, 1.3
  at (two) o'clock a las (dos), 1.3
October octubre, 4.6
of de, 2.3
  of the del (de + el), de la, 2.3
office la oficina, 3.3
OK de acuerdo, 2.6
old viejo(a), 2.2; **(object)** antiguo(a), 3.5
older mayor, 4.1
on en, 3.2
one uno, 1.3
  one hundred cien, 3.3; ciento, 4.2
to **open** abrir, 5.2
or o, 1.4
orange anaranjado(a), 3.6
ounce la onza, 6.6
our nuestro(a), 5.4
outdoors al aire libre, 6.4
outside afuera, 3.3
overcoat el abrigo, 6.1
owner el / la dueño(a), 4.2

P

to **pack (suitcases)** hacer las maletas, 3.1
page la página, 1.4
Panamanian panameño(a), 5.3
pants los pantalones, 6.1
panty hose las pantimedias, 6.1
paper el papel, 1.4
Paraguayan paraguayo(a), 5.3
parakeet el periquito, 4.3
parents los padres, 4.1
park el parque, 1.5
party la fiesta, 1.5
passport el pasaporte, 3.1
pastry el pastel, 2.5

Vocabulario inglés-español

to **pay** pagar, 5.6
pencil el lápiz, 1.4
penguin el pingüino, 4.3
permission el permiso, 5.6
Peruvian peruano(a), 5.3
physical: physical education la educación física, 1.4
pick-up truck la camioneta, 6.3
picture la foto, 1.5
pink rosado(a), 3.6
place el lugar, 1.5
plaid de cuadros, 6.2
to **plan** pensar (ie), 2.6 planear, 5.4
plastic el plástico, 5.2
to **play** jugar (ue) **(game),** 1.2; tocar **(instrument),** 1.5
playing: playing cards las cartas, 4.5
plaza la plaza, 3.2
please por favor, 5.1
pocket el bolsillo, 5.2
police officer el / la mujer policía, 4.2
politician el / la político(a), 2.1
polka-dotted de lunares, 6.2
popular popular, 2.1
post office el correo, 5.1
postcard la tarjeta postal, 3.5
poster el cartel, 3.5
pound la libra, 6.6
to **practice** practicar, 1.2
to **prefer** preferir (ie), 4.5
to **prepare** preparar, 2.5
pretty bonito(a), 3.5
problem el problema, 5.6
professor el / la profesor / a, 4.2
program el programa, 4.5
to **promise** prometer, 5.6
Puerto Rican puertorriqueño(a), 5.3
punctual puntual, 2.1
purple morado(a), 3.6

Q

question la pregunta, 1.4
to ask a question hacer una pregunta, 1.4

R

rabbit el conejo, 4.3
radio (as a medium) la radio, 1.4; **(set)** el radio, 3.5
raincoat el impermeable, 6.1
raining: it's raining llueve, 6.4
to **read** leer, 1.2
to **receive** recibir, 3.1
record el disco, 1.2
rectangular rectangular, 5.2
red rojo(a), 3.6
refrigerator el refrigerador, 3.6
relative el / la pariente(ta), 4.1
to **remember** recordar (ue), 3.1
to **remove** quitar, 5.6
to **rest** descansar, 1.2
restaurant el restaurante, 1.5
restroom el servicio, 3.3
to **return** regresar, 4.6
rice el arroz, 2.5
to **ride** montar, 1.2
to ride a bicycle montar en bicicleta, 1.2
to ride horseback montar a caballo, 1.5
right la derecha, 3.3
to the right a la derecha, 3.3
right? ¿verdad?, 2.5
ring el anillo, 6.1
river el río, 6.4
room (of a house) el cuarto, 3.6
bathroom el baño, 3.6
dining room el comedor, 3.6
living room la sala, 3.6
round redondo(a), 5.2

S

rubber la goma, 5.2
rug la alfombra, 3.6
to **run** correr, 1.2
Russian ruso(a), 5.3; **(language)** el ruso, 5.3

sad triste, 3.4
sailboat el velero, 5.4
sailing: to go sailing pasear en velero, 5.4
salad la ensalada, 2.5
Salvadoran salvadoreño(a), 5.3
sandals las sandalias, 6.1
sandwich el sandwich, 2.5
Saturday el sábado, 2.6
to **save** ahorrar, 3.1
to **say** decir (i), 5.5
I say digo, 5.5
it's said se dice, 5.2
You don't say! ¡No me digas!, 1.6
scared: to be scared tener miedo, 6.5
scarf la bufanda, 6.1
school la escuela, 1.5
science(s) las ciencias, 1.4
science fiction la ciencia ficción, 4.5
science fiction program el programa de ciencia ficción, 4.5
sea el mar, 5.4
second segundo(a), 3.2
to **see** ver, 1.2
let's see a ver, 1.6
to **seem: seems** parece, 4.1
it seems that . . . parece que . . . , 4.3
to **sell** vender, 5.6
to **send** mandar, 5.1
September septiembre, 4.6
to **set: to set the table** poner la mesa, 5.6
seven siete, 1.3
seven hundred setecientos(as), 4.3
seventeen diez y siete, 1.3
seventh séptimo(a), 3.2

Vocabulario inglés-español

seventy setenta, **3.3**
several varios(as), **5.5**
shame: What a shame!
    ¡Qué pena!, **1.6**
she ella, **3.1**
shirt la camisa, **6.1**
shoes los zapatos, **3.5**
shopping center el centro comercial, **1.5**
short (object) corto(a), **4.4**; **(person)** bajo(a), **2.2**
short-sleeved de manga corta, **6.2**
shorts (pants) los shorts, **6.1**
should deber, **3.1**
to **show** enseñar, **5.1**
    game show el concurso, **4.5**
siblings los hermanos, **4.1**
sick enfermo(a), **3.4**
side el lado, **6.3**
silk la seda, **6.2**
silly tonto(a), **2.2**
silver la plata, **5.2**
since desde, **5.3**
to **sing** cantar, **1.5**
singer el / la cantante, **2.1**
sir señor (abbreviation Sr.), **1.3**
sister la hermana, **4.1**
six seis, **1.3**
    six hundred seiscientos(as), **4.3**
sixteen diez y seis, **1.3**
sixth sexto(a), **3.2**
sixty sesenta, **3.3**
to **skate** patinar, **1.5**
to **skateboard** andar en monopatín (m.), **1.2**
to **ski** esquiar, **1.5**
to **skin-dive** bucear, **5.4**
skirt la falda, **6.1**
to **sleep** dormir (ue), **3.1**
    to sleep outdoors dormir al aire libre, **6.4**
sleepy: to be sleepy tener sueño, **6.5**
sleeve la manga, **6.2**
    sleeveless sin mangas, **6.2**

small pequeño(a), **2.2**
smart listo(a), **2.2**
snake la serpiente, **4.3**
sneakers los tenis, **6.1**
snowing: it's snowing nieva, **6.4**
so-so regular, **1.1**
    the weather is so-so hace un tiempo regular, **6.4**
soap opera la telenovela, **4.5**
soccer el fútbol, **1.2**
sociable sociable, **2.1**
socks los calcetines, **6.1**
soda la gaseosa, **2.5**
sofa el sofá, **3.6**
soft drink (noncarbonated) el refresco, **2.5**
solid (color) de un solo color, **6.2**
something algo, **1.2**
sometimes a veces, **2.4**
son el hijo, **4.1**
soup la sopa, **2.5**
souvenir el recuerdo, **3.5**
Spanish español / a, **5.3**; **(language)** el español, **1.4**
to **spend (time)** pasar, **5.4**; **(money)** gastar, **5.4**
sport el deporte, **1.2**
    to play sports practicar deportes, **1.2**
sports deportivo(a), **6.2**
    sports program el programa deportivo, **4.5**
spring la primavera, **6.2**
square cuadrado(a), **5.2**
stadium el estadio, **1.5**
stairs la escalera, **3.3**
stamp el sello, **3.5**
to **stand in line** hacer cola, **5.5**
to **start** empezar (ie), **4.5**
stereo el estéreo, **3.5**
stingy tacaño(a), **2.2**
store la tienda, **1.5**
story (of a building) el piso, **3.2**
stove la estufa, **3.6**

straight derecho(a), **6.3**
    go straight sigues derecho [fam. sing.], **6.3**
straight (hair) lacio, **4.4**
strange: How strange! ¡Qué raro!, **1.6**
street la calle, **3.1**
striped de rayas, **6.2**
stroll: to go for a stroll dar un paseo, **1.2**
student el / la estudiante, **2.1**
to **study** estudiar, **1.2**
    to study for an exam estudiar para un examen, **1.4**
    to study to be a estudiar para, **4.2**
suit el traje, **6.1**
    gentleman's suit el traje para caballero, **6.1**
    lady's suit el traje de dama, **6.1**
suitcase la maleta, **3.1**
summer el verano, **6.2**
sun el sol, **6.4**
to **sunbathe** tomar sol, **5.4**
Sunday el domingo, **2.6**
sunglasses los anteojos de sol, **6.1**
sunny: it's sunny hace sol, **6.4**
supermarket el supermercado, **2.6**
supervisor el / la supervisor / a, **4.2**
supper la cena, **2.5**
sure seguro(a), **3.4**
sweater el suéter, **6.1**
to **sweep** barrer, **5.6**
to **swim** nadar, **1.2**
    swimming pool la piscina, **1.5**
synagogue la sinagoga, **2.6**

T

T-shirt la camiseta, **3.5**
table la mesa, **3.6**
to **take** llevar, **3.1**; tomar, **3.2**

Vocabulario inglés-español

to **take care of** cuidar (a), **4.3**
to take a long time tardar en, **6.6**
to **take out** sacar, **5.6**
to take pictures sacar fotos, **1.5**
to **talk** hablar, **1.2**
to talk on the telephone hablar por teléfono, **1.2**
to talk to hablar con, **1.2**
tall alto(a), **2.2**
tape recorder la grabadora, **3.5**
tea el té, **2.5**
to **teach how to** enseñar a, **5.4**
teacher el / la maestro(a), **1.2**
team el equipo, **5.5**
teeth los dientes, **4.4**
telephone el teléfono, **3.1**
to talk on the telephone hablar por teléfono, **1.2**
television (set) el televisor, **3.5**
ten diez, **1.3**
tennis el tenis, **1.2**
tenth décimo(a), **3.2**
terrific formidable, **2.1**; estupendo(a), **5.4**
thank: thank you gracias, **1.2**
thank you for . . . gracias por . . . , **2.1**
thanks: no, thanks no, gracias, **1.2**
that ese (m.), esa (f.), **6.6**
the el (m.), la (f.), **1.4**; los (m.), **1.4**; las (f.), **1.4**
theater: movie theater el cine, **1.5**
their su(s), **4.1**
them ellos (m.); ellas (f.), **3.1**; les [ind. obj. pron.], **4.1**; los [m., dir. obj. pron.], **6.4**; las [f., dir. obj. pron.], **6.4**
then entonces, **2.3**

there allí, **3.3**
there: there is, there are hay, **3.3**
therefore por eso, **5.6**
these estos (m.), estas (f.), **6.6**
they ellos (m.); ellas (f.), **3.1**
thin delgado(a), **2.2**
thing la cosa, **5.2**
to **think: I think that** creo que, **4.2**
third tercero(a), **3.2**
thirsty: to be thirsty tener sed (f.), **6.5**
thirteen trece, **1.3**
thirty treinta, **3.3**
this este (m.), esta (f.), **6.6**
those esos (m.), esas (f.), **6.6**
thousand: one thousand mil, **4.3**
three tres, **1.3**
Thursday el jueves, **2.6**
ticket (admission) la entrada, **5.5**
tiger el tigre, **4.3**
time la hora, **1.3**; el tiempo, **5.5**
At what time is . . . ? ¿A qué hora es . . . ?, **1.3**
free time los ratos libres, **4.5**
tired cansado(a), **3.4**
to a, **1.5**
to the al (a + el), a la, **1.5**
toast el pan tostado, **2.5**
today hoy, **2.4**
tomato el tomate, **2.5**
tomorrow mañana, **2.3**
the day after tomorrow pasado mañana, **4.6**
tonight esta noche, **2.4**
too también, **1.6**
too much demasiado, **2.2**
town el pueblo, **2.3**
train el tren, **6.3**
to **travel** viajar, **3.1**
trophy el trofeo, **3.5**
Tuesday el martes, **2.6**
to **turn** doblar, **6.3**

turtle la tortuga, **4.3**
TV la tele, **1.2**
twelve doce, **1.3**
twenty veinte, **1.3**
two dos, **1.3**
two hundred doscientos(as), **4.2**

U

ugly feo(a), **2.2**
umbrella el paraguas, **6.1**
uncle el tío, **4.1**
to **understand** entender (ie), **2.6**
United States: from the United States estadounidense, **5.3**
unpleasant (person) antipático(a), **2.2**
until hasta, **2.6**
upstairs arriba, **3.3**
Uruguayan uruguayo(a), **5.3**
us nos [obj. pron.], **6.2**
to **use** usar, **1.4**
to use the computer usar la computadora, **1.5**
used: it's used for . . . sirve para . . . , **5.2**

V

vacation las vacaciones, **2.3**
to go on vacation ir de vacaciones, **2.3**
to **vacuum** pasar la aspiradora, **5.6**
vacuum cleaner la aspiradora, **5.6**
vegetables las legumbres, **2.5**
Venezuelan venezolano(a), **5.3**
very muy, **1.1**
very well muy bien, **1.1**
veterinarian el / la veterinario(a), **4.2**
video el vídeo, **3.5**

video game el videojuego, **2.1**
visit la visita, **5.4**
to **visit** visitar, **1.2**
volleyball el vóleibol, **5.5**

W

to **wait for** esperar, **5.5**
walk: to go for a walk dar un paseo, **1.2**
to **walk** ir a pie, **6.3**
wall la pared, **3.6**
wallet la billetera, **5.2**
to **want** querer (ie), **1.2**
   I want quiero, **1.2**
   I don't want to do anything no quiero hacer nada, **1.2**
   I don't want to go anywhere no quiero ir a ningún lugar, **1.5**
   you [fam.] **want** quieres, **1.2**
to **wash** lavar, **2.6**
to **watch: to watch TV** ver la tele, **1.2**
water el agua, **2.5**
   to water ski practicar el esquí acuático, **5.4**
waves (ocean) las olas, **5.4**
way: No way! ¡Qué va!, **1.6**
we nosotros(as), **3.1**
to **wear** llevar, **6.1**
weather el tiempo, **6.4**
   What's the weather like? ¿Qué tiempo hace?, **6.4**
Wednesday el miércoles, **2.6**
week la semana, **2.6**
   last week la semana pasada, **5.3**
weekend el fin de semana, **2.6**
welcome: you're welcome de nada, **2.1**
well bien, **1.1**; pues, **1.6**
   not too well no muy bien, **1.1**
   very well muy bien, **1.1**

what? ¿qué?, **1.2**; ¿cómo?, **1.4**
   What is he / she / it like? ¿Cómo es . . . ?, **2.1**
   What is it used for? ¿Para qué sirve?, **5.2**
   What's it made of? ¿De qué es?, **5.2**
   What's your phone number? ¿Cuál es tu número de teléfono?, **3.3**
when? ¿cuándo?, **2.4**
where: to where? ¿adónde?, **1.5**
   Where are you going? ¿Adónde vas?, **2.3**
   Where is it? ¿Dónde está?, **3.2**
which: which (one)? ¿cuál?, **4.5**
white blanco(a), **3.6**
who? ¿quién?, **2.2**
whose: Whose is it / are they? ¿De quién es / son?, **2.3**
why: Why not . . . ? ¿Por qué no . . . ?, **2.5**
to **win** ganar, **4.5**
wind: It's windy Hace viento, **6.4**
window la ventana, **3.6**
winter el invierno, **6.2**
with con, **1.2**
   with me conmigo, **5.4**
   with you [fam.] contigo, **5.4**
without sin, **6.2**
woman la mujer, **4.2**
wood la madera, **5.2**
wool la lana, **6.2**
word la palabra, **1.4**
work el trabajo, **2.3**
to **work** trabajar, **1.4**
worried preocupado(a), **3.4**
worse peor, **6.5**
to **write** escribir, **1.4**
   to write a check hacer un cheque, **5.1**
writer el / la escritor / a, **2.1**

Y

year el año, **4.6**
   last year el año pasado, **5.3**
   next year el año que viene, **4.6**
   What year were you [fam.] **born?** ¿En qué año naciste?, **5.3**
yellow amarillo(a), **3.6**
yes sí, **1.1**
yesterday ayer, **5.3**
   the day before yesterday anteayer, **5.3**
you [fam.] tú, **3.1**; [fam. pl.] vosotros(as), **3.1**; [formal] usted, **1.3**; [pl.] ustedes, **3.1**
young joven, **2.2**
   young people los jóvenes, **4.3**
younger menor, **4.1**
your tu, **3.6**; [formal] su(s), **4.1**

Z

zero cero, **1.3**
zoo el parque zoológico, **4.3**

Vocabulario inglés-español

Grammar Index

a when asking or telling time, 28 **(1.3)**; contraction with the definite article, 55 **(1.5)**; after **ir** to express future, 55 **(1.5)**; with **gusta/n** for clarification: **a** + noun (pronoun), 251 **(4.1)**; personal **a**, 284 **(4.4)**
adjectives gender and agreement with noun, 88, **(2.1)**; 96 **(2.2)**; possessive (see possessive adjectives); adjectives used with **estar** to express feelings, 203 **(3.4)**; of quantity, 261 **(4.2)**; demonstrative adjectives, 477 **(6.6)**; of nationality, 348 **(5.3)**
al contraction of **a** + **el**, 55 **(1.5)**
alphabet 66 **(1.6)**
-ar verbs see present tense and preterit tense
articles see definite and indefinite articles
comparatives comparisons of inequality **más/menos...que**, 463, 467 **(6.5)**; of equality **tanto/a/os/as...como**, 463 **(6.5)**; **tan...como**, 467 **(6.5)**; irregular comparatives **menor que, mayor que, mejor que, peor que**, 467 **(6.5)**
con with prepositions and special forms **conmigo** and **contigo** 367 **(5.4)**
dar see present tense and preterit tense
dates days of the week, 149 **(2.6)**; months of the year, 304 **(4.6)**; years, 352 **(5.3)**
de to express origin, 4 **(1.1)**; to talk about things more specifically, 43 **(1.4)**; to express possession, 113 **(2.3)**; contraction with **el**, 113 **(2.3)**; with ¿**quién?**, 113 **(2.3)**
decir present tense, 380 **(5.5)**
definite articles 42-43 **(1.4)**; agreement with noun, 2 **(1.4)**
del contraction of **de** + **el**, 113 **(2.3)**
demonstrative adjectives 477 **(6.6)**
direct object pronouns 454-455 **(6.4)**
-er verbs see present tense and preterit tense
estar present tense, 182 **(3.2)**; to indicate location, 182 **(3.2)**; with adjectives to express feelings, 203 **(3.4)**
gender of nouns, 42-43 **(1.4)**; of definite articles, 42-43 **(1.4)**; of indefinite articles, 214 **(3.5)**; of adjectives, 96 **(2.2)**
gustar me/te gusta + infinitive, 39 **(1.4)**; **me/te gusta(n)** + object(s), 63 **(1.6)**; **le/s gusta** + infinitive, 251 **(4.1)**; **le/s gusta/n** + object(s), 272 **(4.3)**; nos gusta/n, 424 **(6.2)**

hace + present tense with expressions of time, 372-373 **(5.5)**; with weather expressions, 446 **(6.4)**
hacer see present tense and preterit tense
hay 195 **(3.3)**
indefinite articles 214 **(3.5)**
indirect object pronouns me, 328 **(5.1)**, 343 **(5.2)**; **te**, 331 **(5.1)**, 343 **(5.2)**; **le**, 391 **(5.6)**; **les**, 412 **(6.1) nos**, 424 **(6.2)**
infinitive use of, 99 **(2.2)**
ir infinitive with **a/a la/al**, 55 **(1.5)**; present tense, 108-109 **(2.3)**; preterit tense, 355 **(5.3)**
-ir verbs present tense: introduction, 167 **(3.1)**; summary, 170-171 **(3.1)**; see also preterit tense
irregular verbs present tense: **dar**, see present tense; **decir**, 380 **(5.5)**; **estar**, 182 **(3.2)**; **ir**, 108-109 **(2.3)**; **oír**, 380 **(5.5)**; **pedir**, 381 **(5.5)**; **saber**, see present tense; **salir**, 167 **(3.1)**; **ser**, 83-84, 87-88 **(2.1)**; **tener**, 217 **(3.5)**; **traer**, 324 **(5.1)**; **venir**, 437 **(6.3)**; **ver**, see present tense; see also preterit tense
más/menos...que 463, 467 **(6.5)**
mayor que 467 **(6.5)**
mejor...que 467 **(6.5)**
menor que 467 **(6.5)**
nouns gender, 42-43 **(1.4)**; number, 42-43 **(1.4)**; agreement with definite articles, 42-43 **(1.4)**; agreement with indefinite articles, 214 **(3.5)**
number of nouns, 42-43 **(1.4)**; of indefinite articles 214 **(3.5)**; of adjectives, 96 **(2.2)**
numbers cardinal numbers 1-20, 24 **(1.3)**; 20-100, 192 **(3.3)**; 100-500, 264 **(4.2)**; 600 to thousands, 275 **(4.3)**; give years and count to a million, 352 **(5.3)**; ordinal numbers, 176, 179 **(3.2)**
oír present tense, 380 **(5.5)**; see also preterit tense
para to indicate purpose, 340 **(5.2)**
pedir present tense, 381 **(5.5)**; see also preterit tense
peor...que 467 **(6.5)**
plural of nouns, 42-43 **(1.4)**; of definite articles, 42-43 **(1.4)**; of articles, 87-88 **(2.1)**, 96 **(2.2)**; of indefinite articles, 214 **(3.5)**
poder present tense, 311 **(4.6)**
possession expressed with **de**, 113 **(2.3)**; see also possessive adjectives
possessive adjectives mi/s, tu/s, 227 **(3.6)**; **su/s**, 248 **(4.1)**; **nuestro/s**; **nuestra/s**, 364 **(5.4)**; summary, 364 **(5.4)**